ARTISANS OF PEACE

The gospel message, which is in harmony with the loftier strivings and aspirations of the human race, takes on a new luster in our day as it declares that the artisans of peace are blessed," for they shall be called children of God" (Mt. 5:9).

—Pastoral Constitution on the Church in the Modern World
(*Gaudium et Spes*) §77

THE CENTER FOR MISSION RESEARCH AND STUDY
AT MARYKNOLL

Artisans of Peace is the product of collaboration between researchers and theologians in various parts of the world and the Center for Mission Research and Study at Maryknoll (CMRSM), a research and educational institution that shares the charism and traditions of the Maryknoll mission movement. Established in 1995 and governed by a charter with the state of New York, CMRSM has a professional staff of six. The General Council of the Maryknoll Society serves as its Board of Trustees.

CMRSM's mandate is to investigate the trends, contexts, and challenges of global mission and to foster reflection on their practical implications. It has three main areas of work: contemporary research, mission history, and study (conferences, workshops, and an annual summer institute).

In carrying out its research mandate, CMRSM focuses especially on Christians at the grass roots and works collaboratively with international research partners and consultants. Its research is supported by both private foundations and the Maryknoll Society. The work is interdisciplinary in character and strives to give greater voice to local churches and people of faith, especially in the global South, in processes of analysis and reflection. An earlier study, *Popular Catholicism in a World Church* (1999), was also published by Orbis.

For more about Maryknoll and the Center for Mission Research and Study, visit our website at http://www.maryknoll.org.

Artisans of Peace

Grassroots Peacemaking
among Christian Communities

Edited by
Mary Ann Cejka
and
Thomas Bamat

ORBIS BOOKS

Maryknoll, New York 10545

Founded in 1970, Orbis Books endeavors to publish works that enlighten the mind, nourish the spirit, and challenge the conscience. The publishing arm of the Maryknoll Fathers and Brothers, Orbis seeks to explore the global dimensions of the Christian faith and mission, to invite dialogue with the diverse cultures and religious traditions, and to serve the cause of reconciliation and peace. The books published reflect the views of their authors and do not represent the official position of the Maryknoll Society.

To obtain more information about Maryknoll and Orbis Books, please visit our website at www.maryknoll.org.

Library of Congress Cataloging-in-Publication Data

Artisans of peace : grassroots peacemaking among Christian communities /
    edited by Mary Ann Cejka, Thomas Bamat.
        p. cm.
    Includes bibliographical references.
    ISBN 1-57075-463-2 (pbk.)
    1. Peace—Religious aspects—Christianity. 2. Christianity and
justice. I. Cejka, Mary Ann. II. Bamat, Thomas.
BT736.4 .A78 2003
261.8'73—dc21
                                                    2002014784

Contents

Acknowledgments   vii

Introduction
Invisible Artisans of Peace   1
     Thomas Bamat and Mary Ann Cejka

1. God, Justice, Gender, and the Enemy
Issues in Grassroots Peacemaking   19
     Mary Ann Cejka

2. Guatemala
The Challenge of Peacebuilding in Fragmented Communities   35
     Kuldip Kaur

3. Northern Ireland
Peacemaking among Protestants and Catholics   67
     John D. Brewer

4. The Philippines
Bringing Muslims and Christians Together in Peace   96
     Karl M. Gaspar, C.SS.R.

5. Rwanda
Struggle for Healing at the Grassroots   132
     Bernard Noel Rutikanga

6. Sri Lanka
Prophetic Initiatives amidst Deadly Conflict   166
     Shirley Lal Wijesinghe

7. South Sudan
People-to-People Peacemaking: A Local Solution to Local Problems   196
     Julia Aker Duany

8. United States
Places of Sense/Senses of Place: Gang Violence, Positive Cultures
     Leadership, and Peacemaking   226
     John Brown Childs

9. The Mystery of Transformative Times and Spaces
Exploring a Theology of Grassroots Peacebuilding   256
John Paul Lederach

10. A Theology of Power and Spirituality of Empowerment   268
Mary John Mananzan, O.S.B.

11. Grassroots Artisans of Peace
A Theological Afterword   287
Robert J. Schreiter, C.PP.S.

Contributors   301

Bibliography   303

Acknowledgments

Artisans of Peace is the fruit of committed hearts, heads, and hands from all over the globe. We are deeply grateful for the dedication, inspiration, and perspiration of the colleagues, friends, and associates who have contributed to it. Our first nod goes to the research partners and consultants who have borne with us the heat of workdays that stretch back to 1999, and who have put up with us since then. Their careful studies and provocative reflections are the core of this volume.

We also wish to acknowledge those who enabled this project to proceed. The Henry Luce Foundation of New York provided a very substantial and timely grant. Its Program Director for Theology, Michael Gilligan, was enthusiastic from the start and always encouraging. The Maryknoll Society provided the remaining resources. Maryknoll's Superior General, Raymond Finch, and his Council were exceedingly supportive, as were Richard Callahan, M.M., and the personnel of the Society's financial departments.

We likewise wish to thank present and former colleagues at the Center for Mission Research and Study—especially William D. McCarthy, M.M., who spent many an arduous hour preparing the raw data for analysis; Anne Reissner, who organized a stimulating Summer at Maryknoll program on peacemaking in 2001; Jean-Paul Wiest, who helped formulate this project in its early phases and assisted in the search for funding; Donna Bonner, who took notes at our initial research meeting and offered valuable professional opinions from her perspective as an anthropologist and oral historian; and finally but importantly, those who took care of so many demanding administrative, logistical, and secretarial tasks: Maureen Toohey, Clara Araujo, Eileen Finehirsh, and Dianne Doty.

Involvement of the Maryknoll family extended beyond our offices here at Maryknoll, New York. Marie Dennis, Carroll Houle, M.M., and Mercedes Román of the Maryknoll Office of Global Concerns provided both helpful ideas and ideal help, including arrangements for our partners to do a workshop at the United Nations during the Small Arms Conference in 2001. Maryknoll Fathers and Brothers in Guatemala, Kenya, and the Philippines provided generous hospitality, background information, and logistical assistance during our site visits to those countries. The following spent many hours in the tedious but indispensable work of data preparation: Maryknoll Fathers Charles Huegelmeyer, Walter Kelleher, Ken Moody, and John Walsh; Maryknoll Sister Dorothy Mulligan; and Maryknoll Affiliates Ron and Sylvia Guidry.

Joining in the task of data preparation were Hillel Arnold and Sydney Frey of the Jeremiah House Catholic Worker in Bridgeport, Connecticut. Steve Borla, also from Jeremiah House, volunteered to "eat dirt and sleep on the floor" for the privilege of being present during our research meetings—instead, we settled for having him take notes, which he did very ably.

Robert Schreiter graciously accepted a belated invitation to provide a theological afterword. Research psychologists Alice Eagly and Mona Makhijani offered expert advice on the statistical analyses. Michael Leach, Bill Burrows, and the capable professionals at Orbis Books provided constructive, critical assistance in bringing rich raw materials into finished book form. Bob Cejka supplied a laptop computer that made possible many late-night editorial sessions, enabling this manuscript to arrive at Orbis's doorstep on schedule. Thank you all.

These expressions of gratitude would be inexcusably incomplete if we did not include the many research assistants who helped to carry out the fieldwork, and the many hundreds of local people and peace artisans who generously responded to questions big and small. Their participation has provided invaluable contributions to understanding, and some disturbing challenges to complacency.

To all those who toiled in this vineyard, in timely or tireless fashion, we raise our grateful glasses. We trust that they and you will see much of value in this fruit of their labors.

Introduction

Invisible Artisans of Peace

THOMAS BAMAT and MARY ANN CEJKA

The chapters of this book will introduce you to the worlds, the words, and the actions of ordinary Christians coping with extraordinary violence. In places as diverse as Guatemala, Northern Ireland, the Philippines, Rwanda, Sri Lanka, the southern Sudan, and the United States of America, armed violence has etched harsh, indelible marks on their lives. These ordinary local Christians have responded in various ways—sometimes constructively, sometimes not. At times they have failed to respond at all and have become implicated in the violence they chose to ignore. At other times, they have sought to justify their own roles in contributing to the violence. Still other times, they have managed to make a small or even significant contribution toward transforming these conflicts. What they have wrought can often be a source of inspiration.

Jean Banzubaze was a middle-aged Hutu Catholic deeply distressed by the ethnic killing going on in his country. When he spotted his Tutsi neighbor—the author of this book's chapter on Rwanda—on the way home from school one afternoon, he grabbed him and pulled him into the bushes. Hutu strangers were ransacking Bernard's house. Jean told him that he was taking him to his hiding parents and to safety. "If anyone asks who you are," he ordered him gently, "tell him that you are a Hutu and that you are my son."

The Reverend Nirmal Mendis is an Anglican priest from Nugelanda in Sri Lanka, where Tamil and Sinhalese farmers lived and labored together until the Sri Lankan army launched an operation over a decade ago to recapture territory from Tamil militants. Rice paddies became barren killing fields, draining life from Tamils and Sinhalese alike. After two years of meetings promoted by the Reverend Mendis, hundreds of families met again in the year 2000 and embraced one another in this devastated dead zone. Tamils and Sinhalese now cultivate and harvest together in what has become an unofficial peace zone, under banners that proclaim "Peace to the Rice Fields."

Mairead Corrigan Maguire was a Northern Irish Catholic homemaker. When "the Troubles" in Northern Ireland claimed the lives of her two nephews and her niece—all of them small children—she was galvanized into action. Along with a

Protestant homemaker, Betty Williams, and journalist Ciaran McKeown, she organized the Community of Peace People, a grassroots movement that would grow to number half a million Catholics and Protestants rallying for an end to the violence.

José Valenzuela is an evangelical Lutheran layman known as "pastor" to some and, fondly, as "gangsta" to others. Gang life, violence, and drugs menace the Mexican-American and other youth in his Brooklyn neighborhood of Sunset Park. Pastor Valenzuela works tirelessly there to support, organize, and empower the kids. He realizes, he says, that a lot of healing is needed among them, and within American society.

Jean, Nirmal, Mairead, and José are not the kind of high-profile "engineers" of peace processes who usually gain international recognition.[1] They are grassroots "artisans" of peace. But around the world, when ordinary Christians like them bend swords, blunt blows, or build bridges of understanding, they forge grounded hope for a more peaceful world. Strife can often be stymied by the kind of "anonymous" Christians who will seldom be recognized for their achievements (Shenk 2000). Their caring and their courageous craft, however, call each of us to do our part.

ARMED VIOLENCE ACROSS ETHNIC AND RELIGIOUS DIVIDES

The warfare that marks our time in history is not principally warfare between national states. As many scholars and commentators have noted, internal conflicts of various kinds killed far more people during the twentieth century than did conflicts like the First and Second World Wars. Often, the dynamic has been one of government and government allied forces eliminating staggering numbers of people within their own borders (see, among others, Gurr 2000; Rummel 1994; Wallensteen and Sollenberg 1996). The dead in the Sudanese conflict of the last twenty years alone number some two million souls. As Théo Tschuy notes in the introduction to *Ethnic Conflict and Religion: Challenge to the Churches* (1997), the phenomenon of modern ethnic killings, the relationship between ethnic conflicts and religion, and the challenges that both raise for Christian churches should be understood and addressed within this broader context of horror. Large-scale ethnic killing is rarely the work of rival ethnic groups operating on their own; much of it is prepared and carried out by government forces or paramilitary organizations closely allied with them.

Religious communities of nearly all traditions are caught up in the vortex of armed conflicts. One can name Afghanistan, Bosnia, Colombia, India, Iraq, Israel/ Palestine, Mexico, Nigeria, Peru, South Africa, and Turkey, in addition to the

---

1. Mairead Corrigan Maguire is, in this respect, an important exception to the rule. She has been awarded a Nobel Peace Prize.

conflicts included in this volume. Many of these tragic conflagrations involve not only ethnic or racial divides, but also religious ones.

Few of the conflicts marked by a significant religious or ethnic dimension are restricted to, or can be understood within, the confines of modern, national state boundaries alone. Many of these conflicts have been significantly shaped by colonial histories. They readily permeate what are often artificial national borders. They involve a variety of transnational political actors, including powerful foreign governments and a host of international peace brokers.

The horrors of such armed belligerence have been all too familiar to millions upon millions who inhabited the twentieth century. Those of us in the United States of America were largely insulated from direct experiences of them until the attack of September 11, 2001, and its continuing aftermath. We are insulated no longer. Interior psychic landscapes have been as ravaged as that of our country's best-known city—though the national response has been far more violent in its own turn than deeply searching.

A common response to violence of any kind is counterviolence, and religious communities themselves have often been accused of inciting or condoning it. Lately, much of the finger pointing in the West has been at Islam, but it is hardly alone even among the so-called Abrahamic religions. Christianity itself has sometimes been on trial. In his work *Does Christianity Cause War?*, sociologist David Martin (1997) takes up this provocative question with reference to public polemics about the topic in Britain and with his eye on realities like Ulster and Sarajevo among other global hotspots. He insists on the importance of taking into account social and historical contexts and examines a variety of them. His conclusion is that it makes no sense to single out one generic factor such as religion as the cause of conflict. Forms of social identity both unite and separate people. Under certain circumstances they may foster hostility. But it is really a matter of contexts, one of important "markers of identity" such as ethnicity or religion providing "in *special definable* circumstances the preconditions of conflict that are in turn mobilized and reinforced by that conflict" (1997, 19). In fact, as Smock (2002) and others have recently asserted, religion seems better at fostering peace than causing war.

In similarly nuanced fashion, but examining world religions in general and with greater detail and depth, historian Scott Appleby shows that the realm of the holy has more than one valence. In the introduction to *The Ambivalence of the Sacred,* Appleby recognizes the importance of "inquisitions, crusades, pogroms, and wars conducted in the name of God," as well as religious complicity in imperialist expansion and violent extremism wrapped in "religious garb" (2000, 2-4). His emphasis, however, is on the religious resources that can and are being drawn upon in our day to prevent or stem violent aggression, to defend human rights, to transform conflicts as they develop, and to rebuild relations between people.

> Specifically, I refute the notion that religion, having so often inspired, legitimated, and exacerbated deadly conflicts, cannot be expected to contribute consistently to their peaceful resolution. I argue, to the contrary, that a new

form of conflict transformation—"religious peacebuilding"—is taking shape on the ground, in and across local communities plagued by violence. This is a promising development, but it remains inchoate and fragile, unco-ordinated and in need of greater numbers of adequately trained practition-ers, more study and testing, and theoretical elaboration. (Appleby 2000, 7)

The construction of social theory as such is beyond the scope of the case stud-ies and theological reflections contained in this volume. This work, however, is meant to contribute significantly to the tasks of better understanding and, above all, learning important lessons from the Christian peacemaking taking shape at the grassroots in communities plagued by the armed violence that feeds on eth-nic and/or religious divisions.

EVERYDAY ARTISANS

The focus of the vast majority of academic studies on "conflict resolution" or "peacebuilding" is on elite actors. The working rationale seems to be that their power and influence give them privileged potential for success, making them especially worthy of attention. But it is also true that—successes and failures apart—their visibility makes them far easier to study, and their modus operandi may be more readily understood by Western publics than that of some grassroots actors.

Mennonite peace practioner John Paul Lederach, a consultant to this project and a contributor to the volume, has described three different levels of actors in peacebuilding processes—top, middle range, and grassroots—and has attempted to characterize the sorts of practices specific to each. Our focus here is on the often neglected grassroots actors. They are important not simply because they add a large additional number of people to such processes. Often invisible, these makers of peace at the grassroots have a wealth of experience in everyday peace-ful coexistence and considerable experience in dealing concretely with periods of violence and its effects. Their responses, from clever ploys to avoid conscription, to the bold construction of zones of peace, to the use of local traditions to pro-mote community or regional reconciliation, can be astoundingly creative. They are, furthermore, almost always culturally appropriate. Unlike political stake-holders or outside mediators, these actors may be staking their very lives on peace. Their interests are long-term in nature, and their commitment is crucial to making any peace settlement sustainable. In short, while they may be relatively few in number at a given site, weak in might, and in need of greater "empower-ment" or "capacity building," grassroots actors have far more to offer than gen-erally meets the eye. Their grounded wisdom and their often inspiring initiatives also help demonstrate that *everyone* can contribute to peace.

This work is by no means the first to suggest such things or to provide theo-logical reflection on their significance. In addition to articles or sections of works cited above, others bear mention here. *Religion: The Missing Dimension of State-*

craft (Johnson and Sampson 1994) provides important academic accounts of Christian peacemaking activities in Africa, Central America, and Europe. *People Behind the Peace: Community and Reconciliation in Northern Ireland* (Wells 1999) is an enticing look behind the scenes at religious peacebuilding in that troubled land. *People Building Peace: 35 Inspiring Stories from Around the World* (European Centre for Conflict Prevention 1999) is a compendium of promising experiences and a set of reflections on approaches and lessons to be learned. And *The Reconciliation of Peoples: Challenge to the Churches* (Baum and Wells 1997) provides a dozen church-based experiences in conflict-related reconciliation, as well as critical theologizing upon what is seen as the churches' underdeveloped ministry in this field.

The project that led to the production of this book began in 1999. We share many of the assumptions, values, concerns, and conclusions of the works just cited. Our study has probed the experiences of a variety of local, grassroots Christians and of Christian communities seeking peace in the midst of violence. While it has taken into account the official pronouncements and the mediating efforts of church leaders, its primary emphasis has been on the actions of ordinary Christians—laypeople, ministers, and priests engaged at the level of neighborhoods, villages, marketplaces, and schools. We have functioned with the conviction that each time a group of believers attempts to defuse a violent or potentially violent situation, something can be learned that could help others to avoid mistakes or to experiment with new alternatives. We seek to benefit churches throughout the world in their effort to defuse conflicts in volatile areas, to contribute to their mediating actions and their larger endeavor to be a peace-inspiring presence in all spheres of life. We aim to advance the current understanding of the peacemaking role of cross-cultural Christian mission. And we seek to help grassroots Christians themselves, throughout the world church, to learn from one another.We are convinced that only a careful examination of the grassroots experiences of others allows for lessons to be truly learned and adapted creatively in other contexts.

Our research process has also been unique in several ways, and our findings provide some novel contributions. We are aware of no previous attempt to carry out this kind of comparative empirical research on the forms of grassroots Christian responses to violence across cultures. We have employed quantitative methods in tandem with qualitative ones, provided detailed descriptions of the actions taken, and rooted theological reflection in the soil of these systematic, comparative, empirical studies.

GENESIS AND INITIAL DEVELOPMENT OF THE PROJECT

Since its inception a decade ago, the focus of the Center for Mission Research and Study at Maryknoll (CMRSM) has been Christianity at the grassroots. This focus is in keeping with the charism of the Maryknoll mission movement, and with the ethics of global solidarity and a preferential option for the poor. The decision to examine grassroots Christian responses to violence in particular sprang from debate among the international participants at the Center's inaugural consultation. They considered it a pressing priority. The project took further shape as a result of a meeting in 1997 at Maryknoll, New York, of academics and others directly involved in conflict negotiation in volatile areas around the world.

The Center's inaugural consultation of scholars from Africa, Asia, Latin America, and the United States also helped give shape to the way in which CMRSM carries out its research mandate. The Center was envisioned as a potential "beacon of partnership" between local Christian communities. It was recommended that CMRSM foster research based on grassroots experiences, seek to assemble research teams that reflect a diversity of cultures and modes of approaching topics, help to locate and secure funding, assume leadership or facilitating functions depending upon the project, and collaborate in the dissemination of research project findings.

The opportunity to take up the issue of grassroots Christian responses to violence in a comprehensive way was finally made possible by a substantial grant from the Henry Luce Foundation in 1999. In October of that year, the research partners and theological consultants who ultimately participated in this endeavor first gathered at Maryknoll. They had been invited because of their knowledge and understanding of the local conflicts, residency in the affected areas, academic credentials, personal commitments to peace, and willingness to be part of this sort of collaborative enterprise. They were able to meet each other for the first time and to lay the foundations for a working relationship that would last for nearly three years. Partners and consultants gained greater familiarity with the situations of conflict in each of the various sites, worked toward a common understanding of basic concepts, and came to a consensus about the common research questions and methodology that the project would employ.

The sites that had been chosen for the study were intentionally widely distributed around the world. Two are in Africa, two in Asia, two in the United States and Europe, and one in Latin America. All are marked by socially significant and protracted violence that involves an ethnic or religious divide. They differ by design with regard to the duration, stages and intensity of conflicts, the ratio of Christians to other sectors of the population, the role of religion in the hostilities, and church involvements. In each of them, however, grassroots Christians have responded or are currently responding in some significant ways to the violence.

When research partners and consultants gathered in 1999, they reaffirmed the overarching goals of this project, including that of identifying key factors in the effectiveness of grassroots Christian responses to violence, or the lack thereof. It was agreed that in each of the case study sites researchers would explore efforts in which ordinary, everyday people were key actors—no matter who initiated or supported these efforts. Without limiting their studies to actions that involved Christians alone, the emphasis would be on the involvement of those who considered themselves Christians, and it would include the ways in which these people's actions were motivated by their religious beliefs.

Considerable thought was given to the nature of the grassroots responses to violence, and to those making the responses. It was agreed that the study would focus on both direct and indirect efforts to ameliorate conflict and/or bring about peace. It would encompass actions like therapeutic efforts to heal victims of violence or to repair material damages only if such efforts functioned as peacemaking efforts per se—that is, as attempts to bring opposing parties together in a common endeavor. Responses could be spontaneous or planned, but would not include mere instinctual reactions to aggression such as flight or hiding. Convinced of the practical efficacy of many forms of nonviolent action (see Sharp 1973 and the PBS video *A Force More Powerful*) and aligned with it in principle, partners agreed to focus on the nonviolent responses to aggression but to report less clearly nonviolent alternatives, such as the formation of armed night patrols or the destruction of an enemy's weapons.

The grassroots religious actors, participants agreed, could be individuals or groups, including centers, campaigns, or organizations that have facilitated peacemaking in the chosen sites. The actions of individuals were to be considered where possible in relation to a community or communities that may have served as a source of inspiration or support, since individual action is generally part of larger, collective efforts.

Finally, there was a need to delimit the forms of social violence to be considered and not considered in the case study sites. Partners agreed, both because of its contemporary prevalence and because of the need for comparability between research results, to consider only organized, armed violence that involved an ethnic and/or religious divide. Excluded from direct consideration were common crime, domestic abuse, or the "structural violence" of hunger and poverty, though most forms of violence are interconnected. Also excluded were conflicts centered *primarily* on the nature of political regimes, territorial control, or class power—though it was recognized again that such issues often overlap with those of religion and ethnicity.

COMMON QUESTIONS, COMMON METHODS

One of the most important decisions as the project began was the agreement that all researchers would seek to pursue the answers to a set of six overarching "root questions" and their key "branch questions." Other questions could be pursued at the option of individual research partners and their teams. The guiding root and branch questions were the following:

- What have been the grassroots responses to the violence?
  —When and how frequently have specific kinds of responses occurred?
  —Where have they occured?
  —How did they relate to local culture and cultural traditions?

- Who has participated in the actions (numbers, composition, leadership roles)?
  —How have women been affected by the conflict, and responded?
  —How have children and young adults been affected, and responded?

—How have grassroots actors themselves perceived the conflict/problem?
—What do these actors understand by peace?

• How have grassroots actors sought to transform the conflict?
—What were the resources (symbolic, practical, spiritual) employed?
—What were the institutional linkages or broader networks within which the actions occurred, or through which they were enhanced?
—What linkages exist between grassroots actions, intermediate level organizations/initiatives (NGOs, etc.), and those at the state level?
—How do the peacemakers make the connection between these levels?

• What has motivated the grassroots responses?
—How did people perceive their religious faith as related to the responses (if at all)?
—What are people's operative images of God and the sacred?
—What motivates them to engage in peacemaking?

• What problems and constraints were encountered?
—Did people's religion seem in general to help or worsen the situation?
—Was their religion helpful at times, detrimental at others?
—What other factors might have contributed to conflict transformation?
—What resources for peacemaking did people lack?
—What obstacles to Christian peacemaking were there in the setting?
—Did the intervention of an international third party (or parties) make things better or worse?

• What were the effects of the grassroots responses?
—What kind of impact did the actions seem to have (including effects on community solidarity and on civil society)?
—How effective or ineffective did they seem to be in transforming the conflict in some way (by reducing the killing, raising awareness of atrocities, contributing to a ceasefire, encouraging negotiations, etc.)?
—Did any apparent defeat lead to actual victory or vice-versa?

Quite obviously, this study was conceived of as exploratory in nature and aimed at comprehensive descriptions of grassroots Christian responses to violence. The guiding questions provided a common road map to help keep the researchers on the same track.

Both qualitative and quantitative research methods and techniques were initially selected for use by all the researchers. Others were left to the discretion of the individual research partners or teams. The qualitative methods that all agreed to were (a) the use of documentary or secondary sources to examine the broad gamut of known grassroots peacemaking initiatives in each of the case study countries, (b) the collection of autobiographical narratives, and (c) extensive interviewing with both groups and individuals. Each researcher also agreed to attempt a historical periodization of the conflict in question, since responses to violence can vary greatly over years or even months.

Two explorations using quantitative techniques were proposed to the research partners and adopted. The first was to examine whether or not women and men had recourse to different kinds of peacemaking activities and to look for any gender differences in motivation. The second was to use quantitative techniques to examine to what degree perceptions such as personal images of God, images of the opponent, or belief that the world is just tend to predict involvement in peacemaking, motivation for involvement, or the types of involvement, as well as the relationship of these variables to one another. See chapter 1 for a discussion of the quantitative components of this study.

PROGRESS AND PERILS

As expected, the research process itself was fraught with difficulties. At the same time, one might argue, its development was remarkably smooth. Despite dangers, dilemmas, and some unavoidable delays, it was completed without a disaster of any kind.

Partners from the Philippines, Sri Lanka, and the Sudan—where armed conflict has continued—had rightly expected to face serious problems. The other partners had urged them to take no unnecessary risks and to rethink specific research sites if necessary. In the Philippines, fieldwork planned for Sulu and Basilan had to be dropped; fieldwork elsewhere was delayed at times because of local fighting; and communication was sometimes disrupted. In Sri Lanka, research partners were regularly stopped for questioning at military checkpoints. In the Sudan, field research in the Equatoria region had to be canceled indefinitely, and research partner Julia Duany and a female colleague named Nyakang once had to crawl twenty meters across a sorghum field to riverbank bushes in order to hide themselves from marauding soldiers. "Research in Sudan is not a vacation," Julia remarked. "The risks are real, but I think they are worth taking because in the final analysis this project can change the conditions that affect the lives of so many people."

While hardly as dramatic, the establishment of trust among researchers and would-be participants was another serious challenge in several sites. In Guatemala, Kully Kaur found fear and a distrust of anyone asking lots of questions, partly because so many local people had been involved in the killings and rural communities had developed a tradition of silence about them. In Rwanda, Bernard Rutikanga found much the same phenomenon. He overcame much of the resistance by enlisting the support of respected local authorities and by assuring people that he was there to examine not acts of genocide, but acts of peace. In the United States, John Brown Childs was able to establish trust through his own personal presence and reputation in a number of communities and through an open, conversational style of interviewing. As he writes in the introduction to his chapter, such an approach is important given the covert dimensions of gang activity; those seeking to study and help stop the violence must "be on guard not to seem like interrogation police, or to be otherwise endangering those with whom they work."

In some case-study sites, trust was established with the local people because research partners were known not only as academics but also as individuals who are personally commited to peace. This sometimes functioned as the proverbial double-edged sword, however. Researchers had to cope with some role conflicts between the painstaking task of collecting and analyzing data, on the one hand, and the task of actively promoting peace, on the other.

The research process took longer than initially projected. It was slowed down by the need for translation into and out of many local languages, by multiple demands on the time of most of the partners and consultants, by the large number of people who were surveyed in some of the sites, and by the care required to employ the quantitative techniques with professional rigor. In the end, however, the process yielded its anticipated fruits.

It is not surprising that the most difficult root questions to answer were those dealing with the effects and effectiveness of specific actions. The problems stemmed from conceptual complexity, the number of factors at play, and the difficulties that are always inherent in determining causes and effects. In comparative terms, questions about who, what, how, and against what obstacles were far simpler to answer—though the answers were not self-evident. In fact, Shirley Lal Wijesinghe and Deepthi Silva in Sri Lanka and Kuldip Kaur in Guatemala had to struggle initially to find appropriate locations and experiences, and Bernard Rutikanga was amazed when he discovered that so many hitherto unknown and positive actions had been carried out in Rwanda during the very weeks in which the brutal genocide was being perpetrated.

PRINCIPAL RESULTS

This research effort has carefully documented the extent and importance of grassroots peacemaking actions in numerous and varied contexts worldwide. As the chapters that follow clearly demonstrate, these actions are not merely spontaneous or "reactive." Nor are they limited to popular participation in initiatives that originate with other levels of societies or external agencies. Actions by everyday artisans of peace may differ greatly from the practices of the midrange and elite engineers of large-scale peace processes, but they are often creative and sometimes crucial to forging sustainable relationships for peace.

The qualitative and historical research data that our international research team assembled serve to illustrate important arguments that have been made previously by other researchers and scholars. These include such issues as the nonethnic and nonreligious roots of much supposedly "ethnic" or "religious" violence and the potential of embedded economic interests and of certain cultural traditions in perpetuating or transforming conflicts. They include the ways in which the nature and the stages of a given conflict can affect the prevailing modes of peacemaking and the importance of horizontal and vertical social linkages in efforts to make conflict transformation more effective.

Our systematic gathering and analysis of quantified cross-cultural data on forms of and motivations for grassroots peacemaking, gender issues, images of the divine and of the opponent, and belief in a "just world" point to the central-ity of relationship building at the grassroots and raise questions about the notion that women are always the principal relationship builders. They also suggest that people's images of the divine are more strongly related to their peacemaking activities, or lack thereof, than are their images of the opponent (see chapter 1).

CONFLICTS IN CONTEXT

By design, there is a significant ethnic component in each of our case studies. The historical backgrounds presented by the researchers help to demonstrate, however, the mythical and often dangerously misleading nature of the notion that contemporary ethnic/religious conflicts are best understood as eruptions of deep, centuries-old hatred between peoples (see among others Psalidas-Perlmutter 2000). Our studies point out the strong impact of colonialism (and sometimes of Christianity) in shaping many of these conflicts. Rwanda, while hardly unique, provides a devastating example of the impact of both.

A variety of socioeconomic and geopolitical interests have helped to generate and perpetuate these conflicts. The researchers have observed that enduring or deepening poverty and inequality in societies help to feed armed violence. Like-wise, the interests of those who come to reap benefits from a "war economy" (or in the United States a "drug economy") tend to perpetuate it. Unequal or threat-ened access to, or control of, basic resources such as land and water are at the heart of many such conflicts. So are inequitable access to social goods such as jobs and schooling. Dealing with issues such as rights to territory or land (as in the Philippines, Sri Lanka, and Guatemala), water and other natural resources (as in Sri Lanka and the Sudan), or education and employment (as in Rwanda and in Northern Ireland) are obviously essential to achieving just peace.

International geopolitical interests are often key to conflicts and their trans-formation or lack thereof. In our studies, the Cold War policies of the United States, neoliberal economic imposition, and specific issues such as Rwanda's close links to the francophone world, the coveted deepwater ports in Sri Lanka, and international interest in Sudanese oil were all seen as significant in this regard.

GRASSROOTS PEACEMAKING

As mentioned above, our case studies indicate that much more grassroots peacemaking activity is going on than hits the news—and not only the Western news. Several research partners commented about how much they had discovered within their own countries, and how surprised they were by it. At the same time, it is clear to all that such peacemaking is a minority phenomenon. The vast majority of grassroots people in most social contexts seem relatively passive and tend to be readily manipulated by political and/or cultural and religious elites.

A relatively strong civil society seems to provide a matrix that can enhance the extent and effectiveness of grassroots peacemaking efforts. The cases of Northern Ireland and the Philippines clearly demonstrate this. Among our case-study sites they were clearly the countries with the densest peacebuilding networks. Weaker civil society, as in the case of Sri Lanka, seems to be associated with fewer initiatives of this kind.

Unsurprisingly, charismatic leaders are crucial in many peacemaking initiatives and programs. But specific social sectors, such as different types of "elders" and women, often provide the key players for such leadership roles. The Sudan study provides striking examples of the influence of both traditional authorities and of organizations of women.

This research indicates that much grassroots peacemaking takes place not under Christian auspices per se but rather in cooperation with non-Christians (as in the Philippines, Sudan, and Sri Lanka) or in tandem with or under the aegis of secular or nonreligious organizations (as in Northern Ireland, Guatemala, Rwanda, and the United States). Partnership with others appears to be a hallmark of this peacemaking, enhancing its reach and strength.

The character and density of grassroots peacemaking seem to depend on a wide range of factors, including the broader institutional context mentioned above. They also seem to depend on (a) the stage of a given conflict, (b) the intensity and duration of the violence, (c) the resources available for conflict transformation activities, (d) the relative solidarity or fragmentation *within* religious or ethnic communities, and (e) the relative legitimacy or public disdain for such peacemaking actions.

A Tentative Typology for Grassroots Peacemaking

It is useful for purposes of better understanding grassroots Christian responses to violence and for purposes of better enhancing such peacemaking practices, to map out their variety. Appleby (2000, 211-43) recently provided helpful elements for a typology of what he calls "religious peacebuilding" in general, breaking it down into three goal-based "dimensions" and three contextually based "modes" of action. While we could discuss the grassroots Christian peacemaking activities found in our seven case studies with reference to these important dimensions and modes, this does not appear to be the clearest or most helpful way of mapping them here. Grassroots actions tend to have an immediacy, a specific scale, and an everyday character that can be lost if simply subsumed under general "dimensions" like the management or control of conflict or its resolution. The same could be said for subsuming it under the circumstantial peacebuilding "modes" of crisis mobilization, dense organizational saturation, or a web of programs sponsored by intervening outsiders.

A more helpful typology in this particular case seeks to categorize the gamut of grassroots Christian peacemaking actions principally around their timing vis-à-vis armed violence and its levels of intensity. We tentatively suggest the following typology:[2]

---

2. In the chapter on Northern Ireland, John Brewer develops still another set of categories for grassroots peacemaking. He distinguishes between what he calls *passive* and *active* peacemaking, then highlights differences in the two based on the character of group outreach or intervention, the

A. Cross-temporal Initiatives (preventative, or occurring at various stages of a conflict)
   1. Religious events such as organized prayer services or pilgrimages
   2. Demonstrations for peace or human rights (socioeconomic, political, cultural)
B. Activities Carried Out in the Midst of Violent Conflict
   1. Practical efforts to prevent or blunt the impact of imminent violence
      a. Warnings (e.g. drumming, raising flags, sending messengers)
      b. Hiding would-be victims
      c. Accompanying the movement to safety of those in danger
      d. Seeking out or providing spaces of religious "sanctuary"
      e. Protesting against or directly confronting the perpetrators of violence
   2. Longer-range peacebuilding during protracted, less intense periods of violence
      a. Resistance to conscription
      b. Mediation between the parties in conflict
      c. Construction of "spaces" for peace (peace villages, centers, youth camps, training programs)
      d. Relationship building through outreach, dialogue, common economic activities, social exchanges
C. Post-violence or Lingering-violence Initiatives
   1. Providing public testimonies; witnessing to acts of violence, genocide
   2. Memorializing (historical representations; building or maintaining memorials to the dead or to heroic local figures)
   3. Seeking a just peace (reconstructed community, tolerance, respect for human rights, the enhancement of human dignity and development)

Timing isn't everything in peacemaking of course, but there does appear to be a "time to every purpose." Time and intensity tend to frame and structure the realm of the possible.

CULTURAL RESOURCES

Cultural traditions have been identified in some of our studies as rich resources for peacebuilding. Reverence for and concern about the *ancestors* are such cultural traditions. So is the authority of the *elders*, as in the southern Sudan's remarkable people-to-people peacemaking process, and so are traditional community mechanisms for resolving disputes and reestablishing harmony. A good example of the latter is the local *gacaca* tribunals for trying those accused of genocide in Rwanda.

At the same time, certain traditions can serve as impediments to peacemaking. Among these are narrowly clannish identity and behaviors, a glorification of

---

form of organization involved, and issues being addressed. Obviously, there is no single way of categorizing such activities

male aggressiveness, and restrictions on women's freedom of action. The social psychology of a given culture or subculture can be fraught with problems. Collective anxieties about a future that is different (implying shared territory and reconstructed memories) were pointed out by researchers from both Northern Ireland and Sri Lanka as obstacles to peace.

GENDERED RESPONSES TO VIOLENCE

Our researchers suggest that in some situations, violent activity may be fostered not only by traditional patriarchal norms or *machismo*, but also by status crises or "crises of masculinity." In circumstances in which men may find themselves without income, jobs, or other customary claims to status (see, for example, the Northern Ireland and U.S. cases), the appeal of armed aggression can be stronger and the appeal of nonviolence concomitantly weaker.

Women are victimized by armed violence in gender-specific ways. In cases in which their men or their children have been dying or are dead, where they are left dispossessed and grieving, women may occupy specific social roles as forceful peacemakers. A good example is the National Coordinating Committee of Guatemalan Widows known as CONAVIGUA, mentioned by Kudip Kaur in the chapter on Guatemala. Founded in 1988 to demand government support for widows created by the violence, it has also worked for demilitarization and the promotion of human rights in that Central American country.

Women have assumed significant roles as leaders of peacebuilding initiatives in a number of the cases presented in this book, perhaps especially in the southern Sudan and Northern Ireland. At the grassroots, men and women work for peace in surprisingly similar ways; when differences in approach exist, they are apparently determined by constraints placed upon women by the specific culture or conflict. In this regard, the data we collected raise some cautionary flags about glib cross-cultural generalizations. For a detailed discussion of gender and peacemaking, we direct you again to chapter 1.

MOTIVATIONS

Religious beliefs and values were an important source of motivation for many of the peacemakers with whom our research partners and their assistants spoke, but religious motivations were much less frequently mentioned than practical, relational, and ideological motivations—and the latter three often occurred together, with practical motivations being the most common. All these motivational categories, and their relationships to various types of peacemaking as well as to other attitudes and beliefs addressed in our study, are described at length in the next chapter.

EFFECTIVENESS AND SUCCESS

Appleby (2000, 16) notes the need for "a keener appreciation of how effective religion and religious actors already are . . . in preventing and managing deadly conflict, protecting human rights, and promoting more open and participatory forms of government around the world." This need to know more about effectiveness certainly applies to grassroots Christian actors and their own particular successes and failures.

The studies in this book include a rich variety of local success stories. Few are merely tales of individual heroes. Karl Gaspar writes of "the power that can emanate from the group up." In his and the other chapters you will learn of human lives saved, popular resistance to elite manipulation, growing understanding among enemies and strangers, local peace zones carved into war-torn areas in Sri Lanka and the Philippines, grassroots mobilizations influencing higher-level negotiations in the Philippines and Northern Ireland, and widespread peace accords worked out between formerly hostile communities in various regions of the southern Sudan. Local people across our case studies, when asked if their efforts have been effective or not, generally said that they have been.

It would be foolish, however, to don rose-tinted lenses and gaze romantically upon the landscape. Despite Guatemala's 1996 peace accords and popular participation in the process that led to them, discrimination and impunity are still rampant there. Apparent progress in overcoming the ethnic divisions in Rwanda cannot truly be evaluated for years to come. Serious stumbling blocks have emerged in the Sudan's "people-to-people peace process." Gang violence appears to be worsening in at least some U.S. cities, with old truces unravelling (see Winter 2002), and the "positive cultures" phenomenon, of which John Brown Childs writes in his chapter, still limited largely to personal transformations and some stronger neighborhoods.

"Success" has different meanings, of course. Childs prefers to speak of a *scale* of accomplishments that range from merely creating and sustaining a local peace organization, to small-scale and large-scale accomplishments in conflict transformation. We must get beyond equating success, he insists, with nothing less than the "total resolution" of a problem.

At the same time, the ultimate goal in conflict transformation must be precisely such systemic forms of success. John Brewer writes at the end of his chapter about how difficult and frustratingly limited success can be, even in a country like Northern Ireland—where the level of killing is far less than that of other countries, and where the effort to bring it to an end is championed by an entire "peacemaking industry."

The wry, apocryphal beatitude "Blessed are the peacemakers, they will never be unemployed" may, tragically enough, be true. But this does not excuse us from asking how relatively effective or ineffective a given action or set of actions is or may be. Our study describes a host of positive effects that grassroots peacemaking actions have had on individuals, communities, and societies around the world. But it does not measure just how effective such actions were, or predict what might have happened had they never been carried out. This project would have needed a far different methodology—and perhaps miraculous intervention—to provide reliable measures of the effectiveness of these grassroots responses to violence.

Grassroots actors are not always adequately grounded in their own religious heritage, and religious peacemakers as a whole tend to be overlooked, under-funded, relatively isolated, and insufficiently prepared for engaging in conflict transformation (see Appleby 2000, 17). Many of our research partners write that the limited success achieved by local grassroots peacemakers could be signifi-cantly *enhanced* by things like greater resources, more training and formation (as in the Philippines and the Sudan), more institution building (Sudan), greater regional or national networking (as in the United States and Sudan), better reli-gious or ethical education (as in the Philippines), and bridges over the "chasm" that lies between grassroots peacebuilding efforts and those carried out by elites (as in Northern Ireland). Here, churches are among the organizations that can provide the most help.

CHALLENGES FOR CHRISTIAN COMMUNITIES

In principle, virtually all Christians want peace, in their communities and around the world. But pious platitudes are often contradicted by facile justifica-tions for aggression, and prayer is often blindly partisan or accompanied by prac-tical passivity. Fortunately, Christian communities worldwide have in fact been doing more, and not merely saying more, about peace in recent years. Encycli-cals from the time of John XXIII's *Pacem in Terris* and pastoral letters from many bishops' conferences have both grown out of and invigorated practical actions for peace and justice on the ground. The sophistication and scope of modern killing have fueled new debates about the validity and application of tra-ditional "just war" theories. Across the spectrum of the churches, there has been a rich development of theologies of reconciliation and an effort to explore their practical implications. We have witnessed high-profile, turn-of-the-century events such as the Millennium World Peace Summit of Religious and Spiritual Leaders at the United Nations, and major interfaith gatherings in Amman, Jordan, and Assisi, Italy. Religious officials and laypeople alike have led conflict media-tion efforts from Mexico and Nicaragua to East Timor and Mozambique. Churches have participated significantly in the work of national "truth commis-sions" in post-conflict circumstances from Africa to Latin America, and the World Council of Churches has launched a far-reaching educational and action campaign for 2001 to 2010, the "Decade to Overcome Violence."

As important and promising as these developments and others are, most key actors in these initiatives have been high-ranking church leaders, and much of their attention has been on influencing elites. But if armed conflicts involving a significant ethnic or religious divide are those taking the highest toll in victims, and if grassroots "artisans of peace" are indeed crucial to sustainable peace between peoples, Christian churches and communities should be dedicating more energy and resources to transforming these kinds of conflicts in particular (see Tschuy 1997) and to supporting these kinds of actors. They should be cham-pioning the cause of local, lay artisans of peace and channeling more resources toward the enhancement of their capabilities.

There are unique challenges and opportunities for churches and local faith communities in contemporary situations of violence. Often they have both disposable material resources and moral authority among the population (though there are exceptions—such as in Rwanda following the 1994 genocide). They have international networks of communication that offer both means of conveying information and some limited protection for grassroots peacemakers. In extreme circumstances, they may be all that remains of social organization, or one of the few organizations that is able to act.

To take advantage of these peacemaking opportunities, faith communities must be able to read the signs of the times. They must have a reasonably good analysis of social conditions and the ways in which power is exercised within and upon a given context. They must also have a sense of *timing*. They should know when they can take preventive actions, when mediation may be fruitful, and when it is time to witness to past atrocities or focus on rebuilding broken relationships. In this they must be willing to learn from the experiences of others, such as those being shared in a volume like this.

Too often there is excessive partisanship, sectarianism, social passivity, or fear to act on the part of Christian leaders. It is *always* time to defend human dignity. Again, the experiences and example of others not only instruct but also inspire.

As our research partners note, churches have served and can continue to serve as institutional supporters and as allies of grassroots peacemakers. They can encourage risk taking. They can provide spaces of safety, reflection, and a search for meaning. As Mary John Mananzan insists in her theological reflection, they must help to *empower* the local people. They can and should help to provide *hope*, with a vision that beckons toward a future without the violence that they have known.

Paul Van Tongeren has compiled a succinct list of important lessons that can be learned from peacebuilding initiatives worldwide (European Centre for Conflict Prevention 1999, 124-29). These lessons draw on the reflections of many other peacemaking professionals. While they are not specifically religious in character, they resonate deeply with the experiences and reflections of this book. The first seven of them almost seem to cry out for churches, cross-cultural missioners, and local faith communities to respond with the particular gifts and resources they have, in collaboration with others of good will:

1. Involve as many people and sectors as possible in peacebuilding
2. Strengthen local capacities for peace
3. Conceive of peacebuilding and reconciliation as a process
4. Change and transform the conflict pattern; create hope
5. Create dialogue
6. Promote education and enhance professionalization
7. Exchange experiences

The theological reflections of Lederach, Mananzan, and Schreiter ably delve into such practical theological and ecclesial themes. We will not belabor them here. Suffice it to say that they approach this study's findings from a variety of theological perspectives. At times these reinforce one another; at other times they produce distinct emphases or different conclusions. Together, they provide a rich mix of voices with lay and professional, male and female, Northern and Southern, and Protestant and Catholic accents.

PARTNERS IN PEACE WORK

From the day we gathered in 1999 to set in motion the process that has led to this book, it was clear that the assembled group of human beings was remarkable. Not only was it ecumenical, international, and highly diversified by culture and discipline; it was comprised of people with a high degree of personal as well as academic interest in local attempts at peacemaking. The hope was not to make a book but to make a difference. A congenial dynamic has characterized our interactions ever since, and partners' commitments to peacebuilding have grown.

An important part of our commitment is to disseminate the results of the studies and to foster consideration of their practical implications. Some partners have been able to do more in this regard than others. Consultations to discuss results with church leaders and/or other peacemakers have taken a variety of forms, but they have been held in nearly all of the study sites. In Guatemala the research consultation was a small one, while in the Sudan one session to share the findings was attended by two hundred people from the Nuer, Anuak, and Murle ethnic groups and some Dinka church and community leaders. In Sri Lanka, there have been over a half-dozen sessions to discuss the findings, with several of them comparing Sri Lanka and Northern Ireland. Some extended reports on the results of the research have received local media coverage. The report on Rwanda is to be presented to the government's ministry for unity and reconciliation. A book is being prepared in Sri Lanka. The most extensive dissemination, however, has been in the Philippines. There, partners prepared an attractive, illustrated three-hundred-page "reader for peace advocates" (Gaspar, Lapad, and Maravillas 2002), and plan to have it translated into Cebuano and the three principal Moro languages. Popular education materials and study guides for use in some Philippine schools are also planned. In the United States, we intend to publish articles for both popular and scholarly audiences. Maryknoll Productions is likewise eager to prepare a video documentary that will draw on some of the case studies.

As we prepare to go to press, the histories of violent conflict and of conflict transformation go on in Guatemala, Northern Ireland, the Philippines, Rwanda, Sri Lanka, the Sudan, and the United States. Some situations seem more hopeful than when we began. Others do not. The lives of our research and theological partners also go on. The social histories and their personal biographies continue to intersect and evolve. It has been an inspiration for the two of us to work with colleagues whom we now call friends. In the midst of troubling and sometimes very painful realities, and with new forms of warfare now threatening our world, getting to know them has been a privilege. In the pages that follow, we proudly pass on to you that privilege.

1

God, Justice, Gender, and the Enemy

Issues in Grassroots Peacemaking

MARY ANN CEJKA

There is more to grassroots peacemaking than meets the eye. As researchers, we are privileged to explore matters both patent and hidden, to tease out subtle relationships that underlie seemingly obvious processes. The privilege is all the greater when the focus of the research is something that matters, both to the world at large and to individuals facing specific challenges. We hope, with our research, not only to do what scholars do—make "a contribution to the literature" on peacemaking—but to help orient on-the-ground efforts at transforming conflict. Moreover, to be quite frank, researchers entrusted with coordinating a lengthy and costly international project on grassroots peacemaking have a responsibility to obtain as much useful information as possible in the course of the project. So we set out to do just that.

In our introduction to this volume, we listed the "root" and "branch" questions that informed this study. Among them are: What have been the grassroots responses to the violence? Who has participated in them, and why? What have been grassroots peacemakers' operative images of God and the sacred? Within these questions are further questions, at once more specific yet tantalizing in their scope: Do local peacemakers hold stereotypes of opposing religious or ethnic groups, or are peacemakers freer of such stereotypes—are they, in common pejorative parlance, "bleeding hearts" for the enemy? Is their religious faith connected to their work for peace, and if so, to what extent? Do they hold certain motivations in common? Are specific motivations connected to particular kinds of peacemaking? Do grassroots peacemakers see the world as a basically just place, or do experiences of injustice somehow inspire their peacemaking efforts? Do women and men approach peacemaking differently? Finally, how much do the answers to all of the above vary according to country, culture, and specific conflict situation?

Multifaceted studies such as this one call for a multiplicity of methods—some qualitative, others quantitative. Though we have known scholars who seem to be allergic to one or the other, we believe that it is irresponsible to disdain the use of either qualitative or quantitative methods if they are the appropriate methods for addressing a given research question. The partners in this study have therefore chosen to include both kinds of methods, approaching some issues qualitatively and others quantitatively, or both at once, as needed.

You have read some of our qualitative findings in the introduction. We now turn to questions (those presented above) whose investigation required a quantitative approach, or quantitative methods supplemented with qualitative ones. You will encounter findings based on both kinds of methods in most of the chapters from the individual countries included in the study. The task in this chapter is to summarize the quantitative findings from all the countries taken together and to make some comparisons between countries. So as not to clutter the text or scare off nonquantitatively oriented readers with numbers and scientific notation, tables are placed at the ends of chapters. Unless otherwise indicated, all results reported here are statistically significant.

The difficulties inherent in conducting quantitative research in areas characterized by widespread poverty and recent or current conflict bear some mention. So too does that fact that, since each country has its own language, culture, and dominant religions, it is necessary for research instruments to be country-specific yet similar enough to make comparisons possible.

CROSS-CULTURAL RESEARCH

CONSIDERATIONS AND APPROACHES

It is inappropriate or simply impossible in certain conditions (widespread illiteracy, poor roads that make travel difficult, pervasive fear and distrust brought on by the constant threat of attack) to gather potential respondents together, hand them pencils, provide them with printed questionnaires, and ask them to fill them out. For the most part, researchers in this study gathered quantitative data by using structured interviews (in other words, they referred to sets of questions prepared in advance). This was a lengthy and labor-intensive process.

In some cultures, a question such as, "On a scale of one to five, to what extent do you agree with each of the following statements?" would be incomprehensible. Therefore, no questions were phrased using explicit numeric values, but rather using adverbs like "rarely," "sometimes," and "often." With open-ended questions, research teams were instructed not to "prime" hesitant respondents by suggesting certain categories of responses, but rather to let them answer in their own way and at their own pace.

Since research partners represented disciplines as diverse as sociology, anthropology, biblical theology, history, and education, one considerable challenge had to be surmounted before the data gathering even began: the task of agreeing on quantitative procedures that could be implemented in a comparable manner by researchers with varying degrees of experience in such methods. Some of our research partners planned to work with teams, others individually.

Interviews, we decided, were to be kept short. To obtain data via interviews, we had to rely on self-report, with the obvious disadvantage—particularly in areas recently or currently scourged with violent conflict—that respondents might be tempted to present themselves in an exaggeratedly positive light. Consequently, the quantitative data gathering had to be supplemented by some of the qualitative methods described in the introductory chapter, such as group interviews to help counterbalance the statements of individuals.

We had a relatively brief, clearly defined period of time and a generous but finite budget for carrying out a very ambitious research project. This meant that any serious pretesting of questions was not an option. We stuck with established social-scientific measures and modified them when necessary. We would have liked to look at other issues of interest, but decided that this would be up to the individual research teams, who sometimes had to make impromptu revisions of their research plans as a result of news of a morning ambush or a newly established roadblock. Karl Gaspar's team in the Philippines, for example, added a qualitative study of how peacemakers view their own ethnic and religious groups—not just the opponents'. Even in the best of situations, the amount of information local researchers managed to obtain would have been impressive; given what they were up against, it is nothing short of astonishing.

APPROACHING THE RESEARCH QUESTIONS

Assessing gender differences in peacemaking was easy enough. Researchers simply made note of respondents' sex and other easily determined and potentially relevant demographic variables (for example, age, religion, years of education, and sometimes ethnicity), then asked them in a linguistically and culturally appropriate manner what they had done or were doing for peace, and what motivated them. Research on gender was carried out in all countries included in the study.[1]

In Northern Ireland, the Philippines, and Sri Lanka,[2] researchers also investigated what images of the divine, images of the opponent, and belief in a "just world" could tell us about who is a peacemaker and who is not, ways of working for peace, and motivations for doing so.

An approach developed by Pollner (1989) and subsequently adapted by Cejka (forthcoming) was used to assess images of the divine. The latter study employed

---

[1] Gender data from the United States were gathered in a unique manner that will make them a very useful contribution to understanding responses to gang violence in U.S. cities; however, they are not directly comparable to data from other countries included in this volume.

[2] The choice of whether to engage in quantitative research and which of the quantitative projects to undertake was the decision of individual research partners.

a statistical method called "factor analysis,"[3] which surfaced three major categories of images of the divine: *agentic*—God as creator, liberator, redeemer, and father—in other words, a "hands on" God who acts in specific ways in people's lives; *immanent*—God as spouse, lover, mother, and child—in other words, a God in close and intimate relationship with human beings; and *power-over* (God as master, ruler, and judge)—in other words, a God in control of all things, including reward and punishment.[4] In an effort to make this measure more culturally appropriate in Sri Lanka, local researchers added "giver of peace" to the agentic items and "one who punishes the wicked," "one who curses the wrongdoer," and "one who destroys those who do evil" to the power-over items.

Similarly, enemy images included some that were common to all three conflict situations and others that were appropriate to each specific culture and conflict. Images used in all three sites, taken from a study by Amodio (1992), were both positive and negative as follows: power-hungry, hostile, moral, cruel, likable, praiseworthy, evil, and good-natured. Some examples of enemy images that were country-specific referred to "having strong families" (Northern Ireland), to racism (Sri Lanka), and to dictatorial behavior (Philippines).

The "just world" phenomenon is defined as the belief that "the world is just and that people therefore get what they deserve and deserve what they get" (Myers 1993, 407). Studies of this phenomenon, mostly conducted in North America and Europe, have shown that belief in a just world (BJW) is frequently accompanied by right-wing authoritarian views, political conservatism, the Protestant work ethic, anti-feminism, unsympathetic attitudes toward the poor, and other socially problematic attributes.[5] Based on these findings, we hypothesized that belief in a just world would correlate negatively with being motivated to work for peace or with actually doing so. Moreover, we saw potential value in testing these hypotheses internationally, with two countries from the global South (the Philippines and Sri Lanka) well represented.

Back at the offices of CMRSM in New York, volunteers not privy to the specifics of the study were asked to categorize the actions and motivations coming in from the six countries where the data had been gathered. Peacemaking activities were grouped into four categories: confronting perpetrators of violence, relationship building, service, and praying for peace. Two other categories, seemingly less legitimate as efforts at peacemaking but nonetheless interesting in their own right and frequent enough to be included, were as follows: avoidance of members of the opposing group (presumably to prevent a conflictual situation from developing) and very general, nonspecific responses (for example, "I try to

---

[3] Factor analysis is a statistical procedure used to determine whether a measure is multidimensional or reflects a central, underlying concept.

[4] The placement of "mother" and "father" in separate categories was not for theological reasons; factor analyses indicated that people who conceive of God as "Mother" tend to hold immanent images of the divine, whereas people who think of God as "Father" are likely to see the divine in terms of agentic images.

[5] For overviews of literature on the just world phenomenon, see Furnham and Procter (1989) and Montada and Lerner (1998).

be nice to Tutsis," "I am friendly toward Muslims," or "I treat Tamils with respect.").

Confrontational acts of peacemaking were cases of direct intervention in an act of violence about to be committed, or of demands for truth-telling after the fact. These took place mostly between neighbors and fellow civilians rather than against organized combatants, as evidenced by the fact that peacemakers in Guatemala and Rwanda were much more likely to engage in such acts than peacemakers in other countries (see chapters 2 and 5 for descriptions of the conflicts in these countries).

Relationship building included actions such as striking up conversations with members of the opposing group, visiting them in their homes, and attending their special feasts or religious services. Acts of service ranged from the very dramatic (such as sheltering targeted people in an attic or closet) to the mundanely thoughtful (such as sharing vegetables from a garden). Praying for peace took place on an individual basis, as well as in organized church services.

Peacemaking actions reported by respondents were further categorized as to whether they were likely to be of shorter or longer duration (for example, a one-time act like escorting children to safety, or a long-term effort like organizing youths to stage concerts for peace), whether they appeared to be more at the grassroots (for example, taking place in a local barrio or barangay, among homemakers or farmers) or at a somewhat higher level (such as through church or university connections), and whether they appeared to have been carried out individually or in groups. These characteristics were usually evident in respondents' descriptions of their peacemaking efforts.

Motivations for peacemaking were grouped into one of four categories: ideological (for example, "I believe all people are equal," or "killing violates human rights"), practical (for example, "to gain the trust of Unionist Protestants," or "because fighting keeps us poor"), relational (for example, "they are people like me," or "I want to better understand them"), and religious (for example, "God wants us to live in peace," or "The Bible teaches us to love our enemies"). When a specific peacemaking action or motivation appeared to belong to more than one category (for example, "I work for peace out of concern for my childen's safety" could be seen as both practical and relational), it was placed in both or all relevant categories. To be honest, treating ideological and religious motivations separately sparked no little controversy among the researchers and others who have advised and cheered on this project. Whether or not separating them was the right approach will be treated at some length when we discuss our results later in this chapter.

Statistical analyses of data were carried out at CMRSM, and the results were then shared with the research partners. You will find the results for each country, along with local researchers' interpretations of them, in the chapters that follow. The remainder of this chapter will deal with what we learned from all six countries about gender, peacemaking actions, and what motivates them; and from Northern Ireland, the Philippines, and Sri Lanka about images of the divine, images of the enemy, and belief in a just world.

HOW DO PEACEMAKERS SEE THEIR ENEMIES?

A preliminary clarification is in order: we used the terms "enemies" or "opponents" in a rather narrow sense in this study to describe how grassroots peacemakers, as members of an ethnic or religious group in conflict with another ethnic or religious group, view that other group. We are not referring to people who are opposed to peacemaking efforts, though in some cases these are in fact formidable "enemies" and "opponents" of peacemakers.

Taken as a whole, grassroots peacemakers were not inclined to see their enemies in a more favorable light than did their neighbors who are not engaged in peacemaking (see Table 1). Neither peacemakers nor nonpeacemakers averaged enemy images that were negative or positive; both were somewhere in between. In itself, this lack of a difference is noteworthy. It suggests that peacemakers are not motivated by predominantly positive images of members of the opposing group. They push forward with their peacemaking efforts not because of but despite their perceptions of those with whom they are trying to make peace—a finding that held true for all three countries in which this particular study was carried out. Perhaps it is precisely their apprehension of the enemy as having dangerous or sinister traits that instills in them a sense of urgency to work for peace.

Two other findings are of potential interest here: younger respondents and people who worked for peace in groups held more positive enemy images than did older respondents and those whose peacemaking activity was carried out individually. Both of these findings are largely accounted for by a third factor: education. The more years of formal education respondents had received, the more positive were their images of the enemy. Younger respondents had benefited from more schooling than older respondents, and schools were often instrumental in organizing group peacemaking efforts.

Finally, overall images of the enemy were about equally positive among peacemakers in Northern Ireland, the Philippines, and Sri Lanka. See chapters 3, 4, and 6 for more detailed findings on enemy images within these countries.

WHO IS THE GOD OF THE PEACEMAKERS?

Peacemakers overall held more images of the divine in all categories—agentic, immanent, and power-over—than nonpeacemakers (with the exception of Northern Ireland, where peacemakers were very unlikely to hold power-over images of God) (see Table 2). Primarily, however, peacemakers expressed belief in an agentic God—that is, a God who acts in their lives in creative, liberating, and salvific ways (see Table 3). Perhaps the hope required to persevere in peacemaking at the grassroots can only be sustained by faith in such a God. This God is understood to work through them and even sometimes through random events to bring about peace, enabling them to feel that they are not alone and not solely responsible for the outcomes of their efforts. The agentic God they believe in guides their feet onto the way of peace (see Luke 1:79).

It is important to note here that the nature of our data does not allow for causal inferences. In others words, we cannot say whether holding agentic images of the divine motivates people to become peacemakers, or whether people develop such images as a result of working for peace. One of these may be true, but it is also possible that neither is true. Some third factor may account for the finding. Further research may help to tease out this relationship.

Power-over images of the divine were the only category associated with fewer actions and motivations (especially ideological and religious motivations) for peace (see Table 4). In other words, to conceive of God as a ruler, master, and judge—not simply an active God at the service of creation, but a God in complete control—either serves as a de-motivator for peacemaking or is the God of choice for those without much zeal for peacemaking. As theologian Shirley Wijesinghe suggests in chapter 6 on Sri Lanka, "An image of God that emphasizes power over other divine attributes may seem to render human efforts meaningless or unnecessary."

Power-over images of the divine were still high for peacemakers in the Philippines and Sri Lanka, though in the Philippines agentic images were more prevalent, and immanent images were more prevalent in Sri Lanka. Perhaps even peacemakers need some sense of a power-over God who metes out justice, naming the peacemakers blessed as children of God (see Matt. 5:9) and rebounding violence upon the heads of those who are seduced by it (see Ps. 7:17). Peacemakers who had received more education, however, were unlikely to hold power-over images of the divine. More years of schooling may account for the fact that peacemakers in Northern Ireland were low in such images.

RELIGIOUS FAITH AND PEACEMAKING

Overall, peacemakers who cited religious motivation for their work had the following characteristics. They generally did not believe in a just world. Their preferred methods of peacemaking were via various forms of relationship building, and they more often did this in groups rather than as individuals. Except in Sri Lanka, they were unlikely to believe in a power-over God. They were most likely to live in the Sudan or in Northern Ireland, and least likely to live in Guatemala or the Philippines.

Religious motivations, while they were cited frequently enough to be statistically significant, were nonetheless the *least* frequently cited of all four types of motivation for peacemaking. How much less? Quite a bit. Peacemakers overall were one and a half times as likely to cite ideological motivations, three times as likely to cite relational motivations, and three and a half times as likely to cite practical motivations. All of which brings us back to a delicate topic mentioned earlier in this chapter: the matter of whether or not we should have analyzed ideological and religious motivations separately.

The opposing argument goes like this: Is it not artificial to separate these two categories of motivation? After all, both of them have ethical bases. Moreover, beliefs about equality and human rights are not secular for everyone—for some of us, they flow out of religious beliefs. One could further argue that for people of faith, religion is relational and practical as well.

This is a valid point. A statement about motivation that is not worded religiously may still, from the speaker's point of view, have a religious basis. But by the same token, those of us coming at this study from a religious angle have to be painfully honest with ourselves: if we are going to affirm that not everything has to be couched in "God talk" before it can be regarded as religious, then perhaps the next step is to recognize that all motives are "in God," no matter what category they fall under. An act of peacemaking is no less sacred because it is practically or relationally or ideologically based. If it concerns us that in a dire situation, human beings—even religious human beings—may act primarily out of practical motives, or at least be more ready to articulate those motives, then perhaps we do not really know what war is like.

In order to be fair and accurate, a certain "operational reductionism" is called for here—in other words, identifying as religious motivations only those items with explicit religious references (for example, mentions of God, faith, or scriptural sources). The bottom line, however, is not any argument about fairness, inference, or methodological orthodoxy. The bottom line is that if we statistically analyze the categories of ideological and religious motivation separately, and if they perform separately, then they are separate motivational categories. We did, and they are. But to say they are *separate* categories is not to imply that they are unrelated.

Here is how they are alike (see Table 5):

- Peacemakers who held them, along with relational motivations, engaged frequently in relationship building activities, preferred to work for peace in groups rather than individually, and rarely believed in a just world.

- Peacemakers citing both ideological and religious motivations were unlikely to conceive of the divine in terms of power-over images.

- The correlation between ideological and religious motivations is positive, and small but significant.[6]

Here is how they differ (see Table 5):

- The religiously motivated were less likely to favor agentic images of the divine than are the ideologically motivated.

- The ideologically motivated were significantly less likely to conceive of the divine in terms of immanent images.

- The ideologically motivated generally held more positive enemy images than the religiously motivated. They were also more likely to hold relational motives as well, and to engage in acts of service.

---

[6] $r = .12$, $p = .03$.

- Whereas men were more ideologically motivated than women, women and men did not differ significantly in religious motivations.

At the risk of being tedious, we felt it was important to demonstrate here that while religious and ideological motivation have a few things in common, they also differ in many respects. While a few of the within-country studies differed occasionally on the above points, the empirical evidence based on analyses of the overall data overwhelmingly indicates that religious and ideological motivations are separate but related categories.

To be sure, this type of analysis is not for everyone. Analysis of *any* kind is arguably a Western approach to understanding; separating what could be a unified whole will inevitably distort it. Our study, however, was designed and carried out by researchers from both the East and the West, and the motivational patterns we have identified emerged likewise from many cultures. We have proceeded in the belief that reality is more easily distorted by speculation than by empirical observation, despite the fact that the latter is not immune from biases. We leave it to the reader to decide whether our approach is of use.

PEACEMAKING, MOTIVATION, AND BELIEF IN A JUST WORLD

The four types of motivations often related differently to the various categories of peacemaking, and to the attitudes and beliefs our study examined. Understanding how they operate can help us to appreciate their advantages and disadvantages as well as indicate who is likely to hold them.

Not surprisingly, given that all our respondents were living in areas currently or recently afflicted with considerable violence, practical motivations for peacemaking by far outnumbered all the others (except in Northern Ireland, where relational motivations were more common). These were followed by relational, ideological, and religious motivations, in that order (see Table 6). Peacemakers who held relational and ideological motivations tended to be practically motivated as well.

Relational motives, surprisingly, were cited by people who held generally negative enemy images—a finding that is consistent with the fact that grassroots peacemakers were not inclined to see their enemies in a more favorable light than their neighbors who are not engaged in peacemaking, yet they pushed forward in their efforts for peace anyway.

Ideological motives, while they were cited less frequently, were associated with more positive images of the enemy, with service-oriented peacemaking but not praying for peace, and with agentic but not immanent images of the divine (except in Northern Ireland, where ideologically motivated peacemakers commonly did hold immanent images of God.)

Religious motives were more common among older than younger peacemakers. But taken together with ideological and relational motives, they accounted for most acts of relationship building and group peacemaking efforts, and tended not to be accompanied by belief in a just world.

A disturbing finding is that higher levels of motivation—practical, relational, and ideological—were associated with lower levels of formal education (see Table 7). Somehow, schools are failing to empower peacemakers. While they may provide students with the skills and resources they need if they are to work for peace, they are not inspiring or encouraging them to work for peace. Perhaps education promotes a certain cynicism; or perhaps educated people develop other aspirations—for example, financial and material gain—that render peacemaking less of a priority. At the grassroots, however, the relatively well-educated who do choose to work for peace make their major contributions in the areas of confrontational peacemaking and relationship building—both, perhaps, enhanced by the skills and confidence that education can provide.

Another of our findings further clarifies the task facing educators: belief in a just world was associated with lower levels of every category of motivation and with every major category of peacemaking activity except praying for peace (see Table 8). (Respondents who prayed for peace were people who generally believed in a just world.) The more respondents reported believing in a just world, the less likely they were to engage in acts of service or relationship building as forms of peacemaking.

Respondents who believed in a just world had fewer years of formal education than those who did not. It appears, therefore, that educators are succeeding in informing their students of widespread injustice and in providing them with skills for peacebuilding, particularly peacemaking that requires either confrontation or the building up of relationships. But they are not sufficiently motivating their students to work for peace. In fairness, this is not the sole task of educators but of local civic and religious leaders, and indeed all adults who would be role models for future peacemakers.

GENDER AND PEACEMAKING

Given a vast amount of anecdotal evidence and expert testimony on the topic, we expected to find many major gender differences in peacemaking strategies and motivations. Such differences may well exist at higher levels of peacemaking. Our data indicate that at the grassroots, however, women and men are more alike than they are different when it comes to peacemaking.

WHAT WOMEN AND MEN HOLD IN COMMON AS PEACEMAKERS

A document published by the United Nations Development Fund for Women (UNIFEM) quotes women peace activists voicing their conviction that women are more likely than men to hold what our study has referred to as "practical" and "relational" motivations. Women, according to this document, tend to define peace "in terms of basic universal human needs" which leads them to "advocate practical solutions in the building of peace" (UNIFEM 2000, 33). The document contends that in the context of negotiating for peace, women come to the table with different motivations. British Parliamentarian Helen Jackson is quoted as saying that women "come and talk about their loved ones, their bereavement, their children, and their hopes for the future." Similarly, an article in *Fellowship* states that "Women share a concern with how children are traumatized by war" and that "[women] know the need to build a sound economic base for sustainable peace" (Anderson 1998, 15). It has been further argued that as a conflict escalates, "men become preoccupied with military or strategic issues while women are left to deal with the issues of subsistence and day to day survival" (Ramsey Marshall 2000, 18).

It is true that men are far more likely than women to participate as combatants in a given conflict. But when it comes to peacemaking, the above statements could give the impression that men think duking it out on the battlefield is enough to resolve a conflict, whereas women understand the structural requirements and human needs that must be met for peace to come about. Our data indicate that in reference to grassroots peacemaking, men and women are equally likely to have practical *and* relational concerns, and there were no exceptions among the six countries in our study that provided gender data.

It may be possible to break the practical category down into subcategories with more "instrumentally practical" concerns such as economic development, freedom of movement, and protection of property, and "personally practical" concerns such as one's own safety, schooling for children, and subsistence needs such as food and shelter. Attempting such categorical refinement will be a further step in analyzing our study's motivational data. Whether or not it will bring gender differences to light remains an open question for now, with anecdotal and empirical evidence apparently in opposition.

No gender differences in religious motivation for peacemaking emerged in the overall data, but Guatemala and Sri Lanka were exceptions; in these countries, men were more likely than women to cite religious motivations for peacemaking (see the relevant chapters for contextualized interpretations of these gender differences).

In terms of peacemaking activities, men and women were equally likely to engage in acts of service. (The exception was Sri Lanka, where men played a larger role than women in service-oriented peacemaking.)

How Women and Men Differ as Peacemakers

While our study provides evidence that both men and women hold practical and relational motivations, men engaged in peacemaking were more likely than women peacemakers to cite ideological motivations for their efforts. Ideological motivations, being more abstract and seemingly less "grassroots" than practical and relational motivations, might theoretically be the result of higher levels of education. But in our overall sample, men and women did not significantly differ in their years of schooling, and as we have seen above, education apparently detracts from motivation more than it enhances it. So education does not explain this gender difference.

Women were more likely than men to pray for peace. In itself, this finding is hardly surprising, given that women almost universally outnumber men in terms of formal religious affiliation and score higher than men on a number of measures of religiosity (Wulff 1991, 311). In addition, based on a less conservative standard of statistical testing,[7] women are more likely to speak of their peacemaking in very general, nonspecific terms. The fact that women have fewer resources and less mobility than men in many cultures may account for these findings, and cultural pressures upon women may inhibit them from asserting their peacemaking roles, or even from regarding their own efforts as peacemaking.

But if men do have greater mobility and access to resources, evidence that they are more active in other forms of peacemaking is weak. Again, based on a less conservative standard of statistical testing, men (except in Guatemala—see chapter 2) were more likely to engage in confrontational peacemaking. While this finding is consistent with the prevalent stereotype, we also found something that contradicts the anecdotal evidence: men were somewhat more likely then women to engage in relationship building (see Table 9). But again, this is a result based upon a less conservative standard of statistical testing and should be invoked with caution. More research is needed to confirm, qualify, and clarify these relationships.

Our findings do confirm, if anything, the importance of not over-generalizing about women or men as peacemakers. Ramsey Marshall warns against "the tendency to essentialize and universalize women, to assume that 'women' may be treated and discussed as a unitary, homogeneous category and that overarching generalizations may be extended to all women, everywhere" (Ramsey Marshall 2000, 7; see also Waylen 1996). Shelley Anderson, a program officer for the International Fellowship of Reconciliation's Women Peacemakers Program, highlights the difference between "capitalizing on women's strengths" and "perpetuating traditional sex-role stereotypes" (Anderson, 1998, 15). By the same token, neither should we treat "men" as a unitary, homogeneous group, reducing them to stereotypes.

Perhaps with the laudable and important goal of encouraging women's involvement in peacemaking at higher levels, there is a tendency to invoke gender differences in aggression and publicly speculate that women bring more human values and unique skills to peacemaking. At the grassroots, however, it seems clear that gender differences are more nuanced. Caught up in the struggle to survive, women and men respond in ways and with gifts that are more similar than not. Perhaps the most important conclusion to draw from our gender research is that differences in men's and women's actions and motivations for peace are, in large part, determined by the specific cultural, economic, and political context in which they operate.

---

[7] When a finding is "based on a less conservative standard of statistical testing," the probability that it occurred by chance is higher; in other words, it is that much more possible that the finding does not reflect a more common reality.

IMPLICATIONS FOR PEACEMAKING

Several practical implications of these findings should be of interest to peace educators in particular.

We have seen that grassroots peacemakers hold a broad range of images of the divine, but agentic images are prevalent among them. We have further seen that religiously motivated peacemakers are particularly unlikely to believe in a power-over God. Religious educators may thus be in a unique position to form future peacemakers by (a) exposing students to a concept of a God who has many faces and names, while (b) downplaying but acknowledging attributes of God that relate to power, and (c) giving particular emphasis to a God who acts in their lives in creative, liberating, and salvific ways.

Second, we have seen that grassroots peacemakers in our study did not perceive members of the opposing group in more favorable ways than their neighbors who do not work for peace—yet they have persevered in peacemaking. This suggests that working to humanize images of the enemy may not be the critical focus in motivating potential peacemakers. A wide body of literature exists on how enemy images can be used to escalate aggression.[8] It is possible that encouraging the development of more positive enemy images can contribute to a decrease in aggression, but not to active efforts for peace.

Religious motivations for peacemaking were the least common among our respondents. For religious educators, this finding demonstrates the importance of making explicit the faith-based imperative to work for peace. All categories of motivation, however, are operative among grassroots peacemakers, with practical motivations being the most prevalent. Therefore, appeals to motivate involvement in peacemaking may fruitfully invoke concerns related to all four categories. Religious educators should not ignore the motivational potential of practical and relational factors or of secular human values in promoting peace.

Belief in a just world was associated with lower levels of all categories of motivation, and formal education can help people to understand the prevalence of injustice in the world. At the same time, why schools are not succeeding in motivating work for peace at the grassroots must be addressed.

As peacemakers, women and men hold more in common than not. The only major gender differences that surfaced in our overall data were that women are more likely to pray for peace, and men are more likely to hold ideological motives for peacemaking. At the grassroots, gender differences in peacemaking vary on a country-by-country basis. Efforts to enhance women's participation and leadership in peacemaking must be informed by empirical evidence rather than by prevailing stereotypes.

We have attempted to present the overall picture of our findings, along with

---

[8] See in particular Chelsea House Educational Communications (1977), Keen (1986), Sande et al. (1989), and Silverstein and Holt (1989).

some of their practical implications, in this and the previous chapter. We know that the concrete is always more compelling than the abstract, and that the specific delights more than the general. The chapters that follow will introduce you to the diverse flavors of grassroots peacemaking as it is carried out in Guatemala, Northern Ireland, the Philippines, Rwanda, Sri Lanka, the Sudan, and the United States.

STATISTICAL TABLES
ASSOCIATED WITH CHAPTER 1 DATA

TABLE 1. PEACEMAKERS' VERSUS NONPEACEMAKERS' IMAGES OF THE ENEMY

	Peacemakers	Nonpeacemakers
Images of the Enemy*	2.17	2.08
t (187) = 1.07, n.s.		

* Higher scores indicate more positive enemy images. Data represented are from Northern Ireland, the Philippines, and Sri Lanka. Data on the peacemaker versus nonpeacemaker variable were confounded in some regions with sex and age; these were removed from the sample prior to analysis.

TABLE 2. PEACEMAKERS' VERSUS NONPEACEMAKERS' IMAGES OF THE DIVINE

	Peacemakers	Nonpeacemakers
Total Images of the Divine*	8.05	7.53
t (185) = 2.90, $p < .05$		

* "Total images of the divine" is the sum of agentic, immanent, and power-over images of the divine, averaged across respondents. Data represented are from Northern Ireland, the Philippines, and Sri Lanka. Data on the peacemaker versus nonpeacemaker variable were confounded in some regions with sex and age; these were removed from the sample prior to analysis.

TABLE 3. RELATIVE FREQUENCY OF PEACEMAKERS' IMAGES OF THE DIVINE

Agentic	Immanent	Power-over
2.83	2.57	2.62
All differences were significant at or below the .05 level.		

**TABLE 4. INTERCORRELATIONS OF PEACEMAKING ACTIONS AND MOTIVATIONS
WITH POWER-OVER IMAGES OF THE DIVINE**

	Relationship Building	Prayer	Service	Practical Motivations	Relational Motivations
Power-over Images	-.27***	.29***	-.09	-.04	-.06

	Ideological Motivations	Religious Motivations	Average Actions*	Average Motivations**
Power-over Images	-.26***	-.35***	-.16***	-.27***

* Average actions are the sum of all peacemaking activities—relationship building, prayer, service, confrontation, and avoidance—averaged across individuals. (Confrontation and avoidance are not included individually in this table; neither correlated significantly with power-over images of the divine.)

** Average motivations are the average of all motivations—practical, relational, ideological, and religious—across respondents.

*** Indicates that correlation (*r*) is significant at or below the .05 level.

**TABLE 5. SIMILARITIES AND DIFFERENCES BETWEEN RELIGIOUS
AND IDEOLOGICAL MOTIVATIONS**

	Correlations (*r*)	
	Religious	Ideological
Acts of Relationship Building	.29*	.20*
Acts of Service	-.08	.22*
Belief in a "Just" World	-.33*	-.17*
Working for Peace in Groups (vs. Individually)	.32*	.19*
Power-over Images of the Divine	-.26*	-.35*
Agentic Images of the Divine	.01	.23*
Immanent Images of the Divine	.15	-.20*
Images of the Enemy	.10	.23*
Relational Motivations	.14	.17*
Gender**	-.05	-.14*

* Indicates correlation is significant at or below the .05 level.

** Data on gender were confounded with other demographic variables in some regions; these were removed from the sample prior to analysis. Negative correlations indicate that men cited these motivations more frequently than did women, but the difference is only significant with ideological motivations.

TABLE 6. RELATIVE FREQUENCY OF MOTIVATIONS FOR PEACEMAKING

	Practical	Relational	Ideological	Religious
Mean Frequency	1.89	1.62	.88	.56
All differences were significant at or below the .05 level.				

TABLE 7. INTERCORRELATIONS OF PEACEMAKING MOTIVATIONS WITH YEARS OF FORMAL EDUCATION

	Practical	Relational	Ideological	Religious
Years of Formal Education	-.52*	-.20*	-.16*	.01

*Indicates correlation (r) is significant at or below the .05 level.

TABLE 8. INTERCORRELATIONS OF PEACEMAKING ACTIONS AND MOTIVATIONS WITH BELIEF IN A "JUST" WORLD (BJW)

	Relationship Building	Prayer	Service	Practical Motivations	Relational Motivations
BJW	-.17***	.11***	-.19***	-.06	-.17***

	Ideological Motivations	Religious Motivations	Average Actions*	Average Motivations**
BJW	-.12***	-.21***	-.16***	-.17***

  * Average actions are the sum of all peacemaking activities—relationship building, prayer, service, confrontation, and avoidance—averaged across individuals. (Confrontation and avoidance are not included individually in this table; neither correlated significantly with BJW.)

  ** Average motivations are the average of all motivations—practical, relational, ideological, and religious—across respondents.

*** Indicates that correlation (r) is significant at or below the .05 level.

TABLE 9. CORRELATIONAL COMPARISONS OF WOMEN'S AND MEN'S PEACEMAKING ACTIONS AND MOTIVATIONS

	Relationship Building	Prayer	Service	Avoidance	Confrontation
Gender*	-.10**	.13***	-.01	-.05	-.12**

	Practical Motivations	Relational Motivations	Ideological Motivations	Religious Motivations
Gender*	.04	.10	-.14***	-.03

  * Positive correlations indicate that women reported this type of motivation or activity more frequently than did men.

  ** Indicates that correlation (r) is significant at the .06 level.

*** Indicates that correlation (r) is significant at or below the .05 level.

2

Guatemala

The Challenge of Peacebuilding in Fragmented Communities

KULDIP KAUR

My son was fifteen years old when he came and told me he was leaving to join the Guerrilla Army of the Poor (EGP). I said, "My son, this is my red scarf, wear it all the time, it will help you remember that your family is with you. There is no certainty in the world. You may return to no family or we may never see you again. If no one survives, then at least our spirit will survive in others." When he left, I was relieved. Times were bad and I couldn't worry for him as well. He was a man and had to take on his responsibilities.

For years I didn't know whether he was alive or not. Then after fourteen years he appeared one night at the house. It was all done clandestinely because we were still very much under surveillance. We just stared at each other. We couldn't understand the other's experiences, so we just hugged. No words were expressed. It was on that day that I felt that God had given me the chance to reconcile, to see my family exist once again. That day I truly did feel brought back to life.

I have always believed in God and Jesus Christ but I don't believe in peace. My grandfather would talk to me when I was young of wars to come. Christ's story took three hundred years to be written. Our pain will take

My thanks in Guatemala to Clara Arenas and Juan Vandeviere of AVANCSO, who offered not only institutional but also intellectual and emotional support. To Fernando Alonso, Gabriela Escobar, and Carmen Enrique López for their help in the fieldwork process. In England I am grateful to Laurence Allan, James Dunkerley, Olivia Harris, and Rachel Sieder for their editorial assistance and comments. All errors are entirely my responsibility.

*just as long to be recognized. Maybe my great-grandchildren or even theirs
will be able to live and believe in peace.*

—Pachay, San Martín Jilotepeque, Chimaltenango

*The new doctrine that the priests were offering us in the 1970s appealed
to me a lot. Suddenly we began to understand the way in which oppression
worked. We began to look at ways to change this. I became a catechist at a
very young age and soon became a Delegate of the Word.*

*In the 1990s the Recovery of Historical Memory Project (REMHI)
appointed me to collect testimonies. I consider myself a very religious person. The Bible has always helped me to understand things, especially
Christ's life. Christ himself worked for justice. He said, "Blessed are those
who work to denounce injustices." Since my work with REMHI I help my
people in a number of ways. There are efforts to preserve the memory of
our dead. Many people joined to demand exhumations.*

*I also help people in their denunciations against perpetrators of human
rights abuses. There are many here in Rabinal. If they felt some guilt or
remorse for what they had done, then maybe we could start to talk about
reconciliation. But here the victimizers do not want to remember the past
or admit their guilt. This is the injustice we are witnessing today. Many victimizers have changed their religion. Now many are evangelicals and
charismatics. They say we must leave the past behind. Yes, it is easy for
them to say that. My children were burned that day in the massacre. I witnessed the massacre. You do not forget those things. And you cannot forgive, especially when no one has asked for forgiveness. Only when these
people recognize what they did and are taken to court can we start to talk
about peace.*

—Plan de Sánchez, Rabinal, Baja Verapaz

Brutal conflict and violence have marked Guatemala's recent history. A thirty-
six-year period of militarization and armed conflict that reached genocidal pro-
portions concluded in December 1996 with the signing of the Accord for a Firm
and Lasting Peace. The peace negotiations between the government and guerrilla
factions of the Guatemalan National Revolutionary Union (URNG) resulted in
eight substantive accords which committed the government to socioeconomic
reforms, demilitarization, and the recognition of indigenous rights and multicul-
turalism.

On February 25, 1999, the UN-appointed Commission for Historical Clarification (CEH) presented a multivolume report entitled *Guatemala, Memory of
Silence,* which analyzes the causes and history of the armed conflict as well as
its human and economic costs. Focusing principally on the indigenous populated
highlands, the report presents in detail the ways violence was waged against the
indigenous communities during the most critical years of conflict. Between 1980
and 1983 the report notes over six hundred massacres, the destruction of at least

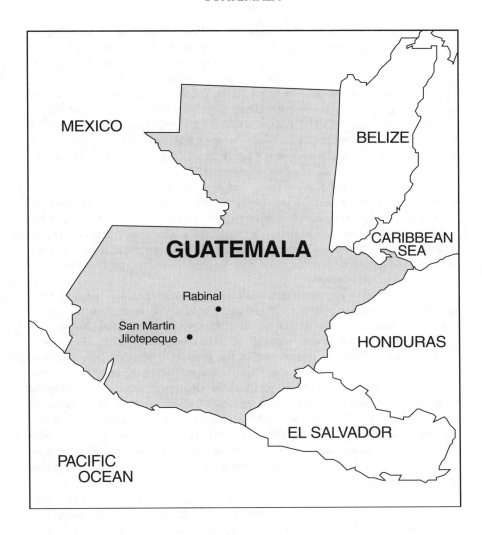

six hundred villages, and the displacement of more than one million people. It estimates that more than two hundred thousand were killed during the thirty-six years, with the majority of deaths perpetrated in the early 1980s. The report attributes 93 percent of the human rights violations to the Guatemalan state and also charges it with the crime of genocide waged against four Mayan indigenous groups in ten different municipalities (CEH 1999, 5:38-48).

Guatemala's population of more than eleven million people is composed of twenty-four ethnic groups. Ladinos, who are of European and indigenous descent, constitute some 50 percent of the population, while indigenous people comprise 45 to 50 percent. Since independence in 1821 the Ladinos have exercised social and political dominance over the indigenous populations, and the state has legitimized Ladino dominance to the detriment of the indigenous peoples, who have historically been denied the rights of citizenship (see Smith 1990).

The armed conflict was not in itself an ethnic conflict. The military counterinsurgency plans were initially drawn up to confront guerrilla forces, whose upper echelons were overwhelmingly Ladino. Yet, when challenged by the armed insurgency in the early 1980s, the military targeted the indigenous population as an "internal enemy" (CEH 1999, 5:29). The CEH concludes that the military developed a deliberate policy of genocide against the indigenous population in this period. Its report estimates that 83 percent of fully identified victims of the war were indigenous, while Ladinos constituted 17 percent (CEH 1999, 5:21).

Jonas argues that the peace accords "are certainly not the product of a revolutionary victory but neither were they imposed by victors upon vanquished" (1997, 6). On the one hand, the military's brutal counteroffensive against the indigenous population precluded further support for the guerrilla factions. On the other hand, since the guerrilla factions were still in existence and there was great international pressure for an end to the violence, the military resolved to partake in a process of negotiations.

With the military clearly in control of the negotiation process, the successful conclusion of the peace settlement did not herald a transition from the *ancien régime* to a new political order. Domestic elites continue to withhold full support for the implementation of the peace accords. The inauguration of the Guatemalan Republican Front (FRG) government in the year 2000 witnessed the return to political power of protagonists who were prominent during the height of the violence. General Efraín Ríos Montt, for example, Guatemala's president during the worst period of human rights abuses (1982-83), became the head of Guatemala's Congress in 2000. Although the presidential election campaign saw many voters turning to the FRG's victorious and charismatic candidate Alfonso Portillo, who offered a populist discourse based on law and order, most of the FRG's membership remained loyal to Ríos Montt; many of its members continue to oppose any initiatives stemming from the peace settlement.

Efforts to understand grassroots responses to violence and attempts at peacebuilding in Guatemala require an appreciation of a number of factors. Here I will refer to just three. First, a climate prevails in which key actors refuse to acknowledge their wartime military transgressions. There is no official narrative of the recent violence. For example, in response to the CEH's findings, Ríos Montt denied intellectual authorship of the massacres: "I never ordered any massacre" (*Prensa Libre,* February 28, 1999, 4). Likewise, Benedicto Lucas, Chief of General Staff during the same period and author of the most brutal counterinsurgency plan, stated that "nothing of major consequence occurred here" (*El Periódico,* May 5, 2000, 4). This refusal to acknowledge the past violence naturally coincides with a perpetuation of impunity. The climate of suppression of dissenting or defiant voices is exemplified by the horrific assassination in April 1998 of Bishop Juan Gerardi, two nights after presenting the Archdiocesan Human Rights Office's report *Guatemala: Nunca Más* (REMHI 1998).

The second factor is the abject poverty that besets the population. According to the latest report of the United Nations Development Program, 27 percent of Guatemalans live in extreme poverty and up to 57 percent in poverty. Although not only indigenous people are poor, they experience poverty more commonly than Ladinos: 74.2 percent of them in contrast to 40.9 percent (PNUD 2000, 41-43). A serious problem is the unjust distribution of the land, one of the worst in Latin America. A mere 2.6 percent of Guatemalan farms occupy two-thirds of the country's agricultural land (CEH 1999, 1:7). As a result, grassroots activities in Guatemala are often hampered by economic constraints.

Finally, religious fragmentation affects all of Guatemala's rural indigenous areas. Historically, Guatemala has been a Catholic country, and its Catholicism was fused with pre-Christian beliefs and rituals. Although the inauguration in 1948 of the Catholic Action movement (discussed below) created some cultural and political ruptures (see Brintnall 1979; Falla 2001), present-day religious divisions in most of the areas in which I worked are between evangelical Protestants, Charismatic Renewal, and other Catholics. According to Garrard-Burnett, by the mid-1980s evangelicals represented one-third of the Guatemalan population (1998, 162).

METHODOLOGY

The main body of this chapter refers to grassroots responses to violence and to grassroots peacebuilding in two municipalities: Rabinal, in the department of Baja Verapaz, and San Martín Jilotepeque, in the department of Chimaltenango (referred to hereafter as San Martín). Between 1980 and 1983 Rabinal's majority indigenous population—the Maya-Achí ethnic group—suffered some twenty massacres, as well as individual killings, rape, destruction of property, and mass displacement, causing the population to drop from 22,000 to 17,000. San Martín's majority Maya-Kakchiquel population was subjected to the same fate. The CEH registers more than 2,000 deaths in San Martín over the same period (CEH 1999, 8:168-271).

Fieldwork was carried out over a period of nine months in 2000. In Guatemala, as in other post-conflict societies, researching the motives behind and responses to violence is a difficult endeavor. A leading preoccupation while carrying out fieldwork was how to address the issue of building trust. This was particularly the case because the interplay of violence and the imposition of silence on victims has created an environment of general suspicion toward outsiders. Prior to this research project, I had no knowledge of San Martín. In light of this, fieldwork there was initially oriented toward building trust, which greatly limited the time in which to focus on grassroots responses. By contrast, I had worked previously in Rabinal. Trust could be established quite rapidly with key actors. I knew whom to approach and I was aware of the limitations of my own questions.

Research was carried out in a number of villages and in the municipality's town center. In Rabinal I worked in Plan de Sánchez, Xesiguán, Pacux, and Pana-jal. In San Martín I worked in Pachay, Sajalá, Estancia de la Virgen, and Choatalum. Most information was received through semi-structured interviews, although a number of life histories and personal narratives were also obtained from key persons involved in grassroots activism. The information presented below is not representative of the local populations as a whole. I approached key actors in these communities, who had been mobilized around a particular concern directly related to the violence. I interviewed local priests, community leaders, grassroots human rights activists, members of a widows organization (specific to Rabinal), community elders, and individual members of communities who have experience in human rights advocacy and peacebuilding. Evangelical and charismatic church leaders were approached. However, although interviews were granted, pastors of both types of churches explained that they do not raise the issue of violence in their services. In fact, the topic is avoided at all costs. Thus the information provided does not convey the views of the evangelicals and the charismatic Catholics, but exclusively those of Catholics willing to address the issue.

Following the gathering of qualitative material, a quantitative study of responses to violence according to gender was undertaken over a period of two months, in both areas of research. Thirty-five interviews were carried out. The results are presented below following the two case studies.

Finally, a workshop was carried out in the offices of the Association for the Advancement of Social Sciences (AVANCSO) in Guatemala City in March 2001. Eight organizations based in the capital attended the one-day session, where the principal results of the research project were shared. Each participant presented his or her organization's own responses to the violence. This was followed by a discussion by all participants of future peacebuilding in Guatemala. The principal results of the workshop form the conclusion of this chapter.

HISTORICAL OUTLINE

By the late 1970s a popular movement had grown to represent a genuine challenge to the status quo in Guatemala. Many of the foundations had been laid during a ten-year democratic experiment that began in 1944, which abolished forced labor. Some modern industry was established and there was limited diversification of export agriculture (see Handy 1994; Rojas Bolaños 1993). For the first time, workers were allowed to unionize (see Levenson-Estrada 1994), and a land reform was attempted by the administration of Jacobo Arbenz (1950-54). The reform, directly affecting landholdings in the possession of the transnational United Fruit Company, provoked strong resistance to the government, which was branded communist and ousted in a CIA-backed coup in 1954. Although Arbenz legalized the communist party (PGT) in 1951, it subsequently won only four out of fifty-six seats in Congress. Arbenz posed no communist threat. As Jonas argues, "U.S. actions were motivated by economic interests as well as ideological anticommunism" (1991, 31). Although the agrarian reform was totally reversed by the counterrevolutionary administration that followed the 1954 coup, the effort to implement it left a precedent for future mobilization in many rural areas (see R. Adams 1993, 188; Gleijeses 1992).

Political rule for the next thirty years was largely military rule. In response to the guerrilla movement and a growing popular movement, the military increasingly deepened its control over the state and civilian authorities. The Rebel Armed Forces' (FAR) initial operations were orchestrated in the Ladino-populated eastern regions in the 1960s. Following a fierce military counteroffensive FAR retreated rapidly but resurfaced, together with the Guerrilla Army of the Poor (EGP) and the Organization of the People in Arms (ORPA) in the 1970s, now operating in the indigenous populated highlands.

Catholic Action, inaugurated in 1948, aimed to establish an orthodox Catholic and anti-communist influence in indigenous communities. However, foreign priests who arrived in the 1960s to work in the indigenous areas replaced the church's prior sacramentalist approach with a developmentalist approach that resulted in many young indigenous people leaving the *cofradías* (Catholic Brotherhoods) for Catholic Action. Until then *cofradías,* based on gerontocratic authority, had functioned as platforms "for all intra-communal juridical decisions, organization of land tenure, the celebration of the saint image of the community, and representation to local and national government" (Wilson 1994, 129). Catholic Action organized cooperatives (see Falla 2001) and development and literacy programs, and backed candidates for local political office, which had traditionally been the domain of local Ladino elites and indigenous elders.

Liberation theology emerged in the 1970s. As Delli Sante notes, precisely because it encouraged people to find for themselves solutions to their problems, its concepts challenged the hierarchical and institutional structures of the Catholic Church as well as those of dominant social classes. In effect, though the theology was endorsed by various dioceses and parishes and promoted by enthusiastic pastoral agents, the church did not have a unified position toward it because "it had essentially been part of the dominant classes in power, sharing in their privileges from the colonial period" (1996, 48).

By 1978 grassroots efforts coalesced to form the Mayan-led peasant organization, the Committee of Peasant Unity (CUC). CUC was the first national organization to group together both Indian and Ladino peasant groups. Its ability to mobilize large numbers of the indigenous and Ladino peasant population in demonstrations against plantation owners was increasingly regarded as subversive, a threat to both the status quo and the military (see Delli Sante 1996). Jonas argues, for example, that the real threat from CUC "materialized in the massive strike of workers on the Southern Coast sugar and cotton plantations in February 1980" (1991, 128).

In response to the popular movement and the heightened guerrilla activity, which had successfully organized large numbers of indigenous people in the central and western highlands, the regime of Romeo Lucas García (1978-82) initiated a campaign of repression. It included the killing of opposition party members together with community leaders, cooperative members, and religious activists in the rural areas. The latter were particularly targeted. For the regime, catechists and "Delegates of the Word" (see below) increasingly became identified with the guerrillas. By 1981 selective terror had become collective as the military treated the population as being either with the army or with the guerrillas.

The threat of a guerrilla victory in 1981 led to a reformulation of the National Plan of Security and Development into five different phases, of which the most salient was the scorched-earth "pacification campaign." Drawn up by Benedicto Lucas, the program entailed the deployment of various Task Forces throughout the rural areas. In their efforts to "win back the indigenous population" and defeat the guerrillas, they destroyed villages and carried out massacres of the indigenous population.

Equally important was the establishment of the so-called Civilian Self Defense Patrols (PAC), which worked alongside military commissioners; and the Poles of Development and Model Villages, effectively concentration camps into which the indigenous people were crowded for greater military control. The "military commissioners" were designated as a military reserve by the counter-revolutionary government of 1954, but from 1976 on their role was restructured with a greater emphasis on intelligence gathering. By 1983 almost every town, village, and plantation had a military commissioner, and it is estimated that up to one million men, mainly indigenous men in rural areas, were recruited into the PAC system (CEH 1999, 2:190).

For a large part of the 1980s the military controlled almost every aspect of rural life. Only with the return of civilian rule in 1985, under President Vinicio Cerezo, did civil organizations emerge once again. In some cases, these were bodies that had existed prior to the violence but had been driven underground, and in others they were new organizations, such as human rights groups.

THE REEMERGENCE OF CIVIL SOCIETY

Although the 1980s were characterized by a military policy of cultivating "historical amnesia" (Zur 1998, 159) through the suppression of dissident voices, the return to civilian rule in 1985 witnessed the emergence of organizations whose focus was on the recent violence. A human rights movement, made up of both a small proportion of Ladinos traditionally affiliated with the Left and various indigenous protagonists, demanded truth and justice for past human rights violations (see Bastos and Camus 1996). A national pan-Mayan movement also emerged, advocating a historical project of memory of five hundred years of Mayan oppression (see Gálvez 1997; Warren 1998). Finally, efforts initiated by a victim-survivor population included not only annual public commemorations and requests for the exhumation of clandestine cemeteries, but also demands for truth, justice, and compensation.

Some of the most important initiatives in the rural areas were undertaken by the Council of Ethnic Communities "*Runujel Junam*" (CERJ) and the National Coordinating Committee of Guatemalan Widows (CONAVIGUA), together with the Mutual Support Group (GAM). CERJ's efforts were mainly directed at the obligatory civil defense patrol. In 1989 alone, basing its claims on several articles of the Guatemalan Constitution and international human rights conventions, it persuaded more than seventy-five communities to withdraw from the PAC system; some five thousand men refused to participate in it (Delli Sante 1996, 162).

CONAVIGUA, founded in September 1988, had some nine thousand members in just two years. Based initially on support for widows, it later joined other struggles for respect for human rights, demilitarization, and an end to forced recruitment. By the early 1990s, together with GAM, it had identified a number of clandestine cemeteries and offered assistance for their exhumation (see Schirmer 1993).

At the same time, the Catholic Church was reconstituted as a leading critic of the government and military. A powerful Joint Pastoral Letter issued in February 1988, entitled "The Cry for Land," condemned the unjust distribution of land and the dire situation in which most indigenous people lived. In 1990 the Archdiocese of Guatemala opened a human rights office, the Human Rights Office of the Archdiocese of Guatemala (ODHAG), which in 1995 launched the Recovery of Historical Memory Project (REMHI).

From its inception REMHI was an interdiocesan church project, involving the participation of ten of the country's eleven dioceses. Up to six hundred religious representatives, referred to as REMHI Promoters, participated in the collection of testimonies, resulting in the compilation of some six thousand interviews from survivors of the violence (Ball, Spirer, and Spirer 2000, 160). Both individual and collective testimonies were gathered. The most notable case of the latter was that of Alta Verapaz. There, the Diocesan Social Pastoral Program gathered eleven community testimonies with the participation of groups of local victims and victimizers (Sister Rosario Celis, personal interview, June 2000). The REMHI project aimed at the recovery and reconciliation of individuals through "truth-telling," and recourse was made to prayer and biblical passages (Fernando Suazo, personal interview, April 2000). The resulting four-volume *Guatemala: Nunca Más* report (REMHI 1998) was presented to the public on April 24, 1998.[1]

Nearly a year later the official truth commission, the CEH, completed its arduous task of investigating Guatemala's history and the violence. It issued an even more detailed report of its own, referred to above in the introduction. Its historical-sociological approach identified the violence as an inherent product of state structures, social inequality, and racism. These two initiatives broke the official regime of denial of atrocities and crimes against humanity. At a local level, not only did they allow survivors to recover some dignity, but they also established a

---

[1] A shorter, one-volume English-language version, entitled *Guatemala Never Again,* was published a year later by Orbis Books (REMHI 1999).

precedent to challenge imposed mechanisms of silence by both national and local agents of immunity.

Various survivor communities, grouped in the Reconciliation for Justice Association (ARJ) and legally counseled by the Center for Legal Action in Human Rights (CALDH), have now filed charges of genocide with the public prosecutor against members of the Military High Command. In May of 2000 charges were presented against three former generals, including ex-President Romeo Lucas García, for ten massacres perpetrated in 1981 and 1982. In June of 2001 charges were presented against five former generals, including ex-President Efraín Ríos Montt, for eleven massacres carried out in 1982 and 1983.

RABINAL, BAJA VERAPAZ

According to the Guatemalan Forensic Anthropology Team, selective repression was experienced in Rabinal as early as 1979 (EAFG 1995, 131). Community leaders, cooperative members, and religious catechists were increasingly subject to threats and torture, with many subsequently killed extrajudicially. Later, selective terror expanded into collective violence. The first act of indiscriminate violence took place on September 15, 1981, when the army, together with paramilitaries and military commissioners, massacred at least 250 people in Rabinal's town square. Over the next sixteen months thousands of innocent men, women, and children were killed as the army rampaged through local villages. By March 1983 Rabinal had been subjected to over twenty massacres, destruction of homes and crops, and mass displacement. Out of a population of 22,733 in 1981 (EAFG 1995, 127) up to 4,411 people had been killed, of which 99.8 percent were Maya-Achí (CEH 1999, 3:361). An investigation carried out by the International Center for Human Rights Investigations concluded that "the common denominator of human rights violations in Rabinal is the massacre, used as an operative tool to eliminate large numbers of the population" (CIIDH 1996, 78).

Although most of Rabinal was identified as a "red zone" by the army, the municipality itself was not an area of guerrilla operations. Even at the height of guerrilla activity from the mid-1970s to the early 1980s, Rabinal was only a support base for the EGP, whose members traversed the municipality's periphery to reach neighboring areas such as El Quiché, Ixcán, and Guatemala City. A number of Rabinal residents joined the guerrilla factions, but they were trained and stationed away from their place of origin. In stark contrast to other areas such as El Quiché, the Ixil Triangle, and Alta Verapaz, where guerrilla action was more pronounced, the handful of local members of the guerrillas in Rabinal remained in their communities and carried out only educational work. Achí involvement with the guerrillas consisted in providing logistical help and foodstuffs. EAFG highlights that the EGP considered the municipality one of its most solid bases, because of its geographical location, and defined its role as providing support for different factions (1995, 96). For the army, however, this confirmed that the Achí were active EGP guerrillas.

It is difficult to ascertain the rationale for the army's repression in Rabinal. The Commission for Historical Clarification attributes it to the fact that Rabinal served as a strategic corridor to operational zones under the control of the EGP (CEH 1999, 3:361). This must have played a significant part in the identification of Rabinal as an insurgent zone, but the army's suspicion of a politicized local population also helped to justify its decision to target the municipality in the counterinsurgency campaign.

THE POPULAR MOVEMENT OF THE 1970s

Liberation theology arrived in Rabinal, as in many of Guatemala's municipalities, in the early 1970s and led to the politicization of a number of Achí. The appointment of Bishop Juan Gerardi to the Diocese of Alta Verapaz (to which the church in Rabinal belongs) and the creation of the San Benito Center for Human Promotion led to an extensive Catholic Action program throughout the departments of Baja and Alta Verapaz (Centro Ak'Kutan 1994, 101). By 1972 a department-wide movement of Delegates of the Word of God (referred to hereafter as *delegados*) was under way. The previously exclusive emphasis on sacramental practice was replaced by a pastoral approach espousing a new economic ethic based on developmentalism.

The new model, which conveyed innovative concepts and tools to confront day-to-day poverty, attracted the attention of a younger Achí generation stifled by the morality of the traditional indigenous authorities, with their elaborate cult of the saints, the *cofradías*. In various communities this led to a frontal attack on the *cofradías*. The *delegados* derided the knowledge of elders and obstructed practices relating to the traditional earth cult. Different conceptions of Achí culture became factors of contention. The questions included (see Brintnall 1979): Who are the natural leaders of the community? What constitutes indigenous morality? What relation does a person have with the earth? Military commissioners who identified with the army (discussed below) subsequently exploited this internal confrontation.

As members of Catholic Action, a number of Rabinal's Achí initially traveled to the San Benito Center for seminar education. They received instruction in Catholic teachings and economic and social awareness. According to one informant, the attendees referred to these sessions as *"El Choque"* (the shock). Shortly thereafter, instruction began in local churches. In Rabinal's case, this was strengthened by the arrival of three new foreign priests during the 1970s. Toward the end of the decade the number of *delegados* and catechists grew substantially, and their presence was visible in almost every rural village in Rabinal.

Following a serious earthquake in 1976, a number of organizations administering foreign aid entered Rabinal. Assistance from the state and from organizations such as the Economic and Social Development for Central America

(IDESAC) and the Center for Family Integration (CIF) expanded the training and education of community leaders, principally the *delegados* and catechists. The most politically motivated of these young members concentrated first on literacy and subsequently on health, agriculture, irrigation techniques, community organization, and commercialization of agricultural products. A preoccupation with combining all these efforts led to the creation toward the end of the 1970s of the municipal-based association *La Huella del Varón Rabinal-Achí.* Most of its members were in the Catholic Action movement. The initial membership included more than five hundred Achís in various villages. Among its many achievements was the running of literacy classes for up to 25 percent of the population, the organization of Betterment Committees in thirty-two communities, and the training of a number of social and health promoters (Alfaro 2000, 27).

THE ENERGY CRISIS, CUC, AND THE EGP

By the mid-1970s, Guatemala was suffering from an energy crisis. In February 1975 the National Institute of Electrification (INDE) announced a plan to build the largest hydroelectric project in Central America. The project was estimated at a cost of $340.9 million (Alecio 1995, 29). The Chixoy Hydroelectric project was funded primarily by the World Bank, to assist the country in its "economic modernization" (see WFP 1995; EAFG 1995, 57). The creation of the reservoir required the displacement of up to fifteen hundred people. The Rio Negro community, skeptical of the government's promise to adequately resettle and compensate the communities, contested the state's decision (Le Bot 1993, 22). The conflict between INDE and the community escalated to such a degree that the residents sought the advice of CUC, which immediately began a campaign against the project. The fact that members of the Rio Negro community had access to CUC was not unusual in Guatemala, since the organization was active in the large plantations of the coastal regions as well as the departments of El Quiché and Chimaltenango. Even in municipalities where CUC had no permanent organization, indigenous people were aware of its assistance, its objectives, and its strategies, because of seasonal migration to the large plantations by different ethnic groups.

CUC's help for the Rio Negro community spread awareness of the organization to other communities. Many of the most politicized *delegados,* catechists, and association members identified with the national organization. Having spent a good part of a decade concentrating on local community issues, they now saw in CUC a way in which their concerns could be addressed nationally.

At the end of the 1970s the EGP entered the area. However, as previously mentioned, its work was limited to propaganda and creating a support base. Although the EGP and CUC were both active in Rabinal, their objectives differed. The latter acted primarily in liaison with the communities to raise consciousness of land, seasonal work, racism, and discrimination. The former addressed communities in terms of an armed struggle, but it never offered weapons or training.

"LA VIOLENCIA" AND MILITARIZATION

With the intensification of the repression at the end of the 1970s, the army and its paramilitary allies targeted many of the politicized community leaders. By the early 1980s, up to 90 percent of the members of the *Huella del Varón Rabinal-Achí* had been killed (Catalino Martínez Toj, personal interview, Rabinal, May 2000). Many *delegados* and catechists were also killed. According to Fernando Suazo, a priest who arrived in Rabinal in 1985, a pre-1970s movement of more than two hundred lay church representatives was reduced to fewer than forty by the mid-1980s. Of this small group all but a few were new (personal interview, June 2000).

One of the military's strategies in Rabinal was to involve the Achí population directly in violence. Civilians were forced to participate in the killings; those who refused to collaborate were labeled guerrillas and were subsequently murdered. At the same time, the military won allies by exploiting local social and economic conflicts, particularly in relation to land.

Rio Negro was one of the first communities to be subjected to indiscriminate violence, because of its resistance to INDE's plans and its collaboration with CUC. Out of a population of over eight hundred, the army, military commissioners, and civil patrollers—who were from a neighboring village, Xococ—(CEH 1999, 3:365), killed some four hundred people. One massacre of 177 people, carried out on March 13, 1982, was solely of women and children (CEH 1999, 6:45-56). The CEH attributes Xococ's violence toward Rio Negro to an incident in February 1982, when members of a guerrilla faction burned down Xococ's market; the Rio Negro community was blamed (CEH 1999, 6:48). Although the two communities had carried out amicable commercial activities prior to the violence, the inhabitants of Xococ had expansionist ambitions vis-à-vis the neighboring municipality, Cubulco, and the Chixoy River valley. Furthermore, Xococ was a very important village in the *cofradía* system (see Ochaita 1974) and venerated the pre-Columbian site of Chwitinamit (see Le Bot 1993), which was under the control of Rio Negro. Xococ's privileged status had led many of its members to join the military since the decade of the 1930s. Surely, all these factors were taken into account when the military chose the community of Xococ to become one of its most favored local allies. Although Xococ was to become the bastion of the PAC contingency and participated in various massacres, so did residents from other villages, such as Las Vegas de Santo Domingo, Pichec, and San Luís.

Much of the Achí population was "internally displaced" by the armed violence and the repression. Only when a number of amnesties were issued during 1983 and 1984 did many of them return to their homes. Poles of Development and Model Villages were not implemented in Rabinal. However, some of the Rio Negro massacre survivors, who returned to Rabinal in 1983 under the protection of the Diocese of Alta Verapaz, were forced to live in Pacux. This was a closed settlement located near the urban center and strictly monitored by the military.

Following the amnesty the military extended its control throughout the municipality, where its barracks remained active until the final Peace Accord in 1996. The PAC system was implemented in all villages and the town center, affecting both the Achí and the Ladinos. A military commissioner was appointed by the army to run every subdivision of a village (*caseríos*), which resulted in up to five military commissioners in each village, in contrast to only one military commissioner per village in the pre-violence period.

Although by 1984 no community experienced open and general violence, people were regularly taken into the military barracks for questioning. At times they were tortured; at other times they "disappeared." The prevailing climate was one of fear, threats, and humiliation, to which war widows in particular were subjected. In Panajal, for instance, over one hundred men had been killed in two massacres, leaving the village with forty-seven widows. Many who had been raped during the violence were stigmatized in their communities; they were labeled "wives of the guerrillas."

Village authority was now conferred upon military commissioners, legitimized by the army under the pretext of protecting villagers from the guerrillas. Many villagers looked upon this authority as illegitimate but were compelled to comply. The new power structures were sometimes welcomed and exploited for personal gain. Villagers who had participated in massacres sought to impose silence and instill apathy. For example, the widows of Panajal were denied access to the site of one massacre in Chilaguna for more than 15 years by perpetrators from Las Vegas de Santo Domingo.

Disbelief, suspicion, and lack of trust toward others defined the 1980s. Silence in many cases was both externally and internally imposed. Villagers, in order to protect their family members from future repression, refrained from broaching the subject of violence. Any form of organizing was prohibited unless approved by the military commissioners, who had to report daily to the barracks. At a municipal level there was little organization, just the Center for Family Integration (CIF) and Caritas International. CIF, under a Ladino directorate, negotiated with the military for the repatriation of thirty-five families. These had been displaced from various villages to the new village of San Pablo, the only other resettled village in Rabinal (Julio Manuel Vásquez, personal interview, May 2000). Caritas operated a limited distribution of foodstuffs:

> After the violence the church received a lot of food but we were controlled closely by paramilitaries to see if the food was being given to the guerrillas. We had quite a lot of projects at that time but each time we wanted to go to the villages we had to ask for permission from the military. Our visits were reduced and when finally we went to the villages people no longer wanted to participate. (Abraham Chen de Paz, personal interview, Caritas, May 2000)

Commemorative ceremonies required the presence of the military commissioners. In effect, many widows were unable to carry out the ritual of mourning for forty days after the deaths of their spouses or to carry out the rite of the Day of the Dead on November 1, so integral to indigenous spiritual and psychological well-being. Villagers had to ask for commissioners' permission to leave their communities; and since commissioners also resolved local conflicts, meaningful responses to violence and peacebuilding initiatives were almost impossible during the 1980s.

RESISTANCE TO SILENCE

The local church was the only institution that offered consolation and help to the Achí population. Father Melchor Fraj remained in Rabinal during the height of violence. Together with various religious sisters, he assisted survivors of violence in a number of ways. First, Father Melchor compiled a list of the dead. Survivors would appear at the church under the pretext of asking for confession to add the names of their dead (Roberto Avalos García, personal interview, April 2000). The list was drawn up shortly after the amnesties, but compiling it was still dangerous. As Father Roberto recounts:

> He [Father Melchor] was a very serious man. Very honorable. His pastoral approach was quite moderate, yet he still had immense solidarity with the people. He never shared the army's attitude but maintained relative contact with it. He measured his distance. Neither did he talk in a way that would risk the lives of more people.

Second, Father Melchor would accompany people to the barracks and mediate with the military in their search for family members. Asking the priest for accompaniment was a means to averting the threat of disappearance. Third, he facilitated dialogue between those who remained in Rabinal and their family members who had joined the guerrillas. According to Father Roberto, the guerrillas had left strategic hideouts where messages were left and taken. Father Melchor himself would take and leave the messages in these hideouts. Finally, whenever possible the church would hold mass to commemorate massacres. For a number of years the church leaders refrained from visiting communities, believing that the military could take advantage of the church's ability to assemble people. In Plan de Sánchez, for example, Fernando Suazo recalls that the community began commemorating in 1985 the massacre of July 18, 1982, in which more than 250 people were burned alive. He was invited to celebrate an anniversary mass. He recounts: "It was of great importance to the people to have a priest there, an authority like the church to bear witness to the fact that, yes, a massacre had occurred *here*" (Fernando Suazo, personal interview, April 2000).

Navarette argues that the number of converts to Protestantism in Rabinal rose in the aftermath of the 1976 earthquake (1999, 41). However, I was informed that while the Nazarene Church had been in Rabinal since the 1920s, other Protestant churches such as the Assembly of God and Bethesda Church did not arrive until the 1980s. Villagers from Xococ and Chipuerta who had participated in massacres did not undergo their conversion to Protestantism or join Charismatic Renewal until toward the end of that decade (personal interviews, Fernando Suazo, April 2000; Benjamin Gerónimo, May 2000). In effect, mass conversions did not occur until after the worst years of militarization. Yet Father Melchor still deemed it imprudent to raise the topic of the violence publicly, since masses were attended by local victimizers and occasionally the army.

RESISTANCE TO MILITARY SERVICE AND CIVIL PATROL

A two-year military service was obligatory for all Guatemalan males, and there was not a generalized rejection of military service in Rabinal. Many youths willingly joined the army, since it was usually the only assured income for them. Yet there were some ways to avoid joining the military. Mothers would often hide their sons when the army sought recruits, usually on festival and market days. On one occasion the *Ixok Ajau* organization of widows took more than twenty young men from Rabinal to the capital city, where they hid with family members (Pedrina Vargas, personal interview, June 2000).

Although a number of villages such as Xococ eagerly identified with the new military structures, many other communities greatly resented them. The 1990s significantly reduced military commissioners' hold over villagers, and more than seventy communities in Rabinal refused to participate in the civil patrols. Alecio attributes this to the decline in state-led repression rather than to community opposition to the patrols or the military: "In many instances, this disbanding reflects the success of the counterinsurgency—it is widely recognized that the patrols are unnecessary because there is no guerrilla presence—and that the social control has been internalized by the population, that there is no need for overt mechanisms of control" (1995, 39).

Nevertheless, most people I spoke with considered their refusal to be a form of opposition. Villages resented the time lost on patrol and successfully argued with the military that such time would be better spent on construction (Juan Manuel Gerónimo, personal interview, April 2000).

The Peace Accords and the return of civilian governments allowed for different kinds of responses in the decade of the 1990s. In various municipalities NGOs began to enter more easily. The imposed silence, so characteristic of the 1980s, began to be contested.

Having been driven out of existence in the 1980s, *La Huella del Varón Rabinal Achí* was refounded in 1991 as *Ixok Ajau* by various widows who had received training outside of Rabinal, principally in the department of Chimaltenango. They set up a project to repay the debts of their dead husbands. These widows have, with others, created projects with midwives, agricultural programs, and a project for weaving and candle production. *Ixok Ajau* also helped to create a Council of Elders to reactivate traditional Achí cultural values, to promote traditional authority, and to reconstruct the fragmented social fabric based on the experience and wisdom of the elders (Catalino Martínez Toj, personal interview, May 2000).

The Association for the Integral Development of War Victims in the Verapaces

Maya Achí (ADIVIMA), the only organization in Rabinal that directly addresses the violence today, was founded in 1993. ADIVIMA is a nonpartisan human rights organization whose initial aim was to contest the silence and fear imposed on the Achí population by creating solidarity and a sense of community for the war victims. Soon it had more than one thousand members, the majority of them war widows. Its focus has branched out to address a number of issues. These include requesting a World Bank review of the Chixoy resettlement plan; securing new land for survivors; creating a scholarship fund for Achí youth; providing popular education courses on human rights; establishing a legal aid center; demanding exhumations of clandestine cemeteries; erecting monuments; and seeking the legal prosecution of perpetrators (see Rights Action 2000).

THE POLITICS OF MEMORY AND MAYAN SPIRITUALISM

The 1990s witnessed a number of efforts to conserve the memory of the victims of violence. When in the early 1990s CONAVIGUA and GAM arrived in Rabinal, survivors were able to challenge the social climate. Both organizations played a key role throughout Guatemala in identifying clandestine cemeteries and demanding their exhumation. In Rabinal, with support of the Catholic Church, they obtained the first exhumations in Rio Negro, Chichupac, and Plan de Sánchez by a national forensics team, the results of which are presented in the book *Las Masacres en Rabinal* (EAFG 1995). ADIVIMA later took over the task of identifying clandestine cemeteries and presently carries out all paperwork associated with exhumations.

Early exhumations were carried out in a climate of risk, since the Peace Accords had not been finalized. In many cases, demands for exhumations have not been supported by all the members of communities, and they are carried out under threats and intimidation. Juan Manuel Gerónimo, an active participant in many exhumations, recounts in relation to the exhumation in Plan de Sánchez:

> In the process some families got involved; others wanted nothing to do with it. They'd say to us, "They're dead, we can't recover them, why do we want to do anything now?" At the beginning we received many threats from military commissioners. Suddenly we'd receive visits from other villagers who'd say, "Don't follow the politics of the guerrilla." But we continued because we had to. (personal interview, April 2000)

Although the practice of exhumation is now easier in Rabinal, there are still threats. During an exhumation that was being carried out in the year 2000 at Pichec, one witness heard: "See, see they were guerrillas; they have the red scarves around their necks."

The reburial of the victims has been followed by the erection of a number of monuments which are scattered throughout Rabinal's landscape. The construction of these monuments has fueled the wrath of local perpetrators who in 1994 defaced and tore down the monument to the victims of Rio Negro. Given that it was erected in the reburial site at the local cemetery close to the barracks, it was assumed that the vandalism had been carried out by the military. Not only did the survivors protest the act in the national press, but they also constructed a much larger monument (Carlos Chen Osorio, personal interview, June 2000). The war monuments not only list the names of all those killed, but also the names of the communities who perpetrated the crimes.

The reburial of victims and the construction of war monuments have also been combined with the renewal of Mayan ceremonies, which, according to widows of Panajal, had not been practiced publicly prior to the 1990s. Promoted by ADI-VIMA, the ceremonies incorporate the spiritual world of the ancestors in order to create unity and protection when mobilizing around exhumations, to fill a spiritual void, and to offer their children (many of whom presently migrate to other areas of Guatemala) an identity connected with the land. The yearly ceremonies to commemorate the dates of massacres and of reburial have been extended to other areas of the survivors' lives, such as the inauguration of projects or petitions for rain.

Mayan ceremonies are not practiced by all Achí. However, the belief that ancestors are part of a living tradition has allowed for the creation of new identities related to the earth cult. This has allowed some survivors to distinguish themselves from the Ladinos, the victimizers, and the Protestant and charismatic converts.

A recent effort to preserve the memory of the dead is the Community War Museum, another ADIVIMA initiative, inaugurated in Rabinal on February 14, 1999. Established through various donations and assistance, primarily from the Union of Community Museums of Oaxaca, Mexico, the museum is the only one of its kind in Guatemala. It displays photos of the dead and of life in local communities prior to the violence. Where possible it combines the photos with life histories of those who perished, recounting their work in the communities and their ambitions to better the lives of those around them. Once again, the motive behind this initiative lies in the desire to allow future generations to understand the recent past and to let perpetrators know that the past cannot be silenced (Carlos Chen Osorio, personal interview, June 2000).

TELLING THE TRUTH AND DEMANDING JUSTICE

In Rabinal various Achís who had strong affinities with the Catholic Church were trained in REMHI's methodology in order to obtain testimonies that contributed to its final report. The REMHI experience led to additional people providing testimony to the CEH, which started collecting testimonies a year later. Juan Manuel Gerónimo recounts:

> REMHI's work was very important for our people. It was a hard task. We were told that it was important to respect the interviewee, only to go to those we could trust. We told the people, "Look here, we're not going to divulge anything, it's very secretive work." But the people understood and they wanted to talk. Even I learnt a lot in this time. So many things we

didn't know about the violence. How other people had suffered it. We had a lack of personnel but we managed to do the job. But then they killed Bishop Gerardi. There was no respect for what had been clarified. The sad thing was that his death made people feel scared once again. (personal interview, April 2000)

Demands for truth have coincided with those for justice. Some local activists have adopted a language of human rights. Survivors' demands for justice tend to have three dimensions. They present themselves as victims of abusive governments; they seek to simply vindicate the truth; and they challenge the local power structures, demanding legal redress from the perpetrators of violence. For some, the main motive stems from a conviction that perpetrators should be held accountable. In other instances, religious conviction prevails. Biblical passages referring to Cain and Abel, as well as to Christ and Judas, are constantly fused into demands for justice.

> . . . victimizers had no feeling towards our kids, towards elders, women. They massacred defenseless people. Today they continue with the same attitude, they continue to threaten people. They feel that they don't need to ask for forgiveness. They say *we* should ask for it for going into the guerrilla, even when they knew there was no guerrilla around. We have the example of who killed Jesus; it was Judas. He was never reconciled because he never asked for forgiveness. In one go, he was condemned. (Benjamin Gerónimo, personal interview, April 2000)

Many survivors explained that the punishment of perpetrators does not entail subsequent forgiveness. But more important for them is the demand for justice as a vindication of their innocence. In the 1980s many people had internalized the military's displacement of blame for the massacres onto themselves. After all, it was said, they had joined the guerrilla movement. In various cases, fellow villagers also blamed the victims of violence for the fragmentation of communities and for the destruction of lives. Judicial proceedings have therefore been sought precisely to demonstrate their innocence to fellow villagers and others.

Yet in the 1980s the line between friend and enemy became so blurred that it is no longer easy to establish who is innocent:

> It's difficult to talk about victimizers and victims in this context. In the 1980s we all did many things to survive. Now people think victimizers are all over the place. Yes, you can say they are, for example, in Xococ. But people would denounce others in the 1980s to protect themselves. Some people were forced to carry out the violence but others don't know they were forced. The enemy here? Well, they were Ladinos, indigenous. They were your family members. Everyone was against everyone. It's not easy to say, "Hey, you did this to me," because they will probably say, "Yes, and you did that." (José Leon, personal interview, February 2000)

Legal Retribution

In 1996 survivors of the Rio Negro massacre, with the support of ADIVIMA and legal assistance from the Center for Legal Action in Human Rights (CALDH), filed a lawsuit against three civil patrollers from Xococ for crimes against humanity. After a number of acquittals, the plaintiffs ultimately secured life sentences in January 2000 against Carlos Chen, Pedro González Gómez, and Fermín Lajuj Xitimul for crimes against humanity. This was the first successful lawsuit in the country against local civil patrollers. What many survivors highlighted after the trial was that, although they were successful, they really wanted to know more about the perpetrators' motives:

> We went every day, the whole community, to see what they would say. Nothing! Throughout the whole trial they said nothing. We wanted to know who gave them orders, why they did it. Instead, they denied their guilt. We've told our truths. We can't say any more. First with REMHI and then the CEH. Now we want to hear their truths. (personal interview, Pacux, June 2000)

A number of Achís, including some from Panajal, Rio Negro, and Plan de Sánchez, are members of the Reconciliation for Justice Association (ARJ). As mentioned above, they have filed a lawsuit against various top military officers for crimes against humanity. In addition, with the assistance of ADIVIMA, a number of villages are presently demanding war reparations from the government. These extend from monetary payments for the loss of family members and livelihoods, to support for weaving and agricultural projects and payment for the construction of memorials.

Building Fragmented Communities

Legal redress is not the only initiative being taken to restore peace. Legal prosecutions are very costly and often drag on for many years. Many communities, divided as a result of the militarization in the 1980s, seek other mechanisms to create or recreate harmony. Here I refer to a few such initiatives.

Deferred Punishment. The *Xib'ineel* mountain spirits, venerated by most Achís, are considered guardians, caretakers of the mountains and land, and arbiters of sinfulness. *Xib'ineel* are called upon to restore harmony with God, ancestors, the earth, and the community. Mayan priests act as mediators when spirits are called upon to right wrongs.

Rather than call upon the spirits to act immediately upon the wrongs of local people, Achí elders of *Ixok Ajau* advocate deferred punishment. Although forgiveness for those who "acted with ambition" is not an option since *Xib'ineel* are expected to exact vengeance in the afterlife, the concept of deferred punishment allows for the interaction of victims with victimizers who are allowed to engage in civil society. Courting the disapproval of widows, elders often argue that such an approach prevents violence and restores local harmony. The sparse evidence to support accusations of human rights violations could result in further hatred, they affirm, so punishment should be left to the spirits, who alone saw everything (Manuel Sesam and José Leon, personal interviews, September 2000).

Mediated Mechanisms for Tolerance. The Catholic Church's ability to mediate in village conflicts was reduced significantly by the presence of military commissioners in the 1980s. The proliferation of converts to evangelical Protestantism and Catholic charismatic renewal, which prefer not to address the violence and not to enter into dialogue with the other churches, has further diminished the Catholic Church's capacity to intervene. Yet Father Roberto plans to elaborate a pastoral program drawing on Christian concepts of repentance and tolerance to bridge the enmity between victimizers and victims—even though no victimizer has yet asked for forgiveness, and survivors have demonstrated resistance to his plans.

Despite difficulties confronting the Catholic Church over the issue of community fragmentation, other, secular initiatives have been undertaken. Here I refer to just two, implemented in Xesiguán and Pacux, communities that have both experienced extreme fragmentation.

Most of the villagers of Xesiguán were sympathizers of the EGP. In the early 1980s three military commissioners and nine of their family members were assassinated. During the years of militarization, two of the group who carried out the killings were themselves appointed military commissioners and subsequently allied themselves with the army. When, in 1993, a dispute arose over a water source between the two military commissioners and two other community members who also participated in the massacre, the community was divided according to prior loyalties with the army or guerrillas.

The Organization of American States' (OAS) nationwide program of conflict resolution for Guatemala was inaugurated in 1996 to train and create a network of community conciliators. Xesiguán was one community in Rabinal involved in the project. Three people from the community were trained in its methodology. However, when they were called upon by municipal authorities in the late 1990s to prevent the village from further division, the efforts of the three conciliators were rejected. Villagers argued that these three conciliators were nominated by authorities external to the community, that the methodology was alien to the community's way of resolving conflict, and also that the problems were profoundly historical. In effect, the conciliators were denied permission to mediate. To this day their role remains superfluous.

In contrast to the effort in Xesiguán, the experience of conflict resolution in Pacux enjoyed some success. In 2000 human rights activists there sought the assistance of the Center of Popular Education. One hundred fifty family representatives were invited to attend a series of thirty-two workshops offered by the Center in the village. Participants were encouraged to talk about their experiences as a community prior to the war. Subsequently, they were asked to reflect and discuss the dynamic of violence. This interaction allowed for the expression of pain, anger, and resentment toward the army and village members allied with the army. The workshops concluded with an analysis of people's own activities, as well as community aspirations (Raúl Najera, personal interview, February 2001).

The fact that the intervention in Pacux was both historical and sociological in its emphasis and was requested by the community itself contributed to its success. In the concluding workshops, community members asked for the replacement of previous authoritarian officials with new, democratic ones. This led to the creation of seven commissions, whose representatives were named by the community.

SAN MARTIN JILOTEPEQUE, CHIMALTENANGO

Grassroots responses in San Martín were significantly different from those in Rabinal. The municipality has a particularly complex history of land tenure and ethnic relations, and it has produced some of the most significant indigenous mobilization in recent history. Chimaltenango was strategically important to the guerrilla factions not only because of its politicized population but also because of its proximity to the capital. The Pan-American Highway, which leads to the large coastal plantations and to the indigenous-populated highlands, also slices through this department. With the threat of an imminent guerrilla attack in the early 1980s, the military made the area a priority. It directed violence primarily against the indigenous Kakchiquel population, with the population in San Martín a particular target.

Historical Antecedents

Social relations in San Martín have always been determined by prevailing patterns of land tenure. With the arrival of coffee plantations toward the end of the nineteenth century, the municipality developed an axis between lowland estates and the highland settlement of their labor force. By 1913, 39 percent of land belonged to local Ladinos (T. Adams 1978, 26), and they increasingly gained control over the Kakchiqueles through lease of land and debt peonage.

Adams argues that until 1944 municipal politics had been largely in the hands of Ladinos (Adams 1978, 36-37). The reform period of Arévalo and Arbenz resulted in indigenous involvement in politics, and in 1952 the first indigenous mayor was elected (Adams 1978, 43; Handy 1994, 114). The subsequent implementation of an agrarian reform resulted in the expropriation of land in five plantations (Adams 1978, 40), and although the municipality as a whole was not affected, there was extensive social mobilization.

In 1963 the department experienced a strong military response to the FAR guerrilla movement. In this period the role of military commissioners changed from a largely symbolic status to actively participating in counterinsurgency operations (McClintock 1985, 66). The U.S.-funded Civic Action for the Development of Communities program proposed new civic-military relations with the population (Schirmer 1998, 36). By December 1973 the Military Academy had opened a stretch of road from San Martín to its neighboring municipality of Comalapa, to create greater mobility in the area. Initiatives were carried out under the Civic Action program in villages such as Pachay and Sajalá as a result of popular organization in the region during the 1960s and 1970s.

The Behrhorst Clinic Foundation, inaugurated in 1962, quickly evolved into a center for health and development activities. It trained health promoters throughout Chimaltenango. World Neighbors arrived in the 1970s to set up an extensive "people-centered development" project, and the San Martín Integrated Development Program resulted in the implementation of new methodologies for agricultural improvement (see Bunch 1982). Doroteo Us recalls that "it was a social agricultural movement which was very much accepted by the local population" (personal interview, August 2000).

At the same time, various trade unions, peasant leagues, agrarian committees, cooperatives, and indigenous associations were set up. In 1972 the peasant organization in Pachay and Sajalá, strongly influenced by the PGT members in the communities and the national Autonomous Federation of Guatemalan Unions (FASGUA), purchased El Centeno. Some 270,000 hectares of land were bought by 120 families, each of which was given some 5,000 acres (personal interview, Pachay, February 2000). Some cooperatives offered credit. Others purchased land and sold fertilizer at reduced prices.

Community members had contacts not only with FASGUA but also with the National Workers Confederation (CNT), whose existence was made known through the radio (Levenson-Estrada 1994, 126). Villagers in Estanica de la Virgen recall the help offered in the mid-1970s by the small CNT legal staff (ibid., 106).

> The Treasury Police abused us a lot at that time. They would turn up in the villages under the pretext of protecting the woodlands and arrest people for making illegal alcohol. They'd turn up in the night and just enter houses. We'd go to the CNT, who would help us in legal matters against the Treasury Police and the National Police. (personal interview, Estancia de la Virgen, July 2000)

Peasant leagues organized around conflicts between peasants and landowners. Cooperatives focused on providing fertilizer, purchasing land, and offering credit; and local committees were concerned with road construction, potable water, and latrines. As Enrique Corral recalls, most of the efforts were still fragmentary:

> When I first went there in 1973 and 1974, what we saw was a lot of activity but it was all in crisis, because the structure of each organization was so formal. They'd have lots of meetings but they were closed to the community. Their demands were economic, they seemed to have no social dynamic. They found it difficult to offer solutions for the peoples' aspirations. (personal interview, March 2000)

Arguably the most important institution in the municipality was Catholic Action, founded and sustained by Father Gonzalo Herrera. He officiated in San Martín, his hometown, from 1963 to 2000. By the mid-1970s he had trained more than six hundred catechists, many more than in other comparable areas. His pastoral approach was conservative, with a strong emphasis on sacramental work and a staunch anti-communism that contrasted with the approach of other Catholic priests in Chimaltenango. His movement experienced severe fragmentation, however, after the 1976 earthquake.

The earthquake, which left twenty thousand dead and over one million displaced (Garrard-Burnett 1998, 120), was a catalyst for coordinated social and political activism. Villages close to its epicenter in the river Montagua were most severely hit. In Chimaltenango 41,677 out of 42,794 homes were destroyed (McClintock 1985, 136). In San Martín alone up to two thousand people had been killed and almost all households destroyed.

The reconstruction effort brought communities together. University students from the city arrived to help. Of more importance was the pastoral work of the Jesuit Enrique Corral, who later left the priesthood for the EGP. Corral entered San Martín for the second time in 1976, to start pastoral work based on liberation theology. Forbidden to celebrate mass and in conflict with Father Gonzalo, he limited his work to a number of villages, primarily Pachay and Sajalá. Liberation theology appealed to a number of catechists who had received instruction in its concepts during meetings in other areas of the country, and they joined Corral. Key community leaders from Pachay and Choatalum became strong opponents of Father Gonzalo, whom they associated with the Ladinos and plantation owners. Within Catholic Action tensions grew between those who followed a more politico-religious approach and those who preferred a purely sacramental one:

> The catechists began to change their discourse. Now they spoke of the rich and the poor. I was here; I saw when the thing started to change. They would say, "God says you must speak directly, that you must speak of the government's injustices." (Catalino Chamaley, personal interview, February 2000)

CUC AND GUERRILLA FACTIONS

Post-earthquake reconstruction coalesced with the politicization of catechists to help form the CUC. A meeting of various organizations in 1978 in El Amate ultimately led to its creation. Many catechists who had abandoned Father Gonzalo for Corral became prominent leaders (Enrique Corral, personal interview, March 2000).

According to villagers from Pachay and Sajalá, the 1978 meeting was a turning point in mobilization. From there on, demands were framed in political discourse. The issues now addressed included respect for the young, the abolition of military service and debt peonage, discrimination, and migration.

What we wanted was a dignified way of life. The plantation system was there to oppress us. The authorities oppressed us. Why is it that only the indigenous were always thrown into jail? Why is it that only the indigenous suffer? Our demands weren't just economic, they were political, ethnic, and social. (personal interview, Pachay, February 2000)

The politicization of San Martín accelerated in 1978 as CUC brought together smaller organizations, such as the youth association of Estancia de la Virgen, whose members came from a number of villages. However, as repression intensified and political space was reduced, CUC's members increasingly joined the guerrillas. Almost all the villagers of Pachay and Sajalá, for example, joined the EGP. Corral recounts:

The process in San Martín was too rapid. Unlike in other areas, we hadn't built a clandestine structure because we didn't have the time. So everyone knew who was who. With the leadership under Comandante Camilo, who wanted insurrection straight away, and with the triumph in El Salvador there was mass support. But it was all too fast and it wasn't going to succeed. (personal interview, March 2000)

Chimaltenango attracted the attention of all guerrilla factions because of its level of organization and geographical location. FAR had contacts with some villages since the 1960s. The EGP had been present in the 1970s, but only began military operations in the area after 1980. An underground hospital, and munitions and uniform workshops were established in the municipality.

Conflicts arose between villagers precisely because of the rapid politicization of the population. For many, armed conflict had become the only viable option, but not everyone shared that view. On occasion, villagers even killed their friends or family members for refusing to join the EGP, with remaining family members fleeing to the town center and outside areas. Perhaps in revenge, or simply to stay alive, these very same people would provide the army with the names of EGP members.

At this time they would say we all had to join them. Some of us didn't want to. My wife's brother turned against me. He said, "Listen, if you don't join us we will kill you." So I left the village. When I returned after the amnesty the people were against us because they said we had joined the army. (personal interview, Pachay, February 2000)

In March 1981 the EGP mobilized the Agusto César Sandino Guerrilla Front (FGACS) in Chimaltenango for a major offensive. The military responded in October with a massive counteroffensive. Within a few months it had killed thousands of people in Chimaltenango, Sololá, and the south of El Quiché (Schirmer 1998, 42-44).

THE VIOLENCE

In contrast to the dynamic of violence in Rabinal, the army's counteroffensive in San Martín did not demand participation by the local people. It was the military's own Task Force Iximché that itself perpetrated the violence. Conflicts within communities resulted largely from acceptance of amnesties by those who had fled during the violence, or it emerged between different religious factions.

Any act of resistance in this period was considered subversion. In many circumstances the first to be targeted were PGT members. Later it was anyone connected with the popular movement. In March 1981, seventy-three teachers sent a letter to the Minister of Education to report that because of the wave of kidnappings and the killings of teachers and students, classes had been suspended indefinitely; but the minister threatened the teachers with dismissal and reprisals (*Inforpress*, April 2, 1981, 437).

Villagers fled en masse, and they placed white flags strategically throughout the area. As the military approached, the flags were removed warning others of the military's proximity. This allowed those in the village sufficient time to flee (personal interview, Pachay, February 2000).

Task Force Iximché carried out the first of the military's scorched-earth "sweeps" and Chimaltenango was the first department to experience this unprecedented military operation. The task force, designed and personally directed by General Benedicto Lucas García, involved more than three thousand soldiers. They burned scores of villages and carried out massacres such as that of displaced people in Estancia de la Virgen at Rio Pixcaya (CEH 1999, 6:75-79). Male villagers from nearby were forced to bury the dead. On their return to the village they warned others not to speak of the massacre or risk death. But some sent a delegation to the U.S. embassy as well as the Guatemalan government to denounce the massacre.

Having pushed back the guerrillas, and with the population of whole villages displaced, the army issued a number of amnesties throughout the country. There were a series of mass surrenders. During this period, those who had already surrendered often helped those who had fled and were still in hiding by providing foodstuffs clandestinely, and by continuing to inform those in hiding about the army's whereabouts. The displaced population of Choatalum, for example, received information from those in Estancia de la Virgen about the military's plans:

> A group of scouts would go each day to the strategic posts to await information from Estancia de la Virgen. We told them when we intended to surrender; to inform the military that the majority with us were children and women, and not to kill us. They would then pass on the information to the army. (personal interview, Choatalum, August 2000)

MILITARIZATION

In 1983 military barracks were set up in the town center of San Martín and in Choatalum, where they remained until the early 1990s. Initially more than two hundred soldiers were stationed in Choatalum—twice the number posted in the town center. Moreover, Choatalum had as many as twenty military commissioners and experienced greater militarization than any other village in San Martín (personal interview, Choatalum, August 2000).

The municipality was also the first to feel the military's next stage of population control, its Plan of Action in Areas of Conflict (PAAC) and the creation of "model villages" (Schirmer 1998, 57). Upon their return to Estancia de la Virgen, villagers were herded into a newly constructed settlement (personal interview, Estancia de la Virgen, July 2000). The New Choatalum Colony initially grouped together villagers from a number of different areas. Subsequently, some families who had fled and were now under the protection of the army resolved to move to it, and they still reside there (personal interview, Choatalum, August 2000). Today Choatalum is one of the most divided villages in San Martín because of the intense military presence it experienced for more than a decade and the social divisions that stemmed from it.

RELIGIOUS CONVERSIONS

In response to the extreme violence, many villagers converted to evangelical Protestantism or joined the Charismatic Renewal movement. Some explain it as a new set of defections from Father Gonzalo. He had been present on the day of the "surrender" of Pachay in Chimaltenango and had demanded that those who surrendered ask for forgiveness not only from the military, but also from the church "because they had offended God by joining the guerrilla movement" (personal interview, Pachay, February 2000). Some people recall his lack of intervention and suggest possible collusion with the military.

Given that conversions in the 1980s were primarily to evangelical Protestantism, some argue that many local people became evangelicals because it was the religion supported by members of the military:

> The evangelicals came in 1983, and the charismatics about nine years ago. It had a lot to do with the violence. Many people went to the coast during that time, and when they came back they brought back evangelicalism. Today most of the divisions are because we don't speak to each other. Maybe once the current priest leaves we'll be able to dialogue with the charismatics. I don't think this will happen with the evangelicals. They won't accept the church's sacraments, and they won't dialogue. (personal interview, Sajalá, March, 2000)

In the villages I worked in, Catholics are still a majority, but a substantial proportion of villagers have gone through a conversion. As in Rabinal, there are villagers who say that such conversions are the result of efforts to appease the military and to conceal complicity in wartime wrongdoings. But the image of the military as an ally of evangelicals or charismatics may also be misleading.

Stoll writes concerning the Ixil region that, although some evangelical churches participated in activities like informing the military of guerrilla locations, it was done because of coercion and as a survival strategy (1993, 102). Siebers argues that the Catholic Church's emphasis on sociopolitical matters and its subsequent identification with the guerillas resulted in the alienation of many members. They joined other churches not only because they were smaller and provided greater personal contact and support, but also because the religious communities were also more spiritual in orientation (1990, 120).

Whatever the motives—and they have probably been diverse in character— conversions in San Martín were direct or indirect forms of grassroots response to the violence. People took personal or group sides in the conflict and sought spiritual solace or protection from danger. But the conversions occurred in, and were clearly affected by, the context of extreme violence.

RESISTANCE TO PAC AND MILITARY SERVICE

Even before the period of the extreme violence, people in San Martín had resisted military service: "Mothers, fathers would go to the military zone with papers saying, 'Look, my son is married,' or 'he's too young,' or 'look, he has an illness'" (personal interview, Choatalum, August 2000). However, as in the case of Rabinal, the army came to represent the only source of income for many, and they willingly joined. Coronado Camay recounts:

> I can't remember if it was '84 or '85 but on one day during recess all students at the teacher training school were rounded up by the army and taken into military service. We went to a number of authorities to complain and, finally, when the military said, "Ok, they don't have to do it," the students refused to return to the school. They wanted to stay with the army. That was it. For that year we had no students to train! (personal interview, March 2000)

In response to the PAC, many villages tried to avoid fragmentation by appointing as their military commissioners people who had the community's interests at heart. For example, Pachay and Sajalá both appointed their own military commissioners. They were initially approved of by the military, but were later replaced (personal interview, Pachay, February 2000).

FEAR AND AVOIDANCE

What is strikingly different from Rabinal is the lack of a human rights discourse or a cultural Mayan revival in San Martín. Fear is a prime reason many give for this. Although a number of exhumations have been carried out in San Martín, such as in El Amate and Tonajuyú, there is no organization in San Martín with a human rights project directly related to the violence. Instead, since the 1990s the municipality has concentrated its efforts on development projects and educational aspirations. In 1995 the returned Kakchiquel refugee Doroteo Us, a native of San Martín, was elected municipal mayor, and nine organizations are now grouped in the Coordinating Committee for Integral Development (Jorge Machan, personal interview, March 2000).

The reasons for this type of narrowly socioeconomic response in San Martín are complex. It could be argued, however, that the absence of a human rights discourse or an indigenous cultural revival movement reflects the intense psychological control that has been exercised by the army, in addition to the strong presence of evangelicals and charismatics who avoid addressing the violence. It was frequently expressed that God will punish those who seek a human rights agenda: "Here the people . . . think God will punish them if they start to go to the authorities and demand retribution" (personal interview, Sajalá, March 2000).

In addition to the effects of fear and of conservative Christianity, it should be noted that the people of San Martín have not had the experience of important national programs such as REMHI. The diocese of Sololá was exceptional in that it refused to assist REMHI in gathering testimonies from local victims and survivors of the violence. The reasons are unclear, but personnel of the REMHI office working in Chimaltenango suggest that the dominant classes in Chimaltenango and Sololá, who have had historically close ties with the institutional church, successfully pressured the diocese not to participate (personal interview, Chimaltenango, March 2002).

Finally, the relative lack of local demands for accountability undoubtedly reflects the fact that it was the military itself that was the principal perpetrator of crimes against humanity in San Martín. Although some communities in the area are presently participating in the Reconciliation for Justice Association under the legal advice of CALDH, there are those who experienced violence from their own village members (Paul Siels, personal interview, July 2000). The military institution was and is still too powerful and impersonal, and too capable of harsh sanctions, it seems, for local people to dare question its past role.

MEN AND WOMEN WORKING FOR PEACE

With women comprising the bulk of survivors of the war, they have been more likely than men to gather in associations such as CONAVIGUA or GAM to organize around their needs and confront perpetrators of the violence. My data on gender reflect these phenomena: women in Guatemala were more likely to work for peace in groups and to engage in confrontational forms of peacemaking (see chapter 1) than were men. On the other hand, men, who more often had received training as catechists and Delegates of the Word, were more likely than women to cite religious motivations for their peacemaking activities. The table at the end of this chapter provides the statistics for these findings on gender.

CHALLENGES FOR THE CHURCH

The Guatemalan people continue to suffer from unjust social structures, continued racial or ethnic discrimination, and the enduring consequences of a history of violence. These factors make it particularly hard for them to address reconciliation and peace. The limited grassroots responses described above, such as some truth telling, the recovery and reburial of victims' remains, legal demands for forms of justice, and religious and cultural rituals of memory, are not representative of the will of whole communities. Furthermore, such grassroots responses confront substantial obstacles.

Peacemaking activities are taking place in a social context still marked by a denial of what occurred. Military impunity remains prevalent. Many victims continue to blame themselves for what happened. The violence has profoundly affected municipalities, small communities, and individuals alike. It has spawned top-down power structures and forced people to adjust somehow to new patterns of life rather than to deal with what really occurred. At the local level there tends to be little outreach to others or relationship building. An experience like that described above in Pacux in Baja Verapaz remains exceptional. At the national level, in this so-called post-conflict society, there is little if any reconciliation.

In the 1990s a variety of social actors emerged who are now challenging the impunity of the perpetrators of violence. Yet, for every survivor who demands retribution and/or restitution, there are many more whose priority is community development or reconstruction, or whose preference is simply to leave the past in the past. According to Rosa María Wantland, who with a team of researchers from OAS-ProPeace has carried out extensive research on attitudes toward reconciliation, it may still be premature to seek reconciliation in the Guatemalan context.

The current situation presents a number of challenges to church people and others committed to peace and social justice. As concluding comments I will refer only to some of the most salient. Each was raised in the workshop held at AVANCSO in 2001 to reflect on the results of this research project.

The first challenge is the absence of effective civil and institutional spaces for dialogue. While many testimonies were gathered by REMHI and the CEH, people are no longer being encouraged to discuss what happened or why. And with legal action emerging as an option for some survivors, there may be even less space for, or interest in, dialogue and reconciliation. Father Roberto's efforts to promote reconciliation in Rabinal are being thwarted in part because many survivors seek legal retribution rather than forgiveness and tolerance.

Another is the absence of a spirit of ecumenical dialogue and religious cooperation. Most leaders of the evangelical churches and the Charismatic Renewal movement, as indicated above, refuse to deal with the massacres and the violations of human rights. They generally reject dialogue with others. Myths about evangelicals abound among Catholics, and vice-versa. And Catholics themselves have internal fissures with which to deal. Drawing on religious resources for peace is virtually impossible, in such circumstances, in many Guatemalan communities.

Furthermore, already divided local communities are becoming even more fragmented in some cases. At the AVANCSO sessions, Miguel Moerth of the Center of Forensic Anthropology and Applied Sciences (CAFCA) pointed out one of the reasons. Because exhumations have tended to be individual rather than community-wide initiatives (and at times have been rejected by community members), the process has often led to further conflict. Father Luis Gurriarán pointed out that the experience of the violence and its aftermath has created local power structures with vertical, authoritarian approaches to community matters rather than democratic procedures that might enable communities to rebuild.

While powerful elites in Guatemala engage in willful denial, many grassroots citizens bear an unjust burden of internalized blame for the violence. Without Guatemala somehow facing up to what occurred on a national scale, reconciliation will remain extremely elusive. In the words of Raúl Najera of the Center for Popular Education, "Only when the blame is shifted from the local to the national level can communities once again begin to rebuild their lives."

Reconciliation means different things to different people. For many in Guatemala today, forgiveness is not one of them. At least not yet. Christian churches need to go beyond solely religious principles, to seek and promote common approaches that can respond to the complex demands and needs of victims and survivors, and to help foster a peace that is grounded in justice. The task is a daunting one.

ACRONYMS

ADIVIMA	Association for the Integral Development of Victims of Violence in the Verapaces Maya-Achí
ARJ	Reconciliation for Justice Association
AVANCSO	Association for the Advancement of Social Sciences
CAFCA	Center of Forensic Anthropology and Applied Sciences
CALDH	Center for Legal Action in Human Rights
CEH	Commission for Historical Clarification
CERJ	Council of Ethnic Communities "*Runujel Junam*"
CIIDH	International Center for Human Rights Investigations
CIF	Center for Family Integration
CNT	National Workers' Confederation
CONAVIGUA	National Coordinating Committee of Guatemalan Widows
CUC	Committee of Peasant Unity
EGP	Guerrilla Army of the Poor
FAR	Rebel Armed Forces
FASGUA	Autonomous Federation of Guatemalan Unions
FGACS	Augusto César Sandino Guerrilla Front
FRG	Guatemalan Republican Front
GAM	Mutual Support Group
IDESAC	Economic and Social Development for Central America
INDE	National Institute of Electrification
OAS	Organization of American States
ODHAG	Human Rights Office of the Archdiocese of Guatemala
ORPA	Organization of the People in Arms
PAAC	Plan of Action in Areas of Conflict

PAC   Civilian Self Defense Patrol
PGT   Guatemalan Workers Party
REMHI   Recovery of Historical Memory Project
URNG   Guatemalan National Revolutionary Unity

STATISTICAL TABLE
ASSOCIATED WITH CHAPTER 2 DATA

See page 63 for an interpretation of this table. See chapter 1 for an explanation of variables.

TABLE 1. CORRELATIONAL COMPARISONS OF GENDER AND PEACEMAKING
IN GUATEMALA

	Working for Peace in Groups (vs. Individually)	Religious Motivation	Confrontation
Gender*	.38	-.34	.36

* Positive correlations indicate that women reported this type of motivation or activity more frequently than did men. Only significant r's ($p < .05$) are reported here.

3

Northern Ireland

Peacemaking among Protestants and Catholics

JOHN D. BREWER

I was born into a very poor Unionist family and was the last of three children. Growing up on a housing estate in Protestant West Belfast, I wasn't aware of the struggle my parents faced to provide the basics for the children. My dad worked so hard for very little financial reward; his main interest outside of work was the Protestant Orange Order. My mother also worked day and night in a hotel but for little reward. We were staunchly Unionist. From a very early age I became a member of the Junior Section of the Orange Order, gradually progressing to the senior post of Worshipful Master. I know that both my parents would later say what so many people in life say with hindsight: "If only we could turn the clock back, how different things would have been."

Both my parents were lapsed Christians, although they made sure the children went to church every week. I found this experience an ordeal and hated Sundays with passion. Church was boring and meaningless to me in my young life and the Christian message I heard in church only reinforced the anti-Catholic message I was receiving from the Unionist society around me. I left school in 1969 at the age of 15 with no academic qualifications. That summer the violence came to the streets of Northern Ireland and at this young age I felt the sectarian feelings rise in me. Within a few years the violence escalated. I became involved with the Ulster Volunteer Force, which is one of the main Loyalist paramilitary organizations. In July 1975 I was arrested by the security forces and sentenced the following year to life imprisonment.

As I settled into the routine of imprisonment, very slowly I started to question my beliefs and values. For the first time in my life I actually read the Bible. As I read about the life of Jesus I came to a conclusion that grows stronger with each passing day – that Jesus preached a message of non-violence and that those who follow Him are called to be peacemakers in this world. It is easy to preach the message of peacemaking, harder to practice it, yet God wants us to live it in our everyday lives. I learnt this in prison and have tried to follow it since.

Upon release from prison* I met my future wife, who is a Roman Catholic from the Irish Republic. From the moment we met we knew that God had brought us together to work in reconciliation and peacemaking. This has not occurred overnight. We first had to learn in our marriage to respect each other's culture, religion, and political viewpoints. This journey has been slow and painful as both of us shed off the baggage that we carried with us from our upbringing in "the troubles." But the lesson of reconciliation we learned in our marriage is relevant, as we later came to realize, for Northern Ireland.

Today, after eleven years of marriage and three beautiful children, we can see God opening the doors to us and using us in the work of peace and reconciliation in the community generally. Both of us have trained as facilitators and, coupled with qualifications in community relations, we have recently started our own business called "Pax Works." Through this name we hope to show that peace does work. As facilitators we have been blessed in having the opportunity to work with all sections of the community in Northern Ireland in trying to bring mutual understanding. It is a joy to watch those who in some cases live only a few streets away from each other come together and talk to each other for the first in a long time or the first time ever.

We know that people's mind-sets will not be changed in one day, yet it is our calling as peacemakers to be prepared for a long journey. After thirty years of violence, pain, and suffering in Northern Ireland, there is much healing to be done, and if my wife and I can in some small way contribute to this process then I firmly believe we have answered God's call to be peacemakers and reconcilers. Our prayer is that others may grasp the vision in their own countries and local communities as it is at the grassroots that the seeds of peace grow.

—Jim McKinley, former Loyalist prisoner

Northern Ireland's conflict is deeply enigmatic, embodying at least four paradoxes. It is supposedly a religious war fought over doctrinal principles between people for whom religion is their primary identity, yet religion disguises the conflict's inherently political character. The conflict is over the legitimacy of the

---

*Despite the sentence to life imprisonment, McKinley was released on good behavior after serving twelve years.—*Eds.*

state and access to its political, economic, and cultural resources, but religious affiliation defines the boundaries of the groups that are in competition. The conflict receives massive world attention, yet the violence is relatively low in intensity. The fact that it is played out in the First World gives Northern Ireland's conflict a media and international focus that conflicts elsewhere, with much higher levels of violence, do not attract. Finally, despite its low-key nature, Northern Ireland has perhaps the most comprehensive "peacemaking industry" of all world conflicts. This leads naturally to the greatest conundrum: why the conflict persists amidst all the peacemaking.

It is a truism that the dynamics of peacemaking are affected by the dynamics of the conflict it seeks to resolve. In Northern Ireland the conflict is such that all can assume the status of victim—Catholics being victims of four centuries of social exclusion, and Protestants being victims of thirty years of terrorism—while both name the other as perpetrator. Mutual blaming and mutually exclusive claims to victimhood complicate peacemaking, for the victims' demands for justice can be divisive unless they are extended to all who have suffered. Given that the character of the conflict shapes peacemaking, the logical way to begin this chapter is with a history of Northern Ireland's conflict. Such a historical overview shows that peacemaking needs to be broadly understood as comprising more than an end to violence, for issues of equality, justice, and political and civil rights also resonate down the ages.

THE HISTORY OF THE CONFLICT

The contemporary conflict in Northern Ireland has its genesis in the social structure created in Ireland by Plantation in the sixteenth century (for general histories see Bardon 1992; Brewer 1998; Foster 1988; Rafferty 1994; Ruane and Todd 1996). Plantation describes the voluntary migration—"plantation"—of English and Scottish Protestants to Ireland. British control of Ireland required Protestant control and hence Protestant dominance. Plantation transformed Irish society as no war of conquest had and initiated a separate pattern of development in Ireland's northeast corner—the ancient province of Ulster. Right from the beginning of Plantation, Ulster was different. Planters saw themselves as embattled because Ulster had Catholic rebels who preyed on the Protestant settlers. The planters in Ulster came from Scotland more than England, bringing with them Presbyterianism and its tendency to separatism, and at the beginning Presbyterians experienced their own exclusion by Anglicans. The Scots outnumbered the English in Ulster by a ratio of five to one in 1640, and their cultural legacy is manifest today in many facets of popular culture and in place-names.[1] The separatism of the planters extended to having their own systems of social control based around the presbytery, to the point that Hempton and Hill (1992) describe Ulster Presbyterians as a self-contained and self-regulating community, virtually independent of the wider structures of the English state. As many others have argued, Ulster Presbyterians saw their task as keeping themselves true to the Reformed tradition, searching out apostates within their community rather than evangelizing among Anglicans or Catholics.[2] At the same time, as Holmes (1985) shows, Irish Presbyterians were also prevented from establishing new congregations.[3] The notion that they were, in terms of Calvinist theology, God's

---

[1] For further background on the Scottish heritage in Ulster, see Akenson 1992; and Gailey 1975.

[2] More extensive treatment of the separatism of Ulster Presbyterians may be found in Hempton and Hill 1992; Miller 1978; and Wallis and Bruce 1986.

[3] Blaney (1996) discusses some early attempts at outreach by Presbyterians.

covenanted "elect" only reinforced the tendency to separatism and has continued to do so ever since.

Throughout the eighteenth and nineteenth centuries, Ireland essentially remained a Plantation society, in that the social structure created at the time of Plantation became set in stone. Its lines of differentiation remained structured around Protestant–Catholic divisions that came to represent all other lines of cleavage. However, Ireland was increasingly unable to live with its past because the old conflicts and fissures caused tremendous strain in its social structure. Protestant and Catholic people developed as solidaristic communities in the nineteenth century, which transcended internal fault lines as they confronted each other as separate communities in a zero-sum conflict. Their interests grew increasingly incompatible. The economy of the Protestant-dominated East Coast developed more rapidly than the rest of the island because of linen and ship-building around Belfast's port. Economic developments in the nineteenth century therefore reinforced the division of the island of Ireland into two identities, mutually sculpted in opposition to each other. It became increasingly difficult to contain both in the one territory. This was not an easy realization, and three Home Rule Bills in the last quarter of the nineteenth century and the beginning of the twentieth, steadfastly opposed by Ulster Protestants, separated the island politically. Social-structural strains eventually developed to the point that the colonial society planted in the sixteenth century was overturned in 1921, at least in twenty-six of its counties, with the partition of the island into two jurisdictions–a Catholic-dominated Irish Republic and a Protestant-dominated Northern Ireland.

Partition was a journey to nationhood for Northern Irish Catholics that they vigorously contested. Two conflicts persisted after partition: Ulster's territory was contested, since partition split their homeland in half, as Catholics saw it; and Catholics in the North felt like second-class citizens compared to Protestants in terms of the privileges, rights, and opportunities they enjoyed. Catholic opposition to both partition and social exclusion brought no easy peace for Protestants, as inequality was challenged militarily and politically. Partition may have kept Protestants from a united Ireland dominated by Catholics, but the old inequalities were transported with them into the new territory, at least initially, and with them the ancient conflicts. Catholics were offered citizenship in the new state but on terms that made their Catholicism and Irishness problematic, and their position in the social structure made them second-class citizens. Accordingly, they mostly withheld legitimacy from the state. Between 1922 and 1972, the conflict spilled over into incidents of violence by Irish Republicans demanding a united Ireland and anti-Catholic riots from those loyal to Britain. A sustained period of civil unrest occurred after 1968, when Catholic demands for civil rights were initially rejected and met with force from both the police and Protestant organizations. This period of violence, known colloquially as "the troubles," has polarized Protestant–Catholic relations and reinforced the zero-sum framework within which group interests are constructed by both communities in Northern Ireland. The violence since 1968 has made traditional hatreds worse, and while a peace process is under way, with a cease-fire since 1994, mistrust and suspicion bedevil it.

Peacemakers in Northern Ireland therefore confront a situation in which ancient religious differences have ensured the survival of separate communities. Through such methods as same-religion marriages, residential segregation, distinct cultural organizations, and segregated schools, the social structure of the two communities ensures the effortless perpetuation of distinct and separate social groups. They live in separate areas, they hold to separate symbols, and they contest rather than share territory. Belfast is a divided city whose geography and physical space vividly portray the conflict. Those working for peace and for reconciliation thus have two obstacles to overcome: the legacy of the past that has created social division and the impact of a social structure that reproduces separateness. A study of those peacemakers and their efforts is the focus of the rest of this chapter.

RESEARCH DESIGN

The research team undertaking this investigation consisted of three people who were very experienced in social research and had worked together on earlier research projects. Two research assistants, Ken Bishop and Gareth Higgins, worked under the direction of the principal investigator, John Brewer. Each member of the team brought not only a wealth of experience in social research but also active involvement in Christian peace work. Access to peacemakers in the research process was facilitated by these personal contacts.

We used a comprehensive research design utilizing a range of quantitative and qualitative methods, such as questionnaires, documentary analysis, in-depth interviews, and case studies. This required us to collect a variety of different data sets, offsetting the weaknesses of one method with the strengths of another. The data are more comprehensive as a result. The methods used and data sets collected include the following:

- An extensive list of church-based and secular organizations involved in peacemaking and cross-community activities and a database of their aims and objectives.
- Documentary analysis of the literature produced by peacemaking and cross-community bodies to explore their mission statements and the principles that underlie their activities.
- Interviews with selected leaders and members of these organizations to expand on the motivations for their activities, to explore the role that Christian faith has played in them, their "theology of peace," the rationale that supports their witness, the opportunities and constraints they experience, and so on. Over forty qualitative interviews were completed. Two sets of guiding questions were developed—a set particularly for Christian interviewees and another set for secular respondents. Each set of questions was

developed to investigate activities and motivation for involvement in peace-making.

- A questionnaire focusing solely on gender differences in peacemaking activity and motivation was administered to twenty-one peacemakers.

- A separate questionnaire administered to a separate sample of respondents assessed differences between peacemakers and nonpeacemakers, Catholics and Protestants, images of the divine, images of the opponent, and belief in a just world. This questionnaire was completed by fifteen Protestants involved in peacemaking, fifteen Catholics involved in peacemaking, four Protestants not involved in peacemaking and two Catholics not involved in peacemaking. (It proved particularly difficult to obtain Catholic respondents who were not involved in peacemaking.) The opportunity also was taken to interview these thirty-six respondents in more depth.

CHRISTIANS AND PEACEMAKING

If it is the case, as some people believe, that the Christian religion in no small way adds to the problem in Northern Ireland, this is but one side of the Janus face. The other is the manifold ways in which Christians engage in practical peacemaking. The conflict is not as intense as many others in the world, but the grassroots peacemaking around it is very well advanced. First World peacemaking involves people who may have greater cultural and symbolic resources to resist the conflict, while a more advanced economy and polity facilitate peacemaking. Because the conflict has a religious appearance, the churches have played a leading part in reconciling differences. Religion has been a principal arena for peacemaking. Therefore, religion is a locus of both conflict and reconciliation.

An important distinction exists between what might be called active and passive peacemaking. *Passive peacemaking* involves commitment to peace as an ideal but without practicing it. Peace is, after all, socially desirable to the point that it equals apple pie as a virtue unchallenged. Passive peacemaking not only involves ritualized expressions of its social desirability but also trenchant denunciations of violence and atrocity. *Active peacemaking* lives out the commitment to peace as a practice. It is broader than attempts at intervention to stop the violence, important as this is. Active peacemaking in Northern Ireland also involves engagement with the terms of the conflict to redefine it in nonsectarian and non–zero-sum terms, efforts to reintroduce and restore justice and equality (since peace is more than halting the violence), and attempts to solve the problems of Northern Ireland's transition to a post-violence society. The types of active peacemaking themselves comprise several different kinds of activity. In this chapter we address six: ecumenical outreach; mediation; cross-community activities; participation in formal peace groups and initiatives; attempts to wrestle with the issue of anti-sectarianism; and dealing with the problems involved in the transition to a post-violence society. People of faith are to some extent involved in all of them; in many instances they work side by side with secular activists. Some of the forms of peacemaking take place entirely at the grassroots; it will be obvious that others have functioned with intermediary help from religious and civil institutions.

The six types of grassroots peacemaking, and their subcategories, are identified in the chart on the next page.

PEACEMAKING IN PRACTICE

The purpose of this section is to present a qualitative description of the analysis undertaken of the aims and objectives, mission statements, and policies of organizations and initiatives involved in the six types of active peacemaking.

ECUMENICAL ACTIVITY

By this we mean activity in which barriers between the denominations are broken down and contact is developed between the churches and their congregations. As evident from the chart on the next page, it comprises several different types of activity.

Church-to-Church Activity

This category relates to ecumenical groups who seek to promote Christian unity and understanding through dialogue between the denominations. This dialogue is promoted within and between the differing Christian denominations through shared teaching, research, and outreach activities, and is marked by efforts toward reconciliation. Within the general category of church-to-church organizations one can subdivide this interdenominational activity into two subcategories: ecumenical communities and interchurch groups that include both clergy and laypeople. Among the most obvious ecumenical communities involved in church-to-church dialogue in Northern Ireland are the Christian Renewal Centre based in Rostrevor, and the Corrymeela Community located in Belfast and Ballycastle. Other notable ecumenical communities include the Columba Community, Columbanus Community of Reconciliation, Cornerstone Community, Currach Community, and the Lamb of God Community.

Central to the aims and objectives of these ecumenical communities are reconciliation and challenging religious ignorance, suspicion, and fear. For all of them, reconciliation is centered on the healing love of Christ and is promoted through prayer, counsel, and retreat. Prayer is an important activity for the ecumenical communities. Daily prayer meetings, weekly prayer and praise meetings, and prayer schools exemplify the importance placed on prayer. However, social awareness and responsibility are not neglected. For example, the Corrymeela Community states that one of its main aims is "to support victims of vio-

GRASSROOTS PEACEMAKING IN NORTHERN IRELAND:
A TYPOLOGY

1. Ecumenical activity (breaking down barriers and stereotypes and developing contact in a religious context)

- church-to-church (joint worship, bible study, prayer)
- clergy-to-clergy groups
- formal ecumenical organizations
- ecumenical public events
- joint declarations of doctrine, belief, and commitment

2. Mediation (conflict resolution)

- formal mediation organizations with local input
- informal involvement in local mediation
- dialogue with protagonists to the conflict

3. Cross-community activities (breaking down barriers in a secular setting)

- large-scale (integrated education, integrated vacation programs, home-building programs, etc.)
- local (neighborhood initiatives, issue-based mobilization on drugs, crime, women's issues, etc.)

4. Self-identified peace groups and initiatives (espousing peace and monitoring the conflict)

- formal peace organizations
- populist peace activity (peace train, rallies, peace marches, etc.)

5. Anti-sectarianism (challenging the conflict and redefining it)

- church and faith-based organizations
- secular organizations

6. Dealing with the problems of post-violence

- working with victims and victim support groups
- dealing with memory and narratives of atrocity
- dealing with the issue of forgiveness
- reintegration of protagonists (ex-prisoner and family support groups, job creation programs)
- citizenship education

lence and injustice, to enable the healing of personal and social wounds." The promotion of pastoral support for local families, individuals, and community groups is encouraged. Importance is placed on sharing common life experiences, struggles, and needs. The Columba Community in Derry, for example, has a visitation program for prisoners, ex-prisoners, and their families. Organizations such as the Cornerstone Community from the Springfield Road in Belfast offer senior citizens' luncheon clubs and support for women's groups, after-schools clubs, and youth clubs. Another key activity for the ecumenical communities in Northern Ireland is offering hospitality and accommodation to specific individuals and groups away from their own neighborhoods. Residential events are common on social, cultural, political, and religious topics. Most of the ecumenical communities in Northern Ireland are registered charities and depend on voluntary service, grant awards, and donations for their funding.

Interchurch groups, including both clergy and laypeople, represent another kind of ecumenism that has an impact on peacemaking. Such groups are locally organized and focus on formal community-relations work, shared prayer and fellowship, and Bible study. Their work concentrates primarily on ways in which churches can cooperate in addressing social and community needs, reconciliation issues, and community life in the local area. The difference between ecumenical communities and interchurch groups is that the latter are smaller, local grassroots initiatives between individual churches and have a much lower media profile. Some groups, such as Churches in Co-operation from Derry, seek to provide joint denominational structures or forums to develop and implement community peace initiatives. Others focus on more informal grassroots community initiatives such as joint services and seminars. Good examples would be the Belmont District Council of Churches, Community Relations and Christians, the Four Churches, and the Magherafelt Inter-Denominational Group. The main aims of these groups are to build relationships of confidence and trust, and to create an "open space" to respond to local community issues.

Some Protestant and Catholic churches have developed a structured twinning relationship with other churches in the same neighborhood or farther afield. Groups where two churches have an ongoing partnership include Clonard/Fitzroy Fellowship; St. Comgall's Roman Catholic Church, Poleglass/St. Columba's Lisburn Church; and St. Matthew's/St. Oliver Plunkett Group. One member of the Clonard/Fitzroy group said of the initiative, "We want to know about each other's denominations. We want to deal with each other to show that we are not all angry stereotypes. We want to show that we can live with our next-door neighbor, whoever they are. We want to make a difference." It is interesting to note that the majority of twinned church relationships are in urban areas. One can argue that this is because urban areas have suffered the most and that there is a greater need for churches and local communities to build trust, mutual understanding, and respect for differences. It is also the case that urban areas are the more progressive; community relations work is generally less well developed in rural areas.

Clergy-to-Clergy Groups

As well as the active organizations described above, there are a large number of clergy groups in Northern Ireland in which Catholic and Protestant clergy come together in acts of reconciliation and for practical benefit. The activities of these groups include prayer and fellowship, as well as sharing resources on pastoral skills and congregational issues. For example, Castlederg Clergy Group states that its main aim is "to promote mutual understanding, respect and tolerance; to help the community to live in peace and harmony." Clergy groups also offer an opportunity for the different denominations to meet informally in order to engage directly in discussion and dialogue about grassroots issues that affect their respective communities. The Ballynafeigh Clergy Group has attempted to mediate in the parade issue on the Ormeau Road, for example. These groups are less formal than interchurch clergy and lay groups; meetings are hosted in private homes or in church halls.

Formal Ecumenical Organizations

There are a number of formal ecumenical organizations in Northern Ireland that have a peacemaking agenda of their own while also supporting the peacemaking activities of the churches, local clergy, and lay groups, by providing resources for training, advice, information and support in community relations, and peacebuilding. Two examples are the Irish School of Ecumenics and the Irish Commission for Justice and Peace. Both were established in 1970 by the hierarchy of the Irish Catholic Church in response to Vatican II, but both are ecumenical in policy and practice. Another organization worth noting is the Evangelical Contribution on Northern Ireland (ECONI). ECONI emerged in 1987 to reflect the shared peacemaking concerns of evangelical Christian leaders who felt that the only evangelical voice on Northern Irish issues was at that time speaking of enmity rather than reconciliation. What makes this organization particularly interesting is that it comes from within the evangelical tradition and is able to utilize the symbols, terminology, and arguments of this tradition in the direction of peacemaking. Another well-known organization, established in 1973, is the Irish Inter-Church Meeting (IICM), a group comprising the Protestant Irish Council of Churches and the Catholic Church. It has departments dealing with theological issues from an interchurch perspective and social issues, as well as the interface of faith and politics. The latter department has been particularly active in challenging the nature of the conflict in the North. The IICM has an extensive peace education program. In fact, all these ecumenical organizations run peace education programs and deal with issues of reconciliation and togetherness in a Christian context. Through education programs, lectures, and the sponsoring of research, these organizations address issues such as forgiveness, sectarianism, identity, and grassroots peacebuilding. Their education programs seek to empower local peacemakers to intervene effectively. The Irish Commission for Justice and Peace states that their emphasis on educational programs is to "encourage mutual understanding and dialogue; to break down prejudice, sectarianism and divisiveness and to help create a society of peace and justice."

Ecumenical Public Events

Ecumenical work is not restricted to the organizations and efforts described above, for there are several public events that take ecumenical policies and practice into the streets. There are occasional ecumenical marches centered on Christian worship and celebration, as well as conferences and other events. The most notable example is the United Prayer Breakfast, which is both ecumenical denominationally and organized across the North and South of Ireland. Key leaders and opinion formers are invited to regular breakfasts held across the island, at which they are enjoined to pray for peace and reconciliation. The organizing team is composed of churchmen and -women from all denominations, as well as public figures with strong personal faith drawn from both sides of the border.

Joint Declarations of Doctrine, Belief, and Commitment

This form of ecumenical activity is not well developed in Northern Ireland. The sorts of joint declarations common in the United States, between, for example, Lutherans and Catholics or among evangelicals and Catholics, are steps too far for Christian peacemakers in Northern Ireland. There are two exceptions. First, the Evangelical Catholic Initiative, run by Paddy Monaghan jointly from Rostrevor in Northern Ireland and Dublin, has produced several pamphlets and books attempting to show the synergy between Catholicism and evangelicalism. *What Is an Evangelical Catholic?* is a pamphlet produced with a view to building bridges between evangelical Christians in the Protestant and Catholic traditions. Other tracts have been published introducing Catholics to reading the Bible as well as collections of the testimonies of evangelical Catholics (see Monaghan and Boyle 1998). A similar impetus lay behind the second initiative. A sixteen-page document entitled *Evangelicals and Catholics Together in Ireland* was prepared in 1998 by a group of fourteen people and endorsed by 130 clergy and leaders from different traditions from the North and South of Ireland. It puts forward an agreed basis of faith between Catholics and evangelical Protestants and calls for Christians to explore their common faith and to build friendships in order to bear joint witness in a divided society. It was launched by the evangelist Jim Packer to an audience of over three hundred clergy and laypeople. It asks all Christians in Northern Ireland to subscribe to a new confession: "We repent of attitudes, words and actions that have fostered hatred and divisions within and among our traditions. . . . We humbly ask the forgiveness of God and one another, and pray for the grace to amend our own lives and to actively seek in every way possible to help change divisive attitudes."

MEDIATION

The second category of grassroots peacemaking is mediation. Mediation involves two processes. The first is assisting individuals or communities to develop their own resources for handling conflicts; the second is direct intervention to contribute to conflict resolution and peacebuilding. Conflict resolution in either sense is particularly relevant in a situation like Northern Ireland, where there are occasional flashes of high-intensity violence which require direct intervention but where the normally low-key character of violence provides some space for local people to learn mediation skills. This sort of peacemaking tends to be of three sorts: that done by formal and professional mediation organizations; informal mediation carried out at a local level by local parties; and dialogue with the paramilitaries and protagonists. Christians by no means do all of the conflict resolution, but there is a pronounced Christian input into all three kinds.

Formal Mediation Organizations

Mediation in terms of empowering local peacemakers with mediation skills is an objective of several bodies for whom this is a major purpose. Ecumenical communities like Corrymeela, Cornerstone, or ECONI engage in this kind of work, as does the Irish School of Ecumenics. The main peacemaking activities common to these groups are mediation in specific instances of conflict, conflict counseling among protagonists, the facilitation of discussions and local consultations, and what is called "Transforming Conflict Training" given to local residents and other involved parties. For example, Columba House of Prayer and Reconciliation based in Derry was formed by Fr. Neal Carlin in 1980 as a response to the need for reconciliation and counseling, "not just about healing the world of divisions within the body of Christ, but about the integration and wholeness of individuals as well." There are, however, few formal professional organizations in Northern Ireland for whom mediation is the sole purpose. One obvious exception is Mediation Network, originally formed as the Northern Ireland Conflict and Mediation Association in 1986 to promote alternative nonviolent approaches to community conflict and disputes. As the organization's vision statement puts it: "The Mediation Network for Northern Ireland promotes the use of third party interventions in disputes, and supports creative responses to conflict in the community." Its principal objectives are the provision of training and support services to enhance the skills of mediators, but the organization offers its own mediation services in instances of conflict. In recent years the Mediation Network has been involved, for example, in mediating a number of high profile disputes, notably the controversy surrounding Orange Parades. Mediation Network also works with individual parishes and congregations of any denomination, as well as local interchurch groups and denominational committees and bodies, in an attempt to empower local Christians in conflict resolution. It has also assisted in bringing to Northern Ireland international conflict mediators, some of them Christian. The majority of the organization's staff are volunteers; some are Christian and one of the principal participants is Mennonite, although the organization is not Christian as such.

Informal Involvement in Local Mediation

Except for its assiduous work in empowering local people with the skills for conflict resolution and mediation, it is questionable whether Mediation Network

is "grassroots." However, more obviously grassroots is the range of nonspecial-
ist groups and individuals involved in mediation at an informal level. This is
characterized less by the training of local residents and parties in their own mediation skills than by ad hoc, emergency-style intervention in disputes in the local
neighborhood. Because of the sensitive nature of the mediation process and the
need to maintain confidence between parties, it is sometimes difficult to identify
those involved informally in any given dispute. At the local level there is the
involvement of community residents, workers, and politicians. Of more interest
in the context of grassroots Christian peacemaking is the role of local clergy in
situations of neighborhood mediation. Northern Ireland has had a long tradition
of clergy from most denominations being involved in mediation of specific
instances of conflict, despite the risk to themselves, their congregations, and
church premises. One Church of Ireland minister recently involved in mediation
commented that he had been threatened by one set of paramilitaries and that he
feared the burning of his church. Another Protestant minister, involved in the
same area, said that he did not fear damage to church premises from Catholics
but from Loyalist paramilitaries who objected to his contacts with Catholic
clergy. Irrespective of the risks, the leaderships of the churches have frequently
taken a proactive stance in facilitating discussion and negotiation. One example
has been the valuable work of the Church of Ireland Primate, Archbishop Robin
Eames, and Presbyterian minister Roy Magee in brokering the Loyalist paramilitary cease-fire in 1995.

Dialogue with Groups in Conflict

A significant part of conflict resolution is the development of dialogue between
Christians and the paramilitary groups responsible for violence. This does not
involve mediation in the two senses used so far but the opening up of constructive dialogue with conflict groups in the hope that it will reap benefits in the
future for other kinds of mediation, and more besides. Most churchmen and
-women have not shied away from meeting members of paramilitary organizations in the expectation of developing relationships that will bear fruit sometime
in the future; some restrict their contact with paramilitaries to those on their "own
side," but others dialogue with all conflict groups. There is a long history of such
dialogue. Some representatives from Protestant churches first began dialogue
with the IRA (Irish Republican Army) in 1974, leading to the Christmas cease-
fire of that year. Since 1990 there has been a regular channel of communication
between some Protestant ministers and Sinn Fein, the IRA's political representatives; these particular ministers have also engaged in dialogue with Loyalist paramilitaries on their "own side," sometimes in combination with Catholic priests.
It is well recognized that Redemptorist priests in Clonard Monastery in West
Belfast have been influential in brokering cease-fires and in facilitating political
agreements. These same priests also facilitated contact between the IRA and the
government in the Irish Republic when such contact could not be admitted. The
Loyalist cease-fire in 1994 owes much to the involvement of Protestant leaders.
These one-to-one contacts continue on both sides. A more systematic and

broader form of dialogue has been in operation since 1999. A group of leading ecumenical churchmen and -women, calling themselves Faith in a Brighter Future Group, holds regular meetings with political parties, paramilitary groups, and politicians in an attempt to shore up the peace process.

CROSS-COMMUNITY ACTIVITIES

One of the most obvious mechanisms for peacemaking is cross-community work, bringing Protestants and Catholic communities together in an attempt to break down barriers. It is the secular equivalent of ecumenical work. But this is not to argue that Christians, as Christians, are inactive in cross-community work. They are active in secular settings, working alongside those with other faiths or none, and in settings where a Christian ethos is missing or is incidental. There are two kinds of Christian involvement in cross-community work, that which is large-scale, often done on a country-wide basis involving specialist organizations and initiatives, and that which is local, done in neighborhoods and in informal ways.

Large-scale Initiatives

Central to cross-community peacemaking is the reconciliation of religious, political, and social differences between Catholics and Protestants. Some large-scale actors fund this kind of peacemaking, such as the European Union, the International Fund for Ireland, Northern Ireland's Community Relations Council, and the Community Relations Unit of the Office of Northern Ireland's First and Deputy First Minister. While these are neither grassroots nor Christian initiatives as such, they fund grassroots groups and initiatives, including Christian ones. For example, the European Union's Special Peace and Reconciliation Program has invested in excess of 1.5 billion pounds in support of grassroots peace and reconciliation activities. Groups like the Community Relations Council, the Northern Ireland Voluntary Trust, and the Northern Ireland Council for Voluntary Agencies have received funding in order to promote and support grassroots community and voluntary activities, such as youth, school, church, and community groups with a cross-community intent. There is an organization, the Northern Ireland Children's Holiday Scheme, devoted solely to organizing vacations to bring together Protestants and Catholics away from the sectarian environs that sustain division.

Other large-scale groups involved in supporting cross-community activities include Co-operation North, Protestant and Catholic Encounter, the YMCA, the Northern Ireland Council for Integrated Education, the Northern Ireland Mixed Marriage Association, and the Sports Council for Northern Ireland. Some of these have had a strong Christian input, most notably the Northern Ireland Mixed Marriage Association and Protestant and Catholic Encounter. The development of integrated education also began in the commitment of individual Christians who wanted to move away from divided education in the belief that Protestant and Catholic children will live together in harmony as adults if educated together while they are young. Integrated education is now well established.

The groups described above represent good examples of what sociologists call "institutionalization"; the personal faith of some committed Christians has become structured into large-scale organizations which pursue the vision on a grander scale but have lost the Christian ethos of the original visionaries. A possible exception is Habitat for Humanity, a large-scale cross-community initiative that is still avowedly Christian, concentrating on bringing ordinary Catholics and Protestants together in home-building programs in which they build homes for each other. Many other Christians assist in the manual labor alongside those who will inhabit the homes. It is also the case that the main churches and ecumenical communities and organizations have been involved in large-scale cross-community activity distinct from their ecumenical work, but as part of their ongoing program of reconciliation and peacemaking. This includes cross-community vacation trips, summer clubs, youth clubs, and identity work with local women's groups.

Local Initiatives

There is a wide range of local secular and Christian cross-community activity in Northern Ireland. The types of groups involved in local cross-community work include community development associations, community interface projects, and children and women's organizations. All seek to promote cooperation and reconciliation through education and understanding in settings in which Protestants and Catholics come together. Groups such as Ballynafeigh Community Development Association are taking "active steps to realize the community relations development potential of a mixed community." The association does this through activities designed to attract both communities, such as workshops and seminars. The Community Centre is a building shared by over twenty groups from the area, representing both traditions.

There is often little Christian input into community development groups—indeed, these bodies are often avenues of action for people committed to cross-community peacemaking activity but who do not want to work in a Christian environment. Churches, however, have often come together to address the social and community needs of neighborhoods in ways that bring Protestant and Catholic communities together. Such projects often promote practical social ministries and community volunteering placements in the context of prayer and fellowship. The Churches' Voluntary Bureau, Clogher Care, and the Downpatrick Area Inter-Church Caring Project are examples of projects that provide a range of services to local neighborhoods on a cross-community basis. Examples of the services they offer include help with the elderly in both communities as well as training and assistance for people with learning difficulties; some organize play groups, youth clubs, and community employment efforts. Forthspring Inter-Community Group states as its objective, "to encourage local people to actively seek for themselves a future free from violence and sectarianism." Another local initiative, Community Dialogue, functions as a bridge between the community development workers interested in cross-community work and churchmen and -women with the same ambition. Community Dialogue was set up in 1997, seeking a "cross-community solution to political, social, and economic problems," and has both community activists and church people as members.

The mobilization of people across the Catholic and Protestant communities in terms of their social needs rather than strictly as members of one religion or another—bringing together categories of people like the elderly, the young, mothers with toddlers, victims of crime, or people concerned about drugs, the environment, or hospital closures—not only unites communities across the sectarian divide but also reduces the salience of religion as an individual's identity marker. This is perhaps most apparent with respect to the cross-community mobilization of women. It is not too much of an exaggeration to claim that local women's groups have had the most profound effect on cross-community activities in Northern Ireland. Groups such as Women Together for Peace and Women's Information Group have actively sought to bring about a cessation of sectarian violence in Northern Ireland and to give women a "voice" in society. This parallels the development of the Women's Coalition, which is establishing itself as a political party to represent women's issues and nonsectarian concerns generally. In terms of more grassroots peacemaking, the Women's Information Group states its objectives as, "to bring women together and provide quality information which can be used to enhance their lives, that of family, project and local community."

The empowerment of women as peacemakers in their local communities is the aim of an initiative based in Armagh and run from the Queen's University outreach campus in that city. Armagh is the ecclesiastical capital of Ireland for the Church of Ireland and the Roman Catholic Church, so it is fitting that the Women and Peacebuilding Program is based there. The program involves joint training courses for women from both traditions to enhance their personal and peacemaking skills to enable them to take up a proactive role in their local communities. The program is a cross-community initiative intended to foster positive relations between women, which they then take into their neighborhoods as grassroots peacemakers. There is a Women's Resource Centre on the campus that facilitates the program as well as providing resource material for local women's groups.

SELF-IDENTIFIED PEACE GROUPS AND INITIATIVES

Two caveats have to be made at this point. First, the examples of Women Together for Peace and the Women and Peacebuilding Program in Armagh illustrate how the analytical categories of grassroots peacemaking adopted here are by no means hermetic. The kinds of activities engaged in by organizations, groups, and individuals can fall into several categories of peacemaking and can overlap. Second, in one sense it appears superfluous to have peace groups and initiatives as a separate category since *all* the types in the analytical framework are examples of peacemaking. It is worth keeping this as a special category however, because there are groups, organizations, and initiatives that constitute and identify themselves in these terms. Peace in these cases is not a by-product of other aims or activities but an espoused ideal and central intention. For this purpose, peace groups also often monitor events and incidents for their threat to peace. One can divide this category also into two subsections: the initiatives of formal peace bodies and populist peace activities.

Formal Peace Bodies and Initiatives

Peace bodies can be described as those formal organizations that seek to promote and support the activities of peacebuilding and that are constituted solely on this basis. Many others can lay claim to having supported peace and assisted in the peace process, but the focus here is on those bodies and initiatives for which it is their raison d'être. Some of the bodies and initiatives are Christian, others not; and some of the secular bodies have Christians working in them. Some Christian bodies and initiatives are local and are tied to specific churches or parishes. Good examples are Hillsborough Parish Bridgebuilders Group, which seeks to examine issues of peace, conflict, and reconciliation in a Christian setting, and Strandtown Christian Fellowship Church's Bridges Forum, which aims to realize peace in Northern Ireland by inviting speakers whose words might inform Christians with the knowledge, skill, and commitment to work for peace. Some are larger scale. For example, the Church of Ireland Diocese of Down and Dromore, which includes the greater Belfast area, has a Diocesan Reconciliation Operational Group, as does the Methodist Theological College. Indeed, in 1999 the diocese developed the "Think Again" initiative, as a systematic program of reconciliation. The Irish Inter-Church Meeting has a peace education initiative, as do the Irish School of Ecumenics and ECONI. The Presbyterian Church in Ireland has also outlined what it calls its "peace vocation." Eighty-two years after its moderator signed the Ulster Covenant, which espoused the narrow sectarian interests of the Presbyterian Church in Ireland, the general assembly passed the following recommendation as enshrining its "peace vocation."

> We affirm [ourselves] to be Christian peacemakers in our own situation. We must therefore be prepared to meet and talk together with those from other churches whose practices and beliefs differ from our own, with those from whom we are politically divided. We understand peacemaking to be an affirmation and accommodation of diversity. Our own particular history makes it imperative that we reassert the Church's proper calling to seek peace and the things that make for peace in our day.

Over the years, outside the churches, a number of small peace organizations have evolved in response to specific atrocities as well as to espouse a more general and sustained campaign for peace and reconciliation. These bodies tend to be independent groups organized by local people who want to do something positive in a conflict situation. One such group is the Peace People. This organization, founded after an incident that claimed the lives of three children, became "a movement dedicated to working non-violently for a just and peaceful society" through cross-community children's work. However, it is but a shadow of its former self and has faced difficulty in sustaining itself after the initial enthusiasm dried up and memories of the atrocity faded. This is a common feature of peace groups founded as responses to specific violent incidents. The Enniskillen Together Peace Group has its origins in the aftermath of a bomb that exploded on Remembrance Day 1987, killing a dozen people, but it no longer has a high profile. The Drumcree Faith and Justice Group first came together in response to the violence associated with Orange parades through Catholic areas; however, it is now little known. Families Against Intimidation and Terror (FAIT) was mobilized by a mother after her son's grievous treatment in a punishment beating by the IRA. For a time the group had a very high public profile in monitoring punishment beatings as a form of violence and in leading the public campaign for peace. FAIT was stymied by various allegations against its founders and its voice is now quite faint.

There are other peace groups that are not mobilized around one specific atrocity and as a result can sometimes sustain their activities more easily. The Peace and Reconciliation Group, Peace Committee, Peace Pledge Ireland Campaign, and Women Together for Peace are good examples. Others include Counteract, a trade union-sponsored organization, and the Non-Violent Action Training Project, which seeks to "explore imaginative, effective and non-violent ways of working in Northern Ireland." Community Dialogue sees as its central aim to promote the Good Friday Agreement, and has undertaken an initiative to encourage community groups to think through peace issues. It has developed a discussion packet, available to community group leaders in order to assist groups in thinking and talking through Northern Ireland's peace negotiations. The Quaker Movement and the small Northern Irish Mennonite community are also involved in peacemaking activities in Northern Ireland on a more general scale. The Ulster Quaker Service Committee aims to "contribute in a practical way to the understanding and reduction of both the causes and results of violence, suffering and social malaise." However, in lacking the initial spark on which to mobilize that often arises from an atrocity, these groups can fail to make a public impact.

Populist Peace Activities

A number of populist activities have had a positive effect on the peacebuilding process. Many of the peace groups mentioned above, such as Women Together and Community Dialogue, hold public meetings at which they attempt to highlight the plight of all who have suffered through sectarian violence and to discuss specific contentious issues like decommissioning or policing as well as the Good Friday Agreement. But populist peace activity is broader. It is mass public participation in peacemaking events, such as the "Light a Candle on Christmas Eve" peace campaign, "Friendship Seats" in parks throughout Northern Ireland, and "Stamp Out Sectarianism Roadshows" in shopping centers, festivals, sports arenas, and the like. Protestant and Catholic Encounter, established in 1968, pursues its peace objectives by means such as drama, carol services, and poetry readings, as well as anti-sectarian projects, ecumenical services, and prayer meetings.

The highest degree of media attention has focused on Women Together's peace vigils and other symbolic events to challenge sectarian violence. The People Moving On project is the best known of these. Coinciding with a difficult period in the peace negotiations, Women Together facilitated the People Moving On initiative by organizing public "peace witnessing" events to give people everywhere an opportunity to show continuing support for the peace process. This initiative was recognized widely as crucial in keeping hope alive during a difficult period.

An earlier example of a populist peace initiative that received wide media coverage was the Peace Train. This involved a series of train journeys between Belfast and Dublin in the late 1980s and early 1990s. Church and civil representatives along with members of the public traveled between the two cities in an act of mutual respect for each other's traditions and in a spirit of reconciliation. The train line was bombed on more than one occasion.

More recently, people have been asked to plant a tree in Israel in a unique gesture of peace and reconciliation. It is called the "Ireland Peace and Reconciliation Forest" and is near Jerusalem. All of the four major churches in Ireland and the government in the Irish Republic support it, and its purpose is to reconcile both Christians and Jews as well as Christians in the North and South of Ireland.

ANTI-SECTARIANISM

A significant part of grassroots peacemaking is to challenge the nature of the conflict by seeking both to name it for what it is, and to redefine its terms. The identification of the problem as one of sectarianism, that is, the use of denominational boundaries in a social project to enforce social exclusion by one religious group against others (see Brewer 1992; 1998), is a contribution to peacemaking because it disabuses the dominant group of any moral superiority in the conflict. The process goes one stage further when the naming of the beast leads to a redefinition of the problem in ways that encourage Protestants and Catholics to transcend sectarian mind-sets and identities. This is what we mean by anti-sectarianism as a form of grassroots peacemaking. It comes in three ways: through church- and faith-based organizations, through secular organizations that have a Christian input, and through the contributions made by individual Christians in business, academia, and community work.

Church and Faith-Based Organizations and Initiatives

Protestant churches were coming to a realization of their culpability since Plantation just when "the troubles" broke out (Brewer 1998, 116), causing the violence to polarize the communities and set back the process of self-reflection. The persistence of that violence, however, impressed itself upon some progressive Protestant churchmen and -women to the point where one could argue today that all the different Christian organizations reviewed here are involved in some way in anti-sectarian activity, just as they are in peace.

What we focus on here, however, is the organizations and initiatives working specifically against sectarianism. From individual churches and other ecumenical organizations such as ECONI and the Irish Inter-Church Meeting, a number of specialized Christian anti-sectarian initiatives have developed. For example, the Corrymeela Community has in the past addressed the issue of sectarianism and produced a booklet (see Williams and Falconer 1993). Perhaps the most thorough confrontation with the issue has been the work done by the Faith and Politics Group of the Irish Inter-Church Meeting. This group represents some of the leading personalities within Irish ecumenism, most being leaders or key figures within peacemaking and reconciliation organizations in the North. The group's thinking is perhaps in advance of most Christians in Northern Ireland but is a good measure of the ecumenical and peace vision of the Irish Inter-Church Meeting. It has addressed through position papers all the contentious issues around sectarianism, including the roots of sectarianism in Ireland (see Liechty 1993), breaking down enmity, how to handle history, especially contested and divided history, the handling of remembrance and forgiveness, and issues like paramilitary funerals and self-righteous boasting. Its most recent publication is *Transitions* (Faith and Politics Group 2001), addressing the issue of identity in a nonsectarian and peaceful Northern Ireland. The Irish School of Ecumenics has also just completed a six-year project called "moving beyond sectarianism," which has resulted in a book (see Liechty and Clegg 2001) as well as a resource packet and materials for use in group work with adults and young people. This is what is significant about all this research; it feeds directly into the practical peacemaking work of organizations, churches, community groups, and other grassroots people who use the resource material and training courses developed from the research. It is through these sorts of training resources and materials that this work on sectarianism moves to the next stage, that in which Protestants and Catholics are empowered and enabled to seek alternatives to the narrow mind-sets and identities of the past. Workshops on identity or anti-sectarianism, for example, teach the skills to help ordinary people assist others in the local community to move on.

Secular Organizations and Initiatives

A large number of secular organizations are also involved in anti-sectarian work. These groups, in which persons of faith are frequently involved, can be divided into such subcategories as those working in local-government, integrated-education, anti-racist, mixed-marriage, and trade-union settings. All have developed anti-sectarian policies and practices over the last thirty years. The development of anti-sectarian social work practices in Northern Ireland (see Brewer 1991) enshrines this as a practice in the larger area of social and community care.

Perhaps anti-sectarian initiatives among children are most worth highlighting. Organizations like All Children Together, for example, challenge sectarianism in segregated education, as does Playboard in the area of voluntary work with children. Playboard took a pioneering early initiative in developing guidelines for anti-sectarian work with children (see Playboard Northern Ireland 1990). The guidelines amount to umpteen pages of useful advice, ideas, and exercises intended to enable childcare workers to deal with instances of sectarian behavior when they arise; promote good community relations through play; instill in children acceptance, understanding, and respect for others; and overcome barriers between children.

There are also many courageous individuals in the universities and churches, in businesses and local neighborhoods who have stood in solitary witness against sectarianism and pushed the idea of nonsectarianism in their particular field.

DEALING WITH THE PROBLEMS OF POST-VIOLENCE[4]

Making the transition from a society racked by violence to one of post-violence is never easy, as the experience in South Africa and some Latin American countries shows. The legacy of bitterness, hurt, and anger acts as a dead weight; the memories of atrocities, with the grief and pain they arouse, just add to its pull. Post-violence societies therefore face acute problems associated with history, memory, and remembrance—the latter being a topic addressed by the Faith and Politics Group (1991; 1996)—especially where all have experience of being victims and perpetrators and have divided memories (on this general issue see Appleby 2000). Ways have to be found in which people's personal plights are recognized, validated, and commemorated while allowing the society as a whole to move forward. Past protagonists need to be wedded to the peace of the future, ex-prisoners need to be socially reintegrated, the guns silenced, and the wounds healed. Dealing with the problems of post-violence is therefore an important peacemaking category.

One dimension of this area of peacemaking is support for victims, though it is not always recognized as a peacemaking activity by the victims themselves. A number of victim groups were originally set up as a response to violent events to help the victims of conflict. After the La Mon House Hotel bombing in 1978, Lifeline was founded to, in its words, "bring together the innocent victims of the troubles"; similarly, the Cross Group was formed after Maura Kiely's son Gerard was murdered. The aims of Women Against Violence Empower (WAVE) are, in its words, "to offer care and support to anyone bereaved or traumatized through the violence, irrespective of religious, cultural or political belief." One interesting group is An Crann/The Tree, which seeks to gather the stories of how individuals have experienced "the troubles" in the hope that the telling of their story will be cathartic and healing for them and the community generally. One of the dangers, however, when divided memories widen the wounds, is that victim support groups can be used to mobilize against peace: the search for justice by victims in these circumstances can, paradoxically, hinder the reconciliation process.

---

[4] Initiatives aimed at dealing with the problems of post-violence are here described as a whole, rather than separated according to the typology in the chart on p. 75.

Another important part of dealing with the transition to post-violence is work with former prisoners and their families. The Northern Ireland Association for the Care and Resettlement of Offenders (NIACRO) is a secular organization involved in supporting former prisoners and their families, as well as being involved in youth justice, crime prevention, and community-level mediation. The Local Initiatives for Needy Communities (LINC) Resource Centre and the Restorative Justice Ministries are examples of two Christian-based organizations formed by ex-combatants to address the issues of former prisoners. In an interview, the director of LINC said that the personal experiences he had as an ex-prisoner were important in his work, but so was his faith: "I became a peacebuilder because I am a Christian." It is worth noting the strong role of the churches in working with former prisoners, assisting their social reintegration. This work is in accordance with the Christian ethic, but it also reflects the high number of religious conversions in Northern Ireland's prisons, producing a generation of former prisoners who have emerged both committed to Christ and to the Christian vocation of peacemaking. Pax Works is one example. Many ex-prisoners in Northern Ireland have also left with educational qualifications earned inside prison, reducing the impact of economic marginalization once they are released, and many work in local community development groups and associations that are themselves active in grassroots peacemaking.

PEACEMAKING ACTIVITIES AND MOTIVATION:
A FOCUS ON RELATIONSHIP

Our research further investigated the actions and motivations of individual peacemakers—whether they worked in groups or on their own. The six types of peacemaking described in the last section constitute the broad framework within which respondents undertook the following kinds of activities. As in the other sites described in this volume, the most frequently cited peacemaking activities in Northern Ireland fell into these categories:

- Activities focused on building relationships, some examples being visits to a church of a different community, dialogue with members of groups who have engaged in violence, and working with former prisoners.
- Service—for instance teaching, peace education, and the sharing of resources, skills, and materials.
- Confrontation of the violence through anti-sectarian activity or conflict resolution.

Prayer was the least commonly reported peacemaking activity—it is possible of course, that respondents prayed for peace, but simply did not report it as a peacemaking activity.

The data showed that Northern Irish respondents are very high on relationship building as a form of peacemaking. This finding perhaps reflects the low-level intensity of the violence, in that it has not been on a scale that has destroyed the search for meaningful relations with the other. Women respondents were more likely than men to participate in relationship building activities, an effect perhaps due to socially constructed gender roles, although it could also be that women are more likely than men to see these activities as a kind of peacemaking.

Typical statements representing the four general categories emerging in this study were as follows:

- Relational: "I've lived in Catholic areas." "It hurts me to watch others suffer."

- Religious: "Obedience to a discipleship command: blessed are the peacemakers." "We should be prepared to compromise, because the incarnation of Jesus was a tremendous act of compromise on God's part." "God wants us to live in peace."

- Practical: "I want a better society for my family." "We have to live together."

- Ideological: "We are all created equal." "I know what it is like to be part of a minority." "Killing violates human rights."

Our survey showed that grassroots activities were more likely to be relationally motivated and oriented toward relationship building than peacemaking activities that take place at higher levels. Christian peacemakers did not place primacy on religious motives, and relational motivations were not restricted to Christian peacemakers.

Older peacemakers tended to be higher in religious motivations for peacemaking than younger peacemakers, and lower in practical motivations. It may be that older respondents are more religious in general, and/or that they have less to gain personally than younger respondents from the benefits of a future peace.

Women were more likely than men to cite relational motives for peacemaking. They also reported (at higher levels than men did) having engaged in service-oriented peacemaking activities (see Table 1). We observed no further gender differences in the activities people most frequently undertook, with the exception that women were slightly more likely to participate in anti-sectarian activities and men in issues of post-violence. The latter may reflect men's greater participation in ex-prisoner issues.

IMAGES OF THE DIVINE AND OF THE OPPOSING GROUP

Only ideological motivations showed any significant relationships with peacemakers' images of God. Peacemakers high in such motivations tended to hold immanent and, to a lesser extent, agentic images of the divine. The explanation for these relationships may be primarily cognitive. Since ideological motivations are more abstract than practical, relational, or explicitly religious motivations, comprehending them might require a higher level of cognitive processing. Peacemakers with highly ideological motivations may have had the opportunity to reflect more on the range of divine attributes and may therefore be more likely than peacemakers with more concrete types of motivations to conceive of God in terms of a broad range of images.

Peacemakers—both Protestant and Catholic—who were high in agentic images of the divine also tended to hold positive images of members of the opposing group. Perhaps persons holding agentic images of God believe that God is as much at work in the lives of members of the opposing group as in their own communities—so they are enabled to see a common bond of humanity between all people, regardless of their political perspective.

Surprisingly, peacemakers who tended to be motivated by the wish to develop good relationships with the members of the opposing group likewise held more negative images of that group. This counterintuitive finding suggests that peacemakers may be convinced of the need for better relationships between the opposing communities while still having negative perceptions of members of the other community.

With respect to views of each other, Protestants in the sample tended to hold more negative images of Catholics than Catholics did of Protestants (see Table 2). It is significant that Protestant peacemakers, perhaps the most liberal section of that community, still conform to the general pattern that members of dominant groups have a more negative view of subordinate group members than the other way around. This again may be based on their Calvinism, with its strong loyalty to the Old Testament ideas of a God who distinguishes severely between the elect and the damned, the sinful and the virtuous. This same theological backdrop might explain a further difference between Protestant and Catholic respondents, in that the former are more likely to conceive of the divine in terms of power-over images. Protestants in Northern Ireland have different experiences of power than Catholics, which might explain this, but it also mirrors theological differences; for Ulster Protestants are noted for being Old Testament Christians, and the Old Testament is replete with such images.[5]

Finally, Protestants are more likely than Catholics to see the world as just (see Table 2). They may, for example, see their society's current patterns of resource distribution as morally unproblematic. This reflects both Protestants' Calvinist work ethic (that people get what they deserve) and the realization that they have benefited more than Catholics from the way the world is currently structured.

CONCLUSION

Northern Ireland's conflict has ensured that Catholics and Protestants have a divided history, a social structure that separates them, and contrasting experiences as victims. However, the relatively low intensity of the violence has

---

[5] See Akenson 1992; Brewer 1998; and MacIver 1987 for examples of Old Testament interpretation among Ulster Protestants and the ways this has affected their self-understanding.

affected peacemaking in a positive way. Civil society has survived the conflict and functions to enhance grassroots peacemaking efforts, permitting an impressive peacemaking industry to develop.

Peacemaking is a many-faceted set of skills. It is carried out in various ways and consists of many activities. Both secular and Christian groups have developed clear aims and objectives for peace and have been successful in developing local initiatives and activities. Some people's capacity for peacemaking is enriched by their faith, some by their past association with violence. The latter is not the only route into grassroots peace work, but some have had experiences as victims that have propelled them into peacemaking. Many others have had experiences as perpetrators that have made them peacemakers too. Former political prisoners, for example, are often found in community development and peace groups. Even outsiders who parachute in as peacemakers know enough to work through local grassroots activists who have connections. The development of grassroots peacemaking is such that Northern Ireland probably has among the most advanced cross-community programs in global conflict situations. Some have been going since the start of "the troubles"; others are more recent. New grassroots initiatives have essentially seized an opportunity created by the ceasefires and the broader constitutional negotiations in the hope of bolstering peace, often utilizing money from the enormous investment in peace initiatives by rich funders. Others have sustained themselves for the last quarter of a century or more.

The sporadic and low-intensity nature of the Northern Irish conflict has permitted civil society to survive. In some conflicts around the world, massacres and widespread violence have eliminated the intermediary level of nongovernmental organizations, community groups, churches, and faith-based organizations. But if there is an indelible mark to grassroots peacemaking in Northern Ireland, it is that the strong personal commitment and motivation of individual peacemakers are tied to the resources and goals of organizations that occupy civil society. Peacemaking at the grassroots is often invisible and carried out by those who have little power and few resources. This is why grassroots peacemaking is often unheard and unseen and usually requires assistance from some component of civil society. Local empowerment of the grassroots by civil society is a strong feature of Northern Ireland's case. Grassroots linkages with civil society in Northern Ireland ensure that strongly motivated individuals in grassroot settings work in conjunction with the resources, skills, and organizational facilitation provided by a myriad of institutions in civil society.

It should also be acknowledged that peacemaking is not a preserve of the churches in Northern Ireland. Christians often have an added dimension to peacemaking arising from their faith commitment, but our research shows that this is not as motivationally powerful as might be expected. Their motives appear to be human as much as Christ-like, and non-Christians are just as concerned with the benefits of peace for all relationships. While Christian peacemakers have religious beliefs that may affect their work, they share with non-Christians a focus on the practical and relational aspects of peace. Non-Christians have no "theology of peace," but they share with Christian peacemakers an ideology that seeks a better future for all, and a practical commitment to see an end to violence.

Precisely because grassroots peacemaking is so developed, it might reasonably be asked why peace appears so far from being achieved in Northern Ireland. It is so near yet still so far, in that a great deal has been achieved in the last thirty years, but the suspicion and mistrust that bedevil the peace process indicate the distance still to travel. Grassroots peacemaking in Northern Ireland faces several constraints. First, there is personal and family safety. Peacemakers at the grassroots often have to put themselves and their families in hard places; if not putting off some people, this can at least predispose them quite naturally to "safer" forms of peacemaking, such as ecumenical work. More dangerous peacemaking, like mediation and conflict resolution, cries out for greater involvement, but this is just the sort of grassroots work that leads people to be accused of "selling out" their community, and it makes them vulnerable to harassment and attack from paramilitary organizations on their "own side." This particularly affects Protestant ministers who might intervene in situations of conflict. Given denominational divisions within Protestantism and the lack of a parish structure, they are generally more isolated and vulnerable than Catholic priests to harassment from paramilitaries.

A second constraint on grassroots peacemaking is the shortage of funds, resources, and skilled assistance. The churches in particular are under severe pressure financially, and peace work in church settings depends on the will and enthusiasm of the congregation. Mediation Network, for example, the primary specialist body involved in conflict resolution is, to quote an interviewee, always in "urgent need for more skilled people." It has been unable to offer mediation in some settings because of staff shortages. Peacemaking is thus limited by lack of funding, trained staff, and resources even in the First World setting of Northern Ireland. Moreover, some peace money has not been spent wisely or productively.

A third problem is that the gap between grassroots peacemaking and that done around the table by the leading politicians is like a gaping chasm. There is virtually no integration of the activities at the grassroots with high-level negotiations, and the spirit and commitment at the bottom does not animate the top. This situation brings added problems. Top-level politicians offer no vision of peace. With a history that divides Catholics and Protestants and with victim experiences that make remembrance equally divisive, Northern Ireland at least needs an agreed future in the absence of an agreed past. Politicians supply the negotiating table but they can lead us to the brink, for with no vision for or stated commitment to peace, the momentum at the top can be difficult to sustain when the negotiations become fraught. This demonstrates the extent of the gap between the peacemakers at the bottom—highly motivated visionaries to a person—and those at the top who negotiate everyone's future. Grassroots people deserve a place at the table: without them we have peacemakers at the top who face peace looking backwards to the past.

A related problem is the short-term expectations of top-level peacemakers, who often do not realize that peacemaking is a "long haul." Failure of the peace process to meet these short-term expectations causes disillusion with peace as an ideal, or exasperation at the process. This is nowhere better demonstrated than by the issue of arms. Arms have been in the Irish conflict for four centuries, but the demand for immediate solutions—full and complete decommissioning all at once and right now—belies the patience required for the long haul. Thus, while the IRA has decommissioned some arms, this is not enough for many Unionist politicians.

This matter of expectations leads to another constraint on peacemaking. As a general principle, peacemaking around the world is enhanced by the experiences of "insider partials" who have a "past." That is, they have biographical experiences as former militants that can be used to develop authority and legitimacy among protagonists in turning them toward nonviolence. Grassroots peacemaking tends to involve a lot of these sorts of people (as well as others with experiences of conflict that urge them to peace, such as victims), but it tends to be the case in Northern Ireland that each side refuses to accept the other's "insider partials" while endorsing their own. Witness the failure of the Orange Order to meet with leaders of residents' groups or Sinn Fein politicians, despite the benefits for peace that this would bring. It is also fair to say that Catholics show more tolerance of the peacemaking vocation of former activists than do Protestants, perhaps because of different theological positions on the notion of sin and forgiveness. Protestants tend to treat former Loyalists who are "born again" in prison differently from Republicans who work for peace, because being "born again" is said to involve a repentance that Republican "insider partials" purposely avoid, irrespective of their commitment to peace.

All of this hints at what is perhaps the most severe constraint on peacemaking in Northern Ireland. Leaving aside those people who want to keep the conflict aflame, too many in Northern Ireland restrict their peacemaking to what is here called the passive rather than the active kind. Very few people in the North of Ireland will disavow peace; it is too socially desirable. But not enough people want to grasp something new or are prepared to live out their aspiration as a daily goal. There are several reasons for this that all amount to the same thing: Peace asks too much of them. It asks them to address their image of themselves, in which they might find bigotry and culpability; it asks them to be more open to the other by embracing the other in trust; it asks them to redefine their identity and group interests away from zero-sum notions and "all or nothing demands"; and peace requires them to share—space, territory, privilege, and power. This is too much for too many people, so they are afraid of peace, at least at the moment. At this juncture, many ordinary people approach the future looking backwards to the past, where they find comfort and security in the traditional hatreds, stereotypes, and relationships. Peace is uncertain and frightening. But this is no counsel of despair. The importance of hope in sustaining peacemakers—both those with religious affiliations and those without—through the travails of peacemaking can scarcely be overestimated. Indeed, when asked, many peacemakers declared that their work was successful, sometimes in the short term but always in the expectation of bearing fruit in the long term. There can be no better point on which to end this chapter than with recognition of such hope.

STATISTICAL TABLES
ASSOCIATED WITH CHAPTER 3 DATA

See pages 90-91 for an interpretation of these tables. See chapter 1 for an explanation of variables.

TABLE 1. CORRELATIONAL COMPARISONS OF GENDER AND PEACEMAKING
IN NORTHERN IRELAND

	Relational Motivations	Service
Gender*	.36	.30

* Positive correlations indicate that women reported this type of motivation or activity more frequently than did men. Only significant r's ($p < .05$) are reported here.

TABLE 2. CORRELATIONAL COMPARISONS OF DENOMINATIONAL DIFFERENCES
IN NORTHERN IRELAND

	Images of the Enemy*	BJW
Denominational Affiliation**	-.39	.22

* The measure of enemy images was constructed such that higher scores would indicate more positive images.
** Positive correlations indicate that Protestants scored higher than did Catholics on this dimension. Only significant r's ($p < .05$) are reported here.

4

The Philippines

Bringing Muslims and Christians Together in Peace

KARL M. GASPAR, C.SS.R.

Ver Albarico and Toto Anig met fortuitously during a time of unrest. The year was 1975, when the war of attrition between the military forces of the Marcos dictatorship and the rebels of the Moro National Liberation Front (MNLF) was raging in the southern Philippines.

At that time, both Albarico and Anig were at the threshold of manhood. Albarico, a son of Bisaya/Christian settlers, was chairperson of the government's youth program called the Kabataang Barangay (Youth of the Village). Anig, a Maguindanaon-Muslim, was an MNLF fighter.

On the day they met, Anig was on the run. Evading the military, Anig found himself in the farm of Albarico's family. When he saw Albarico, Anig sought a favor. "Please don't squeal on me," Anig begged. Without wasting time, Albarico brought Anig inside their house and hid him in the ceiling. The military arrived and asked Albarico if he had seen a young man fleeing in that direction. They even described him. But Albarico did not reveal anything. The soldiers stayed around and asked for food. After eating, they left. Only after the soldiers had left did Albarico ask Anig to come down from the ceiling. The following day, he brought him to a place where he could not be found by the military.

The incident was unforgettable for both of them, especially Anig, who

I acknowledge the contributions of Elpidio Lapad, Jr., and Ailynne J. Maravillas, who served as research assistants in this study. Mr. Lapad helped conduct interviews in Dinas, Bual, Campo Muslim, and Miryamville. Ms. Maravillas did the same in Maladeg, Malabang, Balabagan, Dinas, and Zamboanga City.

has always been profoundly grateful to Albarico. "He saved my life," he often says. Today, people around them say they are like brothers. Today, both are peacemakers actively involved in the peacebuilding efforts of the Dinas Interfaith Movement (DIM) in their municipality, which is located in Zamboanga del Sur on the southern Philippine island of Mindanao. The movement is comprised of members from three ethnic communities resid- ing in the town of Dinas, namely, Bisaya/Christians, Maguindanaon-Mus- lims, and Subanen.

The original inhabitants of Dinas were the Subanen. The Maguindanaons are one of the Moro communities in Mindanao. The name "Moro" arose during the Spanish era. Having encountered the Maurus in their past history, the Spaniards named the Muslims they encountered in sixteenth-century Philippines "Maurus," which later evolved into the name "Moro." The Maguindanaons were originally from the central part of the island. It was in the late eighteenth century that they established a settlement in Dinas in what was the homeland of the Subanen. Most of the Bisaya—Christian settlers whose ancestors came from the Visayas, islands in the central Philippines—arrived in Dinas in the years following the Second World War.

The Dinas Interfaith Movement was organized by Subanen, Muslim, and Bisaya leaders at the time when the Government of the Republic of the Philip- pines (GRP) and the MNLF were holding the peace talks that culminated in the 1996 Peace Agreement. Eventually, the movement was institutionalized into an organization that they called Subanen-Muslim-Bisaya or SUMBIS; today, it is the only local organization that engages in the resolution of conflicts between and among the different ethnic communities of Dinas.

A generation ago, the situation in Dinas was dark, desperate, and dangerous. Armed hostilities were taking place within its territory as well as in adjacent areas. Indeed, much of Mindanao was affected by the conflict in the early 1970s. The period between 1970 and 1972 was marked by violent encounters between Moro militia groups (known as the Blackshirt in Cotabato and Barracuda in Lanao) and the Bisaya fanatical paramilitary group (called the Ilaga).

The chain of violent events started in Cotabato with the eruption of armed encounters between the Blackshirt and Ilaga. Later the conflict spread to almost all parts of Mindanao where Muslim and Christian populations were significant and where there was intense rivalry between Muslim and Christian politicians. The fighting found its way to Zamboanga del Sur in 1972. During this time, hun- dreds of evacuees from Lanao del Norte had sought refuge in some of the province's towns, only to be pursued by the fighting.

Some of the recollections of old-time residents in Dinas bring back memories of the turmoil that the people faced at that time. Cesar Fernandez, a Bisaya Chris- tian, recalls how the neighboring town of Dimataling was torched to the ground by the Barracuda in retaliation for the attacks of the Ilaga. His father and younger brother were killed during this incident, along with the town mayor. Says Fernandez, "I cannot even remember the exact date that they were killed; at that time, there was very little time to mourn their death." The troubles in Dimataling quickly spread to Dinas.

Ustadz Ismael Ambol, a Muslim, remembers one of the most violent events that took place in 1972 when members of the Ilaga raided a Sultan-led settlement in Tarakan, a coastal fishing village. He recalls that a number of people were killed and several houses were burned. Ambol believes that the raid was retaliation for the hostilities of the Sultan's family against the Bisaya. "Prior to the attack, the family had lorded over the area, and the local supporters of the Ilaga must have seen the attack as an opportunity to take revenge on the Muslims." Terrified Muslims fled their homes in motorized boats and sought refuge in a nearby Moro village.

Timoay Felipe Belo, a Subanen, recalls that the village in Sumpotan was "transformed into a ghost village when the war between the Barracuda and the Ilaga broke out." Because of this, the Subanen were forced to retreat to the forested mountain, where they barely survived in makeshift dwellings.

The armed conflict in the 1970s erected a wall between the Christian settlers and the Muslims that has since been reinforced by prejudice. For the Moro people, it validated their age-old perception that Christians were deceitful, and marked the ominous transformation of cultural and religious tolerance into distrust and animosity. The conflict also caused a rift between Moro and Subanen communities, which after centuries of intermarriage, shared to some extent a common ancestry.

When the dictator Ferdinand Marcos declared martial law on September 21, 1972, the conflict intensified. Marcos used the war in Mindanao as one of the major reasons for imposing martial rule on the Filipino people.

The Ilaga–Barracuda skirmishes were soon followed by a protracted war between the MNLF and the government's military forces. This war of attrition further fueled the distrust that had come to characterize Muslim–Christian relations in Dinas. Many Muslims suspected that there were Christian settlers who worked as agents of the military; in turn, Christians believed that the MNLF enjoyed tremendous support from the Muslims. For the people living in Dinas and the nearby areas, martial rule prolonged the violence, which then resulted in displacement of communities and loss of lives.

THE CONFLICT IN MINDANAO:
A SOCIO-HISTORICAL SYNOPSIS

The conflict that arose in the 1970s can only be understood in terms of the historical context of Mindanao.[1] Its history in the precolonial era is closely inter-

---

[1] For further historical background on Muslim Mindanao, see Che Man 1990; Constantino 1975; Majul 1973; Mercado 1999; Rodil 1994; Scott 1985; Tan 1993; 1997; Vitug and Gloria 2000; and Warren 1985.

twined with trade and the introduction of Islam. The trade route that evolved in the ninth century linked Arabia overland across to Central Asia. From there it expanded toward India, China, and Southeast Asia. Eventually, this trade route established connections to coastal settlements in what is now the Philippines.

The trade route in Asia was the passageway for the coming of Islam to the archipelago, where it is believed to have been introduced in the thirteenth century. Those who brought Islam to Mindanao and Sulu came directly from the Malay archipelago. The Islamization process was intertwined with trading activities. As merchant-missionaries established trade stations along the route, they married into the local population, thereby facilitating and hastening the Islamization process.

Islam dramatically changed the political, economic, social, cultural, and religious fiber of the indigenous communities, largely as a result of the establishment of the sultanates, which eventually made the Muslim communities into the most developed areas in the archipelago. The sultanate as a concrete political system took two centuries to come into being after Islam was introduced. The first arose in Sulu in 1450 and another in Maguindanao in 1511. Their coverage was quite extensive. While providing the framework for a political structure, the sultanates had profound effects on other aspects of Muslim society. They imbued Muslims with an identity that would make them distinct from the other peoples of the archipelago. They encouraged resistance to future colonizers, with Islam serving as the anchor of their defiance.

The sultanates' growth and expansion were arrested by the coming of the Spaniards to the Philippines. Spain claimed noble intentions in colonizing the islands. However, the Spanish expedition to the Philippines was, for all intents and purposes, a search for the Spice Islands. On March 16, 1521, the first conquistadores reached what are now the central islands of the Philippines. But it was not until the expedition in 1565 that Spain began to succeed in establishing control.

Though Spain was never able to establish full political control, it imposed crippling trade blockades and instigated continuous war skirmishes against the sultanates. Other factors that eroded the sultanates' power were the coercive measures of the colonial government, with its policy of centralization, and the infighting among the Moro ruling elite. Their losses inevitably brought about a strategic decline of the sultanates, and they were never able to bring back their lost glory.

However, the Moro resistance persisted through the years of retaliatory campaigns into enemy territory. Even as the resistance continued in the South, there were also revolts that took place in the North. Hundreds of revolts all over the islands erupted throughout the Spanish colonial era, but it was not until the 1890s that a viable revolutionary movement, known as the *Katipunan*, arose to become a real threat to the colonial power. This movement declared war on Spain in 1896.

A faction of this revolutionary movement sought American support to defeat Spanish forces. Consequently, the United States evolved a colonization policy vis-à-vis the Philippines. This meant pushing Spain out of the Philippines in order to make them a U.S. colony. The Battle of Manila Bay on May 1, 1898, ushered in the era of the American colonization. The signing of the Treaty of Paris on December 10, 1898, between Spain and the United States, paved the way for the latter to secure "legal" ownership of the Philippines.

The American colonial government's drive to subjugate the Moro people immediately led to hostilities. The first American general of the Moro Province, Leonard Wood, inaugurated the tragic Moro–American War in the early 1900s. Wood's war claimed three thousand Muslim lives. The most infamous was the battle at Bud Dajo in Sulu, where a thousand men, women, and children who resisted the attack were killed by eight hundred American soldiers armed with the most modern weapons of the time.

When the Philippines became independent on July 4, 1946, the Moro people's marginalization deepened. The impoverished reality of the Moro in the south was not a very high priority in the new Republic. It introduced a policy that would hasten their integration into mainstream Philippine society, but in practice this policy did very little to convince the Moro people that the State truly cared about their well-being.

The policy of the Manila government was to encourage landless peasants to settle in Mindanao, and laws were passed for this purpose. A dramatic shift thus took place in the demographic profile of Mindanao. In the 1918 census of Mindanao, 50 percent of the population were Moro (358,968) and 28 percent were indigenous people or Lumad (205,555). Only 22 percent (159,132) were Christian settlers. In 1960 (the statistics included Palawan, the Philippines' westernmost islands), the Christian population increased to 69 percent of the total, while the Moro went down to 23.56 percent and the Lumad to 8.22 percent. Moro and Lumad groups resented the encroachment of the Christian settlers, and the resentment sometimes exploded into violence. In 1947, 1951, and 1961, there were armed clashes between Moro/Lumad bands and government forces. Each time, the rebellions were crushed.

When Marcos came into prominence in the national political scene in the late 1960s, the strained relationship between Muslim and Christian settler communities was a powder keg. It needed only a spark to burst into a conflagration. That spark was Marcos's ill-advised covert operation to invade and reclaim Sabah, previously part of the sultanate of Sulu but which was later annexed to Malaysia. When the Moro young men recruited to this clandestine operation realized what it was all about, they refused to be part of it. For their refusal, they were massacred by their military trainers. The massacre was exposed by media, triggering angry responses from the government of Malaysia and some Moro leaders. Convinced that the government had a policy to exterminate the Moro, Cotabato governor Datu Udtog Matalam set up the Muslim Independence Movement (MIM), which called for the setting up of a state comprising the whole of Mindanao-Sulu. The MIM's call for self-determination eventually led to the setting up of the MNLF.

A new generation of Moro leaders developed after some underwent military training in Malaysia and others studied in Cairo, Egypt. A month after Marcos declared martial law in 1972, a battle erupted in Marawi City between Moro rebels and government troops that left seventy-five people dead. Another month later, the MNLF began their campaign to seize Jolo, leading to a full-scale war between the MNLF and the government military forces. The latter shelled and burned the town; hundreds of people were killed and thousands were rendered homeless.

Meanwhile, the fighting in Mindanao spread. The MNLF were able to seize control over some of the areas, which only provoked the Armed Forces of the Philippines (AFP), engaging them in what seemed like an endless series of battles. One factor that accounted for the persistence of the MNLF organized armed resistance was the support of the Organization of the Islamic Conference (OIC), especially Libya, who brought the Moro problem into the OIC agenda. At the fifth Islamic Conference of Foreign Ministers (ICFM) in early 1972, the OIC officially mentioned MNLF in its resolution by calling on the Philippine government to negotiate with the MNLF for peace in Mindanao.

In 1975, Marcos was forced to respond to the OIC's call for negotiation. The peace talks led to the signing of the Tripoli Agreement between the Philippine government and the MNLF which brought peace to Mindanao. At the heart of this agreement was the granting of autonomy to thirteen of the twenty-three provinces in the south, but within the context of the Philippine Republic's national sovereignty and territorial integrity. But Marcos implemented his own version of the agreement. He reduced the coverage of the autonomous area, weakened the authority of the Legislative Assembly, refused to set up its Security Force, and did not provide the autonomous government with the power of taxation.

Accusing Marcos of betraying the Tripoli Agreement, the MNLF resumed its armed struggle. Fighting once more took place in various parts of southern Mindanao. Unfortunately for the MNLF, Marcos's moves fragmented its ranks. By the late 1970s, serious internal problems within the MNLF had developed. When Marcos sensed low morale among the ranks of the MNLF, he was shrewd enough to employ a divide-and-rule tactic. His cooptation moves were quite effective, as he offered amnesties, political positions in the autonomous governments, livelihood assistance, and access to various business establishments such as lumber concessions and barter market licenses. Within a short time, the once united MNLF splintered into three factions: the MNLF, MNLF-Reformists, and the MILF (Moro Islamic Liberation Front). Still, the armed hostilities between the government and the militant groups persisted.

Then came the collapse of the Marcos dictatorship and Cory Aquino's accession to the presidency following the first People Power eruption in 1986. As soon as she took over, she set up a commission to draft a new constitution. Her government strongly pushed for new provisions favoring autonomy for Muslim Mindanao. Both the MNLF and MILF expressed their desire to negotiate for peace and she responded favorably.

The 1987 Constitution, which was later ratified by a large majority of Filipinos (including the Muslims), provided for the establishment of an autonomous regional government for Muslim Mindanao. The terms by which the new Congress proposed to establish the Autonomous Region of Muslim Mindanao

(ARMM), however, were not acceptable to the MNLF and MILF, who called for a boycott of the plebiscite that would legally validate it. They refused to take part in the ARMM and demanded that the Aquino government implement the Tripoli Agreement. But the Aquino government pushed through with the regional elections in the ARMM and the elected officials assumed their offices.

The establishment of the ARMM did not lead to radical changes in the lives of the ordinary Moro people, and the roots of their frustration with a central government remained unaddressed. Despite the sincere attempts of the Aquino government, there was still no peace in Mindanao. Thus it happened that in 1991, the ICFM meeting in Istanbul called once again for the resumption of negotiations between the government and the MNLF, but these negotiations were not to take place during Aquino's presidency. In 1992, Fidel Ramos was elected president. Immediately after he was sworn into office, he expressed his desire for peace in Mindanao. Ramos's peacebuilding efforts led to the signing of a peace agreement on September 2, 1996. With it, the armed hostilities between the Philippine military and the MNLF ceased. Having succeeded in dealing with the MNLF, the government hoped to also bring the MILF into the constitutional fold.

While skeptical about the government's moves, the MILF nevertheless acknowledged its attempts at addressing the Moro people's sentiments. In September 1996, the MILF indicated its desire to negotiate with the Ramos government. The following month, the government set up a negotiating panel with the MILF. But despite some moves in early 1997 toward beginning the peace talks, armed hostilities between the government and MILF forces continued. After Joseph Estrada took over as president in 1998, the military attacked three MILF camps. The government justified its move by claiming that the MILF was poised to launch tactical offensives.

Despite peace talks initiated by Estrada's government in January and March 2000, it deployed 80,000 troops in central Mindanao. Such a situation made concerned groups and individuals contend that "the government had already made up its mind to crush the MILF" (IBON 2000, 11).

A number of events that followed closely one after another brought back the images of war: military operations, villages bombed, the dead and the wounded, evacuation centers, and ghost towns. Bombs exploded everywhere, including in public markets, bus terminals, restaurants, cinemas, radio stations, and churches. By the end of May, there were close to one hundred people killed and four hundred hurt by the bomb explosions. The peace talks between the government and the MILF collapsed, and the government adopted a policy of all-out war against the armed Moro rebels. Despite the call of civil society groups for a peaceful solution, the Estrada administration persisted in conducting military operations.

The war took a back seat when a corruption scandal rocked the Estrada administration, leading to an impeachment trial. Civic groups demanded Estrada's resignation. The politicization process that came about with the full media coverage of the impeachment trial led to the massing of a million people at the People Power shrine in Metro Manila, demanding Estrada's ouster. Early on the morning of January 20, 2001, close to three hundred thousand people left the shrine to march to the presidential palace. Estrada was forced out of the palace; within hours, Gloria Macapagal-Arroyo was sworn in as the fourteenth president of the Republic of the Philippines. Consequently, the policy of all-out war was scrapped. Within weeks she had called for a cease-fire and the convening of peace talks.

However, it soon became clear that the new president was under the control of high-ranking generals who influenced her toward taking a hawkish position. It is assumed by many political analysts that these generals have never been in favor of resolving the conflict in Mindanao, since their personal interests would be compromised with the reign of peace. The events that took place on September 11, 2001, pushed Mrs. Macapagal-Arroyo to collaborate with U.S. President George W. Bush's "war on terrorism." Eventually this led to her welcoming U.S. troops to the Philippines to assist in neutralizing Abu Sayyaf, a marginal group of Moro militants who have engaged in terrorist acts. Abu Sayyaf reportedly has links to Osama bin Laden's Al-Qaeda network.

These moves have scuttled the peace talks. At the time of this writing, there are no clear signs that Mrs. Macapagal-Arroyo is committed to bringing peace in Mindanao. Consequently, the peace that seemed so possible for Mindanao in mid-2001 has once more evaporated.

OVERVIEW OF CHRISTIAN PEACE EFFORTS

Grassroots peacemaking efforts in parts of Mindanao that have had a positive impact have ranged from spontaneous and informal actions taking place in "the everyday experience" of the people to more organized initiatives. The initiatives that arose in Christian communities emerged because of serious local attempts by the Catholic Church (which holds an overwhelming majority among Christian churches in Mindanao and throughout the Philippines) to face the tension between the Christian communities, on one hand, and the Moro and Lumad communities, on the other. This social movement gained momentum through what the late Bishop Bienvenido Tudtud called the "dialogue of faith and life," also popularly known as interfaith dialogue.

The Second Vatican Council had much to do with the rise of this social movement in Mindanao. Catholic proselytization, as it had been previously understood, was deemphasized by the council. Ecumenism and interfaith dialogue were encouraged. Thus came into being what is now considered the main thrust of the church's presence among the Moro and Lumad communities, namely, a dialogue of faith and life. Various factors pushed urgently for such a dialogue. First was martial law, which created havoc in the lives of all Mindanawons. Second was the birth of the Mindanao-Sulu Pastoral Conference (MSPC), a triennial conference involving all dioceses, where church people came together to discuss their specific situations and generate relevant responses. At the first conference, in 1974, held in the wake of mass evacuations owing to the eruption of hostilities between government and MNLF forces, the delegates tackled this issue and came up with guidelines on how the church could help defuse the tensions and bring forth peace. A deepening of this discussion took place in the MSPC conferences in 1977 and 1980. Third, there were church leaders who actualized the desire to begin the dialogue, beginning at the grassroots level. The major proponent was the first bishop of the prelature of Marawi, Bienvenido Tudtud. He was the first major Christian leader to articulate the need for a dialogue of life and faith. Through a process of study and reflection, he and the pastoral workers of his diocese came up with a vision of how they would deal with the conflict as well as a pastoral strategy to launch the dialogue.

Once they had agreed on a vision and a strategy, they facilitated activities in a few of the parishes that would encourage and prepare grassroots Christians to dialogue with the Muslims. From Marawi, the pastoral call to begin dialogue with the Muslims spread to other local churches. The staff of the MSPC secretariat provided support for such initiatives through a program called *Duyog Ramadhan* (Accompany Ramadhan), which ultimately became coordinated with the Philippine Action for Cultural Ties (PACT) program of the National Council of Churches of the Philippines (NCCP). Duyog Ramadhan became a yearly program aimed at educating Christians about Islam and Moro culture during the period of Ramadhan. As they embraced the spirit of Ramadhan, Christians joined activities where they would learn more about the Moro people. This proved to be an important step in entering into a dialogue process.

Various groups, organizations, and communities adapted this program in order to foster unity and understanding among Mindanawons. Unfortunately, the intensification of human rights violations during martial rule coupled with encounters between government forces and the MNLF made it difficult to organize sessions for dialogue or activities that promoted interaction toward collaboration. Confidence building could not be enhanced. Conflict resolution was most difficult to approach.

Despite the clarity and validity of Bishop Tudtud's prophetic stance on dialogue, many church leaders found his vision threatening. The traditional pastoral response in Moroland (the areas the Moro people regard as their homeland) was, first, to build churches for the Christians as well as schools and hospitals that catered to both Muslims and Christians; and, second, to set up social service programs like cooperatives, nutrition centers, and housing projects. Some radio stations were also established.

Bishop Tudtud's vision highlighted the ministry of presence; consequently, it demanded that the church keep a low profile while maintaining a close rapport with the ordinary Moro people. The church was challenged to give up its once dominant and powerful position. As a result, where the Muslims constituted a sizable percentage of the population, acceptance among Catholics of a church of privilege was very low.

While the process of promoting dialogue was slow, people at the grassroots were beginning to attempt it. The accession of Mrs. Cory Aquino to power gave it a boost. With People Power came an expansion of space for democracy. More sectors became interested in conflict resolution. "Peace" was a buzzword everywhere.

More Catholic religious congregations became interested in working with the Moro people, even as those already involved added personnel to further the agenda of interfaith dialogue. They did this even in the years after 1986, when interethnic tensions were still being expressed in kidnappings, killings, grenade blasts near or inside churches, the burning of the town of Ipil, and other violent acts.

The past several years have seen a number of initiatives. The ones included as case studies in this project are examples of such practices at the grassroots level. There have also been efforts by pastoral groups and nongovernmental organizations (NGOs) to reach out to the middle class in the urban centers, thus including teachers, students, local religious leaders, and personnel of NGOs. Unfortunately, no umbrella organization has emerged to bring together these different groups. An informal group connected to the Asian Journey—a network of Catholics engaged in interfaith dialogue all over Asia—occasionally brings together peace advocates from various parts of the Philippines. However, it remains a loose group with minimally coordinated programs. The Episcopal Commission on Interreligious Dialogue (ECID) provides some loose connection, but its focus is mainly on promoting communications and coordination of inter-religious activities.

The success of the peace talks between the government and the MNLF in 1996 provoked an interest among the various groups within civil society for a more serious campaign for peacebuilding. Among the church people were those with an intense desire to take part in the peacebuilding efforts, even as there were many others who were either quite suspicious of the MNLF's activities or totally against negotiating with them. When a few bishops, social action center directors, and peace advocates attended the Mindanao Peace Congress in late June 1996, they were convinced by the sincerity of the negotiating parties and the importance of pushing forward the peace agenda.

A few of the bishops—both Catholic and Protestant—agreed upon a course of action that would create an impact on peacebuilding efforts in the period following the 1996 agreement between the Ramos government and the MNLF. Led by Archbishop Fernando Capalla of the Archdiocese of Davao, who is the chair of ECID, the bishops sought to open new avenues for dialogue with the Muslim religious leaders.

Still, the most promising aspect of this social movement was what was taking place at the grassroots level. Initiatives arose from the ranks of ordinary people dealing with the everyday reality of violence. These initiatives served as concrete responses among the poor and marginalized—both Muslims and Christians—who have been caught in the crossfire between the government's armed forces and the Moro ideological forces. These initiatives became "weapons of the weak" (J. C. Scott 1985) in response to the machinations of the strong and powerful, who seemed incapable of dealing creatively with the conflict.

RESEARCH DESIGN

An approach that utilized both qualitative and quantitative methods was employed in this study. The qualitative aspects employed historical research through documentary investigation and analysis and appropriation of various ethnographic approaches, including "research as performance" (Lavie 1990, 7), "with-one's-feet-on-the-ground" (Schefer-Hughes 1992, 4), which is multi-sited and engages in advocacy as well as social intervention.[2] These approaches were possible because of the researchers' extended immersion within the communities included as case studies.

Immersion was facilitated by my own direct involvement with the various actors and agencies of this social movement. I worked as executive secretary to the MSPC secretariat with Bishop Tudtud as chair of the board. Therefore, I had a close-up view of how this movement arose. I visited many of the research sites long before this study began and interacted with those who played crucial roles in setting up the initiatives. As the study progressed, there were many occasions to validate the findings during forums, conferences, and round-table discussions, owing to my association with the movement since the 1970s. The research assistants—Elpidio Lapad, Jr., and Ailynne Maravillas—were also familiar with the research sites, spoke some of the local languages, and had extensive experience gathering data for research work.

Interviews of key informants (people who were able to provide important information about their communities) were unstructured and carried out informally, following a conversational style. Note taking was kept to a minimum. Important dates and critical incidents were used as historical locators. Twenty selected Christians and fourteen Muslims from the eight research sites were interviewed extensively. Focus-group discussions allowed for group interaction both in the gathering and the validating of the data. A number of scholars and practitioners in interfaith dialogue were asked to read and critique the study.

The quantitative aspect of this study mainly involved the use of structured interviews, which explored gender differences in peacemaking and how various beliefs and social attitudes might relate to involvement in peacemaking. These included peacemakers' and nonpeacemakers' images of the divine, their images of the opponent, and the extent to which they believe that the world is a just place (see chapter 1). Data were statistically analyzed and findings are described below. A total of 243 respondents participated in the gender study, while 314 were interviewed on their beliefs and attitudes.

THE CASE STUDIES

Research sites in Mindanao included three areas in Lanao del Norte (Maladeg, Malabang, and Balabagan), one in Lanao del Sur (Sapad), one in Zamboanga del Sur (Dinas), two in Cotabato City (Campo Muslim and Miryamville), one in Sultan Kudarat (Bual), and Zamboanga City. The research conducted in Zamboanga

---

[2] See the following for appropriate research approaches: Alejo 2000; Gardner and Lewis 1996; and Marcus 1995.

City was different from that at the other eight sites because its purpose was to document the activities of the Mindanao Peace Week in 2000.

1. Maladeg is one of the nineteen *barangays* (local villages) of the town of Sultan Gumander, which belongs to the province of Lanao del Norte. Sultan Gumander's total land area is 27,756 hectares (107 square miles). Maladeg is home to the Maranaws, who are the indigenous people of Lanao. Presently, 90 percent of the population of Sultan Gumander are Maranaw, while the remaining 10 percent are Bisaya, who were lured to Maladeg in the early 1920s by the opportunity to work on the coconut plantations owned by one clan. The first Bisayan settlers came from the islands of Cebu, Iloilo, and Leyte. Once established in Maladeg, they enticed their unemployed and landless relatives to join them. Thus, many of the Bisaya living in Maladeg are related to one another by blood or share a common place of origin.

Tensions between Muslims and Christians in Maladeg arose through the years. The cause of this can be traced not only to the continuing Muslim rebellion but also to the Maranaw practice of *rido,* which literally means feud or misunderstanding leading to vendetta. Over the years, *rido* has been a phenomenon among the Maranaws all over Lanao, persisting down to the present. There have been occasions when the two causes of armed hostilities (*rido* and interethnic/ interreligious conflict) interfaced with each other.

2. The town of Malabang is located at the southernmost rim of the province of Lanao del Sur. It has a total land area of 16,538 hectares (64 square miles). A majority of the population (75%) are Maranaw-Muslim. Being the indigenous people of Lanao, the Maranaws were the original settlers of Malabang, and they continue to consider this place part of their homeland. Throughout the Spanish colonization, military expeditions were launched to subjugate the Maranaws and to establish a government office in Malabang.

The end of the Spanish colonial era gave way to American colonization. American businessmen were attracted to Malabang to establish cassava plantations. Thousands of hectares of land were given to the cultivation of cassava. The plantations needed docile and cheap labor. The plantation managers hired local Maranaws, but they also recruited laborers from the Visayan Islands, who migrated to Malabang for the job opportunities.

An economic boom took place in Malabang in the years following the end of the Second World War. Because of the economic opportunities, Christians were not the only settlers attracted to migrate to Malabang. Maranaws of the surrounding areas also flocked to this place. The sharp increase in the Maranaw population of Malabang would create problems straining the relations between the Bisaya Christians and the Maranaw-Muslims.

It was inevitable that Malabang in the postwar era would witness the upsurge of the *rido* practice. There were many conflicts between clans and families who were competing for land, livelihood, business prospects, governance possibilities, political favors, and access to fiscal resources. *Rido* became a fact of life, breeding chaos. The cycle of violence triggered by *rido* continues to be an integral aspect of the Malabang sociopolitical landscape.

The years preceding martial law in 1972 would bring more complications to the already complex realities of Malabang. Like many places in Mindanao in the 1970s, the surrounding areas of Malabang became the site of deadly armed confrontations between the Ilaga and the Barracuda. The clashes left countless people maimed or dead. Unspeakable atrocities— harassment, looting, massacres— were committed by both sides and sent terror across the affected land. Government troops were helpless to stop the senseless fighting. Many families were forced to flee to safer areas.

But the war between government forces and militant Muslim groups would affect the lives of the people of Malabang in a different manner. Whereas the Ilaga could not penetrate Malabang, the military—consisting mainly of Christians of various ethnic origins—succeeded in occupying Malabang itself. The gross violation of the human rights of the Maranaws, who were victimized by the military, deepened the animosity between Muslims and Christians in the area.

On both sides, mistrust reached higher levels. Tensions were such that Muslims, especially children, were not brought to the hospital if they became ill, for fear that Christian doctors or nurses would inject them with poison. Christians, in turn, avoided Muslims like the plague. They felt secure only because of the presence of the military.

Another generation has seen the light of day since these events occurred, but children born to Maranaw and Bisaya families in Malabang since then continue to view one another, by and large, with the same prejudiced eyes as their parents and elders.

3. Balabagan is a town adjacent to Malabang. It is also part of the province of Lanao del Sur and is located on the coast. South of Malabang lie the province of Maguindanao and the city of Cotabato. A thirty-minute ride along the Narciso Ramos Highway leads to Camp Abubakar, the legendary MILF camp that once was the Estrada government's primary target for attack.

Such a strategic location placed Balabagan at the heart of the skirmishes between the MILF and the government. The beginning of the series of tragedies befalling the municipality of Balabagan came in 1970 when Fr. Martin Dempsey, the first parish priest assigned to the area, was murdered. Witnesses would point the finger at a teenage Maranaw as the culprit. For the old Bisaya residents in Balabagan, the priest's murder drew the first blood in the increasingly precarious situation in the area. The incident, which to this day they regard as an abominable assault on Christians, left a lasting impression. Previously, expressions of bias had been more discreet, but Bisayan biases against the Maranaws became more pronounced after the murder of Fr. Dempsey. Anti-Moro sentiment would deepen further with the series of atrocities experienced by Christians at the hands of Moro bandits when the Ilaga–Barracuda war broke out.

The Ilaga–Barracuda episode of the early years of the 1970s was welcomed by some Bisaya as an opportunity to fight back against what they believed to be excesses of the Maranaws. That meant taking up arms. The Maranaws echoed the same sentiments. With the cycle of attack and reprisal firmly established, the threat of violence has been a continuing reality in Balabagan up to this day.

4. The municipality of Sapad is one of the interior towns of Lanao del Norte. Its area covers close to 140 square kilometers (54 square miles). Again, the original inhabitants are Maranaws. However, the original Maranaw inhabitants had been pushed out into the mountains, following massive migration of settlers from Luzon (the northernmost of the larger Philippine islands) and the Visayas. In the 1950s, Sapad was proclaimed as a resettlement area by the government and the first settlers to come were former guerrillas who had fought the Japanese during the Second World War.

Eventually the Christians constituted one-half of the total population. The municipality of Sapad had already witnessed the eruption of armed hostilities prior to the turbulent period of the 1970s. It was inevitable that more Maranaws would rise up against the growing threats that the Bisaya represented. By 1965, a number of these Maranaws took up arms and started killing Bisaya settlers they found in the mountain villages. As a result, the Bisaya also armed themselves for protection against the Maranaw raiders. Soon, the systematic violence of the Ilaga-Barracuda hostilities caught up with Sapad's own in-fighting.

The year 1971 would leave a deep wound in Sapad's collective memory with a number of killings that led to evacuations. Those who fled returned to their homes, but peace has eluded them over the decades. The most recent troubles have been the outbreak of hostilities between government soldiers and the MILF in Central Mindanao.

5. Dinas is one of the municipalities of Zamboanga del Sur. Together with five neighboring towns, it forms part of the Baganian Peninsula. With a total land area of 16,238 hectares (about 63 square miles), Dinas is home to the Maguindanao Muslims, indigenous Subanen, and Christian settlers.

The original inhabitants of this place are the Subanen. The Maguindanao Muslims found their way to Dinas only in the late eighteenth century, eventually exercising control over Subanen communities. The influx of the Maguindanaons uprooted the Subanen from their established territories. To avoid conflict, the Subanen gave up their territories and moved farther up into the mountains. Now the riverbanks where they once lived are occupied by a predominantly Manguindanaon community.

Although the migration of Christians had begun in the early part of the nineteenth century, it was only after World War II that Christian settlers from the Visayas and Luzon started coming in waves. These migrant settlers had easily and legally acquired land by virtue of various land acts enacted by the American colonial and postcolonial regimes.

During the early periods of coexistence among the Subanen, Maguindanaons, and Bisaya in Dinas, respect and understanding prevailed. During those times not a trace of animosity or distrust surfaced among the three groups. Even the Subanen, who had harbored a quiet hatred toward the Moro people owing to the hostilities and vassalage their ancestors had endured at the hands of the early Muslims, exercised tolerance. But this situation did not last long.

The period 1970-1972 was marked by violent encounters between the Black-shirts/ Barracuda and the Ilaga. The chain of violent events was sparked in Cotabato. The fighting found its way to Zamboanga del Sur in early 1972. During this time, hundreds of evacuees from Lanao del Norte had sought refuge in some of the province's towns, only to be pursued there by the fighting. No one was spared the consequences of the conflict; Moro, Bisaya, and Subanen all experienced the impact of atrocities.

6. Campo Muslim is in Barangay Bagua, Cotabato City. The area is located along the Rio Grande de Mindanao, which is Mindanao's largest river. One congested portion of this predominantly Manguindanaon territory was selected in the early 1970s for the Campo Muslim relocation site. There were very few people who lived here before the 1970s. In the early 1970s, evacuees who fled their homes in the nearby rural villages, which were the targets of raids and armed skirmishes, began to inhabit this place. Campo Muslim was one of the first relocation sites established by the Reconciliation Center of the Archdiocese of Cotabato for Maguindanaon and Bisaya refugees.

7. Miryamville is another community assisted by the Archdiocese of Cotabato, which established a housing project there in 1987. It is located in the town of Sultan Kudarat, Maguindanao. However, it is only three kilometers away from Cotabato City. The housing project was set up to rehabilitate victims of violence and to reconcile relationships strained by conflict. In this village, there are more Bisaya than Moro. A majority of the Bisaya are Cebuanos (migrants who came from the island of Cebu) who worked in agricultural colonies opened by the government as early as 1913.

8. Bual is a barangay in Isulan, Sultan Kudarat with a total land area of 133,000 square kilometers (51,350 square miles). It used to be called Daguma and it had been home to the Maguindanaons. Christians first arrived in Bual in the 1950s. A sense of mutual understanding developed between the native Maguindanao inhabitants and the earliest migrant settlers in those years. The situation was peaceful. There were Maguindanaons who shared their land with the settlers, though more often than not, they sold land to the newly arrived migrants. Land disputes arose within a generation.

The disputes turned ugly. On December 16, 1996, a group of Christians decided to settle one such dispute by burning Muslim homes; more than two hundred houses were razed by the fire and four persons were killed. Fortunately, witnesses came forward to identify the culprits; a few were eventually arrested and jailed. What pained the Muslims in the village most was that the police and the military did nothing to prevent the burning of the houses, thus raising suspicions among the Muslims that they had somehow collaborated in the crime.

9. Zamboanga City is situated at the tip of the Zamboanga peninsula facing the southernmost islands of the Philippine archipelago, which includes Basilan,

Sulu, and Tawi-tawi. Its history goes back to 1635, when a fort and garrison were established there by the Spaniards, a century after the first conquistadors reached the islands. The Lutao and Subanen were the original settlers of this place. Other ethnic groups came to settle here including the Tausog and the Samal Dilaut. The first Christians from the Visayas arrived as infantry regulars of the Spanish army.

After the war erupted in the 1970s, thousands of evacuees from affected areas in Zamboanga del Sur and del Norte—mainly Bisaya—flooded the city and settled there. Their arrival drastically changed the demography of the city, and the predominant language changed from Chabacano (pidgin Spanish) to Cebuano. As the Moro rebellion deepened, Zamboanga City took on a more strategic importance for both the military and the MNLF. Security in business firms, schools, and churches tightened as bombings took place at the heart of the city.

Since then, peacebuilding and interfaith dialogue have become major concerns for civil society groups, especially church organizations. Among those who responded to the challenge was the group Peace Advocates Zamboanga (PAZ), set up in October 1994. PAZ members pioneered the concept of a Week of Peace in November 1997. Two years later it was adopted by the Bishops-Ulama[3] Forum and other peace advocates throughout Mindanao. The case study presented below is a documentation of the manner in which PAZ conducted the Peace Week in the year 2000.

SUMMARY

The communities included in this study are quite varied. Some are rural communities located along coastal areas, while others are in the interior. A few are found in cities. Some of the peacebuilding efforts take place within one isolated village, such as Maladeg, with its 876 households; others are carried out in larger communities, such as Sapad, with its 2,230 households. In four of the research sites, the Moro are in the majority, for example, in Balabagan, where they comprise 80 percent of the population. The ethnicities of the Moro people in the research sites are primarily Maranaw and Maguindanao; the ethnicities of the Christian settlers in these sites are most commonly Cebuano, Bohol-anon, and Ilongo. In Dinas, close to ten percent of the population is Subanen, the indigenous people of the Zamboanga Peninsula.

The Christian settlers penetrated these areas during three migration waves: the 1930s-1940s, the 1950s, and the 1970s. The majority of people, both Muslims and Christians, in the areas selected as research sites, are farmers and fisherfolk. Those in the cities do all sorts of jobs, from carpentry to selling goods in the market.

The conflicts in these communities go back a long time. For those in Lanao, there has always been *rido* among the various Maranaw clans. In terms of the Moro/Muslim and Bisayan/Christian conflict, some violent incidents took place as early as the 1960s. The major outburst of violence, sweeping across a vast area

---

[3] An ulama is a body of mullas, high-ranking Muslim clerics.

of Mindanao and affecting all the research sites, happened in the early 1970s with the armed confrontations between the Ilaga and the Blackshirts/Barracudas. Many killings took place in these areas. In several instances, the violence led to massive evacuations of those caught in the crossfire.

RESPONDING AT THE GRASSROOTS

Most peacemaking activities could be categorized as formal and institutional versus informal actions that tended to be carried out more spontaneously without institutional facilitation. The latter usually were oriented to relationship building.

Formal and institutional responses included the creation of organizations for peacebuilding and conflict resolution. These included the Sapad Muslim-Christian Association for Peace (SAMCAP), the Dialogue of Life and Faith Program (DLFP) in Balabagan, the Balabagan Youth Muslim-Christian Organization (BYMCO), the Covenant of Peace and Development and Peace Zone of Maladeg, the *Samahan ng Nagkakaisang Mamamayan ng Bual* (Organization of the United Citizens) or SAMAKANA, the Dinas Subanen/Moro/Bisaya (SUMBIS) Interfaith Movement, the Miryamville Christian Fund's Parents Association (MICPA), and Peace Advocates Zamboanga (PAZ).

These organizations have various objectives, including promotion of genuine dialogue between Muslims and Christians as well as understanding of the roots of animosity between the two communities; enhancement of knowledge about the cultures of the different groups, facilitation of the processes of healing and reconciliation; the setting up of peace zones (basically, areas where no weapons are allowed); conflict prevention; the creation of buffer zones or safe havens for those who seek refuge; joint action as a tri-people forum for resolving conflict; establishment of a Reconciliation Center where Muslims and Christians can experience being together; promotion of respect for each other and harmony in relationships; collaborative action with a comprehensive vision of human development; the building of a culture of peace; and promotion of interfaith dialogue. Macaorao Sarip, a Muslim traditional leader in Maladeg explained why he was drawn to work for the establishment of peace zones:

I do not want my children to suffer the loss of a parent due to a conflict. If the situation continued to be critical, my children would not have a bright future. My support for the peace zone is 100 percent because only through this can my children live without facing a lot of worries.

Most of these formal organizations facilitate conflict mediation and dialogue among individuals, families, or clans in conflict with one another. Such mediation sessions take place as the need arises; in some communities, these sessions are quite frequent. In one community, the mediation group even provides counseling to those directly involved in a conflict as a way of sustaining the peace efforts. The group holds regular meetings—weekly, monthly, and quarterly—to monitor conditions and confront emergent issues and concerns. In the case of Maladeg, meetings are conducted by the local organization not just to monitor conflict-related disturbances but also to deal with drugs, gambling, and other vices that often accompany violent crime. Many such organizations conduct prayer sessions or rituals at the start of their meetings or dialogue sessions, since the former are seen as integral parts of the meetings for peace and reconciliation. Gulam Guindo, an ustadz (religious leader) in Maladeg, shared how a local peacemaker group deals with the task of resolving conflict:

> We listen to the cases being presented, settle feuds, solve problems and provide counseling to the people. Before a conflict gets out of hand, we intervene so that troubles could be avoided. All members of the committee are involved in deciding what to do with the cases presented.

SAMAKANA-Bual officers related the story of their grassroots organization:

> The first step was the conduct in 1997 of Culture of Peace seminars. The seminars were attended by various sectors from both Muslim and Christian groups, representatives from the local government, the MNLF, and the military. During the seminars, the participants were challenged to do something to improve their relationships based on the realization that they are not natural enemies. What they did was organize themselves as SAMAKANA.

Various locales provide the space for the conflict mediation, meetings, and other gatherings. These include schools, the municipal hall, a seminary house, the barangay hall, and a Peace Center. In Maladeg, peace advocates built a thatched-roof hut on the beach; it has proven a perfect place for conducting conflict resolution sessions. Parochial and nursery schools also serve as sites to promote mutuality between Muslim and Christian faculty members and students.

These grassroots peace initiatives also include the setting up of projects involving Muslims and Christians to augment their income as well as provide a venue for collaborative efforts. In Bual, a three-year development project is in place; as part of it, programs like cooperatives, small-scale income-generating activities, an ecological farm, and health programs have been implemented. In Miryamville, the MICPA set up a bakery as an income-generating project.

In these communities, Christians are involved in conscious expressions of accompaniment with the Muslims during their religious seasons such as Ramadhan; in return, Muslims join the Christians in religious celebrations such as Christmas. In some of the communities, the formal conduct of interfaith dialogue was introduced. Where this occurred (Balabagan, Sapad, and Miryamville), dialogue continues to take place. However, in one of the communities, the dialogue movement was weakened because local politicians took advantage of it for their political interests. In the case of Malabang, there was under way at one time a formal interfaith dialogue. It did not last, however, for a number of reasons, including the belief of some Maranaw that it was an attempt to convert them to Christianity. More recently, there is renewed interest in the revival of dialogue.

In Balabagan, efforts at dialogue encountered difficulties. Lorna Glimada, one of the dialogue initiators, explained that many of the physical and psychological wounds left by conflict are still too fresh for people to be able to talk to one another:

> Dialogue and reconciliation in our case only sound good in terms of ideas. But in reality, the deep wounds in people's hearts are a stumbling block to genuine dialogue and reconciliation.

In the past two years, there have been joint efforts for the celebration of the Mindanao Peace Week in many parishes throughout Mindanao. It is, however, in Zamboanga City that this celebration is the best organized; after all, Peace Advocates Zamboanga pioneered the Peace Week, during which a variety of activities, including symposia, prayer vigils, song and art contests, parades, sports festivals, and cultural programs take place. In Malabang, Balabagan, and Cotabato, hundreds of Muslims and Christians take an active part in Peace Week.

Innovative approaches have also been implemented by grassroots peace groups. In Campo Muslim, Muslim and Christian women in groups of five come together in a "Circle of Friends" to plan income-generating activities and to offer assistance such as scholarships for children.

In Balabagan, a Muslim-Christian youth group was organized to establish stronger links among the young people through sharing and involvement in joint activities. In other sites where our research took place, Muslim and Christian adults came together to pressure the government to provide for the needs of the community, such as funding the local school and construction of roads.

Aside from the formal/institutional peacemaking activities, relatively informal actions were carried out on a day-to-day basis. Most of these build relationships of mutuality. In many communities, for example, Muslims and Christians invite one another to attend family/clan feasts coinciding with religious holidays/ events. Christians go out of their way to establish cordial relations with Muslims in the community through spontaneous expressions of friendship. Sharing of gifts during special seasons are also ways of deepening friendships.

In Malabang, ordinary Christians have made personal attempts to build peace with Muslims and vice versa. Some have visited their Muslim neighbors, making friends with them and often neutralizing resentments. Others said that if negative comments were uttered in their presence about Christians by Muslims, they would refrain from reacting. A few indicated their interest in knowing more about Muslim culture and religion in order to enhance their relationships with Muslims.

Similar efforts took place in Dinas. One respondent said that he shows respect for the culture and beliefs of Muslims and Subanen through attendance at their feasts and celebrations (Ramadhan for Muslims and D'lumpok for Subanen) as well as birthday celebrations. A woman respondent visits her Muslim women friends and shares her skills in acupressure. Others extend assistance and moral support to Muslims in their times of need such as when a member of their family is sick.

Interfaith dialogue has often taken place in very simple shared religious experiences that cut across the religious divide. The testimonies of three Christian respondents in Miryamville reveal the power of reaching out to one another through their religious beliefs:

> *Nida Mucamad-Dodi:* One of our peacemaking efforts involves the dialogue of life and faith. For example, when the Muslim community celebrates its religious festivities, their leaders make it a point to share with the Christians the significance of the celebration. On the part of the Christians, they invite the Muslims during their fiesta and Christmas celebrations.

> *Helen Villegas*: Another example that symbolizes Muslim–Christian dialogue in our community is our sharing of the multipurpose building for our cultural activities. We Christians hold our liturgies there. The Muslims hold their wedding rites in the same building. So far there has been no problem in regard to this arrangement.

> *Cora Macalib-og*: During the last celebration of the feast of our patron saint (Queen of Peace), a number of Muslim friends gave us a hand in putting up decorations and flyers in the chapel and in the streets. They even made suggestions on how to put up the decorations. It was a very enriching experience of solidarity between Muslims and Christians.

Finally, grassroots peacemaking often involves tapping elements in the local culture or in cultural traditions to develop methods of mediation. For example, the *kanduri* (or coming together of the contending parties to resolve the conflict) was reappropriated to counter the practice of *rido*. Another specifically Moro tradition is a ritual called *apa*, which involves swearing on the Qur'an to contribute to the settlement of a particular dispute.

Overall, the most common peacemaking activities were those in the category of relationship building, for example, Christians striking up conversations with Muslims (or vice versa) and visiting them in their homes. Second most common were acts of service, especially the sharing of resources. Less frequent but still statistically significant were praying for peace and avoiding members of the opposing group in order to prevent conflict from developing. Confrontational peacemaking appears to be very rare in Mindanao. A majority of respondents—especially women—tended to speak of their peacemaking activities in very general, nonspecific terms.

WHO ARE THE PEACEMAKERS?

Various local leaders took the initiative in setting up formal organizations and conducting mediations. In most cases, these people held traditional leadership roles in the community. In Dinas, SUMBIS leaders include a Muslim ustadz and datu (tribal chieftain), a former MNLF commander, a *timoay* (a traditional Sub-anen village leader), and a Christian-Bisaya church lay leader. Some of them are also municipal government officials. Leaders of peace efforts in Maladeg include an ustadz, datus, and a Christian landlord. Community organizers, school teachers, parish lay leaders, and staff members of the Reconciliation Center (including women religious) are the prime movers for peace in Miryamville and Campo Muslim. In Malabang and Balabagan, the parish priests, school coordinator and teachers (Christian and Muslim), and local government officials belong to a peace advocates' group.

Women in Mindanao are generally less involved than men in mediation and conflict resolution, but they often lead initiatives in education, income-generating activities, and the setting up of the "Circle of Friends." Women's peacemaking activities tend to be more informal than those in which men participate.

Children and young adults in Mindanao have been as much affected by violence as adults. They too have been victims of massacres and emotional trauma. Consequently, children too can hold biases and prejudices. Yet there are examples of their involvement in peacemaking. In schools in Miryamville and Campo Muslim, children participate in peacebuilding initiatives. Youth organizations in Malabang and Balabagan join seminars on building a culture of peace, and actively participate in Peace Week activities. Allen Tagbo, one of the teachers at the Miryamville Child Peace Learning Center explained:

> The formation of children's consciousness starts in their early childhood. The Miryamville Child Peace Learning Center assists parents in creative ways in shaping their children's awareness. Through the songs they sing, the poems they read, the riddles and stories they are told, they learn practical values in class.

Finally, our data revealed that Bisaya/Christian respondents engaged in more activity for peace (particularly in the relationship-building category) than did Moro/Muslim respondents. This is remarkable because, as we shall see later in this chapter, Christians' opinions of Muslims were not higher than Muslims' opinions of them—in fact, quite the opposite.

LEADERSHIP IN GRASSROOTS PEACEMAKING

Most peacemakers spoke favorably of the leaders of their local peacemaking efforts, indicating that their leaders hold consultations and employ participative decision-making processes. Others said that the leaders respect the equality of Muslim and Christian group members. A few described local leaders' style as "low-key" and "unimposing."

However, some voiced criticisms as well, observing that the traditional nature of local leadership often made it both male-dominated and very centralized in terms of authority. Some, like Pedro Nantes of SUMBIS-Dinas, found local peacemaking leadership insufficiently democratic and inclusive of people at the grassroots.

HOW OTHERS SEE PEACEMAKERS

In general, respondents had positive views of the peacemakers they had encountered. Peacemakers appeared to be well respected; they were often seen as wise, fair, and well versed in laws, customs, and traditions. In some areas, peacemakers are highly regarded even by the military. In Maladeg, the local government was so pleased with their services that it provided them with an allowance, since they serve as the justice arm of the local government. Some Christian peace advocates are esteemed by the Muslims, who would warn them if they were ever in danger.

However, some respondents held unfavorable opinions about local peacemakers. It is not uncommon for grassroots peacemakers, rightly or wrongly, to be regarded as biased against one side or the other. A few, said respondents, are corrupt and easily bribed by those in power. In some of the research sites, government officials and politicians who engage in peacemaking activities are particularly suspect. One frustrated respondent said local peacemakers in their place help to resolve conflicts arising out of *rido*, yet the same "peacemakers" engage in *rido* themselves. Indeed, people involved in grassroots peacemaking were sometimes ambivalent about their convictions. In an interview, one left us with this contradictory assertion: violence is never justified, he said, but he would still carry a gun for his own protection.

RELATIONSHIPS AMONG PEACEMAKERS

Any group can suffer from tensions or contradictory interests among members, and groups whose primary purpose is peacemaking are no exception. But members of these groups generally spoke warmly of their fellow activists. They reported deeply trusting one another and enjoying a sense of acceptance and tolerance within the group, which in turn facilitated their ability to work together to settle conflicts. One important factor to which they attributed their strong bond of trust was their shared collaborative experiences. Peacemakers also appeared to have a profound respect for one another's culture and religion. Another bond they widely shared was a common desire to work together for the good of all.

PREJUDICE AND BLAME

IMAGES OF THE ENEMY

Those we inteviewed provided insights into the roots of the conflict. Land is one contested issue between Muslims and Christians. Land disputes in turn were caused by conflicts over territorial boundaries or by the Moro wanting to take back land from the Christians that had once been theirs. Long-standing biases, prejudices, and distrust exist on both sides. Christians often think of Muslims as traitors, criminals, and troublemakers; Muslims perceive Christians as unclean because of their vices. Columban Father Rufus Haley, a priest active in peace-making in Malabang, was murdered by an armed Moro band not long after we interviewed him. He had shared with us these observations:

> Two cultures co-exist in Malabang. The Muslims always have this attitude of superiority; they are a proud race. The Christians, on the other hand, consider themselves an endangered species. They believe the Maranaws oppress them. What the Muslims consider rightful, the Christians think is unlawful. When a Christian is killed, they rely on the law to bring justice. But the Muslim relies on family for support and protection. When one of them is killed, they demand retribution; they seek to avenge the death of their kin. This is why *rido* happens all the time. . . . Christians are in the minority and they feel that they are always at a disadvantage. . . . The hatred deep within is mounting and nothing you can say or do can change their opinion about the Muslims.

Statements of those we interviewed tended to corroborate the late Fr. Haley's remarks. When we asked Christians their perceptions of themselves and other Christians, they largely portrayed themselves as victims but morally superior to the Muslims. One respondent believed that Christians are members of an "endan-gered species." Many saw themselves as powerless and oppressed. On the other hand, Christians were generally of the opinion that they are better educated than the Muslims (though in regions where it was possible to compare Christian and Muslim eductional levels, we found no statistically significant difference) as well as more diligent, industrious, open-minded, fair, law-abiding, and God-fearing. Their prejudices appear to be rooted in the belief that their families have suffered the brunt of violence. They are commonly of the opinion that Christians should tolerate differences but fight back if provoked.

Christians' images of the Moro were quite negative; indeed, Christians appear to be far more prejudiced against Muslims than the latter are against them. Many Christians believed that Muslims are fierce, warlike, more prone to violence owing to their warrior tradition and the practice of *rido*. They further regarded Muslims as troublemakers who are always ready to start a fight, and as traitors who cannot be trusted. The following remark made by a Christian in Malabang is typical:

> In the early 1950s, we used to be quite close with some of the Muslims. They were very friendly and respectful. When you hired them, they worked hard. Then came those stormy years; it was never the same again. After martial law, the Maranaws went all the way to show what they really are—aggressive, fierce, warlike, proud troublemakers.

Another commonly held stereotype was that Muslims are untidy (both in terms of personal hygiene and their environment). Finally, because Muslims are more family- and clan-oriented, some Christians believed that they would go to extremes to protect and avenge the members of their families and clans. Pedro Nantes of SUMBIS-Dinas observed:

> After the major conflicts that arose in the 1970s, things have never been the same. Camaraderie and friendship in Dinas gave way to hostile relations. The Bisaya have since dealt with the Muslims with suspicion, perceiving them as murderers and traitors not worthy of any trust. Now it is the Muslims who are on the offensive.

Obviously, just *how* negative enemy images were depended on which religious and ethnic group held them, with Bisaya/Christian respondents holding more negative images of Muslims/Moros than Moro/Muslim respondents held of them (see table at end of chapter). It also varied according to research site. Both Moro/Muslim and Bisaya/Christian respondents in Bual, Miryamville, and Dinas held significantly more positive images of the opposing group than did respondents in Malabang, Sapad, Campo Muslim, Maladeg, or Balabagan. Among the Bisaya groups, respondents who identified themselves as Ilongo had the most positive images of the Moro people, while the groups holding the least positive enemy images of the Moro were Siquijodnon and Cebuano. Moro groups did not significantly differ from one another in their images of the Bisaya.

WHAT—AND WHO—IS TO BLAME?

Moro and some Bisaya respondents widely believed that the decades of conflict are the result of Bisaya settlers' encroachment into Moroland, the government's neglect of the Moro people's problems, its disregard for their rights, and its continuing policy of waging war against the Moro people at the slightest provocation. But governmental transgressions are bolstered by some Christians who believe that Muslims want to control the whole of Mindanao. Others say that the conflict is the result of pride on the part of Muslims and the need for Christian families to protect their honor. Still others think that the conflict has resulted from the government's manipulative moves to create a wedge between Muslims and Christians; they contend that the war in early 2000 could not have erupted if not for a "third party" that fueled the conflict, just as when the war began in the 1970s.

VIEWS ON PEACE: WHAT IT IS, HOW IT HAPPENS

Longings for peace were expressed by respondents during the interviews even as they explained what it meant to them. A few defined peace as the stemming of violence and the resolution of conflict, resulting in Muslims and Christians living in harmony with each other. Others said that peace reigns when there is friendship, unity, and understanding between Muslims and Christians. Some saw peace as the possibility of living without fear of their neighbors and sleeping peacefully at night without worrying. Many expressed hope in the establishment of peace zones. Finally, there were those who believed that peace would be the result of addressing the root causes of the conflict: peace would arise when all have access to land and other resources, when progress and development guarantee a better future for everyone, and when the government responds to the needs of the Muslims.

The following are reflections on peace shared during interfaith meetings and interviews among the peace advocates who are members of SUMBIS-Dinas:

> Our concept of peace is concrete, namely, getting rid of prejudices among the Moro, Subanen, and Christian settlers. Our biases towards one another hinder all efforts at peacebuilding. Aside from this, the rights of the Moro and Subanen to their ancestral domains must be recognized. Respect for people's culture and identity leads to the acceptance of their being part of society. With all of these, there will be peace.

In Bual, some expressed their views on peace as follows:

> There is peace where Muslims and Christians follow wholeheartedly the commandments of God and the teachings of the Qur'an. Peace does not necessarily mean the absence of conflicts because people are different from one another. There will still be conflicts but people are empowered to cope and rise above these conflicts through peaceful means.

> If peacemaking is the concern of the interfaith movement, they should have brought it down to more people at the bottom level. The initiative is limited only to a few who wield influence in the municipality. This does not augur well for the continuity of any peacemaking initiative.

WHAT WORKS AND WHAT DOES NOT: PEACEMAKERS' IMPRESSIONS

Many peacemakers have witnessed positive results from negotiations and mediations as well as joint efforts to alleviate poverty, such as the livelihood projects set up by the Circle of Friends. Others strongly believe in interfaith dialogue to help bridge the gap between Muslims and Christians and to promote reconciliation.

Bob Anton, a Christian leader involved in peacebuilding in Maladeg, spoke of the importance of respect for dissent within the negotiating process:

> Unlike other groups, our committee uses persuasion and understanding of the root cause of the case presented for resolution. No coercion tactics are

used to persuade the antagonists. The slightest doubt observed during the course of the settlement will not be left unexplained to the last detail for total satisfaction from both sides. In other words, when the case is resolved, the committee sees to it that no stone of doubt on both sides will be left unturned.

In Balabagan, thanks to grassroots efforts, there is now a group that can deal with local conflicts in the absence of appropriate responses from the government. In many research sites, the efforts of local peacemakers have led to the establishment of friendly relations between Christians and Muslims. In Dinas, grassroots efforts have empowered traditional and governmental leaders to take direct action in dealing with conflicts. In Malabang, the involvement of young people in peacebuilding has made them better able to confront their own prejudices and transform potential conflicts into opportunities for cooperation.

In various sites, respondents believed that grassroots initiatives have had a favorable impact on government, making civil officials more sensitive to peace issues. Murders still occur, but some killings have been prevented; and where grassroots peacemaking efforts are well established, murder rates are down. Perhaps the ultimate achievement of local peacemaking efforts has been their impact on youth, many of whom have embraced them—and even their enemies—with enthusiasm.

There is no question that many grassroots initiatives have had a positive impact on the lives of the people, both Muslims and Christians, residing in the areas where research was conducted. However, peacemakers were critical of certain initiatives. Pedro Nantes, for example, says of SUMBIS-Dinas:

Interfaith activities have been going on for a few years now. But it is sad to note that until now, violence remains a common story in Dinas. A person still gets shot, or if he is unlucky, gets killed. I can only believe that the interfaith movement is successful if it is able to at least minimize the killings.

Sr. Stella Llerin, O.N.D., says of the Reconciliation Center's initiatives in Campo Muslim:

The present program has not risen to the more significant challenge of interfaith dialogue. Helping people through livelihood endeavors is a noble objective. But it is only a single element of an integral whole. If the program were to be true to the vision of genuine dialogue and reconciliation, the conduct of livelihood services must be viewed in relation to how it can inspire Muslims and Christians to work together towards a culture of peace.

Despite substantial gains, there remain many obstacles to peace, such as the ongoing existence and activity of militant Moro groups as well as of the military and paramilitary groups called CAFGU (Citizens Armed Forces Geographical

Unit); the persistence of the *rido* system; leadership problems; lack of education and training in interfaith dialogue and conflict resolution approaches; inadequate access to indigenous or traditional grassroots peacemaking approaches; and lack of funds. In recent years, the most formidable obstacle to peacebuilding, across the board, has been the armed hostilities that erupted between Moro militants and the Estrada government.

The grassroots peacemakers we interviewed overwhelmingly expressed an urgent need for the mobilization of resources, reasoning that peace advocates could take advantage of such resources from various agencies: government (local government and agencies like the Department of Trade and Industry), parishes (which could provide meeting facilities), and NGOs (such as the Reconciliation Center and the Christian Children's Fund). Traditional leadership systems, both religious and civil, were also mentioned as a resource, as were the personal funds and the facilities of the ustadz.

MOTIVATING FACTORS BEHIIND
GRASSROOTS INITIATIVES

Many peacemakers in our study were motivated by their own experiences of the tragic consequences of war—for example, losing a member of one's family or having to evacuate. The need to provide for one's family, the hope for a brighter future, and simply feeling tired of the violence were other reasons cited.

In Mindanao, all four motivational categories—practical, relational, ideological, and religious—were significant among peacemakers. However, the most common motivations were practical, followed by relational. Ideological and religious motives did not differ significantly from one another in frequency, but both were cited less frequently than practical and relational motivations.

A CLOSER LOOK AT RELIGIOUS MOTIVATIONS

Peacemakers who did cite religious motives believed that their faith empowered them to be engaged in peacemaking. "My belief in Divine Providence triggered my involvement in peacemaking," stated one. Another declared, "Faith helps us in what we are doing to promote peace." Some Catholic peacemakers said that their faith sustains their peacebuilding efforts because it "demands that they work for peace" and teaches that it is "a moral responsibility on their part to work for peace." They believed, they said, in a God who is "a God of dialogue." As one peacemaker reasoned, "If we believe in a God, why can't we believe that the reconciliation between Muslims and Christians is possible?"

As the remarks quoted above suggest, grassroots theologizing takes place within the communities engaged in peacebuilding. "God's word brings peace," said one respondent. "We must put God first in all our endeavors, and this will result in having peace," said another. Forgiveness, they believed, was an inescapable precondition for lasting peace. Some saw divine inspiration in particular peace efforts. Macaorao Sarip from Maladeg, for example, remarked:

"The idea of creating a peace zone was heavenly inspired. I believe that Divine Providence triggered it. We were so busy with war to ever think of peace, so I believe God touched the heart of some people to give them the inspiration to create a peace zone."

Some religiously motivated peacemakers said that their faith had helped them in moments of danger. One of these expressed the belief that "in spite of all the troubles, God is with us to protect us." Or perhaps *especially* "in all the troubles," as some reflected that God was most present to them and active through the harsh conditions they had faced.

BELIEFS ABOUT GOD AND JUSTICE

Agentic images of the divine were the most commonly held in Mindanao. Power-over images were the next most common, and immanent images were the least frequent. Bisaya/Christian respondents held more total images of the divine than Moro/Muslim respondents (see table at end of chapter). Christians were apparently comfortable with a broader range of divine attributes than were Muslims, perhaps owing to differences in Christian and Muslim theology.

Peacemakers were more likely than nonpeacemakers to hold agentic images of the divine, and peacemakers who conceived of the divine as agentic reported having engaged in more total acts of peacemaking, especially in the relationship-building category, than those low in such images. As suggested by the section on religiously motivated peacemakers, those believing in a God who acts on behalf of creation may have found themselves empowered to act as well.

Moro/Muslim respondents were more likely than Bisaya/Christian respondents to believe in a just world (see table at end of chapter). In some ways, this is a surprising finding, given that Muslims/Moros are an oppressed minority relative to Bisaya/Christian respondents. Perhaps it reflects a Muslim religious belief in the absolute justice of Allah rather than the daily sociological realities of the Muslim respondents themselves.

Both Muslim and Christian respondents who believed in a just world tended to be low in agentic and immanent images of the divine. Among Christians only, belief in a just world was associated with less motivation to work for peace.

CHALLENGES TO THE PARTIES IN CONFLICT

Immediately after Gloria Macapagal-Arroyo took over as president in early 2001, many people in Mindanao were hopeful that her government would reverse the war policy of her predecessor. Her peacebuilding initiatives (ending the government's war policy, calling for peace talks with the MILF, and setting up the Peace Panel) brought a sense of hope to all those dreaming of peace. Their hope was anchored in the belief that her moves would put a stop to the violence that has defined the Mindanawon landscape for decades. The MILF's favorable response to her initiatives—which led to the convening of a meeting between the government's panel and that of the MILF in Kuala Lumpur in mid-2001—provided the occasion for many to believe that this process would parallel the gains of the 1996 Peace Agreement between the State and the MILF.

But as of this writing in the spring of 2002, such hopes have been quashed. Many peace advocates today believe that President Macapagal-Arroyo does not possess the political will to end the war in Mindanao and that the top generals of the military hold full control over her. This became very clear after the events of September 11, 2001, when she very quickly fell in line with U.S. President George W. Bush's "war on terrorism." Using the provisions of the 1999 Visiting Forces Agreement—opposed by most sectors in civil society then and now—she allowed the deployment of three thousand U.S. military troops for the *Balikatan* (literally meaning "mutual shouldering of responsibilities," but it actually refers to joint war games) military exercises that began in March 2002. The first *Balikatan* operation led to the presence of fifteen hundred U.S. troops on the island of Basilan, purportedly to train Filipino soldiers so they can obliterate the Abu Sayyaf guerrillas. The second *Balikatan* operation, which started in April 2002, has brought more than thirteen hundred U.S. troops back to the former Clark Air Force Base for military exercises in Luzon.

These moves were opposed by many local and intermediate-level peace groups as well as by Moro communities throughout the country, especially those in the big cities of Manila, Cebu, Davao, Cotabato, and Zamboanga. President Macapagal-Arroyo's moves led to the suspension of the peace talks between the panel she had set up and the MILF. The latter had reason to be afraid that it, too, would be the target of military operations in the near future. However, opposition to President Macapagal-Arroyo's alignment with the Bush government has not been widespread; polls have shown that the majority of Filipinos approve of her policy. These developments have caused frustration among peace advocates, whose work has suffered a setback. They fear that the U.S. troops' presence in Basilan could lead to the resumption of violence. In fact, during the last week of April and first week of May 2002, bombings took place in the Mindanawon cities of General Santos and Cotabato. Contrary to the promise of President Macapagal-Arroyo, her recent moves have led to the deterioration of peace in Mindanao.

Many peace advocates today are concerned that any peace process must operate at both the state and the grassroots levels. In a troubled society, they argue, it is a matter of common sense that action be coordinated among the different stakeholders to guarantee their active involvement at every stage of the process and to ensure maximum participation in the implementation of the agreements.

The two contending parties—namely, the government and the MILF—will need to be convinced that forging an acceptable peace agreement is worth pursuing. Its positive outcome will provide a win-win solution to the long-festering problem in Mindanao. Mindanawon civil society—constituted by church groups, NGOs, the media, and universities—which has started to come together over the peace agenda for Mindanao, should aggressively place itself within the very heart of the peacemaking experiment. It should push for an inclusion in the peace process, with or without full support from the government or the MILF. Fortunately, there are key people in the government and the MILF who do welcome the active involvement of civil society in seeking a peace agreement that will benefit the whole country.

If the peace process that involves the government and the MILF is to fulfill its promise of effecting peace, both parties must work toward binding consensual norms, which might include, for example, the declaration of a cease-fire or the cessation of hostilities that would allow evacuees to return to their homes. Both parties have to commit themselves to analyzing the conflict, clarifying the issues at hand, identifying the barriers to a win-win solution, and developing viable strategies that have long-term impact.

It is the state, however, that has the greater responsibility to make sure that the processes involved in bringing together the contending parties would influence the flow of the peace talks. The state should use all its resources and tap all possible support systems to establish the right atmosphere for mediation, a crucial factor that could make a big difference in accomplishing successful negotiations. This involves searching for the most favorable site for the peace talks (Kuala Lumpur seems to meet the criteria), empowering the key agents of both sides to speak honestly and sincerely, providing adequate time for venting thoughts and emotions, facilitating a process where the panelists' voices are well considered, and creating a space that allows for the free flow of opinions that generate sustained feedback.

Such a setting allows for the key agents to articulate their views on the causes of and possible solutions to the conflict. The state in particular must listen intently to the MILF's validity claims both in terms of why the latter has waged a long-term struggle for self-determination, and the demands it is making on behalf of the Moro people in Mindanao. It is critical that MILF members feel unencumbered in venting their demands, even if these seem totally unacceptable during the early part of the negotiations. The MILF peace panel should appropriate to themselves all that would promote adequate discussion of the issues and exhaust all possible resources at their disposal to make their case. However, they, too, should play by the rules of dialogue, namely, taking care that communication is never distorted or compromised.

It is in this context that there is need for an appropriate public sphere that would guarantee the maximum involvement of all sectors of society in the peace agenda. The public sphere guarantees that the peace agenda is not monopolized by the contending parties but is shared by all stakeholders, including the people at the grassroots. The public sphere is the arena where civil society could engage the state and the MILF to make sure that stalemates are avoided, conflicts are resolved, and agreements are reached as well as implemented.

CHALLENGE TO THE CHURCHES

Various organizations, groups, and associations constitute Mindanawon civil society. In terms of the Mindanao peace agenda, civil society is represented by the *Kusog* Mindanao (an NGO engaged in pursuing a political agenda favorable to Mindanao), *Kalinaw-Mindanaw* (an NGO engaged in promoting peace, especially between Muslims and Christians), the Bishops-Ulama Forum, Peace Advocates Zamboanga, People United for Peace in Iligan City, Davao United People's Movement for Peace, the Mindanao Peace Advocates Conference, the Mindanao Congress of Development NGOs (MINCODE), the Mindanao Council of Women Leaders, the Muslim-Christian Movement for Peace and Development, the Institute for International Dialogue, and other local groups.

Groups of Christians, local churches (through base ecclesial communities,[4] parish organizations, social action centers, etc.), Catholic religious congregations, and pastoral associations are very much a part of civil society. They have a particular role to play in generating support to consolidate civil society so that it can pressure the state and the MILF to work toward a peace agreement. If this happens, it would mark an improvement over the process that led to the 1996 Peace Agreement. Because the state and the MNLF did not thoroughly involve civil society in the process, the implementation of the agreement has been fraught with difficulties.

At the level of consolidating civil society, there is still much that needs to be done by Christians and local churches, despite the fact that they have become more committed to peacebuilding in the past decade. Dioceses that have parishes with sizable Muslim populations (the Archdioceses of Zamboanga, Cotabato, and Davao; the Dioceses of Kidapawan, Marbel, Mati, Pagadian, and Iligan; and the Prelatures of Marawi, Ipil, Isabela, and Jolo) still need to identify peacebuilding and interfaith dialogue as pastoral priorities, as well as allocate personnel and financial resources for such programs. The church's program for setting up and strengthening base ecclesial communities has yet to integrate peacebuilding and interreligious dialogue. Catholic educational institutions at all levels—kindergarten, elementary school, high school, and college—still need to find ways to actively promote a culture of peace. Catholic radio stations could make a difference by broadcasting programs that combat prejudice. Religious congregations, established lay organizations (such as the Knights of Columbus and Legion of Mary), and pastoral agencies still need to allocate resources to support the efforts of the local churches for peacemaking and dialogue. All should aggressively be engaged in drives that would popularize "peaceableness . . . as an action concept, involving a constant shaping and reshaping of understandings, situations, and behaviors in a constantly changing lifeworld, to sustain well-being for all" (Boulding 2000, 1). All must work toward "a much wider recognition of the actual peace processes at work . . . and a wider awareness of the success stories of conflicts resolved and wars avoided" (ibid., 28).

Christians in the local churches, religious congregations, and pastoral organizations—including theologians, pastoral agents, liturgists and artists, community

---

[4] For the purpose of this study, base ecclesial communities are aggregates of around six to nine neighboring families who become a community in the process of sharing their life and faith as they gather around the Word of God and the Eucharist. See Mendoza 2001.

organizers, and human rights advocates—can do much more to promote peace. They could help provide training in conflict resolution and the conduct of interfaith dialogue, raise resources for peace projects, motivate grassroots leaders to engage in peacebuilding, and do research in indigenous and traditional grassroots peacemaking approaches that could be appropriated for contemporary use.

For those Christian leaders who are committed to the peace agenda, we make the following recommendations:

1. Recognize that all religions have internal resources that could help stop the violence and facilitate conflict resolution. The themes of "reverence for all living things and compassion for fellow human beings are found in the teachings of indigenous peoples" (Boulding 2000, 57), as well as in religions with an international presence, such as Christianity and Islam.

2. Find time to read, study, and discuss some of the major writings on the theology of religious pluralism, interreligious dialogue, theological issues in Muslim–Christian dialogue, and liberation issues.[5] In particular, the following texts may be useful:

> (T)he dialogue does not serve as a means to a further end. Neither on one side nor on the other does it tend to the "conversion" of one partner to the religious tradition of the other. Rather it tends to a more profound conversion of each to God. The same God speaks in the heart of both partners; the same Spirit is at work in all. By way of their reciprocal witness, it is this same God who calls and challenges the partners through each other. They become, as it were, for each other and reciprocally, a sign leading to God. (Dupuis 1997, 383)

> Dialogue understood and undertaken as communication and sharing of divine life, as journeying together in a common search of the work of the Spirit, removes prejudices and helps mutual understanding and enrichment. Involving both individuals and communities, dialogue proceeds from exterior aspects of living and working to more interior aspects of spiritual life. (Emmanuel 1999, 266)

> Dialogue . . . means "a passage" through one's own horizon, in order to deal with questions and problems raised by the very presence of the other on one's own horizon, or from within another's horizon itself. The very openness to dealing with the other changes the boundaries and character of one's own horizon. The emergence of the other on one's horizon, and the willingness to be in dialogue immediately changes the nature of the hori-

---

[5] Major writings on the theology of religious pluralism include CBCP and CIRD 1991; Dupuis 1997; Ecumenical Association of Third World Theologians 1996; Tilley 1995; Tracy 1988; and Tudtud 1988; on interreligious dialogue, CBCP and CIRD 1991; Dupuis 1997; Emmanuel 1999; Tilley 1995; Tracy 1988; and Tudtud 1988; on theological issues in Christian–Muslim dialogue to engage the liberation issues, Mercado 1990; Rodil 1994; Salgado 1990; and Tudtud 1988.

zon from which one proceeds; in particular, it prevents our horizons from becoming ossified into fixed dogmas. (Fernandez 1999, 92)

There exist different forms of interreligious dialogue . . . a. The dialogue of life, where people strive to live in an open and neighbourly spirit, sharing their joys and sorrows, their human problems and preoccupations. b. The dialogue of action, in which Christians and others collaborate for the integral development and liberation of people. c. The dialogue of theological exchange . . . where specialists seek to deepen their understanding of their respective religious heritage, and to appreciate each other's spiritual values. d. The dialogue of religious experience, where persons, rooted in their own religious traditions, share their spiritual riches, for instance with regard to prayer and contemplation, faith and ways of searching for God or the Absolute. (CBCP and CIRD 1991, 16)

3. Be engaged in dialogue, in one way or another, with all the key dialogue partners in your local area. There is no use studying and discussing dialogue if we are not engaged in the actual praxis of interreligious dialogue. In this regard, it is important to acknowledge the various problems that could be encountered in entering into dialogue with Muslims. From his own experience, Fernandez (1999, 97) has written:

The endeavour to build up co-operation and relationship with Islam is an arduous task for the following reasons: a) It inevitably criticises, as a principle, both the Christian conventional theology as well as its shallow understanding of Islam, and it aims at finding out ways for a mutually solid co-operation, working for justice, peace and socio-political change; b) There exists a great rancorous prejudice, inherited particularly from the days of the Crusades, and conventionalized institutions which make the task an uphill battle; c) Many an external political situation has considerable influence on any relation between local Muslims and the followers of other religions . . . d) An increasingly bitter propaganda war that has been going on between secularist powers and Muslim organizations . . . e) Actual conflicts in the name of religion [are] going on in Kashmir, Palestine, Bosnia, Indonesia, Philippines, Egypt, Sudan, Algeria, [and elsewhere].

4. Support various creative initiatives that promote peace, including (a) peace zones; (b) indigenous and traditional conflict resolution approaches or "existing local practices of dealing with conflict" (Boulding 2000, 71); (c) the involvement of women, children, and youth actively in such processes beyond their traditionally passive roles; (d) artistic contributions of all types to grassroots peacemaking.

5. Provide support to grassroots initiatives in whatever way possible so that these local efforts will thrive even as new ones arise.

In many peace initiatives, only those who are seen to have direct access to power, authority, status, technology, armies with high-powered guns, and other resources are brought into the inner circle of the negotiations. Grassroots communities are treated as if they hardly matter in the whole peace process. And yet, in the end, it is the grassroots communities who suffer the brunt once the negotiations fail. This is why it is of the utmost importance to involve grassroots communities in peace negotiations. "Peace culture visions must keep reminding us that social compassion begins in the small, the local," says Boulding (2000, 55).

The findings of this research study have revealed to us the power that can emanate from the ground up once ordinary people are able to mobilize the resources of their communities in the context of everyday reality. They can assert their collective ability to carve spaces of peace in the midst of hatred and strife. They can push away the encroaching waves of violence so that their families can live, at least temporarily, in tranquillity. They can evolve " weapons of the weak" that help to resist the machinations of the strong and mighty who do not hesitate to violate the people's rights in order to advance their selfish interests. This study reveals the ordinary people's "strategies of conflict resolution over time, uniquely rooted in local culture . . . built on the knowledge of local environment and lifeworld and the historical memory of times of crisis and change . . . [which are] the hidden peacebuilding strengths of every society" (Boulding 2000, 91).

With or without support from the institutional churches and religious leaders, these grassroots Christians, in conjunction with the Muslims in their communities, have undertaken formal and informal approaches to peacebuilding. These approaches have allowed them to build harmonious relationships with Muslims, provide them with services, and collaboratively resolve conflicts. Such efforts have saved lives, freed the children of both communities from the fear of being caught in a crossfire, and forged friendships across boundaries. They still dwell in war's darkness and "death's shadows," but their "feet are guided to the way of peace" (Luke 1:79).

Many respondents in this study echo a sense of hope:

Jun Cillado, Malabang: I have hope. We have to continue to have hope that, in time, maybe next century or next millennium, the Muslims and Christians will eventually see eye to eye.

Connie Balindong, Malabang: There is hope that Muslims and Christians will be able to accept each other. But it will take a long time for this to happen. I do not see it happening in this decade; still I am hopeful.

Ana Corpin, Balabagan: Although difficulties have marred our efforts at dialogue, this is not reason enough to lose hope. Our efforts failed because both Muslims and Christians dwelt on our differences. We were also grappling with the lack of proper perspective and orientation to pursue a more effective approach. With lessons learned, I believe firmly that our journey will eventually lead us into reconciliation.

Norma Candia, Sapad: Peace and reconciliation are only possible if we work for genuine dialogue with one another. It may not happen this year or in the next, but we shall not lose sight of it. Soon, we shall be able to realize it, [soon we shall] hold it in our hands.

On my last trip to Dinas, I found Ver Albarico and Toto Anig singing. Joining voices with their Muslim and Christian friends gathered at one of their interfaith sessions, they sang a song that expressed their dreams and commitment to peace perhaps better than anything our research methods could bring to light:

> *Ayaw wad-a ang paglaum, bisan tuod sa mga kadag-um*
> *Kay luyo sa mga panganod, nagasidlak ang adlaw.*
> Do not lose hope, despite the dark clouds
> Because behind those clouds, the sun shines.

STATISTICAL TABLE
ASSOCIATED WITH CHAPTER 3 DATA

See pages 120 and 124 for an interpretation of this table. See chapter 1 for an explanation of variables.

TABLE 1. CORRELATIONAL COMPARISONS OF ETHNIC AND RELIGIOUS DIFFERENCES IN THE PHILIPPINES

	Images of the Enemy*	Total Images of the Divine**	Belief in a "Just" World
Ethnicity***	.57	-.59	.37
Religion****	.56	-.60	.37
All correlations (*r*) reported here are significant at or below the .05 level.			

* The measure of enemy images was constructed such that higher scores would indicate more positive images.

** "Total images of the divine" is the sum of agentic, immanent, and power-over images of the divine, averaged across respondents.

*** Positive correlations indicate that Moro respondents scored higher than did Bisaya respondents on this dimension.

**** Positive correlations indicate that Muslim respondents scored higher than did Christian respondents on this dimension.

5

Rwanda

Struggle for Healing at the Grassroots

BERNARD NOEL RUTIKANGA

Whoever saves a single life is as one who has saved an entire world.
                                                    —Mishnah, *Sanhedrin* 4:1

The Christian Centenary Jubilee, a yearlong series of celebrations marking the 100-year anniversary of the arrival of the first missionaries in Rwanda concluded on February 8, 2001. Led by a special envoy of the Pope, Cardinal Roger Etchegaray, the national celebrations took place in Kigali, the Rwandan capital. Thousands of people from neighboring countries attended the celebrations. After religious leaders and the Prime Minister addressed those gathered, a speaker representing grassroots Christians was invited to the rostrum. Her words mesmerized the audience. Many eyes filled with tears as she recalled the terrible events of April 1994. Saverina Niragire was from Musha parish in the diocese of Kigali.

> *When the 1994 genocide started I couldn't run away because I had just had a baby. My children, being young, couldn't seek refuge without me. Then the killers came. Without an iota of pity they killed my three sons, but they spared my three daughters because, at the beginning of the genocide, the females were not targeted. I lost my head and appealed to them to finish me off with my daughters.*
>
> *They refused and walked away triumphantly. I followed them, but they insisted that their instruction was to eliminate Tutsi males only. I was so desperate and chagrined that I decided to commit suicide.*

I wish to thank the many people who helped me in carrying out the fieldwork for this study in Rwanda, and Fr. Carroll Houle at Maryknoll, New York, who provided me with useful background materials.

I headed to a nearby river. On the way there, I met an old Hutu woman. She sensed my feelings, and when she tried to comfort me I just pushed her aside and rushed toward the river. She might have guessed what I intended to do, so she approached me and she took the children from me. She took them to her home and looked after them.

I waded into the middle of the river but it was not deep enough to drown me. After a long time wasted in wading up and down it, I walked back to the woman's house and recovered my children. I sought the killers out and when I finally located them, they told me that their latest instruction was to exterminate all Tutsi regardless of sex and age. However, they said that they would not harm me and they asked me to go away.

I wandered in the bush for days until I was found by the liberation forces, who took me to safety. After the defeat of the former regime, I returned to my village. He who laughs last, laughs best. I felt that the time of the victims to revenge and avenge had finally come. I sent many people to prison and extorted money, cows, and properties from others. I struck fear among Hutu in my neighborhood, and many bribed me in order to remain free.

I had been a good Christian before the genocide. But due to the church's betrayal of the victims when they most needed its assistance, I stopped praying and going to church. I had only one obsession, to get revenge. However, gradually I started to pray and I started to read the Bible voraciously. I came across Saul accepting the Lord and I started going to church, and I prayed hard asking Jesus Christ for forgiveness for having turned against the church and having been vengeful. I started also praying for courage to forgive those who had wronged me.

I started to feel pity for the Hutu who were suffering themselves from the consequences of the genocide. I forgave all those who had injured me directly or indirectly. I didn't believe it, but it was happening to me.

I started to feel warm toward the families of those who had killed my children. I started to greet them. Previously, we exchanged cold stares and we by-passed each other without even nods of acknowledgment. Gradually, we started to pay each other visits.

The Tutsi survivors were not happy with this. They started to scold me about this relationship. Then one day, I picked two Hutu young children from the street and took them to my home. They were homeless; their parents had perished during the war. This was too much to the survivors. They gave me an ultimatum, either I drive them away or I jeopardize their assistance in repairing my house. I turned down their ultimatum; so they stopped helping me to rebuild my house. I have done what I can, and some Hutu friends have given me

*a helping hand. So now I am in my rehabilitated house with my chil-
dren and the homeless Hutu children.*

*I have asked forgiveness from all those I terrorized immediately
after the war. I have already returned properties and money I
extorted from my neighbors. By the grace of God, I have forgiven
those who have killed my children. Recently, I tried to have them
released. The prosecutor called them to meet me. When they were
informed about my forgiveness, they said that as long as they were
innocent they didn't need any forgiveness. They suspected that we
wanted to trick them into confession.*

*With my meager resources I am giving food to wives of the geno-
cide detainees and when I am free, I look after their children when
they are visiting their husbands. I have also sent the homeless children to school. I feel happy with my life, I remember everything but
I have forgiven all, thanks to prayers, which have invigorated me.*

ORIGINS AND NATURE OF THE RWANDAN CONFLICT

What is history but a fable agreed upon?
—Napolean Bonaparte

Precolonial Rwanda had never experienced any Hutu–Tutsi war. Nor did
problems of this kind emerge under German colonial rule (1896-1916). Ethnic
division was introduced under Belgian colonialism (1916-1962). Influenced by
the European racial theories of the nineteenth century and writings of early trav-
elers in the Great Lakes region, missionaries and colonial officials started concerted campaigns in their writings, preaching, and education about pronounced
differences between Tutsi, Hutu, and Twa. A Belgian social scientist, Didier Goyvaerts, asserts that the process of ethnic formation comes into being in the following manner:

> When certain categories are favoured over others or consistently receive
> preferential treatment, members of all categories concerned begin to
> develop a stronger sense of belonging and the categories stop being cate-
> gories but become groups. . . . When groups are given or give themselves
> a particular history, then the groups in question stop being mere groups but
> become ethnic groups. (Goyvaerts 2000, 281-82)

Belgian colonial officials used data from a 1929-1930 census to establish rigid
group identities. Anyone who had more than ten cows was identified as being
Tutsi (14% of the population), and anyone with fewer was identified as Hutu
(85% of the population); the few who lived on pottery and hunting were identified as Twa (1% of the population). From that time onward, identity cards bearing one's ethnic affiliation were issued, a policy that was to have far-reaching
repercussions some years later.

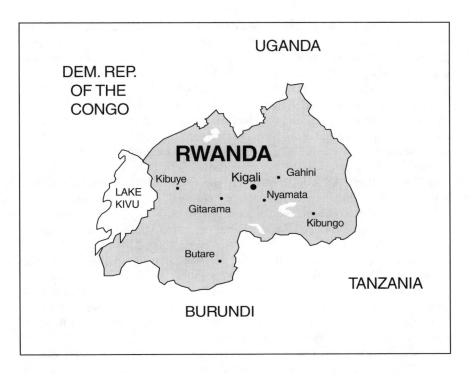

The tragic irony is that there are virtually no differences in modern history between the Tutsi, Hutu, and Twa. For centuries they have spoken the same language, lived together in the same culture, and shared the same socioeconomic and political organization. The "Divide and Rule" policy practiced in colonies was aimed at creating differences among the people and favoring one group, which enabled the colonial officials to consolidate their rule.

Through "anthropological hallucination" (Sitbon 1998, 18), colonial agents, missionaries, and Western pseudo-scientists divided the Rwandan population into three distinct groups: the stereotypically "superior and intelligent" Tutsi, "the inferior, less intelligent" Hutu, and "the sub-human" Twa. This "romanticizing and at times plain fantasizing" (Prunier 1995, 5) became such an obsession that "scales and measuring tapes and callipers" were needed to deal with Rwandan cranial, nasal, and facial sizes and shapes (Gourevitch 1998, 55). An Annual Report for Nyanza Province in 1925 describes a Twa as "a member of a worn out and quickly disappearing race. . . . With a monkey-like flat face and a huge nose, he is quite similar to the apes whom he chases in the forests" (Prunier 1995, 6). On the level of intelligence, the Tutsi were praised to the sky in the same report, and they were alleged to be beyond comparison with the other groups. As for the Hutu, the colonial propaganda emphasized that they were like children: "shy, lazy, and usually dirty" (Goyvaerts 2000, 274).

The superior-inferior ethnic group ideology of the Catholic Church and colonial agents was the first nail in the coffin of Rwandan social cohesion and solidarity. However, ideology alone would not have obliterated the peaceful coexistence of Tutsi and Hutu. Since the Tutsi were favored by the church and the colonial state in education (see the table on the following page) and employment, and were generally protected from many backbreaking colonial forms of labor, wide fissures started to appear in the Rwandan social fabric.

Traditional Rwandan administration had long recognized three equal local chiefs: the chief of the pasture, the chief of the land, and the chief of the army. Chiefs of the pasture and army were drawn mainly from the Tutsi, chiefs of the land mainly from the Hutu. The Belgian colonial administration changed this system; all three positions were amalgamated into one, and only the Tutsi remained as chiefs. All Hutu chiefs were dismissed. Bishop Léon Classe contributed much to devising pro-Tutsi colonial policies. In his 1923 Annual Church Report, Classe insists on the employment discrimination against the Hutu, stating, "Surely, however limited the number of places may be in the administration they must be reserved for young Tutsi" (Goyvaerts 2000, 279).

Education, too, was monopolized by the Tutsi. Statistics shown in the table below reveal how Tutsi from Rwanda and Burundi (both countries under Belgian colonial rule and with the same ethnic composition) dominated at Butare Secondary School, the only postprimary institution in existence at that time in the two countries. Hutu in Burundi were less discriminated against than those in Rwanda, which is why they had more representation at the school.

Gradually, the colonial policies were creating rifts between the Tutsi and the Hutu. When the colonial agents introduced unpopular measures in agriculture and animal husbandry, and forced labor in constructing schools, health centers, and roads, the Tutsi became overseers of all these projects and mistreated the Hutu. Belgian colonial officials also let the Tutsi exploit the Hutu without much interference.

As the winds of nationalism started to blow across Africa in the 1950s, however, the Tutsi elite jumped on the decolonization bandwagon, thus antagonizing the Belgian colonial establishment. The Tutsi nationalists' challenge to the Catholic Church's monopoly of education undermined the formerly strong support for the Tutsi from foreign priests and nuns.[1] Moreover, the arrival in Rwanda of Belgian priests who sympathized with the majority Hutu increased the opposition against Tutsi domination. The tide was about the turn. Tutsi opponents led by Bishop André Perraudin and Jean-Paul Harroy, the vice-governor general for Congo and Ruanda-Urundi, started to prepare the Hutu to take power. Moreover, the arrival of many Belgian priests in the early 1950s who sympathized with the exploited Hutu started to oppose the colonial policy of Hutu exclusion.

At this time, Rwanda was a Trusteeship Territory of the United Nations (UN). The UN approached Belgium, asking it to democratize Rwanda and lead it to independence. The Catholic Church and the colonial government began to do

---

[1] The Catholic Church owned and ran all primary, secondary, and vocational schools in the country. Today, not much has changed in this regard.

Tutsi-Hutu admission at Butare Secondary School, Rwanda, 1932-1954*			
Year	Tutsi *Rwanda & Burundi*	Hutu *Rwanda*	*Burundi*
1932	45		
1933	21		
1934	26		
1935	41		
1945	46		3
1946	44	1	8
1947	44	2	10
1948	85	2	11
1949	85	5	9
1953	68	3	16
1954	63	3	16

* This table was compiled by René Lemarchand in 1970; it is cited in Goyvaerts 2000, 280.

this, but in a fashion conducive to their own interests. This entailed the replacement of Tutsi political domination with Hutu political domination.

When Rwanda's King Mutara III (Charles Léon Pierre Rudahigwa) died in July 1959, his successor, King Kigeli V (Jean-Baptiste Ndahindurwa), lacked the necessary experience, diplomacy, and maturity to defuse escalating ethnic tensions. Political parties grew out of those tensions. On the Tutsi side there were UNAR (Rwandan National Union) and RADER (Rwandan Rally for Democracy). On the Hutu side, there were PARMEHUTU (Party for the Emancipation of Hutu People) and APROSOMA (Association for the Social Promotion of the Masses).

As political parties started campaigning, divisive ethnic charges, counter-charges, scuffles, and fights pitting Hutu against Tutsi started to destroy their age-old peaceful coexistence. A spark was needed to unleash violence, and this came on November 1, 1959, when Dominique Mbonyumutwa, a Hutu subchief and a PARMEHUTU activist was beaten up by Tutsi UNAR youths. The violence spread like fire in the wind, and within a short time the Hutu were killing the Tutsi by the thousands, destroying their property, and looting.

In the ensuing violence, the colonial state found a pretext to break the backbone of the Tutsi nationalists. All Tutsi chiefs and subchiefs were replaced with Hutu. Thousands of Tutsi were killed. Others fled to the neighboring countries of Tanzania, Burundi, Uganda, and Congo. Some remained in their homes. Still others took refuge in the southeast of Rwanda in Nyamata, which was then infested with tsetse flies; many of them succumbed to diseases and food shortages.

The upheaval, popularly known as the Hutu Social Revolution of 1959, did not solve the Hutu–Tutsi conflict. Instead, the two ethnic groups reversed positions. The Hutu appropriated power and privileges hitherto monopolized by the Tutsi.

Social injustices against the Tutsis under the First Republic (1962-1973) of President Grégoire Kayibanda and under the Second Republic of President Juvénal Habyarimana (1973-1994) led the Tutsi to resort to armed struggle. In the early 1960s, bands of Tutsi guerrillas (popularly called *inyenzi* or "roaches") were attacking Rwanda. Before they petered out in 1967, their only achievement had been to escalate the conflict.

Indeed, the entire Great Lakes region has been rocked by political instability since the 1960s. In 1981, the current President of Uganda, Yoweri Museveni, started a guerrilla war in Uganda, and five years later he took power. About four thousand Rwandan refugees were in his army; shortly after victory, Ugandans' hostility against them became intense. Also in some rural areas, competition for pasture rights set Ugandans against the Rwandan refugees. Their needs to return home became pressing. In Burundi and Congo as well, Rwandan refugees had problems that motivated them to join the RPF (Rwandan Patriotic Front) when it was formed in Uganda in 1987 with a main objective of repatriating Rwandan refugees.

The repatriation of refugees was the last thing the Rwandan regime wanted to hear. President Habyarimana often declared in his speeches, "Rwanda is like a glass full of water. You can't add more water to it." This was an allusion to the overpopulation of Rwanda, which had the highest population density of any country in Africa (248 people per square mile) (Dorsey 1994, 2).

On October 1, 1990, RPF invaded Rwanda from Uganda. The war that ensued lasted for four years and aggravated the internal Hutu–Tutsi conflict. The regime's extremists' hate propaganda, broadcast through radio RTLMC (Free Radio-Television of Thousand Hills) and through print media, called for violence against the Tutsi. It is in this context that Ten Hutu Commandments, the rallying ideology of the extremists, were written and disseminated throughout the country. They were intended to destroy Tutsi–Hutu relationships and to prepare the Hutu to commit genocide.

The spark that ignited the genocide came on April 6, 1994. The plane carrying President Habyarimana and the President of Burundi home from peace negotiations was shot down as it approached Kigali airport. This act forced the long Rwandan conflict to its climax. A genocide ensued that continued for three months, until it was stopped by victorious RPF forces. It is estimated that nearly one million Tutsi and moderate Hutu were killed between April and July 1994.

The end of the genocide was not the end of Rwandan suffering. When the defeated Hutu army and the regime's political officers began to flee to the neighboring countries (Congo, Burundi, and Tanzania) they forced millions of Hutu to follow them. These refugees were used as hostages by the former regime officials, who wanted to show the international community that the new regime was unacceptable to millions of Hutu, and to get international assistance. Moreover, they recruited some of them to return and invade Rwanda from Congo.

Because of the threat posed to Rwanda by these refugees, the Rwandan army and Congolese rebels invaded Congo in 1996, and forced the majority of the refugees to return to Rwanda. In this war, the Congolese government headed by Mobutu Sese Seko was toppled because of its support for the former Rwandan regime's officials, who were plotting against the new government of Rwanda.

Many Hutu refugees died in the Congo, and some of those who returned to Rwanda were arrested and imprisoned for their role in the genocide. Others, on reaching their homes, found that their properties had been destroyed or taken over by Tutsi returnees, and some became victims of the survivors' revenge.

PERPETRATORS AND BYSTANDERS DURING THE GENOCIDE

There are no devils left in Hell. They are all in Rwanda.
—A Roman Catholic missionary[2]

Political violence has been a long-standing problem in Rwanda. In 1959 it was used to end the Tutsi grip on power. In the 1960s, it escalated as a result of the attempt by Tutsi refugees to regain power. In the 1970s, the northern Hutu used violence to overthrow the First Republic dominated by the southern Hutu, and in the 1980s the opposition to the Second Republic was silenced through repression and assassinations.

The pre-genocide violence and the 1994 genocide itself were aimed at safeguarding the status quo. In carrying it out, the ruling MRND (Revolutionary Movement for National Development) did the following:

- disseminated hate propaganda through newly established papers and journals (For example, to incite the predominantly illiterate Hutu population, radio RTLMC was established in 1993; it dehumanized the Tutsi and broadcast songs and programs intended to set the Hutu against the Tutsi.)

- formed a militia (*interahamwe*) and an extremist party CDR (Coalition for the Defense of Democracy) whose aim was to use violence to consolidate the regime

- procured and distributed arms to its supporters

- used bribery and intimidation to divide opposition parties, especially the Liberal Party, the Republican Democratic Movement, and the Social Democratic Party

---

[2] Quoted in *Time*, May 16, 1994; cited in Peterson 2000, 245.

The extremist propaganda, apart from setting the Hutu against the Tutsi, was aimed at encouraging and justifying the eventual violence against the Tutsi. According to Alison Des Forges, an American human rights activist at Human Rights Watch (Kimonyo 2000, 44-45), great pains were taken to convince the Hutu of the following:

- The Tutsi who would be given government posts under the Arusha Peace Agreement were related to those who held power before 1959.

- All the Tutsi inside the country had strong ties with RPF, which had recently invaded Rwanda from Uganda.

- If the Tutsi-dominated RPF took power, it would oppress the Hutu as the Tutsi had before 1959.

- The Tutsi were foreigners who should be driven out of the country.

- If the Hutu did not take preventive measures, the Tutsi would subjugate them again.

- Previous killings of the Tutsi and driving them out of the country had not solved the "Tutsi problem," so their total elimination was an indispensable solution.

- The Tutsi had the intention of eliminating the Hutu, so striking first was necessary.

The perpetrators of the genocide included the following:

- high-ranking civilian and military officials and big businessmen who were afraid of losing their positions and privileges in a future power-sharing arrangement

- middle-level leaders who wanted to advance their careers by implementing orders from the top

- grassroots leadership and the masses who blindly executed orders from above

- people who were coerced or intimidated to take part

- people who wanted to settle an old score

- poor people who wanted to loot or take over the victims' property, land, or animals

- people who were intoxicated by drugs or alcohol distributed by the leaders

- Hutu refugees from Burundi who were conscripted

The majority of the Hutu population did not participate in the violence. Some felt helpless because the ruthlessness of the killers prevented them from helping the victims. Some Hutu who had hidden Tutsi were forced to ask them to leave when it became dangerous to be found hiding them. A survivor in Kibungo told me that when the militia started searching Hutu homes, his host had told him emotionally : "Please go away to look for another hiding place. If they find you here, they will kill you and they won't spare me and my children."

In another incident in Kigali, a woman married to a soldier hid a girl on top of a room's ceiling. As the ceiling was made of old cardboard, the girl's body made a conspicuous bulge and her presence would have been obvious to anyone who looked up. After just a few days, the nervous woman, choking with tears, asked the girl to leave.

If Rwandan Christians—who were 88 percent of the population (62% Catholics and 26% Protestants) before the genocide (African Rights 1995, 868n)—had opposed the violence, Rwandan history would have been different. But before 1959, Tutsi domination was consolidated under Bishops Léon Classe and Laurent Deprimoz. The architect of the 1959 Revolution was Bishop André Perraudin, and Archbishop Vincent Nsengiyumva was the pillar of the Second Republic. All along, the Catholic Church ignored social injustices prevailing in society; its policy was to see no evil and to hear no evil.

The Catholic Church was divided also along ethnic lines. Local religious leaders had strong ethnic sentiments. Foreign religious leaders, too, were involved in ethnic politics and were partial toward either the Tutsi or the Hutu. This partiality is dramatically underscored in a legendary (if unverifiable) confessional exchange between a foreign priest and a Rwandan Catholic in Rwanda around 1959. I heard slightly different versions in the 1960s; the one I remember well is as follows :

Penitent: Father, I would like to confess that in the recent ethnic clashes I killed a person. I did not do it deliberately, circumstances forced me to do it. I place myself at the feet of our Lord and ask forgiveness.

Foreign white priest: My son, I sympathize with you and I am sorry that you are tormented by your conscience. But considering that a revolution is taking place, killing someone in self-defense like you did is excusable. My son, I am sure the Tutsi man you killed was one of the troublesome monarchical-communist-agitators. For the good of the Eternal Kingdom of our Lord, go in peace and co-operate with others to defend yourselves against those atheists. When victory has been consolidated, come back to me and I will give you an absolution for all your revolutionary transgressions. Meanwhile recite the Hail Mary . . .

Penitent: Sorry Father, I am a Tutsi and I killed a devout-Christian-revolutionary Hutu who wanted to kill my family. Give me an absolution now because within a few hours I will flee into exile.

Foreign white priest: (Blushing and fuming as he darted to his office to phone the police) Son, be patient and wait for me.

Penitent: Father, good-bye and best wishes in your struggle against
             monarchical-communists. It is becoming very late and I want
             to cross the border before nightfall.

All across Rwanda, respondents of this study have blamed the Catholic
Church for having failed to resolve the ethnic conflict over the years. They say
that the church was good at giving humanitarian aid to the oppressed rather than
working for peace and justice.

When violence started in the 1990s, religious leaders' ethnic loyalties overwhelmed them. Many Hutu priests and nuns supported the genocide in word and
action. Some are now in prison; others have fled abroad. Two Benedictine nuns,
Julienne Mukabutera and Consolata Mukangango from Butare diocese were
arrested in Belgium because they were alleged to have participated in the 1994
genocide. After a long trial in Brussels, they were found guilty of assisting the
militia in killing more than five thousand Tutsi who had sought safety at their
convent in Sovu. Sr. Consolata was sentenced to fifteen years in jail, and Sr.
Julienne to twelve years.

Some of the foreign church leaders exacerbated the conflict and violence
rather than resolving them. Two Catholic priests, Gabriel Maindron, a French-
man, and Carlo Bellomi, an Italian, have been implicated in the execution of the
genocide. The latter was imprisoned after the genocide but was released after a
short time due to poor health and advanced age.[3]

More than fifty Roman Catholic priests and nuns are believed to be in hiding
because of their participation in the genocide. At the International Criminal Tri-
bunal for Rwanda (ICTR) there are two Catholic priests, one Anglican bishop,
and an Adventist pastor awaiting trial for their roles in the 1994 genocide. By
condoning violence, such church leaders trampled on the sanctity of human life,
and their followers participated in it with the assurance of their approval.

FOREIGN INVOLVEMENT

The long Rwandan ethnic conflict was ignored by the international community for decades. When the RPF invaded Rwanda in October 1990, Rwanda's
conflict was suddenly in the limelight. Beginning in 1990, RPF rebels began
receiving material and diplomatic support from Uganda, while France backed the
predominantly Hutu Rwandan government. But Rwanda is a small, poor country
with no minerals or oil, and its agricultural production cannot satisfy the nutri-
tional needs of its own population of about 7.5 million. Rwanda is a landlocked
country of no strategic value to big powers. Some writers (Prunier 1995, 103-7;
Shawcross 2000, 126) have explained France's strong support for the Rwandan

---

[3] The French Christian publication *Les Dossiers de Golias* (1999) has extensively documented
both local and foreign priests' and nuns' participation in the genocide.

government on the basis of the personal friendship that existed between the countries' presidents at that time, François Mitterrand and Juvénal Habyarimana. In addition, France's military, financial, and diplomatic support were said to be tied to the historical rivalry between the anglophone and francophone powers. The RPF rebels who attacked Rwanda from Uganda were considered by France to be a tool of United States and Britain, meant to subjugate a francophone country. Michel Sitbon (1998, 38) rejects this reasoning; for him, France's main motive was economic leadership of the region. Rwanda is near mineral-rich Congo, and the French were afraid that anyone who controlled Rwanda would have the key to the Congo.

While the extremists prepared the genocide and the Rwandan government delayed the establishment of a broad-based transitional government, the international community ignored the warnings of General Roméo Dallaire of the UN peacekeeping forces about the impending violence. His 2,500-member police force of the United Nations Assistance Mission to Rwanda (UNAMIR) had been sent to the country in December 1993 to help in the establishment of a transitional government. But UNAMIR had no appropriate mandate, logistics, or weapons to defend the menaced population.

When the genocide began, the international community lacked the compassion and will to stop it. The Rwandan genocide was regarded, to borrow the words of British Prime Minister Chamberlain in the 1930s, "a quarrel in a faraway country between people of whom we know nothing" (Dobbs 2000, 36). The United States was reluctant to act. As late as June 1994, when asked about the situation in Rwanda and the position of the United States government, State Department spokeswoman Christine Shelly said: "We have every reason to believe that isolated acts of genocide have occurred." But when she was asked, "How many 'acts of genocide' does it take to make genocide?," she could not answer (Peterson 2000, 296).

When the genocide began in earnest, the UNAMIR peacekeeping force, inadequate in the first place, was reduced to 250 men. According to General Dallaire, if a UN force of five thousand men with an appropriate mandate and necessary weapons had been sent to Rwanda, the genocide would have been prevented. Des Forges asserts that the genocide was not prevented because "the Americans were interested in saving money, the Belgians were interested in saving face, and the French were interested in saving their ally, the genocidal government" (Shawcross 2000, 145).

DATA COLLECTION AND METHODOLOGY

When fieldwork for this project on grassroots responses of Christians in situations of violent conflict began in Rwanda early in 2000, the prevailing conditions influenced my sampling procedure. The evolution of the Rwandan conflict over decades had led to the emergence of specific groups that shared similar problems and expectations. These groups had come into being depending on the roles they had played in the conflict. My data collection took these groups into consideration, though as time passes their boundaries are becoming indistinct. The groups are as follows:

- earlier generations of refugees, mainly Tutsi who had gone into exile in 1959, the 1960s, and 1973, to Burundi, Uganda, Tanzania, and elsewhere

- Hutu who fled into exile in 1994 when the genocidal regime collapsed, and later returned to Rwanda

- genocide survivors, i.e, the Tutsi who did not go into exile between 1959 and 1994

- the Hutu who did not go into exile in 1994

- prisoners charged with genocide (men, women, and children), who numbered about 135,000 in 2000

- Twa, who constitute 1 percent of the population and are found side by side with all the groups mentioned above

To examine their different experiences during and after the violence, my research covered four provinces: Kibungo, Kigali-Rural, Butare, and Mutara. In Kibungo, one rural district, Rukira, was covered. In Mutara, Gahini was chosen because of its Anglican predominance and its long, clean record of fighting to end the Tutsi–Hutu divide. Three other rural areas covered were Nyamata in Kigali-Rural province, and Mbazi and Kigembe in Butare province. Nyamata interested me because of its large Tutsi population, which dates back to the settling of Tutsi refugees from many parts of Rwanda during the 1959–1960 violence. Kigembe and Mbazi districts in Butare province have Hutu and Tutsi returnees from Burundi and Congo, as does Rukira district in Kibungo province.

To take into account rural-urban differences, the research included Butare and its university campus, Kibungo, and Kigali, the capital. Interviews were also done in four prisons: Butare, Kigali, Kibuye, and Gitarama.

The sources of data that were used in my study are as follows:

- Primary sources such as official documents, reports of commissions and organizations

- secondary data sources such as published and unpublished literature and conference proceedings

- qualitative questionnaires (These were distributed in four provinces. About 600 questionnaires were distributed because Rwanda has a high rate of illiteracy and I expected that some would be poorly completed, others would be illegible, and some would not be returned at all. Of the questionnaires distributed, 486 were returned. A third of these came from urban areas. Only 190 women, 64 of them from rural areas, completed the questionnaires.)

- semi-structured and open interviews (These were carried out in rural and urban areas, and involved 45 people: 30 were peasants or professionals, 3 were high ranking prison officials and 12 were genocide prisoners). Prisoners who were interviewed included a former cabinet minister, a nun, a pastor, a priest, a driver, a peasant, and middle-level professionals. To encourage more honest answers and freedom of expression, a tape recorder was not used; respondents feared that government agents could use what they said against them.

- quantitative questionnaires assessing gender differences in peacemaking actions and motivations (These were completed by 72 people, including both women and men: 42 were Hutu and 30 Tutsi.)

- my personal observations and experiences (When the conflict escalated in 1959, I was old enough to observe the different responses of my neighbors. After 1959, when my family fled to the Congo, I was a distant witness of the growing conflict in Rwanda. Almost four decades later, after repatriation, I began to participate in peacemaking educational activities at the grassroots.)

PEACEMAKING EFFORTS AND MOTIVATIONS

By far, the most frequently reported form of peacemaking in Rwanda was relationship building (for example, striking up conversations with members of the opposing group, visiting them in their homes, etc.). This was followed by acts of service (e.g., sheltering people in danger and sharing of resources) and confrontation of perpetrators of violence. Praying for peace was not frequently mentioned, and it was an activity that women engaged in more than men (see Table 1).

The most common motivation for peacemaking was practical (e.g., "to gain the trust of the Hutu" or "because fighting keeps us poor"), followed by ideological (e.g., "I believe that we are all equal," or "I oppose discrimination and impunity"). Less frequently cited motivations were relational (e.g., "for the sake of my children," or "because I can't stand to see other people suffer") and religious ("I try to be a good Christian," or "God wills for us to live in peace") (see Table 2).

GRASSROOTS CHRISTIAN RESPONSES TO VIOLENCE

Some were educated, others barely literate. They weren't all religious, they weren't all brave. What they did share, however, was compassion, empathy, an intolerance of injustice and an ability to endure risk beyond what one wants to believe.

—Block and Drucker 1992, 31

During the Rwandan genocide, many Hutu men and women worked for peace, and many lives were saved as a result of their compassion. They are unsung heroes whose simple and sometimes bold acts made a difference. Many lost their lives in the course of aiding others.

As their houses burned, as they fled from their killers, as their properties were being looted or destroyed, Tutsi in many parts of the country ran or fell into the helping arms of Hutu, some of whom they knew while others were complete strangers. This happened repeatedly even during the genocide, when helping victims meant risking one's own life and the lives of family members.

During the 1994 genocide killings, apart from some instances of bribery, many who helped others did not do so for personal gain, but out of compassion and love. How endangered Tutsi and moderate Hutu were helped was conditioned by factors such as the extent of one's willingness to take risks or one's depth of Christian morality; the number of victims involved, the availability of necessary means; the expected duration of assistance; the relationship of the victim and the helper; the nature of the surroundings; the number of killers in the vicinity; and the nature and intensity of their operations.

Prior to the genocide of 1994, neighbors did much to help those targeted for political violence. Without helpful neighbors, my family and I would have perished in 1959. I remember well the role they played.

It was November 1959. I was in class. I saw smoke billowing from many burning houses. Gradually, the sky was being enveloped in darkness. Without explanation, our headmaster sent his pupils home. Approaching my house, I was shocked to see strangers going back and forth from our house, carrying away our possessions. As I stood there uncomprehending, a Hutu neighbor materialized from nowhere and pulled me stealthily into the bush. He started to run while pulling me along. After a short distance, he stopped and told me sternly, "If anyone asks you who you are, tell him that you are a Hutu and that you are my son. Don't be afraid, I am taking you to your parents." I did not know then what Hutu meant, but I was too afraid and confused to worry about definitions. He took me to my parents, who were huddled in a dark corner of another neighbor's house.

Our neighbors divided tasks to protect us and to feed us. We stayed in hiding for three weeks before we came out into the open. For a while the situation was calm, then it started to deteriorate. One dark morning before cockcrow, I was yanked from bed and my family fled into exile.

Many Tutsi like my family were saved by their neighbors during periods of violence in the 1960s and 1970s. Where neighbors were unreliable or unable to help, particularly when great numbers of refugees were involved, the victims went to nearby churches. Before the genocide, churches had been safe havens; no one dared to harm anyone on the holy premises. Clergy then protected the victims until it was safe for them to return to their homes, or assisted them to flee abroad.

During the 1994 genocide there were no widespread organized efforts to help potential victims apart from those undertaken by RPF. However, spontaneous assistance was given to thousands of refugees who had sought safety around church compounds such as Kabgayi in Gitarama province; the churches of St.

Famille, St. Michel, and St. Paul; and St. André Secondary School in Kigali. At St. Famille, many survivors were aided by Missionary Sisters of Charity of Mother Teresa. The mother superior is fondly remembered for her kindness, courage and mollifying spirit.

In some parts of Rwanda, government-sponsored massacres did not take place as envisaged; some security agents and local leaders sided with potential victims. In Cyangugu province about ten security agents refused to participate in killings; instead, they comforted the Tutsi who were being held at Kamembe stadium and joined with them in prayer. The extremists tried several times to involve these agents in the killings but they refused. They paid for their righteousness with their lives.

Some leaders at the grassroots level also resisted the violence and tried to defuse it. Examples can be found in Giti district in the eastern province of Byumba and in two districts of Butare province: Ntyazo and Nyabisindu.

Giti is the only district in Rwanda where the genocidal government failed utterly to draw the population into committing massacres. This was mainly due to its mayor, Edouard Sebushumba. Before the genocide, he did all he could to root out ethnic division, partisan dissension, and the recruitment of party militias. When the massacres started in April 1994, the mayor successfully prevented them from occurring. The mayors of Ntyazo and Nyabisindu districts, Narcise Nyagasaza and Jean Marie Vianney Gisagara respectively, opposed the genocide and mobilized grassroots forces to resist it. But in the end, they were defeated and killed.

Righteous people, lacking organization, coordination, and leadership during the violence, tried as individuals to help those in need. Some of their good deeds ended happily, but others had some catastrophic consequences. Examples follow.

A woman named Pamela was hidden along with three other people by the owner of a small shop in the town of Gisenyi. They were concealed under sacks of groceries with such ingenuity that they were comfortable, and yet when the killers came to buy supplies they suspected nothing. As the groceries became depleted and as the raging war prevented the acquisition of new supplies, the grocer was forced to find a new hiding place for the four people. He came up with a brilliant plan: at his grocery he built a false wall with a small window. Behind this wall a tiny, ideal hiding place was created.

In the middle of June, some of the killers let it be known that if any Tutsi in hiding paid $50, he would be given passage to Congo, just a few miles away. The refugees at the grocery store had no money, so the grocer paid the $200 ransom, probably by dipping into his life savings and by borrowing. They were given a safe passage and the grocer himself escorted them up to the border. Pamela narrated this story to me in December 1999, when she was admitted at the University in Butare.

A kind Hutu man was forced by circumstances to kill a young Tutsi boy in order to save many Tutsi lives, as well as the lives of his family and himself. After the genocide, he was arrested; he is now awaiting trial. He had hidden many

Tutsi, young and old, in his home. To deflect suspicion, he would regularly arrive at a nearby checkpoint early in the morning and would shout extremist expletives against the Tutsi until his voice was hoarse, in order to convince his colleagues that he was strongly anti-Tutsi.

One morning, tragedy struck. A young boy crawled unnoticed from the hiding place and went for a stroll, looking for playmates. He was too young to understand why he should be confined to a dark room. He was spotted simultaneously by the militia and by the man sheltering him. The man knew what awaited him, his family, and all the refugees if the boy were interrogated. So the man made a terribly painful decision, perhaps the best under the circumstances. He dashed toward the boy shouting insults against the Tutsi, and with one machete blow he killed him. I was told about this while on fieldwork in Kibungo province.

Some people helped potential victims because of preexisting friendship or acquaintance, while others accepted bribes to help, and still others proved their humanity by assisting strangers. Some parents and their children in Butare were running for their lives. They came across a woman who was working on her farm. As their pursuers were very close at their heels, they dove for cover not far away from the woman. Within minutes, the killers reached the woman and asked her which direction the fugitives had taken. Without hesitating, the woman pointed at the path they had allegedly gone down. Long after the killers had vanished, the kind woman went to her house and brought ripe bananas for the family. She showed them the shortest route to the Burundi border and wished them luck. I interviewed one of these family members in June 2001.

Some people capitalized on the situation but, nonetheless, discreetly helped some of those who were in danger. A man in Butare survived because he came face to face with such a person just before he was about to be killed. He was in a pickup truck that was taking him to a killing site. The survivor told me:

> The pickup truck was speeding towards the killing site. The policeman kept looking at me. Then he told me, "If you give me your watch, I can reward you more than you expect." I did not understand that sort of proposition. When he repeated it, I removed my cheap watch and handed it to him. After all, in my position I had no use of it any more. No sooner had I handed it to him than he gave me a strong kick and shove and I found myself flying from the truck and landing on the tarmac. Fortunately, the truck was moving slowly. I lay sprawled on the tarmac for some minutes, then I realized what the proposition was all about. As I crawled to the side of the road, I saw another man falling from the truck.

DEFIANCE AND RESISTANCE, VIOLENT AND NONVIOLENT

From 1959 until the 1994 genocide, Tutsi engaged in various forms of defiance and resistance. Tutsi resistance in 1959 and in the early 1960s was easily suppressed by the Belgian and Congolese soldiers. An old man who participated in resistance in Gikongoro remembers that on several occasions, in order to undermine resistance, the army flew over their positions in low-flying helicopters and sometimes dropped bombs.

The Tutsi who had remained in Rwanda devised various ways to survive and prosper in a hostile environment. To get ahead, Tutsi forged alliances with Hutu through marriages and bribed officials to change their identity cards. Tutsi businessmen in quest of protection gave free shares of their businesses to prominent Hutu. For the majority of Tutsi, closely knit associations and partnerships were formed to ensure their security as well as their educational and business interests.

When the genocide began, those targeted used all possible means to survive: bribery, lying about one's ethnic affiliation, and hiding in every available place, as well as fleeing to safety in neighboring countries (Democratic Republic of Congo, Burundi, and Tanzania), RPF-controlled areas, and a few safe areas under the surveillance of UN forces.

The victims' responses to violence depended on many factors, such as the distance to a neighboring country, the distribution of the Tutsi population (especially in rural areas), physical characteristics of the surroundings (such as forests, hills, and swamps), the local leadership's attitude toward violence, and the disposition of the enemy.

In rural areas where Hutu were opposed to extremist ideology, Hutu and Tutsi organized themselves and defended their communities against attacks from the outside. In the first weeks of April 1994, acts of joint resistance were common in Butare and Gitarama provinces. But the show of force by the government and the propaganda on radio RTLMC discouraged most Hutu, and they stopped resisting.

The major examples of Tutsi armed resistance took place in Butare, Kibuye, Kibungo, Gikongoro, and Kigali-Rural provinces, areas that had large Tutsi populations and a tradition of resistance since the 1960s. Resisters during the 1994 genocide were poorly armed. Some carried spears, machetes, and clubs. Others had nothing to resist with apart from stones, bricks, and sticks. When the Tutsi who had sought refuge at schools and churches realized the inevitability of their extermination, they used anything available to confront the killers. In the cases of the Nyange and Kibeho churches, the enemies were repelled several times but both churches were eventually destroyed in order to kill all those sheltered inside.

The resistance of these Tutsi was hopeless in the face of the forces allied against them. But according to a resister who survived in Kibungo, sometimes a variety of objectives were achieved, including dying an honorable death rather than dying on one's knees while begging for mercy from unmerciful killers; engaging the enemy long enough to give old people, women, and children the opportunity to run as far away as possible; delaying mass killings in expectation of the RPF's arrival or the international community's intervention, such as that of UNAMIR forces; or denying the enemy an easy victory by inflicting heavy losses upon them.

Tutsi resisters chose hilly and wooded areas in order to fight more effectively. In Butare and Gikongoro provinces, refugees sought safety in the Bitare hills. Prolonged resistance there enabled small groups of refugees to flee in different directions toward Burundi. In leaving the Bitare hills, small groups were preferred to avoid detection and to minimize casualties in case of ambush.

The most celebrated resistance during the genocide took place in the Bisesero hills in Kibuye province and lasted for three months. In April 1994, about fifty thousand Tutsi took refuge in the Bisesero hills. Attacks against them were repelled by well-organized action; pitched battles raged from April to June 1994. The resisters had many disadvantages; lack of arms, food, reinforcements, and medical supplies, combined with heavy rains, severely weakened them. The importance of the Bisesero resistance was not the number of people who survived—only about one thousand people did—but the resisters' spirit of courage, unity, determination and resilience.[4]

Many targeted people engaged the killers on an individual basis in desperate combat in order to die with dignity or to save their loved ones. Many others did not raise a finger against their killers, but jeered them with their last breath. Killers were taken aback when their victims spat in their faces and taunted them.

Long after the genocide, armed supporters of the former regime continued killing the Tutsi. In March 1997, they stormed into Nyange Secondary School in Kibuye province and in one of the classrooms told the students to separate themselves according to their ethnic origins: the Hutu were to stand on one side and the Tutsi on the other. If the students had done it, they would have risked the lives of the Tutsi, so they refused. Before they abandoned the site, the assailants threw grenades at the students, three of whom died. The students of Nyange have won national accolades for standing up against the instigators of ethnic division.

As documented by Muligande (2000, 94), the Episcopal parish of Gahini has played a significant role in peacemaking. When violence broke out in 1959, the Gahini church became a sanctuary for all those who were in danger. The victims were given humanitarian aid and sometimes smuggled out of the country. The church's assistance to the Tutsi did not please Belgian colonial officials; consequently two of its leaders, Joe Church and Geoffrey Hindley were asked to leave Rwanda in 1961.

During the 1994 genocide, Gahini once more became a safe haven for the Tutsi, and after the genocide the church helped the returnees to build new lives. Six years after the genocide Reverend Simon Banyanga, a Hutu, told me how his parishioners helped many Tutsi refugees by hiding them in the church. This was corroborated by Canon Enoch Kayumbo, a Tutsi, when I interviewed him in February 2000. According to Canon Enoch, Gahini parishioners did this because they "had been imbued with strong Christian faith which could not be exchanged with politicians' promises of worldly wealth and prestige."

There were also Catholics who sacrificed their lives during the genocide. The most celebrated martyrs are Felicité Niyitegeka, a Catholic lay worker from Gisenyi town, and Fr. Jean Bosco Munyaneza of Mukarange Parish. Before the genocide, Felicité, a Hutu, was a champion of peace. When the genocide began,

---

[4] The Biserero resistance is well documented in African Rights 1999.

many Tutsi sought refuge at St. Pierre Center where she worked. She assisted them with their daily needs, and she helped some to flee to safety; when the killers came, she refused to leave. Her brother, an army colonel, sent her many messages asking her to leave the Tutsi, but she refused and died with them (Des Forges 1999, 248). In 2001 she was declared a national hero by the government; she will be reburied in the Heroes Cemetery in Kigali.

Fr. Jean Bosco Munyaneza, a Hutu, died under similar circumstances. He refused to leave the Tutsi who had sought refuge at the Mukarange Parish. A survivor told me that when Munyaneza was asked by the killers why he could not leave them to their fate, he told them that he was a shepherd working for the Lord and could not leave his flock. During the genocide, many priests could have avoided suffering or death had they just walked a few meters away from the Tutsi crowds. But in almost all dioceses there were priests who risked their lives to save lives (Les Dossiers de Golias 1999, 246-49).

Some foreign religious leaders refused offers of evacuation when violence escalated. Many of these decided to remain in order to help those who were in need. At St. André Secondary School, Father Henri Blanchard from France and Otto Mayer, from Germany, fed, treated, and tried to save the Tutsi from the killers. In all corners of Rwanda, Christians have their local heroes. In the parish of Kaduha, Gikongoro province, survivors recall with gratitude the moral courage and compassion of a German nun, Sr. Milgitha Kosser, who fed, hid, and helped refugees to escape. A plot to murder her was hatched partly because of her opposition to killings and partly because "she confronted one of the priests for selling foodstuffs donated to refugees."[5] She went into hiding for a short time, before coming back to resume her humanitarian work. After the genocide, Sr. Milgitha and other survivors worked hard to erect a memorial for the almost twenty thousand Tutsi who perished at Kaduha church. The memorial was inaugurated in July 2001.

POST-VIOLENCE HEALING EFFORTS

By the time the genocide came to an end in July 1994, the country had been devastated. The genocide had aggravated the Hutu–Tutsi divide; the social infrastructure had been destroyed; and insecurity and lawlessness were rampant. About one million Tutsi and moderate Hutu had been killed, and three million Hutu had been forced into exile. Thousands of orphans, widows, and unaccompanied children roamed and foraged in rural and urban areas. Thousands of genocide suspects were increasingly overcrowding prisons.

The first step in dealing with these problems was to form a government. The Transitional Government of National Unity was formed in July 1994 and is still composed of eight political parties. One important aspect of Rwandan reconcili-

---

[5] Online source: http://www.nationaudio.com, Amnesty Lessons from Rwanda July 19, 2001.

ation has been the attempt to ensure power sharing between the Tutsi and Hutu. This was built into the formation of the current government, which is based on the Arusha Peace Agreement of August 1993. The Agreement has five protocols: rule of law, power sharing, repatriation of refugees, integration of armed forces, and miscellaneous issues. Since its inception, the government has instituted power sharing not only among the eight political parties but also among Hutu and Tutsi at all levels. Institutionalized discrimination based on ethnicity is being combated. In civil service, employment is based on merit, and access to educational opportunities depends on passing examinations.

In restoring security and ending lawlessness, the government has ended killings of the Tutsi by genocidal forces, as well as revenge killings and persecution of the Hutu by survivors. It has restored Hutu property and land occupied by the Tutsi returnees.

To promote good governance, the Transitional Government is in the process of democratizing and decentralizing the society. In March 1999 and March 2001, grassroots elections at cell, sector, district, and municipality levels were held. According to an official of the National Electoral Commission, the elections consolidate peace and empower "competent, willing and responsible people capable of motivating the population to participate in their own socio-economic development" (Bazivamo 2001, 3). A new constitution is being prepared by a Legal and Constitutional Commission relying on a nationwide consultation, which aims to collect views on the type of constitution and legal reforms the country should have.

No one can build peace on an empty stomach. Measures to alleviate poverty are being undertaken in partnership with bilateral and multilateral donors. Much has been done and is still being done to assure that every Rwandan has decent food and adequate shelter as well as easy access to clean water and to health care and educational services.

There are conflicts that need resolution so that a lasting peace can be attained. Some external Hutu and Tutsi opposition groups are trying to undermine the reconciliation process through propaganda. There is also a new party inside Rwanda —the Party for Democracy and Renewal (PDR-*Ubuyanja*)—whose ethnic rhetoric does not augur well for reconciliation.

Genocide memory is another source of conflict. Some Hutu argue that it revives anger among the survivors and arouses guilt among the Hutu. The survivors argue that historical memory is essential to the society to constantly combat all causes of violence. It both honors the dead, they say, and appeases the survivors. Historical memory is a delicate matter that needs to be handled carefully if all are to live in peace.

The healing of Rwandan society cannot be achieved outside the regional context. Ethnic and political wars in the Great Lakes region must be resolved before each country can attain durable peace. Today Congo is a complex theater of war, pitting Rwanda, Uganda, Burundi, and Congolese rebels against the Congo, Zimbabwe, Namibia, Angola, and rebels from Rwanda, Burundi, and Uganda. The

Lusaka Peace Accords, whose major provisions are disarmament, repatriation, and reintegration of rebel forces from Rwanda, Burundi, and Uganda as a precondition for withdrawal of their forces from the Democratic Republic of Congo, must be respected if Rwanda and the region as a whole are to enjoy a sustainable peace.

Some progress has been made in healing the society. To demonstrate this, I will highlight the activities of five institutions that are much written about and were often referred to by my respondents. These are the National Unity and Reconciliation Commission (NURC), the National Human Rights Commission (NHRC), the Ministry of Justice's *gacaca* judicial system, the National Fund for the Assistance of the Survivors of the Genocide and Massacres (FARG), and the churches. While not initiatives of grassroots people, these institutional efforts involve a great deal of popular participation, especially NURC's solidarity camps, *gacaca*, and church activities.

UNITY AND RECONCILIATION INITIATIVES

Because unity and reconciliation are the foundations of sustainable peace and development, a great deal of energy and resources are being invested in them. The official process began with a series of Reflection Meetings (between May 1998 and March 1999), which brought together 164 participants drawn from the government, civil society, the private sector, and educational institutions. As a result of these meetings, participants recommended the formation of a national commission. In March 1999 the National Unity and Reconciliation Commission was established (NURC 2000b, 2). It has nine objectives, which revolve around raising popular awareness about issues such as harmonious coexistence, the ideals of unity and reconciliation, and the importance of joint socioeconomic programs.

In planning and implementing its activities, NURC regularly consults civil society, government institutions, professionals, vulnerable people, students, and business people. Foreigners and Rwandans residing in diaspora are also involved in consultations.

In its peacemaking efforts, NURC has three main activities: civic education, community development initiatives, and conflict mediation. Civic education undertaken by NURC has had a positive impact in the country. This education takes place mainly in solidarity camps (*ingando*), whose participants are youth, students, leaders at all levels, security agents, and former rebels. Between June 1999 and June 2000, some eleven thousand people participated in solidarity camp activities (NURC 2000b).

It has been asserted that, "since wars begin in the minds of men, it is in the minds of men that the defenses of peace must be constructed" (European Centre for Conflict Prevention 1999, 161). The solidarity camps help instill in the participants the tenets of the rule of law, democracy, tolerance, and patriotism. They also impart to them skills to better understand their own history. Moreover, solidarity camps encourage interaction of people from different ethnic groups, different regions, and different social backgrounds. The transparency encouraged in the camps extends beyond them after the participants complete their courses.

Every group has its special emphasis. The students and youth are taught the virtues of tolerance and solidarity and their country's history. The former rebels are prepared for integration into civilian life and are taught about unity and reconciliation. Leaders are taught skills based on equality, justice, democracy, and transparency. A newly admitted student at the National University of Rwanda, who had just completed a solidarity camp course, told me in May 2001 that what impressed him in the course was "the forging of good inter-ethnic understanding and transparency in discussing our tragic past."

NURC also collaborates with civil society in its civic education programs. Catholic Relief Services (CRS) from the United States sponsored the Catholic Church's organization of solidarity camps in the Byumba, Kigali, Butare, and Kabgayi dioceses. CRS also supported the Episcopal Church in its organization of camps in Gahini and Ruhengeri dioceses. Local associations and groups such as the Muslim Youth Council, the National Youth Council, and the National Women's Council are also working with NURC. And in schools and institutions of higher learning, students themselves are organizing clubs. A high school student in Kigali, telling me about his school's unity club (May 2001), had this to say:

> We organize discussions and lectures about unity and reconciliation. We invite political and religious leaders as well as academicians. The attendance is often big but this depends on the popularity of the guest speaker and the subject to be dealt with. Last time, when our topic was "Collective Guilt versus Individual Responsibility," our hall was overcrowded. We have also a cultural group that composes reconciliation songs and performs drama.

In its civic education program, NURC does not depend on solidarity camps alone. It has a newsletter that is disseminated across the country and a weekly radio program. Its activities are well covered by the print media, radio, and television. Nor does NURC underestimate the role of the arts and athletics in peacemaking. It promotes sports, songs, poems, and dances dedicated to unity and reconciliation. Now and then, the NURC organizes competitions which attract many artists.

In its community development initiatives, NURC promotes unity and harmonious coexistence while at the same time promoting the economic well-being of people. Poverty breeds violence, so alleviation of poverty is the second major activity NURC is using to build peace. The target groups are multiethnic associations and clubs. Those who benefit from this program include the handicapped, the aged, street children and orphans, Twa, genocide widows, demobilized soldiers (both from the Rwandan Patriotic Army and from the army of the former regime), the homeless, and child-headed families. Economic activities supported by NURC include agriculture, animal husbandry, poultry farming, and small businesses such as carpentry, metalworking, sewing, and trading. As a result of the destruction of houses during the genocide and the repatriation of the "old caseload" refugees, there are many people who either have no home or who live in dilapidated buildings or makeshift plastic-sheeting shelters. NURC helps some organizations to build houses for the needy.

HUMAN RIGHTS AND PEACE

> Sinhalese politician: *We should live in peace.*
> Tamil woman: *First let us enjoy our rights, and then we will talk about peace.*
> —European Centre for Conflict Prevention 1999, 170

One of the most important ways of healing Rwandan society is to consolidate respect for human rights. If people live in fear, if they are denied civil, political, social, and economic rights, then the healing process cannot succeed.

The current government established the National Human Rights Commission (NHRC) on March 12, 1999. The main activities of the commission are "to investigate and follow-up any violation of human rights committed by state institutions or individuals," to sensitize and educate the population about its rights, and to inform relevant authorities to "initiate judicial proceedings in case of human rights violations by anyone" (NHRC 2000, 10).

Before it prepared its three-year plan of action, the commission consulted the population through visits to all provinces. During those visits three questions were administered to one thousand people. People were asked which were the main human rights problems in Rwanda that should be urgently addressed, how to eradicate the culture of impunity, and how to make every Rwandan know his/her rights and respect his/her neighbor's (NHRC 2000, 45).

In 1999, the commission conducted sensitization campaigns about human rights among students in solidarity camps, grassroots leaders, middle-level leaders, and nongovernmental human rights activists. It also established links with external human rights organizations. But its early attempts at human rights protection were disappointing. The commission's advocacy and investigative activities are becoming more successful due to its newly opened provincial offices and its close collaboration with police, army, the judiciary, educational institutions, and human rights organizations through their umbrella organization CLADHO (Collective of Leagues and Associations of Human Rights).

In 2000 the commission's sensitization campaigns involved 900 security agents, 2,400 grassroots leaders, and 120 middle-level leaders. It organized meetings with local human rights organizations and conducted meetings in rural areas (NHRC 2001, 26-31).

The complaints brought to the commission have involved labor and education disputes; ownership disputes over land, property, and animals; killings; and arbitrary imprisonment. Any complaints that the commission is unable to redress are redirected to appropriate agencies (NHRC 2001, 21-23).

There is still a long way to go. Many people's rights are still being violated. Fortunately, grassroots organizations, civil society, and government institutions are working hard to promote the basic rights of all, regardless of one's sex, creed, and ethnic origin.

TRUTH AND JUSTICE

The Rwandan judicial system was destroyed by the genocide. Many judges, prosecutors, lawyers, and law clerks were killed or imprisoned or fled into exile. In a prison population numbering some 135,000 in December of 2000, only 5,229 had been tried in four years' time. If the speed of trials in Rwandan courts did not increase, it was estimated that it would take more than a century to try all the genocide suspects!

The Rwandan government has thus resorted to a traditional participatory system of justice called *gacaca* in the Kinyarwanda language. Traditionally, many offenses (excluding crimes like treason or murder) were dealt with by the families and neighbors of offenders and plaintiffs. Led by elders (presumably the wisest community members and the most conversant with customary law), the *gacaca* participants normally congregated in the open, on a lawn somewhere in the village (the literal translation of *gacaca* is "lawn"). This allowed many people to participate.

Gacaca served (and is now expected to serve) four important functions in the society: it brought together the offender and the offended; it sought the truth; it addressed the conflict; and it reconciled the parties. The government is tailoring traditional *gacaca* to the current Rwandan situation. The hope is that it will contribute to the healing process because, if it works properly:

- the truth about the long Rwandan conflict and genocide will be established
- those presumed guilty will get a platform to defend themselves
- it will consolidate the struggle against impunity
- it will speed up genocide trials
- it will appease the victims who could otherwise resort to retribution
- it will encourage offenders to ask forgiveness and the offended to give it
- it will foster unity and reconciliation
- it will promote democratic participation and interethnic cooperation, since it is "owned" by all ethnic groups
- it will be a permanent conflict mediation organ in the society
- genocide negation and historical revisionism will be dealt a blow

Gacaca trials will now take place at all four tiers of the country's administrative hierarchy: cell, sector, district, and province. In accordance with the Gacaca Organic Law of 1996, the genocide perpetrators have been divided into four categories depending on the nature of crimes allegedly committed between October

1990 and December 1994. The first category will be tried through the classical judicial system (rather than *gacaca*) and is composed of leaders and people who planned, supervised, and zealously committed genocide crimes. It also includes people who committed heinous sexual crimes. The district will try the second category, which is composed of perpetrators of criminal acts which resulted in deaths. The sector level will try the third category of people, those who are charged with assault. The cell will try the fourth category, composed of people charged with crimes related to property.[6]

Those found guilty will be punished according to the Gacaca Organic Law. The first category's maximum penalty is death, and the second category is life imprisonment. The third category's maximum penalty is imprisonment and the payment of reparations. For the fourth category, there is no imprisonment but only the payment of reparations. Those prisoners who confess their crimes will receive reduced punishments.

Sensitization campaigns about *gacaca* have been in full swing since its inception. These have been undertaken by the government, civil society, and grassroots organizations. They use radio, television, seminars, meetings, leaflets, and pamphlets. To reach larger audiences, songs, dances, and sports events are organized. According to the widely distributed *gacaca* leaflets, these events are meant to encourage the population to attend meetings about *gacaca;* to reveal the truth when *gacaca* trials begin; to be part of *gacaca* process; to elect honest and patriotic persons in the *gacaca* judicial system; to fight corruption, bigotry and despotism in the *gacaca* trials; and to work in full freedom without fear.

As of this writing, the *gacaca* trials were scheduled to begin in May 2002. About 260,000 people at the grassroots have been elected to participate in the trials, and their training is under way.

There are fears that *gacaca* may not be effective because of insufficient preparations, lack of adequate financial and material resources, incompetence, corruption, dishonesty, and the slow pace of trials. Nevertheless, with no other solutions to judicial problems in sight, the nation is placing its hope in *gacaca* as a culturally appropriate initiative aimed at healing the society through community justice.

SURVIVING SURVIVAL

In its healing efforts, one of the government priorities is to give the survivors of the genocide and the massacres assistance that will enable them to "survive survival." The survivors lost everything—their families and their properties—and some were traumatized. To help them and so to facilitate reconciliation, the government has established the National Fund for Assistance to Genocide and Massacre Survivors (FARG). The government is to contribute 5 percent of its fiscal and nonfiscal revenues to the fund (FARG 2000d, 8-9). FARG raises additional funds from various other sources.

---

[6] See Gasibirege and Babalola 2001 on the categorization of Rwandan genocidal crimes.

In June 2000, the number of official survivors stood at nearly three hundred thousand. The elderly, the handicapped, orphans, the homeless, and impoverished widows have been given assistance. Another major humanitarian activity was the burial with dignity of the remains of genocide victims found scattered across the country.

To rebuild people's lives, FARG helps survivors to establish profit-generating businesses and to access education, housing, health care, and legal assistance. To start businesses, individuals and survivors' associations receive low-interest loans. Rural survivors benefit from FARG's "A Cow for a Family" project. This aims at giving the survivors animals that are the source of milk, money, and compost. Over twelve thousand cows have already been distributed in all provinces (see FARG 2000b).

FARG supports orphans and youth from families impoverished by the genocide. It admits them to secondary schools, technical schools, and institutions of higher learning. To deal with traumatic problems suffered by some of them, students can attend psychosocial training, including how to deal with trauma.

During the genocide, the victims' houses were demolished. FARG is assisting the survivors with accommodations, settling them in planned villages, helping them to rehabilitate their houses whenever possible or constructing new ones for them, buying houses for the needy, and helping those with bank loans to repay them lest the banks take over their houses.

Most of the genocide survivors are too poor to meet their medical costs. Some of them need normal medical services while others need special medical treatment, for example, women who have disabilities as a result of genital mutilation or repeated rapes, and those afflicted with sexually transmitted diseases such as AIDS. There are also many women and men who have bodily disabilities inflicted by their assailants. Many, too, are suffering from psychological trauma. FARG collaborates with survivors' associations such as AVEGA AGAHOZO (Association of Genocide Widows), which runs services for trauma, rape, and sexual mutilation victims. Survivors who have visual problems are provided with glasses. Those who lost arms or legs receive orthopedic assistance. Survivors who have complicated health problems may be sent abroad for treatment, especially to South Africa, Belgium, Germany, and Italy (FARG 2000c, 26).

FARG gives the survivors legal assistance. This enables them to lodge genocide complaints in the courts, acting as witnesses, claiming reparations, and participating in other matters related to justice.

The management of FARG has faced many problems: lack of adequate staff, corruption, mismanagement, and lack of data about those who deserve to be assisted. Sometimes well-off survivors receive assistance to the detriment of the needy ones. In its three-year plan 2001-2003, FARG aims to improve its project management by working with religious organizations such as Caritas, the Josephite Brothers, and the Missionary Sisters of Charity of Mother Teresa.

Survivors do not depend only on FARG for their socioeconomic well-being. There are many associations working to improve their living conditions, to heal their psychological wounds, to keep alive the genocide memory, and to struggle against historical revisionism and negation. Apart from IBUKA, an umbrella organization of all survivors' associations which runs FARG activities, and AVEGA AGAHOZO (which has twenty-five thousand widow members) there are many other survivors' associations in all provinces.

HEALING BODY, MIND, AND SOUL

If we go wrong and you keep quiet, one day you may have to answer our mistakes, as the nation today needs a conscience and you, the church, are that conscience.

—Mzee Jomo Kenyatta,
First President of Kenya

After the genocide, the Catholic Church began working hard to heal Rwandan society. It is now putting great effort into reviving Christian faith, helping to reconcile the victims and the perpetrators, and providing humanitarian and developmental assistance to the population.

The weeks and months following the genocide were difficult. Problems were many. Not least among them was the severely eroded moral authority of an institution with many leaders who had been complicit in the genocide. Nevertheless, church leaders, Christian organizations, and many ordinary Christians have worked tirelessly to heal society spiritually and physically. Their activities have included reviving the spiritual and faith development activities of church organizations and Christian groups, launching ecumenical activities, conducting a three-year special synod about peacemaking, and cooperating with the government in peacemaking activities.

In line with the instructions of Jesus Christ to his disciples (see Matt. 28:19-20), evangelization has been aimed at dispelling hatred, despair, vengeance, and disunity. Church leaders preach love, compassion, solidarity, and the value of humanity. They castigate bigotry, disunity, and violence. They challenge Christians for their passivity and for condoning violence. They call for soul-searching that leads to confession and asking for forgiveness. They appeal to the victims to be merciful and forgiving.

In peacemaking, Christian sermons are supplemented by activities of church organizations. In Butare town, in January 2000 there were fifteen organizations, such as the Legion of Mary, the Young Student Christian Organization, Caritas, the Charismatic Renewal, and others. At the University of Rwanda, located in the same town, there were eleven. They encourage peaceful coexistence between Hutu and Tutsi and between people from different regions. Members organize prayers and discussions, and they help each other when members face problems. They participate in their parish's activities and provide humanitarian assistance to the needy.

Catholic Christian neighborhood groups (*imiryango remezo*) are important promoters of unity and reconciliation. The members range from twenty to eighty, depending on the number of Catholics living in a given area. These groups have the same functions as the Christian organizations described above, but in some areas they also form cooperatives to improve the living standard of their members. It is from these groups that the parish gets leadership, sets its agendas, and implements its activities. The Catholic Church's grassroots justice and peace committees cooperate with neighborhood groups in promoting solidarity, social justice, and peaceful coexistence. These groups strengthen relationships at the grassroots. A Tutsi survivor in the eastern part of Rwanda told me that his attitude toward the Hutu changed as a result of his membership. He realized through discussions that they too had suffered a lot during the violence.

In 1997 a three-year special national Synod was launched in preparation for the year 2000 celebration of the Rwandan Christian Centenary Jubilee. The Synod dealt with three issues: ethnic conflict, the weakening of the family, and the lack of adequate education for youth.

Christians from all walks of life, from the grassroots to diocesan staff members were brought together for a soul-searching exercise. Christians were called to free themselves from hatred, fear, intolerance, and vengeance, and they were asked to work for a new era characterized by unity, reconciliation, and forgiveness. To get at the truth, they were challenged to ask themselves whether they did the right things during the violence, what they were doing to heal the society, and what they were doing to prevent a recurrence of the tragedy.

Dialogue among groups in conflicts is a prerequisite for reconciliation. The synod brought face to face the survivors, spouses, and relatives of genocide prisoners, intellectuals from both major ethnic groups, and neighbors who were not on speaking terms because of past conflicts. All aspects of the conflict were discussed with relative transparency. A Christian grassroots leader in Butare told me:

> By grace of God we were courageous enough to talk about everything related to the conflict. We opened scars and we squeezed them, it hurt too much but we needed to do it to take out the pus once and for all, for the sake of genuine healing. We exposed issues no one dared to talk about for decades. At the end of the day, we felt relieved to have spilled out all we had held in the secret recesses of our hearts.

If some of the following synod resolutions are fulfilled even in part, then the healing process will be enhanced. These resolutions, published in the Catholic journal *Kinyamateka* (April 2000), are the following:

- to eradicate ethnic distrust and discrimination
- to uproot extremist, malicious, divisionist remarks, writings, and actions that could compromise the healing process
- to use all means available to achieve sustainable peace
- to promote respect for human rights, Christian values, and the truth

- to unite the church, which has been divided on ethnic lines, and to encourage its leaders to be exemplary

- to consolidate love and peace in the family and revitalize Christian grassroots organizations

- to be compassionate and helpful toward all vulnerable groups such as genocide victims, orphans, widows, the handicapped, prisoners, and their families

- to impart to youth the knowledge and skills necessary for their welfare

Besides the efforts of individual churches, ecumenical activities are playing an important role in peacemaking. The impulse for them came in 1995, thousands of miles away from Rwanda, when a Rwandan theologian, Dr. Fulgence Rubayiza, supported by the ecumenical community of Detmold-Hiddesen (Reformed, Lutheran, and Roman Catholic Churches), brought together fourteen Rwandans living in Europe to discuss how to make peace in Rwanda. A second conference took place in December 1996 and was attended by twenty-four persons, including priests, pastors, laypeople, and a delegation from Rwanda composed of Hutu and Tutsi. This conference came to be known as the Detmold Confession, because Hutu and Tutsi participants confessed and apologized for the crimes committed by the members of their respective groups.

The Hutu apologized for the crimes committed against the Tutsi between 1959 and 1994 and especially the heinous nature of the crimes: "torturing, raping, slitting pregnant women open, hacking humans to pieces, burying people alive . . . forcing people to kill their own relatives, burning people alive" (Detmold Confession 1996, 51).

The Tutsi apologized for "repression and blind vengeance which members of our group have taken, depassing [sic] all claims to legitimate self-defense." They also apologized for "certain arrogant and contemptuous attitudes shown to [Hutu] throughout our history in the name of a ridiculous complex of ethnic superiority" (Detmold Confession 1996, 51-52).

Western participants apologized for having sowed the seeds of Rwandan division and violence, for having aggravated violence by delivering arms, and for having neglected the suffering of Rwandan refugees.

Inside Rwanda, interfaith consultations in the form of seminars, meetings, and solidarity camps have been organized to deal with reconciliation, promotion of human rights, security, and combating community social ills. In 2001, the Kabgayi Diocese organized solidarity camps for 735 youths drawn from many faiths. Apart from prayers, the youths learned that they will need "to live together as brothers or perish as imbeciles," to borrow the words of the Reverend Martin Luther King.

The church is treating the genocide prisoners as prodigal sons (see Luke 15:11-32). They are being brought back to the fold; their humanity is being affirmed; and they are being prepared to reintegrate into their communities on their release. Prison pastoral activities have a large constituency: an estimated prison population of 107,000 people in 2001. The gospel is being promoted in prisons. After Bible studies and examinations, prisoners are receiving baptism, communion, and confirmation. Partly through prison evangelization, a substantial percentage of imprisoned genocide suspects have confessed their crimes and asked for forgiveness.

Sr. Genevieve Uwamariya is one of many church leaders who have dedicated themselves to working for reconciliation. She is a Tutsi who survived the genocide because she was abroad when it began. After her return, a prisoner who had killed her father confessed to her in public. Sr. Genevieve impressed the prisoners and all those in attendance when she embraced and forgave him. This was the beginning of her reconciliation project in Kibuye prison, which has 3,700 inmates. By July 2001, about three hundred inmates had confessed and asked for forgiveness publicly or through writing letters to those whom they had wronged. But Sr. Genevieve does not work among prisoners only. She organizes meetings between the perpetrators and the victims, and encourages them to forgive those who express contrition verbally or through letters.[7]

After the genocide, numerous nongovernmental organizations, many of them Christian, rushed to Rwanda to give emergency assistance to millions of displaced people, survivors, orphans, and widows. After the emergency phase, they launched development projects such as repairing schools and health facilities, building durable shelters, providing water to villages, and assisting economic production in the sectors of agriculture, animal husbandry, and small businesses. To improve the living standard of the people, these organizations have imparted skills and knowledge and facilitated easy access to resources necessary for production.

Some of the international Christian organizations that are involved in reconstruction today are Catholic Relief Services, Christian Aid, World Vision, Caritas, and the Lutheran World Federation. Apart from taking care of the material welfare of those in need, these organizations also work for peace. For example, World Vision encourages dialogue among Rwandans in order to build a society based on love, tolerance, and solidarity. It seeks to combat hatred, prejudice, and intolerance by consolidating Christian faith and practices. In its meetings and seminars it challenges youth to rekindle their faith, and to love neighbors as they love themselves.

In the recent past there have been three issues that have caused misunderstandings between the Catholic Church and the government. One was the case of Bishop Augustin Misago of Gikongoro Diocese. When he was imprisoned in April 1999 on charges of participating in the genocide, the relationship between the church and the government cooled. But a year later, relations improved after the court found him innocent.

Four Catholic church buildings, Ntarama, Nyamata, Kibeho, and Nyarubuye —where many Tutsi were killed during the genocide—were turned into memor-

---

[7] Online source: http://www.nationaudio.com, Amnesty Lessons from Rwanda July 19, 2001.

ial sites. The church opposed this appropriation of its buildings but the survivors, supported by the government, refused to have the churches used again for Christian services. The church now intends to build new churches.[8]

The other recent issue of contention involves the failure of the Catholic Church to apologize for its leaders' participation in the genocide. The institution's position is that individual religious leaders must account for their deeds, but that the church as such has no responsibility for this. As these issues are being addressed, the government and the church are now working together with increasing ease.

CONCLUSION

Fr. George, a Tutsi, is a Roman Catholic priest in Cyangugu Diocese. He narrowly escaped the 1994 genocide. He now dedicates himself to pastoral activities in prisons. His main concern is to clothe the prisoners, many of whom are in rags and tatters. One day he had the following experience, as recounted to me by one of his close acquaintances:

Fr. George was distributing second-hand clothes among prisoners. One of the prisoners got his share but did not go back to his cubicle. At the end of the distribution, when Fr. George was preparing to leave, the prisoner approached him and said, "Father George, I have something I would like to tell you." Fr. George was tired and told him so, and he suggested a meeting the following day. When the prisoner insisted, he took him with resignation to a bench and asked him what was on his mind. The prisoner, with tears welling up in his eyes, told him, "Father, I would like to tell you something which has been heavy on my heart since you started working with us. It pains me to see you working for our comfort while some of my colleagues here and I killed your mother, taking everything from her house including the clothes on her body." The prisoner started to cry, and Fr. George became like someone who has been struck by lightning. After a long moment of silence, Fr. George left the scene. Shortly thereafter he went on a spiritual retreat.

The prisoner, overwhelmed by a guilty conscience, had wanted forgiveness. After some weeks, I was informed that Fr. George had sought out the prisoner and forgiven him. The prisoner later confessed his crimes to the authorities.

While some Rwandans are courageous enough to confess to those whom they wronged and to the authorities, others fail to summon the courage to say, "I am sorry" or "Forgive me." They find the words too heavy.

Some Rwandans seek forgiveness in an indirect way. They show their remorse

---

[8] In a recent development the Catholic Church, the government and the survivors agreed to divide Kibeho church into two parts, one to be used for prayer and the other as a memorial site.

physically and symbolically and expect forgiveness without asking for it in words. For example, if a husband wants reconciliation with his wife after a quarrel, he may not admit his misdeed and ask forgiveness as such, but instead he tries in various ways to make his wife happy by buying her an exotic present, or returning home early and making a fuss over her. In the search for reconciliation and forgiveness, many Rwandans are relying on this kind of indirect approach. In both rural and urban areas, people are finding various ways to mend broken relationships, such as by socializing with those they wronged, working with them, and helping them in their daily lives.

In general, the healing process is bearing tangible fruits. However, more effort is needed to consolidate what has been achieved and to come up with new initiatives necessary for a sustainable peace, resistant to the various threats remaining in the country and in the region.

Close cooperation, shared visions, and efforts between the government, civil society, the churches, and the people are indispensable in this task. The starting point of this long journey is to imbue individuals with great compassion, as described in this Buddhist prayer:

> *Great Compassion makes a Peaceful Heart.*
> *A Peaceful Heart makes a Peaceful Person.*
> *A Peaceful Person makes a Peaceful Family.*
> *A Peaceful Family makes a Peaceful Community.*
> *A Peaceful Community makes a Peaceful Nation.*
> *And a Peaceful Nation makes a Peaceful World.*
> *May all Beings live in Happiness and Peace.*
> —by Maha Ghosananda
> European Centre for Conflict Prevention (1999, 220)

STATISTICAL TABLES
ASSOCIATED WITH CHAPTER 5 DATA

See page 145 for an interpretation of these tables. See chapter 1 for an explanation of variables.

TABLE 1. RELATIVE FREQUENCY OF PEACEMAKING ACTIONS IN RWANDA

	Avoidance	Confrontation	Prayer	Relationship Building	Service
Mean Frequency	.21	.44	.18	1.44	.88

Relationship building was more commonly reported than all other types of peacemaking ($p < .05$); service was more frequent than the remaining types of peacemaking ($p < .05$). Avoidance, confrontation, and prayer did not significantly differ from one another in frequency.

TABLE 2. RELATIVE FREQUENCY OF MOTIVATIONS FOR PEACEMAKING IN RWANDA

	Practical	Relational	Ideological	Religious
Mean Frequency	1.57	.53	1.24	.50

Practical and ideological motivations were more commonly reported than relational and religious motivations, $p < .05$. However, practical and ideological motivations did not differ significantly from one another in frequency; neither did relational and religious motivations.

6

Sri Lanka

Prophetic Initiatives amidst Deadly Conflict

SHIRLEY LAL WIJESINGHE

It was around 9:30 in the morning at the border villages of the districts of Batticaloa-Amparai. Tamil refugees—men, women, and youth—were going back to have a glimpse of the villages they had been forced to aban-don ten years ago. Their land was now overgrown with bushes and weeds; the houses where they were born had been destroyed.

This is how I recall the day when the Sinhala farmers awaited the Tamils' arrival anxiously at the Kandaiar-Vattividai Junction. While they waited, they kissed, embraced, shook hands with each other, and took turns holding welcoming banners. Finally, the Tamils arrived.

We walked from the junction, about a mile away along a bund overgrown with weeds and thick bushes due to non-use of the regular path; recently, though, it had been cleared enough for us to walk single file. There was music blaring, very appropriate indeed: Nalai Namathe (Tomorrow is Ours), arranged to the delight of all by the Sinhalese themselves! If that is not the meeting of hearts and minds, what else is?

The idea for that day was for people to engage themselves in "shra-madhana," volunteer work. It did not happen. Although people had come prepared for it with "kathies and kodalies," knives and axes, the occasion was emotionally overpowering for both the Sinhalese and the Tamils pres-ent. The elders spent the day exchanging views and recounting memories, while the younger adults engaged in chitchat and loud laughter and snapped photos of one another, thus reliving their childhood days.

I am deeply grateful to the members of the research team, Reverend Father Oswald B. Firth, O.M.I., and Mr. Deepthi Silva, for their tireless assistance in carrying out this research project. I also wish to thank the Peace Committee of Batticaloa, the United Peace Committee of Nugelanda, and *Kitusara* youth for their generosity and cooperation.

The stream with flowing water along the bund attracted the youth, who got into the water saying, "At least let us dip our feet and wet our faces in our water!" A meal cooked by the hosts, a very tasty meal indeed, was served. Samba rice with hot dry fish curry cooked in the Sinhala way and white curry of breadfruit made a wonderful menu. Even the plates and cups were shared. All added indeed to the strengthening of the ethnic, linguistic, and religious bond broken several years ago, now happily beginning to mend itself.

—Father J. Joseph Mary, S.J.

The ethnic conflict between the Sinhalese and the Tamils in Sri Lanka is multifaceted and complex. Its origins date back to European colonization, but in the years following independence, it has been aggravated by the government's discriminatory policies against the Tamil minority. For the past twenty years, the conflict has taken the form of a civil war between the Sri Lankan government and the Liberation Tigers of Tamil Eelam (LTTE).

This chapter describes the findings of a two-year research project, offering a brief summary of the origins of the conflict, some description of the war and its victims, an account of grassroots peacemaking efforts taking place in Sri Lanka, and the motives for them. Our study also examined gender differences in peacemaking and the relationship of images of the divine, images of the enemy, and belief in a just world (see chapter 1) in relation to peacemaking actions and motivations. Ingredients to be considered in developing a Sri Lankan theology of peace are suggested, as are the challenges posed to the churches by the conflict itself and by the experiences of peacemakers at the grassroots.

ORIGINS OF THE CONFLICT

Sri Lanka was known in earlier days as Tambapanni, Taprobane, and then Ceylon. This island in the Indian Ocean is a tropical paradise of sandy beaches, mythic mountains, breathtaking waterfalls, lush rainforests, and abundant wildlife. It is heir to four great religions: Hinduism, Buddhism, Christianity, and Islam. Throughout the centuries people from all over the world have journeyed to Sri Lanka, attracted by its mystic silence, smiling people, and perennial streams of deep spirituality. But the fires of war and destruction have marred this island's tranquil beauty.

Sri Lanka is inhabited by nineteen million people. Categorized according to religion, they are roughly 69 percent Buddhist, 15 percent Hindu, 8 percent Christian, and 8 percent Muslim. The ethnic distribution of the population is 74 percent Sinhalese, 12 percent Sri Lankan Tamil, 5 percent Indian Tamil, 8 percent Muslim,[1] and 1 percent Eurasians and others, including a tiny minority of

---

[1] Sri Lankan Muslims, mainly descendants of West Asian merchants, are considered to be an ethnic entity.

indigenous people (*Statistical Abstract of the Democratic Socialist Republic of Sri Lanka* 1991, 45, 49). Most Buddhists are Sinhalese; Hindus are more likely to be Tamil.

History records wars between Sinhalese and Tamil kings, but their direct impact on the present problem is disputed. What *is* known is that the Tamils, along with Christians of all ethnic entities, benefited more than the Sinhalese Buddhists from missionary education during the colonial era, and especially under British rule. As a result, the former groups enjoyed better employment opportunities than the latter. Post-independence policies, determined primarily by the Sinhalese Buddhists who took power, attempted to redress the situation. But the measures taken resulted in discrimination against Tamils as well as Christians. As the scope of this chapter does not allow for a detailed account of Sri Lankan history, I shall provide a summary of the main events that led to the present conflict.

For the sake of convenience and control, Britain ruled Sri Lanka from 1796 to 1948 through a highly centralized system of government. At the moment of independence, the rights of minorities were granted by the Constitution. At that time, the question of sharing power with the minorities was raised, though not until the creation of the Federal Party did the idea of a federal-style sharing of power emerge. But the majority of Sri Lankan Tamils living in the north and east had been comfortable with the centralized system of government—many of them held government posts or had business connections in Colombo. They had no reason at that point to be concerned that they would become the victims of discrimination by the Sinhalese majority.

The tide turned in 1956, however, with the introduction of the "Sinhala Only" bill in Parliament, which marked the beginning of Sinhalese nationalist sentiment. Peaceful protests against the bill by Tamils were met with waves of violent reprisals. Tamils were further annoyed with the introduction of post-independence colonization schemes to settle landless Sinhalese farmers in Tamil areas, resulting in significant demographic changes.

In July 1957, Prime Minister S. W. R. D. Bandaranaike and the leader of the Federal Party, S. J. V. Chelvanayagam, signed a pact that recognized the Tamil language as the language of a national minority. The pact included the cessation of state-aided colonization and guaranteed a large measure of regional self-government; it also secured the right of every Tamil-speaking person in every part of the country to transact all affairs with the government in Tamil. But the pact was unilaterally abrogated by the Sinhalese leadership due to strong opposition from the extremist Sinhalese elements provoked by the United National Party. To this the Federal Party reacted with a nonviolent campaign of civil disobedience that culminated in the 1958 communal riots. On February 17, 1958, the Tamil Language (Special Provisions) Act was passed in parliament, among whose provisions included the use of the Tamil language for purposes of correspondence and "prescribed administrative purposes" in the northern and eastern provinces. But in the context of serious inequalities this measure was far from sufficient, and the Federal Party continued its nonviolent protests.

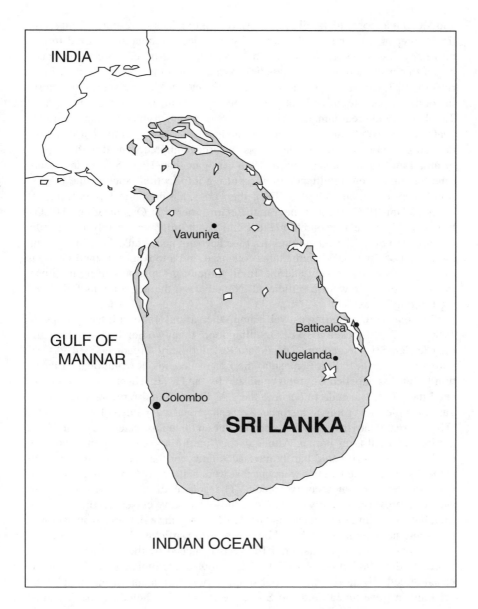

Other pacts and attempts at reform failed to guarantee equal opportunities for the Tamil minority. Instead, the situation was aggravated by the educational policy of "standardization" in 1972, which was intended to give rural youth greater access to university education by reducing the number of urban youth—who had better educational opportunities—entering universities. But this measure proved to be a great disadvantage to the students from the Tamil-dominated, urban Jaffna district. It was also not useful to youth in the northern rural districts of Mannar and Vavuniya, home to Tamil majorities, owing to a lack of resources and facilities to prepare students for the university entrance examination. Barred from a university education, Tamil youth felt increasingly frustrated. Violent militancy began to stir in the north. The situation further deteriorated with the anti-Tamil riots in 1977, the burning of the Jaffna market, and the subsequent ruthless burning of the invaluable Jaffna library by Sinhalese extremists. A riot in 1983 against Tamils living in predominantly Sinhalese areas, which erupted in response to the deaths of thirteen Sinhalese soldiers at the hands of armed Tamil youth, had the tacit approval of the government. It was "a carnage unprecedented in the sequels of anti-Tamil riots commencing in 1958" (Loganathan 1996, 87). In the meantime the Tamil youth militancy grew, splitting into factions such as the Liberation Tigers of Tamil Eelam (LTTE), the Peoples' Liberation Organization of Tamil Eelam (PLOTE), and the Tamil Eelam Liberation Organization (TELO). Indian soil became a second home to Tamil youth militancy. In July 1985, India attempted to bring the warring parties together with peace talks held in Thimpu, the capital of Bhutan. When the talks collapsed, India took a firm stand vis-à-vis the Sri Lankan government and the Tamil militant groups, pressuring both parties into working toward a settlement. Nonetheless, the negotiations failed and the fighting intensified.

Tensions were mounting as well among the various Tamil militant groups. In 1986 the LTTE attacked the TELO, killing more than two hundred members and their leader, Sri Sabaratnam. The Eelam Revolutionary Organizers and PLOTE withdrew from the Jaffna Peninsula; the Eelam Peoples' Revolutionary Liberation Front was expelled from the peninsula by the LTTE. These events strengthened the LTTE's agenda to become the sole liberator and representative of the Tamil people. According to historian Ketheshwaran Loganathan (1996, 119-20), "LTTE's real strength . . . lay in its accumulation of sophisticated weaponry from the international arms bazaar. Although the Tamil diaspora was contributing to the LTTE coffers, it could hardly have accounted for the quantum of weaponry at the disposal of the LTTE—weapons that were neither given by India nor seized from the Sri Lankan security forces." The source of the LTTE's supply of weapons remains a mystery even among those who have closely studied the conflict, but, according to Loganathan (1996, 120), they have developed an "autonomous international network based on narco-arms trafficking."

A major offensive against the LTTE was launched by the Sri Lankan armed forces in May 1987. As the LTTE was being routed, the Indian government intervened directly by air dropping relief supplies over Jaffna, an act resented by the Sri Lankan government and the Sinhalese leadership, including the Buddhist clergy.

The incident occasioned fresh negotiations, and the outcome was the Indo–Sri Lanka accord of July 1987, intended to ease Tamil grievances and ensure the unity of the nation. A result of the accord was the deployment of the Indian Peace Keeping Force (IPKF), a contingent of Indian soldiers, to disarm the Tamil militants. Although the people of Jaffna were enthusiastic about the arrival of the Indian army, the relationship between the LTTE and the IPKF turned sour. The LTTE attacked the IPKF on October 10, 1987, thus beginning a new war in the north and the east, much to the detriment of the Tamil population. The IPKF eventually withdrew from Sri Lanka leading to a fresh war in June 1990 between the LTTE and the government known as Eelam War II. Peace talks that had resumed in October 1994 between the LTTE and the government ultimately failed. When the LTTE bombed the Sacred Buddhist Temple of the Tooth in Kandy, the government banned the LTTE. A unilateral ceasefire by the LTTE from December 2000 to April 2001 was not reciprocated by the government. The United National Front government, which came into power in early December 2001, immediately brought about a new cease-fire, which has been in effect since then.

THE WAR AND ITS VICTIMS

The battle between the Sri Lankan government and the LTTE is a guerrilla war, fought mainly in the jungles of the northern and eastern provinces. There is no conscription to join the government security forces, and whether the LTTE practices compulsory enlistment is disputed. The Sri Lankan military is largely indebted to widespread poverty and unemployment for its recruits, who frequently join because they have no other options for supporting themselves. In the case of Tamils joining the LTTE, there are probably mixed motives at work. They might do so in response to heavy LTTE propaganda, succumb to social pressure to join, or, like their Sinhalese counterparts, they are driven by poverty.

At the beginning of the war, both sides fought with simple hardware like machine guns, but later on mortars were introduced. During the last few battles before the current cease-fire was declared, the government was fighting with multibarrel rocket launchers capable of destroying targets in ranges exceeding thirty kilometers with high-volume firepower.

The war is fought between Tamils and Sinhalese; except for a few militant Muslim groups, the Muslim minority has had no direct role in the conflict. Nonetheless, it has suffered death and displacement at the hands of the warring parties. For the most part, Muslims have been caught in the crossfire. Most of them had settled in the east, where the fighting has been very intense. Their villages are often contiguous with Tamil villages, and at times Tamil militants have suspected Muslims of supplying information to government forces. Muslims have been chased out of the north by Tamil militants. At present, most Sri Lankan Muslims are refugees in the south.

Most of those who die in the war—at least, as direct casualties of combat—are men. They leave behind widows, orphans, and impoverished families, as most of them are sole breadwinners. It is estimated that there are about ten thousand war widows among the Tamils and Muslims and an equal number among the Sinhalese.[2] The widows not only suffer the psychological effects of having lost a

---

[2] No comprehensive data are available on the number of war widows. The total number of deaths due to war is estimated to be over 50,000. It is speculated that there are about 20,000 widows (*The Economic, Social and Human Cost of the War in Sri Lanka* 2001, 40-41).

spouse, but in certain cases their trauma is aggravated by witnessing the killing of children, sometimes their own, the burning of their homes and all their life's possessions, and/or being brutally assaulted and raped. Many war widows are in their twenties; they often have to care for little children, yet must carry on without spousal support. Therefore they are compelled to earn a livelihood through hard labor, and at the same time they become sexually vulnerable. War widows often do not find partners to remarry. Desperate to earn a few rupees, widows are easily exploited sexually. Insecurity, anguish, and uncertainty loom large in their lives. "I had seven classmates who joined the army and six of them were killed in battle, leaving widows," explained Mahinda Namal in an interview. Namal is editor of *Kitusara*, a Catholic monthly that advocates nonviolent solutions to the conflict (see Case III below). "The women married to soldiers have a very intense sexual life during the latter's brief home visits. These widows will have to struggle with their feelings of aloneness, their sexuality, and a lack of intimacy in the years ahead."

Rape has also been a common feature of the war. In most stories of rape, government soldiers are the perpetrators and Tamil women are their victims; they were likewise reported to be the victims of the visiting Indian Peace Keeping Force. "[Rape] was carried out with considerable brutality and impersonality, where the victims were publicly defeminized and destroyed," according to Daya Somasundaram (1998, 244-45). "Chastity is traditionally considered one of the supreme virtues of women, to be safeguarded with the same diligence as their life. The screams and pleading of a young, attractive girl, whom three soldiers were trying to rape at gun point, still echoes in my ears. She fell at their feet and begged, 'Please, brother, shoot me, but don't do this.' Fortunately for her, her pleading got through to an officer who took pity and let her go, after slapping her. A young rape victim in Tinnavelly immediately attempted to commit suicide by jumping into a well." A young girl who is raped may never be able to marry; if a married woman is raped, she runs the risk of abandonment by her husband. No female is immune to this danger; even women well past menopause have been brutally raped.

Prostitution is another malaise of the war. The presence of a large number of women prostitutes in the port capital of Colombo and the recent incidents of male prostitution attached to the tourist industry in Negombo and Hikkaduwa are driven by abject poverty and may or may not be related to the war, but the prostitution practiced in the sacred city of Anuradhapura is a product of the war economy; soldiers make up most of its clientele, while destitute young women from the villages on the borders of the war zone have become its victims.

Women living in refugee camps suffer enormously. Families are often forced to live in cramped quarters. Children are born and raised, attain puberty, and even marry under these tragic circumstances. Married couples, especially those with children, have little privacy. During the day, men have the opportunity to leave the camps, but the women are trapped there. Some of the men who get their rupees through a day's labor come home drunk, and at night force their wives into having sex in the presence of the children sleeping in the same tiny space.

The war has likewise victimized children in specific ways. Playgrounds have become battlefields. The army occupies them. Worse, the war has orphaned the children who once played in them. When a father is killed, the mother has little time to care for her children. If she goes to the Middle East for employment, the children are left with their grandmother, uncle, aunt, or cousins. These children bear an enormous burden of loss. Speaking of the children of war, Mahinda Namal observed: "These children have lost their childhood. Only the adults can remember a childhood worthy of children. There are no smiles on the faces of these children. Even when they smile, there is pain in it. Children carry the burden of war forced on them by the adult world. A lot of children die because there is a lack of medicine in the Vanni area [of northern Sri Lanka]. Unwilling to watch their children suffer from malnutrition, some mothers have put poison into their children's food and themselves committed suicide. The south [of Sri Lanka] laments the problem of malnutrition elsewhere in the world, not knowing that it is at our doorstep. Children resembling old photos of victims of the famine in Ethiopia are now in Vanni."

Sri Lanka at war faces another severe problem: the widespread recruitment of child soldiers. More than adults, children are easily brainwashed and exploited. There is a cruel irony in the fact that the adult world is fighting a war for the liberation of future generations at the same time that it is victimizing the very future of the nation. Most of the children in war-torn areas suffer from physical or psychological trauma, or both. Some have been injured themselves; these and others, often enough, have witnessed their parents, brothers, and sisters being raped, killed, and sometimes dismembered. They live with nightmares. What today's children are experiencing will prove to be a major problem for the future of Sri Lanka. The plight of children in the border villages of the war zone is particularly pathetic. They spend their nights in the jungle for fear of rebel attacks. How can these children who hardly sleep at night be expected to study at school the following day?

METHODOLOGY

This chapter documents some examples of grassroots Christian peacemaking efforts in Sri Lanka. Only a few of the peacemaking efforts we found were exclusively Christian; members of Christian communities often engage in interreligious activities for peace, and such efforts have been included in this investigation.

Oswald Firth, Deepthi Silva, and I—the three of us comprising the research team in Sri Lanka—had been involved in grassroots peacemaking efforts before undertaking this study. This involvement facilitated our work on the study, since people who are deeply engaged in peacemaking are often reluctant to provide information to outsiders, fearing that the release and subsequent publication of such information could jeopardize their hidden peacemaking efforts and put their lives in danger.

Both qualitative and quantitative methods were employed in the research. Qualitative research included interviews and written questionnaires to obtain information about the range of grassroots peacemaking efforts that are under way, religious and cultural resources for peacemaking, problems and constraints encountered by peacemakers, and the impact of peacemaking at local and national levels. A total of 265 individuals from eleven research sites provided data for the qualitative research. Based on this research, the following section will begin with an overview of grassroots peacemaking efforts in Sri Lanka, then focus on three outstanding examples as case studies.

Two quantitative investigations were included in the study: one on how images of the divine, images of the opponent, and belief in a just world (BJW) relate to peacemaking actions and motivations; and the other on gender as a factor in peacemaking efforts (see chapter 1). There were 107 respondents from three sites for the investigation into images of the divine, images of the opponent and BJW; respondents from two of these sites and respondents from two other sites also participated in the gender study, whose sample totaled 139 (see table on p. 185). Data were obtained through use of structured interviews rather than questionnaires, as many respondents felt safer addressing controversial matters orally rather than in writing. A second reason was cultural: Sri Lankans in general would prefer to share information in the course of a conversation rather than via a written questionnaire.

GRASSROOTS PEACEMAKING IN SRI LANKA

As we conclude work on this project, we are aware of little previous research on grassroots peacemaking in Sri Lanka, perhaps because it is, practically speaking, a difficult topic to study. The conflict is a delicate issue, and we learned the hard way that enlisting cooperation for research that addresses it in any way is no easy matter. Indeed, we had moments of wondering if we would even find anything to research; so much grassroots peacemaking that takes place in Sri Lanka must necessarily be carried out quietly and in secret that few Sri Lankans, even among media professionals, are aware of these efforts. Consequently, literature on the subject is scarce.

But grassroots peacemaking efforts in Sri Lanka do exist, as we found, and many of them are remarkable. They deserve to be widely known and understood. This section is intended to provide a panoramic view of these efforts. As an overview, it will describe not only Christian peace initiatives but also interreligious and secular peacemaking efforts.

WILDFLOWERS OF PEACE IN A VIOLENT WILDERNESS

Although the armed struggle in Sri Lanka began as a reaction to the politics of marginalization, today it persists owing to the institutionalization of the conflict in the social and cultural ethos of the country. A thriving war economy provides employment to Sinhalese and Tamil youth, personal profit to arms dealers, and power, prestige, and wealth to both government forces and militants. Those who benefit from the war economy shudder at peace initiatives. Their influence is so widespread and entrenched that there is no massive grassroots movement for peace in the country. Any such movement in the making would come under attack from both extremist Sinhalese and Tamil sectors. Yet small prophetic peace initiatives—often quietly undertaken and unnoticed outside their immediate regions—are present at the grassroots. Like wildflowers, they bloom and die in a brief span of time. But the culture of goodness created by these small peace efforts continuously inspires new initiatives.

The town of Vavuniya is situated at the southern section of the northern province. It has a mixed population of Tamils, Sinhalese, and Muslims.[3] They belong to the four major religions of Sri Lanka: Hinduism, Buddhism, Christianity, and Islam. Vavuniya is also the doorway to the LTTE-held territory called Vanni. The Buddhist temple, the Roman Catholic Church, the Assembly of God Church, and the Scouts of Vavuniya have initiated peace efforts in this troubled milieu.

In 1990, the government forces in Vavuniya began to arrest hundreds of Tamil youths on suspicion of being involved in militant activity, and many of those taken into custody disappeared. In this situation, Reverend Siyambalagasweva Wimalasara Thero, chief monk of Vavuniya Buddhist Temple, led a group of concerned citizens to locate those who had been detained and to facilitate visitations in the detention camps with their families. In 1997, the same group formed the Vanni Peace Foundation, composed of twelve committee members. Through a fruitful dialogue with the LTTE, the foundation has succeeded in preventing attacks on the civilian Sinhalese population. Today, Tamil–Sinhalese dialogue continues to take place in the Buddhist temple.

During Lent in the year 2000, Fr. T. Navaratnam, pastor of Vavuniya's Roman Catholic parish, introduced the practice of daily prayer and fasting for peace. These spiritual disciplines have borne fruit in solidarity for collective peace-building as the parish has endeavored to transform the armed conflict into a non-violent struggle for justice. One year later, the initiative had spread from Vavuniya to all the Catholic parishes in the Diocese of Mannar.

Both Tamils and Sinhalese are members of the Assembly of God denomination in Vavuniya. Inspired by Christian values, they live together in a village called Tekkawatta. In a milieu dominated by armed conflict between the two ethnic entities, this community is a living example of ethnic harmony.

The Tamil, Sinhalese, and Muslim Boy Scouts in Vavuniya have had the opportunity to meet when camping. The experience has strengthened solidarity among all three ethnic groups. In January 2000, they marched together through the town of Vavuniya, demanding peace.

South and east of Vavuniya is the coastal town of Batticaloa. Here Paul Hogan, a Canadian visual artist who had worked with traumatized children in

---

[3] See n. 1 above.

Toronto, founded a haven for Tamil and Muslim children affected by the conflict. He named it the "Butterfly Garden." Groups of children from both ethnic groups come here for play activity. Jesuit Fr. Paul Satkunanayagam serves as co-director along with Paul Hogan. The nine-month program, a fascinating experiment in long-term peacebuilding with and among children, provides an opportunity for healing and friendship. The two directors are planning to expand the program to other parts of the country.

In Colombo, the Sri Lankan capital city, the Centre for Society and Religion (CSR) was founded in 1971 by Reverend Fr. Tissa Balasuriya, a priest of the congregation of the Oblates of Mary Immaculate (O.M.I.). Under the initiative of the present director, Fr. Oswald Firth, also an oblate, CSR has initiated both village-level and school-level programs. One village-level peace effort was a massive peace rally in April 1999 under the theme of *Sama Jeevanaya* ("Lifegiving Peace") which brought together hundreds of youth from village-level grassroots peace groups scattered throughout the country. Many others joined the rally. Their appeal to the political, religious, and civic leaders of Sri Lanka read: "We the youth of this country refuse to kill or be killed. We do not wish to carry forward a conflict created by our political ancestors. We wish to till our land and live in peace and harmony. We call on you, our leaders, to work out an acceptable, honourable, just and sustainable solution to the present conflict" (*Sama Jeevanaya "Youth for Peace"* 1999, 1).

CSR's school programs include one that brings together Sinhalese school-children from Moratuwa—a town situated twelve miles south of Colombo—and Tamil schoolchildren from Batticaloa; and another in Colombo at the Holy Family Convent's secondary school for girls, which facilitates dialogue between Sinhalese and Tamil students. These school programs have been very successful.

A number of grassroots peace efforts of a secular nature have not been included in the present study. These are *Sarasavi Diyaniyo* (an association of Tamil and Sinhalese university women), *Rukada* (a traveling puppet show for peace), *Sunila* Women's Development Movement (aiding women and children traumatized by the war), *Ginikandulu* (a photo exhibition), *Bingusara* (a street drama group), and *Sadujanarava* (music and poster campaigns to raise awareness of the suffering caused by the war).

While not all grassroots peacemaking efforts in Sri Lanka could be described in detail in this chapter, three case studies presented below could be considered a cross-section of grassroots peace efforts in general. The first is the Peace Committee in Batticaloa, which is mainly a Tamil effort in a Tamil area; the second is that of the Tamil and Sinhalese farmers of Nugelanda who live and work together in border villages; the third is the *Kitusara* group, which is mainly a Sinhalese effort in a Sinhalese area. Hence the three selected cases represent a pattern in the membership and the geography of grassroots peacemaking efforts in Sri Lanka, namely, exclusively Tamil efforts in Tamil areas, interethnic peacemaking in areas where the population multiethnic, and exclusively Sinhalese efforts in Sinhalese areas. The origin, development, and impact of each of these efforts will be studied.

Case I: In the Land of the Singing Fish

Situated on the eastern coast, Batticaloa boasts of clear, shallow seas and lagoons teaming with shrimp and crab. Under the Kallady Bridge, generations have listened to the singing fish—an extraordinary phenomenon—whose concert is at its best on nights brightly lit by a full moon. But since the war came to Batticaloa, their singing seems more like mourning for the many who have left this town. The intelligentsia and the rich who once lived in this haven of the East have long since departed; those left behind must cope with checkpoints, armed personnel, and the blasts of gunfire at night.

The Indian Peace Keeping Force arrived in Batticaloa in 1987. When it left in November 1989, the LTTE occupied the town. The Eelam War II began in June 1990, and as the Sri Lankan army was gaining ground, the LTTE left Batticaloa and receded into the jungles. But before withdrawing, they killed an estimated nine hundred Sinhalese policemen, broke into government warehouses, and took away sacks of flour, sugar, *dahl* (a local legume), and everything else they could carry. Most shops in Batticaloa belong to Muslim merchants, who at that time feared coming into town. Batticaloa was suddenly engulfed in chaos, as civilian looters began to attack Muslim shops. Abruptly, the looting stopped. A group of forty courageous residents had intervened. Thus was born the Peace Committee of Batticaloa.

Meanwhile, as the Sri Lankan army was advancing toward Batticaloa from the north and the south, it destroyed shops and houses on the side of the road. People in its path fled to refugee camps in fear of a fierce attack. In this situation, some members of the Peace Committee realized that the soldiers would destroy the town and raze it to the ground. They took courage and went to the two entrances of the town waiting for the army to come. On its arrival the Peace Committee informed those in command that the militants had left Batticaloa and asked them to enter the town without destroying it. In July 1990, the Sri Lankan army peacefully occupied Batticaloa.

But the worst was yet to come. Suspecting that some LTTE cadres were hiding among the youth, government forces began to round up teenage boys and imprison them. One high-ranking army officer alone is believed to be responsible for three to four thousand deaths. The Peace Committee began to keep lists of those missing, and by August of 1990 the number was up to 407. At the time of this writing, over seven thousand people have disappeared in the Batticaloa area, but the committee has achieved some success in reducing disappearances by insisting that the army and police be accountable for everyone taken into custody.

As a result of this sort of pressure and the insistence of the international community, the Sri Lankan government enacted a law in 1994 that if a person is arrested on charges of terrorism, the arresting officer must give a receipt to the person's next of kin. Despite the reluctance of police and military personnel to implement the law in Batticaloa, they had to do so under pressure from the Peace Committee, whose membership has at times been as low as six. The same law has apparently not yet been implemented in Jaffna, Mannar, Vavuniya, Trincomalee or anywhere else on the island.

Another factor that reduced disappearances in Batticaloa was the practice of the government holding security personnel accountable for their subordinates' actions before commissions and court tribunals. Every senior officer is subject to being brought before the tribunals to explain the behavior of those under him. Since the Peace Committee witnesses to any misbehavior of the government forces, the senior officers serving in Batticaloa are very careful about enforcing discipline among their junior officers. The Peace Committee has also been instrumental in convincing senior security personnel to remove barbed wire from checkpoints in Batticaloa and to replace it with nylon cords, and also to allow people on motorcycles—a very common means of transport in Batticaloa—to ride up to the checkpoints instead of having to stop the motorcycle far away and push it towards the checkpoint in the burning sun or torrential rain. Before this change, any extra passenger—often the wife of the rider, carrying a heavy load of goods from the market—had to go through a separate line to be checked.

One of the most remarkable accomplishments of the Peace Committee was its role in resolving a grisly eruption of violence between Tamils and Muslims in Batticaloa. Locally, these two groups had often been compared to rice and curry—in other words, inseparably united. They had lived together for centuries, and no one ever dreamed that they could be divided. The situation drastically changed in July of 1990, when over seventy Muslims in Kirankulam, eighteen miles south of Batticaloa, were abducted, presumably by unidentified Tamils, and never seen again. After that, it was not safe for Tamils to go to the Muslim village of Kathankudy, nor was it safe for a Muslim to come to Batticaloa. That same month, a massacre took place in the Kathankudy mosque; over a hundred Muslims were slaughtered as they prayed. The next month, another hundred Muslims were massacred in Eravur, a village north of Batticaloa. Culpability for the massacres has yet to be established, but it is widely believed that the LTTE was responsible for the Kirankulam incident. The initial Tamil attacks had apparently been instigated by the LTTE to demonstrate their hegemony over Muslims in the area and to pressure them into becoming allies. Muslims retaliated by attacking nearby Chenkaladi and killing more than twenty Tamils in August 1990; the following month, according to human rights activists in the area, members of the Muslim Jihad and some off-duty army personnel were reported to be involved in a massacre of 184 Tamils in villages near Batticaloa.

After these horrendous events, the Tamil and Muslim communities were alienated from each other for four years. The deadlock was broken when the Peace Committee, working with a branch of local government, and the Eastern Rehabilitation Organization (an independent agency involved in rehabilitation work in war-torn areas of the eastern province) initiated talks between the Tamil and Muslim communities in conflict. The negotiations were successful, and Tamils and Muslims in Batticaloa are once again living and working together.

Case II: Keth Bimata Samaya (Peace to the Rice Fields)
Descending the slopes of Sri Lanka's central hills, the Kandy-Ampara truck route crosses the Mahaweli River at Mahiyangana. Beyond this ancient town, the

road runs along the flat lands of Bintenna. Turning off toward the north from Piyangala Junction, one comes to Nugelanda, a new settlement that is part of the Gal-Oya irrigation scheme found in the eastern province. Nugelanda is surrounded by traditional villages: Rajagalatenna, Bakki-Ella, Pullukunavai and Puthumunmaricholai. In this area, both Tamils and Sinhalese lived together in peace until 1990, when the Sri Lankan army launched a military operation against the LTTE to recapture the eastern province from them. This operation was launched from Nugelanda and brought disaster to the Tamils there. Some were killed; many women were raped; most of the houses were demolished; and the survivors were chased away. Following the Tamils' departure, Sinhalese rice farmers began to cultivate most of their paddy lands under the protection of government security forces. In spite of this protection, while the Sinhalese farmers were working their fields, some were attacked and killed by Tamil militants, who regarded the paddy land as their territory.

In 1995, some of the displaced Tamil farmers returned to their former habitat and began to cultivate their fields. But they ran the risk of being attacked by the government security forces, who suspected them of being the LTTE. Indeed, anyone entering the disputed territory ran the risk of being killed, and hence, the Sinhalese and Tamil farmers who had once lived and worked together were completely separated. Friends and neighbors were now enemies and strangers.

In November 1997, some Sinhalese farmers asked the Reverend Nirmal Mendis, an Anglican priest then in charge of the church in Nugelanda, to intervene on their behalf—by approaching religious leaders with high-placed connections in the government—and obtain for them some protection from militant attacks as they cultivated their fields. Mendis helped them to see that their former friends and neighbors, the Tamil farmers beyond the disputed territory, were perhaps facing the same problem and invited them to devise a plan for protection that would benefit both them and the Tamil farmers. Having discussed Mendis's suggestion, the Sinhalese farmers presented a fresh request to him in December 1997, asking him to intervene both on their behalf *and* on behalf of the Tamil farmers.

Returning home from Batticaloa to Nugelanda in October 1999, Mendis unexpectedly came upon some of the Tamil farmers at the small village of Palamunai. This incident opened the possibility of communication between the Sinhalese and Tamil farmers. As a result, the two groups met at Kalmunai, south of Batticaloa, with forty Sinhalese and seventeen Tamil farmers in attendance. Later that year, a second meeting took place in which the United Peace Committee was formed, consisting of twelve Tamil and six Sinhalese farmers. At the third meeting in January 2000, the seventy-five farmers in attendance decided to meet at the disputed territory.

The next month, about a thousand women, men, and children from Sinhalese and Tamil farm families met at Palaiyadyvattai in the disputed territory to prepare the fields for cultivation. But upon seeing each other, emotions overflowed; they embraced one another in tears and celebrated the reconciliation with a festive meal right in the heart of the disputed territory. From that day onward, the

Sinhalese and Tamil farmers have worked together in their fields under banners reading *Keth bimata samaya*, "Peace to the Rice Fields." Henceforth, both the government forces and the militants would learn that the presence of banners meant that there were unarmed farmers in the fields. Furthermore, the farmers pleaded with the warring parties not to roam the rice fields, the unofficial peace zone of the farmers.

During the months of April and May 2000, the farmers worked together under the peace banners, cultivating the disputed territory for the first time in ten years. In April alone, they cultivated six hundred of the area's twelve hundred acres. Everything seemed to be going well until one day in late May, when Tamil militants took away by force a tractor belonging to a Sinhalese farmer. This was a blow to the peace initiative of the farmers. As a consequence, the United Peace Committee became inactive; Mendis received death threats and was attacked in the parish house on September 1, 2000. His assailants were not from among those involved in the process of reconciliation, but some Sinhalese farmers who were opposed to it. Mendis was forced to leave Nugelanda and take up residence in Ampara, twenty kilometers away.

Meanwhile the situation in the fields continued to deteriorate. Some Sinhalese farmers went to the extent of asking the government forces to protect them while they worked in the fields, as they had done in the days before the reconciliation. As a result, a few armed military personnel were sent to the fields. But soon Tamil militants attacked them and killed two home guards (Sinhalese villagers recruited to guard the villages against militant attacks) and one policeman. The official protection of the Sinhalese farmers was discontinued. Presuming that Tamil militants would not attack them while the Tamil farmers worked their fields, the Sinhalese farmers watched for the Tamil farmers to appear far away in the horizon. On the days that the Tamil farmers worked their fields, the Sinhalese farmers also worked. Both sides harvested in tears the fields that they had sowed in song.

Just as everything seemed to be falling apart, about fifteen Sinhalese farmers took the initiative to evaluate the situation in November 2000. At this meeting, Mendis invited them to join him in visiting the Tamil farmers. The visits took place in January 2001. A group of Sinhalese farmers met a group of Tamil farmers at the Palamunai refugee camp, and then another group of Tamil farmers in Kaluwanchikudy, south of Batticaloa. These encounters helped to build up the damaged solidarity between the Tamil and Sinhalese farmers. They recommitted themselves to strive together for a peaceful future.

It was once the case in Nugelanda that a few farmers were killed in every agricultural season. But since the beginning of the reconciliation process, no farmer has been victimized in the rice fields. The disputed territory in Nugelanda is perhaps the only one in Sri Lanka that is routinely traversed by unarmed civilians. The territory has become an unofficial peace zone. Sinhalese farmers can cultivate their fields without the protection of government forces, and Tamil farmers are able to cultivate their fields after ten years of banishment. This successful initiative revealed to both sides that dialogue and communion are possible.

Case III: Peace Initiatives of Kitusara

Meaning "Light of Christ" in Sinhalese, *Kitusara* began as a group of Roman Catholic youth who came together to reflect on the tragic events of the 1980s in light of their Christian faith. The decade of the 1980s witnessed the greatest number of large-scale massacres in Sri Lankan history. The disastrous Tamil riots took place in 1983; an insurrection of Sinhalese youth in late 1980s was ruthlessly suppressed by the government, killing thousands. These two massacres were the loci for action, reflection, and prayer for the *Kitusara* group.

Since August 1990, the group has been publishing a monthly news magazine, *Kitusara*, which has proven to be a useful instrument for raising consciousness among people in the south about their ability and obligation to advocate for the rights of the Tamil minority. Ending the conflict is *Kitusara*'s goal, and most of the articles aim at shaping a value system as a foundation for living in community as brothers and sisters. The group published a book called *Sanvedi* ("Sensitivity"), detailing at length the futility of war. Some groups involved in peacemaking have borrowed ideas from this book for their antiwar campaigns, such as the slogan, "The war destroys both you and your family." *Sanvedi* attempts to convince the Sinhalese population that war offers no victory to the people; the multinational arms trade and its local allies are war's only victors.

Oliei Nokki ("Towards Light") is a Tamil magazine published by *Kitusara*, which features the writings of Tamils suffering because of the war. *Oliei Nokki* is unique in being a Tamil-language magazine for peace published by a group of Sinhalese youth. It was established as a grassroots response to a pressing need for authentic communication between north and south after an encouraging reaction from Tamil sectors to a Christmas message published and distributed by *Kitusara* group in the north. It is perhaps the only medium of communicating to the north about the true situation in the south. The sad plight of soldier families, widows, and orphans; the poverty that drives young men and women to become soldiers; the inalienable right of Tamils to their land; protests in the South against the war; and the enormous war expenditure are some of the issues addressed in its pages. Despite major financial difficulties, it continues to be published quarterly.

With the arrival of the IPKF in the north in 1987, trains began to operate between Colombo and Jaffna, and *Kitusara* youth were the first Sinhalese peace group to visit the north. They traveled two to three times a year, often in small groups and occasionally in larger groups of about forty youth. These encounters opened the eyes of southerners, who had been kept ignorant of the sufferings of the people living in the north. They were shocked to find, for example, that a particular refugee camp which accommodated eight hundred refugees did not possess a single toilet.

Recalling these visits, *Kitusara* editor Mahinda Namal said:

> Having discovered the naked truth, we felt obliged to communicate it, hence we planned musical programs. So far we have staged over 300 such singing events. Flowers are the same whether they blossom in the North or

South, and similarly the children. From a Christian perspective, the children who die because of the war are neither Sinhalese nor Tamil but God's children. We continue to convince people that the human person is stifled by the war irrespective of race, sex, or religion.

Apart from its musical programs, the group has organized numerous seminars and discussions on the need for peace; over two hundred such meetings have been held in the south, and over fifty in the north.

The *Kitusara* group has been a challenge to Christian churches and organizations which lack consistency in their approach to ethnic issues. The very Sinhalese and Tamil Christians who profess brotherhood and sisterhood during liturgies and services of worship often rejoice over the deaths of members of the opposing group in their day-to-day life. *Kitusara* youth have been confronting the hypocritical attitudes held by some institutional churches and individual Christians.

In another act of solidarity, *Kitusara* advocated for the just allocation of resources for schools in the north. The ministry of education is charged with distributing textbooks needed for the schools at the beginning of the year. Often such supplies are delayed to marginalized schools. Tamil schools in the Vanni area, and poorer Sinhalese schools in the South have suffered from a lack of textbooks. *Kitusara* launched a poster campaign and insisted that the authorities, including the president of Sri Lanka, attend to this need. The poster campaign was perceived by the Tamils in Vavuniya as a gesture of Sinhalese brotherhood and sisterhood struggling for the rights of marginalized Tamil students in Vanni. On another occasion, when LTTE detainees were attacked and killed in the Bindunuwewa Rehabilitation Center, *Kitusara* launched a poster campaign protesting the heinous crime.

Having observed that there are many who are ready to die for the war, and hardly any who wish to lay down their lives for peace, *Kitusara* published a book on the lives of four priests who sacrificed their lives for peace: Fathers Mary Bastian in Mannar, Chandra Fernando in Batticaloa, Michael Rodrigo in Buttala, and Srilal Ameratunga in Negombo. Recalling a liturgical celebration in Mannar attended by vast crowds to commemorate the anniversary of Fr. Mary Bastian's death, Namal observed: "Just as the blood of Jesus created new relationships, the blood of these martyrs has made us a family. I do not know your language, and I am not from your area, but I have become a relative of the Tamils of Mannar through the blood of Fr. Mary Bastian."

The major achievement of *Kitusara* is the formation of a group of youth who are able to understand the ethnic conflict in Sri Lanka from the perspective of the oppressed.

PEACEMAKING ACTIVITIES AND MOTIVATIONS

For those concerned with inspiring others to work for peace, it is important to understand what motivates grassroots peacemaking and which sorts of peacemaking activities may be within the realm of the possible for most people, as well as more neglected forms of peacemaking. In addition, we undertook studies of gender differences in peacemaking, images of the divine and the opponent, and belief in a just world (see chapter 1).

By far the most common peacemaking activities in Sri Lanka were those in the category of relationship building (see chapter 1). Acts of service were also common. Less frequent but still statistically significant were reports of having avoided members of the opposing group, presumably in order to prevent a conflictual situation from developing. Praying for peace was the least frequently reported mode of peacemaking activity in Sri Lanka. A majority of respondents tended to speak of their peacemaking activities in very general, nonspecific terms, yet these respondents were more likely to report having prayed for peace than those who were specific about their peacemaking actions.

All four motivational categories (see chapter 1)—practical, relational, ideological, and religious—were statistically significant in Sri Lanka. Practical and relational motives were the most commonly reported; ideological motives were the next most frequent, and religious motives the least frequent. Given the devastation and deepened ethnic enmity wrought by decades of war, the primacy of practical and relational motivations is not surprising. Many Sri Lankans long for peace if only so that they can tend to their basic needs and those of their children. They long for an end to the terror and poverty inflicted by the war. As the Nugelanda and *Kitusara* case studies suggest, people at the grassroots also long for communion and solidarity with their fellow Sri Lankans, be they Tamil, Muslim, or Sinhalese.

In the multireligious milieu of Sri Lanka, with its nontheist majority of Buddhists, the relatively low priority of religious motivation for grassroots peacemaking is understandable. Christians are culturally conditioned to abandon "God talk" when they speak about issues of concern to everyone, regardless of religious affiliation—such as peacemaking, economic development, and environmental protection. Christian "God talk" in particular is alien to Buddhists, Hindus, and Muslims. Hence, it is avoided outside the confines of the Christian communities in general. In addressing social issues, many within Sri Lanka's religiously pluralistic milieu are therefore more comfortable using the relatively secular and ideological rhetoric of human rights. In addition, the religious training many Christians received as children makes it difficult for them to relate their religious faith to social issues. These phenomena could also explain why praying for peace was reported relatively rarely—prayer may focus more commonly on personal or familial matters or may simply not be regarded as a peacemaking activity.

The sample for our study of gender differences in peacemaking activities and motivations included members of *Kitusara*, the Roman Catholic parish of Vavuniya, and Tekkawatta Village. From among these, Tekkawatta and a smaller sample of respondents from the Vavuniya Catholic parish were individually interviewed on their images of God and of the opponent, as well as on the extent to which they believed that the world is just. Also included in the latter study were students from the secondary school at Holy Family Convent in Colombo.

The table on the following page provides demographic information about the samples used in both the gender study (I) and the study of images of the divine/images of the opponent/BJW (II). The larger number of Catholics than Protestants in the sample reflects Sri Lankan demographic realities; while Catholics make up about seven percent of the total population, all the Protestant denominations together form only about one percent (*Statistical Abstract of the Democratic Socialist Republic of Sri Lanka* 1991, 49).

GENDER DIFFERENCES IN GRASSROOTS PEACEMAKING

In Sri Lanka, men involved in peacemaking were more likely than women to engage in acts of service and to cite religious motives (see Table 1). These findings may be due to men having more resources or mobility to engage in acts of service and more access to religious education than women. In the case of Catholic peacemakers, however, women have equal access to traditional catechetical instruction; in fact, a larger number of women receive traditional religious education than do men. But as the foregoing discussion of religious motivation suggests, traditional religious education does not always enable people to relate their Christian faith to social issues. Men have greater access to new thinking in theology by way of informal reflection sessions conducted by progressive groups. Contemporary theology helps people to relate Christian faith to social issues such as the ethnic conflict, environmental protection, and good governance. But often these discussions are held after sunset. On account of cultural constraints and danger to personal security at night, most of the women are forced to confine themselves to their homes after dark.

IMAGES OF THE DIVINE, IMAGES OF THE OPPONENT, AND BELIEF IN A JUST WORLD

The more peacemaking actions of any variety that respondents had engaged in, and the more motives they cited (with the exception of religious motives), the less comfortable they were with *any* images of the divine—agentic, immanent, or power-over (see chapter 1). This may again be due to peacemakers' sensitivity to the religious pluralism of Sri Lankan society, in which Buddhism, a nontheistic religion, claims the majority of adherents.

Peacemakers citing religious motivations, however, tended to hold a relatively wide range of images of the divine, particularly immanent and power-over images. These respondents were also more likely to believe in a just world than those lower in religious motivation.

Respondents who were particularly high in power-over images of the divine

Kitusara Youth (I)

Sinhalese/Female/Roman Catholic	17
Sinhalese/Male/Roman Catholic	17
Total	34

Roman Catholic Parish of Vavuniya (I only)

Tamil/Female/Roman Catholic	19
Sinhalese/Female/Roman Catholic	1
Tamil/Male/Roman Catholic	18
Total	38

Roman Catholic Parish of Vavuniya (I & II)

Tamil/Female/Roman Catholic	9
Tamil/Male/Roman Catholic	12
Sinhalese/Female/Roman Catholic	5
Sinhalese/Male/Roman Catholic	2
Total	28

Tekkawatta Village (I & II)

Tamil/Female/Protestant	9
Tamil/Female/Roman Catholic	1
Tamil/Male/Protestant	10
Sinhalese/Female/Protestant	11
Sinhalese/Male/Protestant	7
Sinhalese/Male/Roman Catholic	1
Total	39

Holy Family Convent School, Colombo (II)

Tamil/Female/Roman Catholic	11
Tamil/Female/Protestant	2
Tamil/Female/Hindu	7
Sinhalese/Female/Roman Catholic	20
Total	40

tended to report having engaged in very general, nonspecific types of peacemaking acts. Belief in a powerful God who is able to change the course of history at will may serve as a demotivator for engaging in concrete peacemaking initiatives. An image of God that emphasizes power over other divine attributes may seem to render human efforts meaningless or unnecessary.

Protestants held a wider range of images of the divine than did Catholics (see Table 2). This may be due to the fact that there is a greater biblical emphasis in Protestant churches than in Catholic churches. Indeed, the majority of Catholics in Sri Lanka receive relatively little in the way of biblical instruction. Biblical texts present a God who is multifaceted: a vulnerable infant, a good shepherd, a pillar of fire, a leader of armies, a lamb enthroned.

Furthermore, Protestants—both Sinhalese and Tamil—held more positive images of the "opposite" ethnic group than did Catholics (see Table 2). In other words, Sinhalese Protestants perceived Tamils more positively than did Sinhalese Catholics, and Tamil Protestants perceived Sinhalese more positively than did Tamil Catholics. Being smaller in number than Catholics, Protestants in Sri Lanka likewise have smaller communities, and therefore there is likely to be more interaction among the membership of Protestant groups than in Catholic groups. Thus the opportunity is greater for encounter between Tamils and Sinhalese in Protestant churches than in Catholic churches. It is easier to get to know and make friends with people of another ethnicity in Protestant churches than in Catholic churches. Furthermore, Protestants' more positive images of the "opposite" ethnic group could also be due to different emphases in Protestant and Catholic missionary methods. While Protestant missionaries stressed Christian identity over and above the sense of belonging to one's ethnic group, the Catholic Tamils and Sinhalese still identify themselves more strongly with their ethnicity than with their faith community.

On the other hand, Catholics reported on average more peacemaking actions and motivations than Protestants (see Table 2). First, it should be said that Christian churches in general—Catholics as well as Protestants—are not involved in grassroots peacemaking except perhaps in the form of prayer; some distribute food and clothing to some victims of the conflict. Among the thirty-nine Protestant respondents in this study, thirty-six belonged to the Tekkawatta community in Vavuniya, which is affiliated with the local Assembly of God church. For practical reasons, they may confine themselves mostly to the membership of their own community in their acts of relationship building and service, thus having fewer peacemaking activities to report. Catholics in our study belonged to several communities; their larger network in Sri Lanka could facilitate efforts outside the ecclesial community and result in their having more opportunities for taking part in grassroots peacemaking efforts.

A couple of other matters relating to religious affiliation warrant mention here. Among Catholics only, more positive images of the opponent were associated with higher numbers of peacemaking acts. Finally, though there were some Hindu respondents in our sample, they were all teenage girls and all enrolled in the Holy Family Convent School in Colombo; moreover, their numbers were insufficient to include in our statistical comparisons.

Peacemakers who scored high in belief in a just world cited fewer motivations for peacemaking than those whose BJW scores were low, especially in the ideological and practical categories. They were also particularly unlikely to engage in acts of relationship building, the largest category of peacemaking.

PEACEMAKING AND ETHNIC DIFFERENCES: A "NON-FINDING"

We found no evidence for ethnic disparities in peacemaking actions and motivations—in other words, Tamils and Sinhalese did not differ in the type or number of the peacemaking activities they engaged in, nor in the type or number of motivations they cited for their peacemaking. This "non-result" is in itself noteworthy. It indicates that in Sri Lanka, though many Tamils and Sinhalese are mortal enemies of one another, ethnicity is not a major factor affecting motivations or actions for peace. This gives us reason for hope. In the end, though some of us disagree on the causes of the conflict, we are far more alike than we are different when it comes to how and why we work for peace.

ELEMENTS FOR A THEOLOGY OF PEACE IN SRI LANKA

This section, while not pretending to offer an integrated theology of peace for Sri Lanka, will identify some important factors that would need to be taken into account in developing any such local theology: concepts of violence and peace, scripture as a resource in peacemaking, the ministry of leadership in peacemaking, and obstacles to peacemaking. These are both perceptions and realities of the world in which grassroots peacemakers operate.

CONCEPTS OF VIOLENCE AND PEACE

Many in Sri Lanka, peacemakers included, believe that the Tamil voice was not heard by the Sinhalese majority rule until the Tamil militants became a threat to the government. If they had not taken up arms, their demand for equality might have been ignored. In that sense, it may be argued that violence had some positive value. The militants were, after all, reacting to the repressive government policies of the post-independence era. When Tamil leaders tried to fight for the rights of the Tamils through nonviolent means, they were marginalized and victimized.

But peacemakers believe that there has to be a limit to violence. Under no circumstances should innocent civilians be targeted. Furthermore, they would argue that violence settles nothing and that an ardent effort should be made to solve problems through negotiation. War is a distorted response to injustice; people need to evolve other, more creative forms of resistance. Peacemakers struggle to convince the government, the militants, and the people that a settlement can be reached only through a political solution and not by defeating the enemy militarily. Even when the war stops, they warn, there will be large numbers of young women and men who will have severe problems as they try to integrate into civil society. These women and men hold onto their guns and use them to settle disputes of all kinds. It may take half a century to abolish the gun culture from among the young women and men who are today using guns in the battlefield. Finally, peacemakers believe that violence is a result of inequality and therefore, assurance of equal rights would diminish violence.

Surprisingly, a majority of those we interviewed who are involved in grassroots peace efforts had to struggle to describe their understanding of peace. They were quick to articulate what peace was *not*. Breathing the air of hostility, facing the disaster of war and violence, it was easier for them to put into words the negative experiences which haunted them day in and day out. When there is war, when thousands of young women and men carry arms, when there are checkpoints, when people are arrested, tortured, and killed—then there is no peace. But grassroots peacemakers were unanimous that peace is far more than the absence of war; yet as long as there is war, peace cannot be. They hope for peace as a future still to be realized, as the awakened nature of woman and man, as the dream of God. Peace can take root wherever there is love, joy, patience, kindness, goodness, faithfulness, gentleness, justice, and righteousness.

SCRIPTURE AS A RESOURCE IN PEACEMAKING

As mentioned earlier, land is a critical issue in the Sri Lankan conflict. We have heard peacemakers quote Genesis 15, the story of God's promise of land and descendants to Abraham. Human beings have a right to the earth, to be free on the earth; as the land belongs to all, all must have their share. "They shall sit every man under his vine and under his fig tree, and none shall make them afraid" (Mic. 5:4).

Peacemakers also clamor for the beating of swords into ploughshares, and of spears into pruning hooks (see Mic. 4:3). The government defense expenditure in 1982 was Rupees 48,000,000, but in 1999 it swelled to Rupees 40,670,000,000 (93 rupees = 1 dollar) (*The Economic, Social and Human Cost of War in Sri Lanka* 2001, 16). Commenting on this colossal amount, Mahinda Namal said, "As Christians we can never approve this. There ought to be a massive protest worldwide against such expenditure." The allocations for the high-defense budget drain money from the health and education sectors. In the final analysis, the finances which should be spent on uplifting the poor are used to cripple and kill them. Christian peacemakers understand the will of God to be in direct contradiction to the allocation of money for the war. Prayer alone is not sufficient here, for God calls us to a greater commitment: "What does the Lord require of you but to do justice, and to love kindness, and to walk humbly with your God?" (Mic. 6:8), "[to] execute justice and righteousness in the land" (Jer. 23:5)—that is, in the north and the south, among Tamils and Sinhalese. For in Christ there is neither Jew no Greek, there is neither slave nor free, there is neither male nor female—and there is neither Sinhala nor Tamil—for all are one in Christ (see Gal. 3:28).

The dream of the poor and victimized is the dream of God: a world without violence where "the wolf shall dwell with the lamb . . . the lion shall eat straw like the ox" (Isa. 11:6-7). Peacemakers hope against hope for a new Sri Lanka, when young women will not be victimized as war widows or prostitutes, when children are no longer orphans or refugees. They hope for a day when tears will be wiped away, and when mourning, pain, and death will disappear from this land (see Rev. 21:4).

The Ministry of Leadership in Peacemaking

The dynamics of leadership in each of the groups in the case studies presented above—the Peace Committee of Batticaloa, the Nugelanda farmers, and *Kitusara* —are participatory. While male clerics have figured prominently in the leadership of each, the groups follow democratic procedures in all their decisions and function with minimal bureaucracy.

The Nugelanda farmers in particular exhibit enormous diversity. They are women and men belonging to two ethnic groups, three religions, and diverse political affiliations. They are Sinhalese, Tamils, Hindus, Buddhists, and Christians, from both the right and left ends of the political spectrum. The village leaders in Nugelanda took the initiative for the Nugelanda peace effort. Undoubtedly, the Reverend Mendis bore a heavy weight of responsibility and leadership in this venture. Everybody realized that, at one stage, Mendis was on his own, dragging the whole reluctant throng toward peace. But now the leadership is shared among many. The group has learned to bear the burden of responsibility together.

The norm in leadership of grassroots peace initiatives in Sri Lanka is diversity. Buddhists, Hindus, and Muslims (as in the Vanni Peace Foundation), laywomen (as in the *Sunila* Women's Development Movement), and laymen (as in the *Bingusara* drama group) have played vital leadership roles in grassroots peace efforts. The ministry of leadership for peacemaking at the grassroots is evolving away from authoritarian models toward democratic, participatory, and inclusive approaches that invite and enable the talents and strengths of diverse individuals.

Obstacles to Peacemaking

Obstacles are part of the real struggle of grassroots peacemakers. They are therefore a legitimate and necessary locus for theological reflection. *Kitusara* interprets obstacles as an experience of impasse and impossibility, calling for profound thinking and committed action. Its members believe that the Christian vision has the potential to enlighten the faithful in any crisis situation and to lead the way to a fruitful ministry of reconciliation.

In the present study, the main obstacles that we encountered to peacemaking in Sri Lanka were as follows: contradictory concepts of peace, historical memories of terror and oppression, the war economy, lack of commitment to peace on the part of religious leadership, and an inability to mobilize a mass movement for peace.

Contradictory Concepts of Peace

According to the majority of Sinhalese, peace means the end of the armed conflict. These people assume that on the day the LTTE withdraws from the areas it has occupied and hands over the weapons of war, peace will dawn in Sri Lanka.

But for most of the Tamils, peace is a question of language rights, land rights, and federal autonomy. These are two conflicting notions of peace.

Historical Memories

History records that Tamils destroyed the ancient Sinhalese capitals such as Anuradhapura and Polonnaruwa. When reading the history of Buddhism in Sri Lanka, the Sinhalese tend to equate the present Tamil population with the wrong-doers in these historical crimes. On the other hand, Tamils have lived with post-independence majority Sinhalese policies that have denied them freedom and equal opportunity to education, suppressed their language, and threatened their lands with colonization. Meanwhile both sides have ruthlessly killed thousands of innocent civilians. While the Tamils see Sinhalese as oppressors, the Sinhalese see Tamils as terrorists.

The War Economy

An economy dependent on war is a severe obstacle to peace in Sri Lanka. Those involved in the war industry are reported to be earning fabulous sums of money. In a sense, both the Sri Lankan military and Tamil militia have gained through the war. Some enjoy economic benefits and power that would be unthinkable in peaceful circumstances. This is true even at the grassroots level, where the home guards resist peace efforts for fear of losing their employment.

Lack of Commitment among Religious Leaders

For the most part, institutional religion has become an obstacle to peace in Sri Lanka. Buddhist, Hindu, Christian, and Muslim organizations have not been consistent in their stance on the ethnic conflict. Instead of declaring a clear and unequivocal position on the war and maintaining it at any cost, the religious leadership of this country has vacillated and accommodated the opinions of war agents. When the political leadership plans for war, the religious leaders bless the soldiers; when they talk peace, the religious leaders too preach peace. This lack of consistency on the part of the religious institutions is a major obstacle to the peace process.

Inability to Mobilize for Peace

In Sri Lanka, people involved in peacemaking are very few. It seems an impossible task to convince the majority of people—who drift from one opinion to another regarding war and peace—to become involved in peace efforts. The handful of people struggling for peace at the grassroots has as yet been unable to make a significant impact on the peace process. The lack of a massive movement at the grassroots frustrates hopes for peace.

CHALLENGES TO THE CHURCHES

Will the Christian churches, in the spirit of *Kitusara*, recognize the obstacles to peacemaking listed above as challenges to living the gospel? The example of

Christian peacemakers in Sri Lanka demonstrates that an authentic, contemporary commitment to follow Jesus Christ calls for a radically new understanding of the mission of Christian churches. Traditional Christian theology is not up to this task. The basic schema of creation-fall-redemption does not adequately interpret the Sri Lankan crisis. A new paradigm in theology is needed to address the phenomenon of conflict.

The point of departure for the new paradigm is the Exodus event: the struggle between the lords of Egyptian civilization and its victims, the liberation of Hebrew slaves, and a pact of the divine with the liberated toward a sustainable freedom. Freedom is defended by journeying with the God of slaves and refusing to bow down to gods of kings. Exodus is not only departure from Egypt but also having a portion in the promised land. This is not the inalienable right to land as interpreted in Zionist theologies but the ownership of the means of production. Slavery and economic destitution demand the conversion of slave masters. It is a call to renounce power, prestige, and wealth so that everyone may have freedom, a share of the means of production, and human dignity.

This was also the mission of the prophets. A careful analysis of the prophetic literature leads us to the same conclusions. Tyrants bring oppression, and the concentrated ownership of the means of production creates destitution. Jesus of Nazareth identifies himself with the prophetic tradition of John the Baptist and rejects the options taken by the Sadducees, Pharisees, Essenes, and Zealots. Jesus' call for conversion meant rejection of power, prestige, and wealth—the temptations Jesus faced in the desert (see Matt. 3:4-11 and Luke 4:4-13). The message and praxis of the reign of God were a call to restore human dignity, to freedom, and to ownership of the means of production. This is what it means to declare the year of the Lord—the old concept of jubilee when the means of production is restored to everyone who had lost it. Jesus' commitment to jubilee justice led to his death because the mighty of the earth would not tolerate it. But Jesus' God, the God of slaves, confirmed him in the resurrection.

The early church witnessed to Christ's death and resurrection, and thus to his continuous struggle to restore human dignity to the slaves of the earth. No church which claimed to witness to salvation in Jesus Christ could speak of spirituality apart from the message and praxis of God's reign for freedom and ownership of the means of production.

Without this paradigm shift (from a theology of creation-fall-redemption to a theology anchored in the God of slaves), the involvement of the churches in the struggle for peace in Sri Lanka will be useless and even damaging. Those churches which have the courage to make this paradigm shift might begin to see spirituality in a broader perspective and initiate a fruitful dialogue for peace in this land.

Putting it bluntly, most grassroots peacemakers in Sri Lanka are poor. The majority of the victims of war are poor as well. An ongoing radical involvement with the poor is a major challenge for the churches and a prerequisite for working toward reconciliation. The churches could facilitate encounters between Tamil and Sinhalese victims of war, such as disabled government soldiers and disabled Tamil militants, war widows, refugees, and orphans from both sides. *Kitusara* successfully organized an encounter between the families of dead Sinhalese soldiers and families of dead Tamil militants. It was the first ever meeting between the victims of warring parties. They wept together for each other on that day. Such experiences of sharing suffering and compassion on a human level need to be multiplied throughout the country. The churches could be catalysts for these exchanges.

Some issues are common to both Tamils and Sinhalese. One such issue was the distribution of textbooks in government schools, as mentioned above in the account of the third case study. When Tamil schools in the Vanni area and poorer Sinhalese schools elsewhere did not receive these resources, the youth of *Kitusara* campaigned on their behalf, and the Tamils considered it a great gesture of solidarity from Sinhalese youth. Similar issues could be addressed by the churches. These common struggles create solidarity among Tamils and Sinhalese, and grassroots peacemakers testify that they are roadways to ethnic reconciliation. At the moment, Sinhalese and Tamil fishermen face a severe problem in common: they are barred from fishing in certain areas because of security concerns of the government. Yet foreign fishing trawlers frequent Sri Lankan seas, plundering the resources of the poor fishermen for whom it is a question of life and death. This is a challenge for the churches: to be a voice for Sinhalese and Tamil fishermen.

What constitutes "truth" in communication about the war is a major issue in Sri Lanka. People do not have access to accurate information. Many Sinhalese soldier families are still expecting the return of a son or a husband or a father who is reported to be missing in action. They think that these loved ones are in LTTE custody and will come home in the near future. According to the LTTE, most of these "missing" are in fact already dead. Successive governments are believed to have concealed the truth about missing soldiers. Christian churches, however, are in a unique position to gather information, being located in both Sinhalese and Tamil territories. They could create an information bureau to obtain, verify, and release information about persons, incidents, repressive policies, and human rights violations. Media are controlled by the government and at times influenced by extremist elements. In these situations, churches could be a voice for truth.

The agents of the war economy must be exposed. Extremist groups are fueled by those who benefit from the war economy, such as arms dealers and certain high-ranking government officers. They rally against sustainable peace. It is the prophetic role of the churches to reveal their crimes and injustices, and to cry out against blood money. In a situation of a prolonged conflict like Sri Lanka's, even the poor can become dependent on the war economy. The home guards referred to above are an example of this phenomenon. They fear that with the peace process, they will lose their livelihood. If the war economy is to be transformed, people must be made aware of it, and alternative avenues of employment for the poor who depend upon it must be created. This could be a common project for the churches, undertaken with the help of nongovernmental organizations.

The majority Christian community in Sri Lanka, the Roman Catholic Church, could facilitate encounters between Sinhalese and Tamil parishes to create good will and understanding. If fifty Sinhalese parishes could embark on an ongoing fellowship project with fifty Tamil parishes, it would be a significant contribution to a peace culture in Sri Lanka. The churches could facilitate a major inter-religious peace effort involving Buddhists, Hindus, Christians, and Muslims. Although there are a few religious leaders who are aware of this need and acting on it, they have not succeeded in engaging people at the grassroots. Inviting and coordinating the participation of over 500 communities belonging to four religions could be the beginning of a massive peace movement inspired by religious values. Our research demonstrates that religious motives were the least frequently cited by the grassroots peacemakers. Religious values are an underutilized resource for peacemaking. If the core values of religions are to be tapped, an interreligious understanding of peace, or a peace philosophy/theology acceptable to people belonging to the four major religious traditions of Sri Lanka must be developed. This is a task for the theologians and scholars of religion that can be carried out only in dialogue with the people at the grassroots.

The churches have a vital role to play in sustaining the cease-fire in effect since December 2001. People are tired of the war and they do not want the government or the LTTE to go back to fighting. At this hour of hope, the churches must be vigilant, and urge warring parties to stop choosing war as the only solution to the ethnic problem. As custodians of nonviolence, they should exert pressure on both sides to abandon the armed struggle and call for a negotiated political settlement. Nonviolence is constitutive of Buddhism, and an unflinching dialogue with Sinhalese Buddhists at the grassroots could make it the norm in Sri Lanka. Since a political settlement would demand renunciation on the part of the warring parties, it would, in a sense, be a spiritual journey. The role of religions is vital in this respect, and the churches face the challenge of initiating and sustaining this process.

CONCLUSION

The conflict in Sri Lanka has roots in European colonization and has mushroomed into a civil war as a result of the repressive government policies of Sinhalese majority rule. The poor are the most affected by the war. The great majority of those who have been killed in this conflict through direct fighting, attacks on civilians, accidental killings, and collateral damage, are mainly poor. This is not simply because the majority of Sri Lankans are poor, but rather because the political and economic structures expose the poor to the violence and exploit them as cannon fodder. The majority of fighting cadres among Tamils as well as Sinhalese are poor. Rich Sinhalese are not compelled to send their children to join the government security forces, and rich Tamils are able to escape LTTE recruitment by leaving the war zone. Most of the rich Tamils either migrate to Western countries or resettle in Colombo. Most of those who die in the conflict are their family's breadwinners. Women, on the other hand, have been raped, widowed, or compelled to take up prostitution as their means of livelihood. The country is left with a multitude of traumatized orphans.

People from the grassroots of society have been implicated in the ethnic conflict, making reconciliation a long process. Extremist positions on both sides of the conflict generally leave little room for grassroots peace initiatives. Their initiators have been attacked and threatened with death. As a result, only a few have been willing to accept the risks of grassroots peacemaking. In the early stages of our research, many of those involved in grassroots peace efforts refused to share information with us, and even when they did, it was not meant for publication. Fortunately the ceasefire has changed the situation.

Having presented an overview of initiatives which could be categorized as grassroots peacemaking, we next described three particular cases at length. They are the Peace Committee of Batticaloa, the United Peace Committee in Nugelanda, and *Kitusara*. The Peace Committee in Batticaloa has been a custodian of human rights in defense of innocent victims—against the powerful war machinery. Sinhalese and Tamil farmers of Nugelanda initiated a peace effort to safeguard their livelihood. Even when their efforts were frustrated, they kept alive the goal of ethnic reconciliation. *Kitusara*, whose members are mostly Sinhalese youth, based their work for peace on building relationships by visiting and engaging in dialogue with Tamils.

Ethnicity is not a major factor affecting motivations or actions for peace, and the most frequently cited motivations were practical and relational. These are signs of hope for the future. They indicate that Tamils and Sinhalese can work together toward reconciliation. Relationship building, the most common form of grassroots peacemaking, builds a foundation for truth, justice, and reconciliation. Religious motivations were relatively infrequent; most grassroots peacemakers avoid "God talk" or religious language because of the interreligious nature of this work, and due to the failure of traditional Christian indoctrination to relate spirituality to social involvement.

The concepts of peace and violence, scripture as a resource for peacemaking, the evolving nature of leadership, and obstacles to peace are important elements for a contemporary Sri Lankan theology of peace. The main obstacles encountered by grassroots peacemakers are contradictory concepts of peace, historical memories of terror and oppression, the war economy, lack of commitment for peace on the part of religious leadership, and an inability to mobilize for peace on a large scale.

The identity of the Christian churches is tied to reconciliation between God and human beings, and among human beings. The task of mediating reconciliation in this conflict is part and parcel of the churches' mission. The churches will fail to grasp this challenge in correct perspective without a paradigm shift in their understanding of salvation. A commitment to the poor, relationship building between Tamils and Sinhalese at the grassroots, courage to expose the truth, creating alternatives to the war economy, efforts toward mobilizing a broad-based, interreligious peace movement, dialogue toward nonviolence, and insistence on a politically negotiated settlement constitute challenges to the institutional churches.

Finally, a settlement negotiated at the highest levels will not on its own extinguish the fires of ethnic strife. Any such settlement will require massive support at the grassroots if the dream of peace and reconciliation is to become a reality.

STATISTICAL TABLES
ASSOCIATED WITH CHAPTER 6 DATA

See pages 184-186 for an interpretation of these tables. See chapter 1 for an explanation of variables.

TABLE 1. CORRELATIONAL COMPARISONS OF GENDER AND PEACEMAKING
    IN SRI LANKA

	Religious Motivations	Service
Gender*	-.18	-.19

* Positive correlations indicate that women reported this type of motivation or activity more frequently than did men. Only significant r's ($p < .05$) are reported here.

TABLE 2. CORRELATIONAL COMPARISONS OF DENOMINATIONAL DIFFERENCES
    IN SRI LANKA

	Total Images of the Divine*	Images of the Enemy**	Average Actions***	Average Motivations****
Denominational Affiliation*****	.54	.31	-.18	-.25

* "Total images of the divine" is the sum of agentic, immanent, and power-over images of the divine, averaged across respondents.

** The measure of enemy images was constructed such that higher scores would indicate more positive images.

*** Average actions are the sum of all peacemaking activities—relationship building, prayer, service, confrontation, and avoidance—averaged across individuals.

**** Average motivations are the average of all motivations—practical, relational, ideological, and religious—across respondents.

***** Positive correlations indicate that Protestants were higher on this dimension than were Catholics. Only significant r's ($p < .05$) are reported here.

7

South Sudan

People-to-People Peacemaking:
A Local Solution to Local Problems

JULIA AKER DUANY

The Jikany and Lou are two of the largest Nuer groups in South Sudan. To survive dry seasons, the Lou leave their villages and move to cattle camps along Nile River tributaries, in Jikany territory. In early 1993, after seasons of mounting tension, a minor incident set off a feud between the Jikany and Lou that became widespread in short order. Instead of spears or clubs, men carried guns supplied by both local liberation armies and the government of Sudan. Escalating cycles of attack and retaliation decimated villages and left over a thousand dead, including women and children.

In late 1994, efforts of the Presbyterian Church and local women to initiate a peace dialogue succeeded. Jikany and Lou came to a conference and made a covenant of peace.

But Nyaluak, a Jikany woman married to a Lou man, who lived among the Lou people in central Upper Nile, was among those who wondered, "Would it hold?"

I wish to express my deep sense of appreciation to the Workshop in Political Theory and Policy Analysis at Indiana University and especially to Vincent and Elinor Ostrom, Patty Dalecki, Gayle Higgins, Linda Smith, and all the visiting African scholars of the Workshop, particularly Amos Sawyer. I am deeply grateful to those who served on the research team in the Sudan—Galik Gatlou Riak, Doyok Chol, Stantino Makur Kot, and Mary Nyacin Chol—as well as to Gabriel Y. Doak and Gabriel Riam, and to the Sudanese churches, particularly the New Sudan Council of Churches and Presbyterian Church of the Sudan. Finally, heartfelt thanks to Isabel Hogue for her editorial work on this manuscript.

One day, a group of young Lou men—men not known in the Lou village where Nyaluak lived—went into Jikany territory and stole twenty cows. They brought the cattle to the river near Nyaluak's village, thinking they could escape the Jikany by hiding among the Lou.

When the people of Nyaluak's village saw new cattle near the river, they first thought a Jikany family had moved into the area. This was good news, because it meant that the covenant of peace was holding. But when Nyaluak and other women went out to welcome the family, they found only young men with guns. Nyaluak became suspicious when the men would not reveal their lineage, but she said nothing. The following day word came that Jikany cattle had been stolen.

Nyaluak knew that if she accused the strange Lou men, the village might turn on her because she was Jikany. But she let the words come out. Fortunately, other women shared her suspicions. They went with Nyaluak to the Lou chief. The chief then confronted the local liberation army commander and demanded an investigation. When the truth was discovered, the Jikany cattle were returned and the Lou men detained.

The voice of one woman had inspired an entire village to uphold the peace process by restoring justice and order. The story spread like wildfire throughout the region.

A brutal war has ravaged the Sudan for the past twenty years, pitting northern, largely Arab people against southern, black Africans. A war within the war has been raging in the south, pitting peoples like the Jikany and the Lou, or the Dinka and the Nuer, against one another. The Sudanese conflict has received relatively little world attention, despite the fact that two million people have died and the level of human suffering is beyond description. This chapter looks at the responses of grassroots Christian communities to violent conflict in South Sudan.[1] Its grassroots focus reflects a recognition that faith-based responses to violence originate on a moral level beyond the control of governing authorities. Though this study does not examine the broader civil war in Sudan, I will review the root causes of the North–South struggle to establish a context for the responses to violence in the southern part of the country. Then I will present the cases of grassroots intercommunity peacemaking occurring in the regions of Bahr el Ghazal, Equatoria, and Upper Nile. I will conclude this chapter with challenges for the Sudanese churches as they struggle to live up to their values and their ability to become trusted peacemakers.

This study is by no means a "final word." As Christian people, we have much to learn about the approaches and processes of grassroots peacemaking in different communities and cultures around the world. Above all, our learning must

---

[1] Both "South Sudan" and the broader term "the southern Sudan" are used here and in other reports and studies. "South Sudan" refers not to an officially recognized country, but to the regions of Bahr el Ghazal, Equatoria, and Upper Nile, defined since Sudanese independence in 1956 as "South Sudan." Movements for self-determination are centered on, but not limited to, South Sudan.

transform our practices, so that we truthfully "follow after the things which make for peace" (Rom. 14:19).

ROOT CAUSES OF THE NORTH–SOUTH STRUGGLE

"Thirty-seven years of the civil war have taken away the fresh blood, the young people," said a woman from South Sudan, mourning her three sons. Her words reflect a prevalent grassroots sentiment there. Since 1983, Sudan's war has killed an estimated two million people and displaced an estimated four million (Human Rights Watch/Africa 1994, 12; OLS 1995, 2). Most victims are civilians from the southern Sudan and Nuba Mountains. The Sudanese government, a military regime dominated by an Arab/Islamist elite, bears primary responsibility for this devastation. But a 1991 power struggle among the southern elite began a brutal, interfactional war among the liberation armies that turned southerner against southerner. That struggle too has taken many young lives.

War in the Sudan must be understood in terms of the larger issues rooted in its history. These issues include religion, race and identity, the centralization of state power together with its control of natural resources, and the consequences of colonial policies. I will briefly touch upon each of these.

RELIGION (MUSLIM VERSUS NON-MUSLIM)

The modern Republic of the Sudan came into existence in 1956. It is Africa's largest country, populated by thirty million people of very diverse ethnicity, religion, and culture. Among Sudan's 597 ethnic groups, more than 400 different languages and dialects are spoken. The two major religious groupings are Islam and Christianity, but many Sudanese also practice traditional African religions.

Although the roots go deeper, the southern Sudan's present troubles emerged in the early nineteenth century, as Arab-Muslim groups moved south up the Nile River Valley with an unshakable conviction of the superiority of their civilization and a religious motivation for assimilating black African peoples. The southern Sudan became then, and remains, a fierce battleground for religious conquest. For the non-Muslim southerner, "this period fixed a collective memory that the northerner was the primary source of danger" (Lesch 1998, 38).

RACE AND IDENTITY (ARAB VERSUS AFRICAN)

Modern northerners believe their ancestors came as traders and Islamic teachers to Sudan from the Arabian Peninsula, before and during the seventh century C.E. (see Holt and Daly 1986). Racially they consider themselves Arabs, and the southerners black Africans or original inhabitants. Most southerners accept this racial designation. In our interviews, a common response of Nuer and Dinka people to the question, "What do you think is the problem between the North and the South?" was, "We are black and they are Arabs." A Dinka from Bahr el Ghazal said:

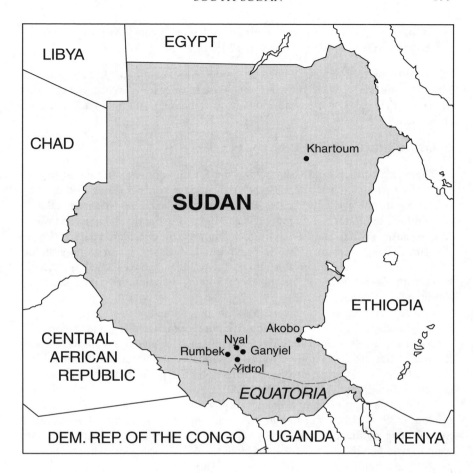

They are Arabs. We are Africans. They are Muslims. We are Christians—
not all of us, but a large part. We are black. They claim to be brown . . .
there is hostility deep inside us. The hostility is because of domination.
They want to dominate us; we want to control our country . . . they came
here as Arabs and settled. This is African land and they control it.

A Bari respondent from the Equatoria region observed, "We are parallel lines.
We do not meet. We are just like water and oil. We do not mix."

A Nuer man in the Lou community told us:

There is a cultural difference between us. North claims to be Arab while
we are African. The northerners marry their cousins. In our society you
have to find someone who is not your relative. They are Muslims . . . many
of them use the derogatory term *abid,* which means slave, in their private
conversation, and sometimes in public, in reference to southerners. We are

reminded that in the past, the southern part of the country was a source of slaves to be sold in the North and the Middle East.

A majority of respondents tended to agree. As one remarked, "They say it directly: *abid,* slave. Slave is the term they use to refer to us. When you talk and get angry, they call you *abid* and walk away. Sometimes you fight back and confront them."

POLITICAL AND ECONOMIC CONTROL IN THE SOUTH

There is a further, vital issue behind the Sudan conflict: differential power. Since the first encounter of Arabs and Africans, the conflict over resources has been clear. In the early 1800s, the British colonists had a considerable stake in controlling Mediterranean trade routes, and Egypt's geopolitical landscape was a link to European markets. At that time, Sudan was still considered part of Egypt. But British aims were frustrated in part because, over the centuries, migrations of Arab and black African groups into northern Sudan had weakened the ancient bond with Egypt. Many of the northern Sudan's peoples had come to reject Egyptian identity and control.

In 1881, a northern Sudanese Muslim proclaimed himself the *Mahdi*, a divinely appointed guide who would drive out Ottoman and Egyptian rulers and establish an Islamic state. The *Mahdi* led a rebellion, threatening both British and Egyptian interests. They joined forces to suppress it. The Sudan remained the scene of a power struggle involving British and Egyptian interests for years to come (Beshir 1968, 84; Collins 1999, 120).

The British administered what was known as the Anglo-Egyptian Condominium (1899-1955), according to their tradition of indirect rule. They divided Sudan along political, cultural, religious, and ethnic lines. The British did not want to risk disturbing political stability in the Arab North, especially by raising political aspirations in the African South. They held off economic and social development in the South, and took steps to isolate the southern population from much contact with Arab/Islamic hegemony (see Collins 1999, 121; Lesch 1998, 48; Wai 1981, 90). This helps explain why the Arab/Islamic polity was protected in the North while the culture, languages, religions, education, and polity of the African South came under the Western influence of English-speaking Christian missionaries.

The long-term consequence of separating the northern and southern administrative regions was to institutionalize a northern cultural tradition of identity politics (Arab Islamic) and a southern expectation of self-rule. The dichotomy became identified in the North under the rubric of "the Southern Problem" (Albino 1970, 45; Collins 1999, 113).

During the 1940s, the Condominium's stability was challenged by the rise of a northern nationalist movement. This political development exacerbated the religious and political differences between Islam and Christianity and further excluded any voice the southern people might have had then in determining their political future.

During the transitional years of 1953-1955, dominant nationalist parties in the Sudan pushed hard for political independence from Egypt. They held out, as bait to lure southern leaders to side with their resolution, a promise of federal arrangements to allow for southern self-rule. But once the anti-Egypt parties took control of the constitutional proceedings, it became clear that the Arab North had no intention of sharing power with the African South. The South was up in arms. The first civil war broke out a few months before the flag of the Republic of Sudan was raised on January 1, 1956. A succession of northern governments has been unable ever since either to impose full hegemony upon the South or to bring the conflict under control.

THE YEARS SINCE INDEPENDENCE

The civil war that broke out in 1955 continued until 1972, when President Muhammad Nimeiry's government signed the Addis Ababa Accord, establishing an autonomous regional government in the South. There was a decade of relative tranquillity. But the Accord did not last, because the foundation for a pluralistic, democratic society was simply not there (Beshir 1968, 87; Wai 1981, 188).

During the 1970s, Sudan had a good relationship with the Soviet Union. Many economic experts were sent to Sudan. But the failure of Nimeiry's socialistic economic development schemes pulled the Sudan away from the influence of the Soviet Union and strengthened its ties with Egypt and Saudi Arabia. The shift renewed interest in correcting "the Southern Problem." The government began implementing additional policies forcing the South to adopt Arab culture, language, and religion. The economic crisis, however, continued to worsen.

It was the discovery of mineral and petroleum deposits in the South during the early 1980s that offered Nimeiry's failing government the miracle it so desperately needed. To seize the wealth, Nimeiry had to regain control of the South. In an effort to rally support from the northern political parties, in early 1983 he instituted *Sharia*, or Islamic law, as Sudan's civil law. This move was key, since "if Sudan was an Islamic state, non-Moslems would be denied political positions—and so southerners would be denied any influence on how the oil money would be spent" (Rasmusen 2000, 8).

In mid-1983 Sudan exploded into a second period of civil war. Southern resistance was fragmented, but John Garang, a military man with Marxist credentials, organized the Sudan Peoples' Liberation Army (SPLA) and seized power by eliminating his rivals (Lesch 1998, 48). Marxist-Leninist ideology dominated the SPLA, bringing devastating consequences as the leadership attempted to transform "liberated" areas in the South into a model "New Sudan."

Nimeiry was forced out of power in 1986. His replacement was, in turn, overthrown in 1989 by General Omar al-Bashir and the charismatic fundamentalist leader of the National Islamic Front (NIF), Hasan al-Turabi. Sudan became an Islamic dictatorship.

Cut off from political power, the northern parties formed an opposition camp, the National Democratic Alliance (NDA), which, in 1990, included the SPLA.

This unlikely alliance was cobbled together not so much because Garang was in sympathy with the northern parties as because he needed their strength to control the South. Under Garang's leadership, the SPLA directed the war campaign through a cadre in tight control of power, rather than a broad base of grassroots participation. It was inevitable that under mounting, top-down pressure, the SPLA would fracture (Malwal 2000, 2).

In 1991 Garang lost his grip on the SPLA and the organization split into warring factions. The government of Sudan took advantage of the split, co-opting one faction and pitting it against another. Fighting escalated, involving nearly every community in the South. Violence raged with no end in sight, and the southern Sudan became "one of the world's darkest humanitarian nightmares" (Duany and Duany 2000, 168).

SOCIAL FACTORS CONSTITUTING A JUSTIFICATION FOR VIOLENCE

Politically in the Sudan, religion, identity, and race have become factors of social control and social change. Violence, employed either to increase or decrease levels of social control as well as to promote social change, has been justified on all sides.

SOCIAL CONTROL

Religion/Values/Beliefs

According to Indiana University's Wal Duany, who has been involved with the People-to-People Peace Process in South Sudan since its inception in 1993, religious justification for violence is not so much a matter of theology as it is a matter of the political function of religion in the society:

> What is happening [in Sudan] is a moral re-orientation of Sudanese society away from individual faith and toward state-imposed religion. While institutions of faith and those of government may have a symbiotic relationship, their interests remain distinct. However, once linked to a particular political system or party, religious authority comes to be seen no longer as a shaper of the heart and mind, but as the strong arm of the state. For example, Arabic is known as the language of the Qur'an, the language of Allah. When the State established Arabic as the language of instruction, the move was seen as an imposition of Islam. (W. Duany 1997, 6)

Identity and Race

Identity as a factor of social control is rooted in the assumption that individuals are defined by membership in a racial or ethnic group. Bonds of identity may have both positive and negative social effects, but in polarized situations can be turned to deadly effect by skillful agitators. Identity in the Sudan is extremely polarized: Arab/Islamic on the one side and African/Christian on the other. Ethnic divisions also exist among the people of the South Sudan.

Racial factors are biologically rooted and closely linked to identity or ethnicity as a polarizing issue. Lines of racial and ethnic distinction blur over time, particularly in regions where diverse peoples intermarry. Yet, when people feel threatened by the proximity of groups or subgroups of different race or ethnicity, they may sharpen such distinctions. In Sudan, those identifying themselves as Arab generally regard black Africans as a lower form of life, referring to them as *abid*, or slave. The SPLA has also turned negative ethnic perceptions to its advantage, particularly in Equatoria. As a control strategy, the SPLA gave weapons to certain communities as a defense against cattle raiding. The intended consequence was an outbreak of aggression of increasing magnitude between ethnically identified communities, with the SPLA stepping in to offer "protection."

SOCIAL CHANGE

When Sudan became an independent republic in 1956, the Arab-dominated government set about to correct the "Southern Problem" by imposing a blanket of uniformity over the South through forced Arabization and Islamization measures. The policies have been meant to eradicate both the influences of Western language, religion, and culture in the South, and the African languages, religions, and culture. The objective is to "re-unify" Sudan under one government, one language, one religion, and one culture. The underlying assumption is that the southern people "would have naturally adopted Islam (with Arabic as its linguistic vehicle) through gradually expanding contact" (Lesch 1998, 220). The effort is not to force conversion to Islam, but rather to bring an end to forces that oppose it. The northern government views the civil war as a mutiny and a military problem, and the killing of two million southern people as an issue of national security.

While southerners have viewed as a mistake Britain's policy of unifying the South and the North in one Condominium Administration, they were at one time generally willing to accept unity with the North under one secular, pluralistic system of governance. But in the current Islamic State, non-Muslims are not full citizens. From the southern perspective, religious and racial differences are now elements of resistance to coercive social change. Violence has become justified in the defense of their beliefs, identity, and homeland. When religious identity and racial factors solidify into policies or legislation, violence breaks out—sometimes with shocking rapidity and inhumanity.

ESCALATION OF POWER STRUGGLE
INTO INTERCOMMUNITY CONFLICT

Southern peoples' resistance to the SPLA's Marxist ideology of social change was the engine driving its fragmentation. John Garang's dream of a secular, united, egalitarian "New Sudan" promised to create a new national identity for all Sudanese people. The dream required "total social revolution" under the guidance of the SPLA. Having "cleansed" certain groups in the rural areas of southern Sudan, the SPLA commenced to "purify" the population by eliminating "useless elements," mostly southern intellectuals who opposed its dream. The SPLA reign of terror led to extensive, endless destruction of peoples and property. Ironically, the great failure of secular social revolution is that it never ends, having no moral basis for forgiveness and reconciliation, and no institutional means of conflict resolution other than coercion.

The government of Sudan took quick advantage of the internal divisions within the South in 1991, by encouraging dissidents within the SPLA ranks to break off. The SPLA split was largely along ethnic lines, with some SPLA commanders making alliances with the government (see Duany and Duany 2000). The split brought devastation to communities across the board. Suddenly people who had lived side by side for centuries turned modern weapons upon each other. They burned villages, raped women, kidnapped children, and stole cattle. While cattle raiding has a long history among the Nilotic people, the matter got worse. The fighting caused an enormous refugee problem, internally displacing thousands upon thousands of southern peoples from their homelands and livelihoods.

The power plays of liberation movement leaders, who ostensibly represent the interests of the people, all too often have obscured the fundamental principles at stake. Patterns of self-preservation, competition for power, and personal accumulation of wealth are well documented, particularly with respect to the primary rivals, John Garang of the Sudan People's Liberation Movement/Army (SPLM/A) and Riek Machar of the Sudan People's Democratic Front (SPDF). Even during the years leading to Sudan's independence, successive northern governments displayed consummate skill in manipulating the personal aspirations of southern leaders and rivalries among ethnic groups, keeping the South divided and weak (J. Duany 1997, 23; Human Rights Watch/Africa 1994, 136). The consistent failure of southerners to form a unified political and military front has served to convince northerners that the civil war can and should be resolved on the battleground, no matter how costly and no matter how long it might take.

NEW VOICES: THE PEOPLE-TO-PEOPLE PEACE PROCESS

By 1994, the southern people had grown weary of interfactional fighting. Christian church leaders began an advocacy process encouraging traditional leaders and local liberation army leaders toward reconciliation. This was a significant challenge for churches, as the only functioning social institutions in the devastated South. With human suffering increasing every day, the church had no option but to intervene as bridge builder. The first church move was to appeal to all communities for an open dialogue. The response was overwhelming. The call to dialogue had coincided with a significant, emerging grassroots peace sentiment. Communities began to organize themselves to address the issues, and the church became the institutional connection, giving rise to formal peacemaking.

The first intercommunity peace meeting was the 1994 Akobo Peace and Reconciliation Conference between Jikany and Lou Nuer in the Upper Nile region. The Ikotos Conference in Equatoria followed this in 1995. A larger intercommunity peace conference between the Dinka and Nuer was convened in January 1999 at Wunlit in Bahr el Ghazal. There have been numerous smaller conferences, but these three are representative of the approach now known as the People-to-People Peace Process, which is the focus of this study.

COMMUNITIES STUDIED

The three major regions of the southern Sudan, the Upper Nile, Equatoria, and Bahr el Ghazal, are populated primarily by Nilotic and Bantu peoples. Nilotics are the majority, but they are subdivided into many localized yet extensive communities that include the Dinka, Nuer, Shilluk, Anuak, and others. The Bantu are subdivided into small Sudanic groups including Zande, Ndogo, and others. The Nilotic and Bantu peoples of southern Sudan derive their character and way of life from their historic homeland and the traditions of their ancestors. The Sudd, the Nile River flood plain, provides vast, shared fishing and grazing grounds as well as trade and communication arteries. It also is a source of frequent intercommunity conflict.

Christians of all three regions share traditional values as well as values based on Christ's teaching. Although present responses to violent conflict are worked out in the context of traditional approaches and institutions, Christian values are also used to guide dialogue. While the regions and their communities have much in common, including a sizable population of Christian believers, approaches to conflict resolution vary.

METHODOLOGY

Field research was conducted over a one-year period. Three research teams of two men and one woman each, using Arabic, English, or the local language, as appropriate, interviewed people in several comparable communities. Teamwork involved establishing contacts, conducting interviews, and attending community meetings. When necessary, follow-up interviews were conducted with the original respondents or with other relevant contacts, for the sake of verification. Most interviewees participated in multiple, in-depth interview sessions lasting from one to one and a half hours. The repeated contact and personal visits provided opportunities to build trust, witness nonverbal cues, and observe meetings among peacemakers. When tape recording was not possible, only notes were taken. The researchers reviewed the notes with interviewees to ensure accuracy.

We concentrated our research on specific peace activities in the three regions of South Sudan. In the Upper Nile, we did fieldwork in Akobo, Ganyiel, and Nyal. In Bahr el Ghazal we gathered data in Yirol and Rumbek. We gained access to communities in Yei and Kaya, but dangerous access to Equatoria nearly eliminated this region from the study. Fortunately, we discovered at the borders of northern Uganda a community of recently arrived Sudanese refugees from Equatoria who permitted us extended research visits.

One sample of thirty-five grassroots peacemakers—eighteen women and seventeen men, ranging in age from nineteen to sixty-five, from various groups and villages in the southern Sudan—responded to questions that allowed us quantitatively to assess gender differences in peacemaking activities and motivations.

A second sample of men and women, some involved in peacemaking and some not, responded to questions about their values, the relationship of their beliefs and culture to the war and efforts to make peace, and their perspectives on the effectiveness of spiritual leaders and community elders in local peacemaking initiatives. This sample included community residents, chiefs, liberation movement commanders, soldiers, local churchwomen, and youth group leaders, all of whom were asked to identify and describe the organization that was their key point of reference within the community.

Members of the New Sudan Council of Churches (NSCC) and other individuals shared official reports, detailed documentation of peace meetings and conferences, internal memos, and maps. A few high-ranking liberation movement commanders in Nairobi, Kenya, some of whom officially represent their movement's positions, were interviewed in depth. These commanders were selected either because liberation movement personnel directed us to them as "key contacts," or because other interviewees suggested them as important contacts.

The chart on the next page shows the numbers and types of leaders interviewed, and regional breakdowns of others interviewed.

To facilitate open, honest communication, all interviewees were assured that comments would not be attributed to them individually in any written report.

GRASSROOTS POTENTIAL FOR PEACEMAKING

How the Communities Define Peace

During the field research, it became clear that peacemaking was the major concern of many of the southern Sudanese interviewed. The respondents were asked to tell us "what peace means to them." A majority of them said that peace was a right for all humans, Arabs or Africans. They saw peace as a way of life characterized as much by a freedom to participate in all areas related to human dignity and self-satisfaction as by the absence of conflict. One elder said, "Peace opens the way to confronting a legacy of chaos and conflict." These understandings of peace are significant, since effective approaches to peacemaking must be logically related not only to the issues at the root of the conflict but also to the ways the actors view peace itself.

INTERVIEW RESPONDENTS

A. Leadership Sample

Chiefs (five from each region)	15
Church Leaders and Staff (Catholic, Presbyterian, and Episcopal)	15
Liberation Movement Commanders	13
Leadership Total	**43**

B. Regional Sample

Upper Nile	89
Bahr el Ghazal	75
Equatoria	68
Regional Total	**232**

Most literature on conflict resolution points to the idea that peace is an equitable and democratic system of human relations, a cooperation based on common interest, intimately bound up with the respect for and safeguarding of human rights (Ostrom 1997, 227). The southern Sudanese women I interviewed in 1995 and 1996 for a separate study nearly all defined peace as, in some fashion, "a total way of life." These women had their own individual understandings of peace, but understandings that nevertheless reflected their daily living.

In this study as well, the majority of women stated similar kinds of things. A woman from the Acoli community said, "Peace is understanding and respect for others and humanity. The SPLA and the government of Sudan do not understand the word peace, because none of those leaders are going hungry. Their children are in schools. They live the high life of rich people, so they are not missing anything." A Dinka woman living in a Nuer community said, "Peace is a daily thought of every southern Sudanese. People get up every day and yearn for when they will go home. They say, 'I wish peace comes and we can go home.' So, peace is something waited for, like a baby in a woman's womb. You never know when the baby will come. You just have to be ready to receive that baby." A Nuer women said, "*Mal ee mieth.* Peace is food. We have to feed families. Our husbands are no longer living with us to provide. We are now the providers. For me, peace is access to basic needs, shelter, food, health care and security, and protection of my family against hunger." Peace then, is doing things that nurture life.

WAR AND GRASSROOTS VIOLENCE

The women's definition of peace as a "total way of life" sheds light on why the southern Sudanese tend to accept civil war between North and South, but not interfactional conflict in the South. The majority of respondents, both men and women, stated two primary reasons for civil war in the Sudan. First is the continuation of colonial patterns of unequal development between North and South (with the North controlling the resources of the South). Second is the imposition of Arab/Islamic domination upon the African/Christian South. As long as southerners view the war as a North–South conflict, they are more inclined to accept it as necessary, because they believe it will lead to freedom, justice, and peace. However, since 1991, when the SPLA split into factions, interethnic fighting in the South has become a more pervasive threat than northern control. As violence spilled over into the communities, grassroots people began to raise serious questions about the motivations behind this fighting. One Dinka commander commented, "I just do not understand why we have to kill our brothers."

To assess people's levels of concern regarding war and grassroots violence, we asked, "Tell us which things going on in the Sudan currently concern you? And how do you perceive the other ethnic groups?" The majority of respondents gave answers relating to violence, such as government attack, interfactional fighting, cattle raiding, widespread distribution of guns, and the breakdown of law and order in the communities. In addition, respondents identified violence committed by renegade militia, including the looting of villages, raiding cattle, and the abduction of women and children.

The most frequent response to the second question pointed to the tension between northerners and southerners. Telling comments included: "I think it's the inability of northern Sudanese to see southern Sudanese as equals." "The northern Sudanese say the southerners are not human." "They [northerners] think, if you're not a Muslim you do not have culture or religion." "They play up religion to discriminate against southerners. The reality is, the North wants the resources of the South."

Next to antagonistic racial and religious relations, southern Sudanese mentioned political frustration as a cause of violence. People of the South feel that their rights are being violated. They want to be recognized as equals and exercise full rights as citizens. Southerners feel that the North is not willing to share the power and not ready to accept the African identity of southerners, as evidenced by continuing northern efforts to transform the South by imposing Islamic and Arabic culture. The majority of respondents mentioned racial and religious discrimination as a cause of dissatisfaction and frustration. The majority of respondents specifically mentioned race and religion as a source of infringement of rights, and "people not being given their rights" as a cause of war and violence. Two-thirds of respondents blamed war and violence on the North specifically, as the group dominating the affairs of the country. Nearly all respondents mentioned separation of the South from the North as the way to stop violence in the country. However, a few respondents also stated that they would accept an arrangement that would give southern Sudanese equal rights within a united Sudan.

Southern Sudanese perceive that the cause of war and grassroots violence lies somewhere in the social, economic, and political condition of the Sudan as a divided nation state. The emphasis on social factors as major causes of violence became even more apparent when respondents were asked to identify how violence affected them personally. These responses confirm what scholars have repeatedly cited as southern Sudan's primary problems: discrimination based on race and religion, political and economic exploitation, and substandard education.

The majority of respondents reported that intercommunity conflict generally occurs over grazing lands, water pools, fishing grounds, and other shared natural resources. Concern with violence and disorder within communities is extensive. Concern is greatest with respect to collective violence along ethnic lines within the South, as encouraged by liberation movement leaders. In addition, the government encourages groups to fight one another and supplies arms and ammunition, thus inflaming violence among the southern communities.

In most interviews, communal violence was regarded both as an outcome of interfactional fighting and as the initial motivation for grassroots peacemaking. Communal violence refers to calculated targeting of grassroots communities, particularly of women and children, for control, terrorism, and retaliation. "Conflict confronted us everywhere," one pastor explained. "Every day people are violated, not only by armies committing acts of 'ethnic cleansing,' but also by random acts of violence in our communities and villages."

CULTURAL CONTRIBUTIONS TO GRASSROOTS PEACEMAKING AND MOTIVATIONS

Since the South Sudanese, particularly Nilotic people, see conflict as something gone wrong with people's relationships, they view conflict resolution as restorative, leading to the re-establishment of social cohesion (Evans-Pritchard 1968, 185-88). In the Sudanese culture, peacemaking is construed as a communal process of rebuilding, of bringing justice into an unjust situation. Lasting peace requires reconciliation.

The southern Sudanese overwhelmingly hope for such reconciliation. The majority of the respondents, both men and women, are of the opinion that a lasting peace can be achieved on all conflict levels if there is respect among Sudanese in all aspects of life. Sudanese leaders, both North and South, must seek peace and justice for all citizens.

CULTURAL VALUES

Social Solidarity

Africans recognize that conflict is a part of life, yet its expression can indicate a wrong that must be corrected in order to bring society back into harmony. In an African context, an individual is never considered to be "alone." Each person represents the family, clan, or community. During the interviews, a Dinka or a Nuer would not finish speaking without referring to their brotherhood and sisterhood. The respondent would say, "We are brothers (or sisters)." The role of an individual in the African community is that of one part of a functioning body (Mbiti 1970, 31). A Nuer chief stated the proverb: "If one eye hurts, the other cries." In most African societies, the most important mechanism for preventing conflict is dialogue grounded in respect for human dignity, justice, and equal treatment, regardless of ethnicity or religious beliefs. The majority of the respondents indicated that violent conflict could be prevented if communities would use their existing social mechanisms that allow for resolution. In South Sudan there are existing institutions that just need to be applied. One church leader stated that, "Peacebuilding is a long-term process, and to prevent, resolve, and transform the violent conflict we have today, we must allow full participation of local groups who are committed to peace. Strengthening grassroots capacities may take forms that include education and training, nurturing the commitment of these communities."

Telling the Truth

Another key belief is the value of "truth telling." Women tend to conceive their special role in society as that of keepers of the truth. When hearing a person fail to tell the truth during grassroots peacemaking sessions, women have threatened to expose anyone not wanting to reveal what they know.

Local Autonomy

The strong tradition of local autonomy that pervades communities in South Sudan should be recognized, enhanced, and formalized. Since 1983, the SPLA has pressured for strong, centralized control over the South through a call for a "New Sudan." Local people have found this social reorientation difficult to accept, because it undermines the traditional clan autonomy and the decentralized management of natural and productive resources.

Among groups of people in the South, politics are based on the sharing of a common understanding among the clans, families, and elders. Tradition runs deep. Clans will, if necessary, fight for the preservation of their access to land, water rights, and grazing territory. Yet no elder believes that he can impose a military or political hegemony on others. Instead, each seeks only to preserve access to and control of his clan's livelihood resources, within a system of reciprocity. Traditionally, ethnic groups in South Sudan are equal in power and practice time-honored, give-and-take relationships, based on traditional rules and agreements. The command-and-control structure of the SPLA's "New Sudan" would remove the authority of local elders and override traditional institutions such as spiritual leadership and age groups.

In spite of years of devastation, grassroots communities still value the structures of traditional institutions, local autonomy, culture, and community welfare. Current voices of anti-centralization come as a direct reaction against the excesses of SPLA oppression. Some voices have emerged as grassroots movements, demanding full participation in their own affairs. Some are asserting a right to self-determination by region. In the Upper Nile, some people have organized under the institution of the South Sudan Liberation Movement (SSLM) to defend their communities against government and SPLA aggression. SLPA leadership has not been willing to allow full participation of local groups in the South, yet grassroots people value broad-based participation, both as an echo of the past and as a search for a more participatory future. Institutions of civil society, such as local nongovernmental organizations (NGOs), the NSCC, and women's groups have joined together to reinforce the values of peacemaking and peacebuilding.

Linkages

Social linkages are the keys to social cohesion. Horizontal linkages in south Sudanese society play out in community events, informal networks, associations, and institutions, including the church.

A question in this study was the role the church could meaningfully play in response to violent conflict. The majority of respondents said that the church was the only institution left functioning in southern Sudan. In the midst of violent conflict, the church has had to reexamine its mission and role in the communities. The church has been left with a huge gap to fill in South Sudan, particularly in promoting dialogue among the ethnic groups and political parties. "It would be erroneous to ignore the extremely fluid and often rough terrain within which the church operates," stated one church leader. "It takes a lot of courage to speak out against policies that are inhumane before a government—or even a liberation movement—that is not flexible toward dissenting views. The church as an institution is certainly in a better position to articulate the issues involved, but right now in Sudan the church lacks the required capacities."

The Christian churches walk a fine line when it comes to political involvement. Islam, on the other hand, has been transformed in Sudan into a tool of state oppression. "While institutions of faith and those of government may have a symbiotic relationship," writes Wal Duany, "their interests remain distinct. Once linked to a particular political system or party, religious authority comes to be seen as the strong arm of the state" (W. Duany 1997, 3).

Nevertheless, the majority of respondents in this study see the church as a legitimate facilitator for grassroots political action. "We shall continue to support legitimate initiatives," one church leader said. "Peacemaking is hard work. It has to involve the beneficiaries at all stages of design. Then it stands a better chance of success." Thus far, the New Sudan Council of Churches has been able to remain neutral regarding the interfactional conflicts within the liberation forces. It is incumbent upon church leadership to withstand its own internal power struggles and resist the strong pressures to take on a narrow political agenda. On the personal level, it has often been a struggle for individual church leaders to decide how far to commit to political involvement. For example, Catholic Bishop Paride Taban's decision to speak out against liberation movement corruption resulted in his arrest and torture. Today, however, he is one of the leading voices for peacemaking and reconciliation in South Sudan.

Institutional linkages also take shape through nonreligious organizations and associations. Most Sudanese communities are at pains to find local remedies for their problems through voluntary, locally based community organizations. Yet efforts to organize or network have generally failed, due mostly to lack of accountability. The majority of our respondents believed that local groups, organizations, and associations have a role to play in peacemaking and peacebuilding. A few emphasized that the role of institutions, particularly in the present circumstances, will be undermined if they are not responsive to society and to the processes at hand. This warning is summed up in the words of one respondent: "The atmosphere in the country has generated lots of apathy, as people fail to see the benefits of a liberation movement that does not take into account its own people."

Perhaps the most fundamental social linkage in the southern Sudan is the alliance of clans through intermarriage. Women become community resources, providing information across clan lines that can lead to dialogue, and this can keep broader intercommunity relations positive. Clan elders manage and resolve conflict using customary law, but elders do not have authoritative power to determine the outcome of a conflict. Rather, they merely represent the preferences of their clans. Traditional, official, and informal leadership in the village or community also influence social linkages. The majority of respondents reported that the relationship of these leaders to the community is critical to peacebuilding and peace management. The nature and quality of community leadership determines the level and quality of the exchange of information, and of local patron–client relationships. We observed two cases in which cattle raiding was the central issue. These could hardly be described as "legal" cases. Of course the evidence from both sides was heard, but one is on shakier ground when one deals with theft. The judgments led to ceremonies of reconciliation. In one case the elder who chaired the process ordered the parties to have a ceremonial meal, to gather in a healing ceremony. In another case, the village elders ended the case by returning the stolen cattle and asking the young men involved to pay a fine to the community. These young men paid two bulls, which were later killed in a reconciliation ceremony in which members of the two communities ate, shook hands and forgave one another.

Vertical community linkages include relations with the government, liberation movements, NGOs, and the business sector. Indigenous Sudanese NGOs, like most NGOs elsewhere, depend on donor support. One church leader said, "Much as Sudanese appreciate the presence and good work of the foreign NGOs, they will not always be here. It is therefore imperative that local NGOs receive adequate support to build their capacities." The majority of the liberation movement leaders indicated that the local NGOs need to network to develop their advocacy competence, so as to contribute meaningfully to the design of grassroots community approaches to peacebuilding. The primary task is to develop outreach programs targeted at educating people about their civic responsibilities. Because of their central and strategic role, the Christian churches are certainly in a position to encourage leading NGOs in articulating peace and reconciliation issues.

MOTIVATIONS FOR PEACEMAKING

In South Sudan, the most commonly cited motivations for peacemaking were practical—for example, "to combat poverty" or "to stay alive." Many respondents simply expressed a desire to end the "interfactional fighting" that they believe is prolonging the war, and the power struggles among members of the southern elite. A smaller number of respondents wanted to see "widespread distribution of arms in the villages" brought to an end.

After practical motivations, relational motivations for peacemaking were most common. Less frequently cited were ideological and religious motives (see chapter 1). Those who did cite religious motivations, however, were able to articulate them in some detail. "We Sudanese must forgive each other, as God's children and as Africans," one woman said. "Peace is to seek for similarities rather than differences."

Two themes that emerged in group discussions of faith-based peacemaking were *covenant* and *life*. *Covenant* making is critical to the cohesiveness of African society. One church leader stated, "We are one people, a covenanted people who honor very ancient bonds, bonds between the living and the dead, and, as Christians, we are told by the Bible to respect our neighbors." Binding, cleansing, and healing can be ritually symbolized in a covenant as follows: a white bull stands for God's creation, the bull's blood for life, and eating the meat of the bull together for the restoring of life.

African concepts of *life* also play an important role in African peacebuilding, because the understanding of "life" shapes the understanding of what is "good" and, therefore, has profound ethical implications. The Nuer say *Kuoth aa Kouth*, meaning that God is God and as source of life, God acts in a living way; that God is creator and God alone can give life.

African religious beliefs presuppose a concern for the welfare of their communities here and now, for health and prosperity, success in life, happy and productive marriages, and so on. As one Dinka chief stated, "When there is conflict, the community has to be involved; we cannot just sit and wait while people are fighting."

Religious Affiliation, Age, and Motivations for Peacemaking

Catholics in the sample cited religious motivations for their peacemaking activities more frequently than did Protestants. Younger respondents tended to cite more relational and practical motivations for peacemaking than did older respondents (see table at end of chapter). It is likely that younger respondents have a greater need to form new, mutually supportive relationships as they approach the life tasks of marriage, child-bearing, and child-rearing. In addition, older respondents may not anticipate living to experience the practical fruits of a nation at peace.

GENDER, CONFLICT, AND PEACEMAKING

As interfactional fighting has consumed communities, one family in three has lost at least one member in the southern Sudan (J. Duany 1997, 25). When respondents in our study were asked how the violence has affected women and children specifically, they said that the war had destroyed their communities and families. Respondents spoke of the toll taken by the violence in terms of (a) lost loved ones, (b) large numbers of people displaced, (c) an increase in the numbers of physically disabled people (as a result of landmines), (d) starvation imposed as a weapon of destruction, (e) an increase in abuse, rape, and abduction of women, and (f) a lack of health care and educational services in the communities.

During the interviews, more women than men mentioned the war as a matter of concern. They said, "The war has taken too long." Many women expressed the belief that fighting among the liberation movement factions serves no purpose other than to benefit a few individuals.

Among the Nilotic people there is the saying, "Childbirth teaches women the value of life." This thought was echoed during group interviews, as women talked about issues of community life such as care for family, showing respect and harmony within the community, and using nonconfrontational approaches to conflict resolution. One woman said, "I hate these guns around here. Men just take and shoot anything around them." Said another, "We women, having given life, always know what life costs. Men just go out and kill. It is easier for them to destroy life than to create it." Women mentioned their concerns about the involvement of young people in the military as contributing to the breakdown of law and order. One woman stated, "Young men have nothing to do, so they have to join the military."

To our surprise, however, analyses of data from the quantitative study indicated that South Sudanese men involved in peacemaking were slightly more likely than women to name practical motivations for their activities (see table at end of chapter). Men more than women spoke specifically of their desire for an end to cattle raiding and the abduction of women and children. In the larger sample that included both peacemakers and nonpeacemakers, men described their concerns about communal violence in terms of the defense of the family, community, or nation, for which they assumed responsibility. Those who had participated in the violence viewed their doing so as a performance of their familial and civic duty. During interviews, men expressed more interest in obtaining things that would make them more powerful, such as weapons. A man might build up his pride by engaging in activities that demonstrate physical strength and the ability to use force. As one Nuer commander stated, "We need to defend ourselves by showing Arabs that we are men too, and that we can fight as well." One South Sudan Liberation Movement (SSLM) soldier stated, "I have the right to defend my community. I am proud to carry this gun every day and make sure no one gets hurt. If any group attacks, I will be the first to die because of being in the front line."

Among peacemakers, men and women in our study were equally active in peacemaking and equally motivated to do so. However, a majority of the women interviewed seemed to perceive themselves as initiators of efforts for harmony and peace. It is characteristic among Nilotic women, especially if conflict escalates into violence, to push in small ways from behind the scenes for resolution or reconciliation, until finally the men come to the front and take the necessary action. Nilotic women typically use "back channels" and communication networks within the community to rally moral, attitudinal, and social influence for nonviolent social change, rather than resort as readily as do the men to coercion and violence. A woman, for example, might talk to her husband or her brother, urging him to disengage from violent activities. One woman recalled about a recent grassroots peacemaking effort, "Men go through visible motions of conflict resolution, but the real work in reconciling was done in advance by the invisible mediation of women working through the network of relatives, coalitions, and personal relationships." The pressure women can exert upon men is illustrated by a Nilotic saying about the way a tiny fly can rouse a great elephant. "Women are on our nerves these days," one man said. "They think we are making a lot of problems and they are the ones who suffer most."

GRASSROOTS RESPONSES: PERCEPTION AND PRACTICES

When we asked our respondents what should be done for peace, most of the respondents said that only the local communities themselves could find solutions to resolve their local problems. They also strongly stated that a reduction of arms in the communities could reduce raids and the abduction of women and children. The majority of church leaders believed that rebuilding civic and social institutions, along with social and economic improvements, would prevent violent conflict. On balance, the respondents appeared not to have lost faith in the society as a whole.

Our hundreds of interviews with traditional healers, community leaders, church leaders, women's groups, youth, liberation movement commanders, and politicians illuminate the essence of an extraordinary South Sudanese spirit of reconciliation. Today there is a rising force of peace activities that are ingenious and inspirational. Distinctively African and particularly Sudanese, they are forging a quiet change that holds immense promise for the future of South Sudan.

WHO IS WORKING FOR PEACE, AND HOW ARE THEY DOING IT?

Peacemaking in the Sudan generally takes the form of some sort of relationship building, but it is also approached through acts of service. It is impossible to provide a comprehensive account of all South Sudanese peacemaking groups and initiatives, but a few selected examples suggest the overall profile. Because conflict is seen as group crisis, rather than as an individual or interpersonal issue, the primary concerns have been the restoration of relationships, a return to functional cooperation, and the reconstruction of the communities. The fragmentation of the South in the aftermath of the SPLA's split opened a space for local people to play a role in restoring their communities. This allowed ecumenical groups to seek unity and understanding. "Since 1991 the NSCC as a church organization [has] adopted a positive role in trying to heal the rift between the southern Sudanese communities. It has seized the opportunity and effectively stepped into the unknown, committed to assisting the promotion of peace among southerners but unsure where that aspiration would lead the organization," said Telar Deng, Peace Coordinator for the NSCC. He added, "The job of the church leadership is to lead from behind, like a Dinka herdsman leads his cattle from behind."

The central aims and objectives of the church body are reconciliation and forgiveness centered on the healing of Christian love. This is promoted through prayer as an important activity for bringing the communities together. Also, social awareness and responsibility are taken into account so as to welcome non-Christians in these activities.

There are also a number of local women's organizations, such as the Sudanese Women's Voice for Peace (SWVP), which are networking to work for and maintain peace. SWVP is an indigenous NGO that is involved in several peace activities from women's perspectives, entailing the creation of mutual bonds between women in the communities and various traditional institutions in southern Sudan. SWVP organizes peacebuilding training, creates peace demonstration centers in Sudanese villages, and supports small-scale local development projects. In 1995 the SWVP began training individual women to become peace facilitators in their villages and surrounding areas. Also, the SWVP women based in Nairobi, Kenya, are involved in peace advocacy on the international level.

Another women's organization is the South Sudanese Women's Association (SSWA), a women's network that operates a series of peace programs connecting women in rural areas of South Sudan. SSWA advocates awareness and does capacity building for female community leaders at the grassroots level on conflict resolution and peacebuilding. SSWA is targeting local leaders for peace training. The organization also started a local campaign to ban landmines and work for AIDS prevention. SSWA cooperates with the local churches. It has conducted a number of workshops to train women leaders in their communities, with the help of international NGOs.

The Sudanese Women's Association in Nairobi (SWAN) is an organization of women refugees from different ethnic and political groupings. It works for reconciliation and respect for human rights within the Sudanese refugee camps in Kenya. SWAN aims to contribute to the political empowerment of Sudanese women.

PROCESSES OF DIALOGUE

Over the years, substantial amounts of money has been spent by neighboring African states and Western countries in organizing consultations and meetings between the government of Sudan and the SPLA. The most prominent effort is the Inter-governmental Authority for Development (IGAD) forum. Its meetings are often held in Nairobi, Kenya. There is generally no community or grassroots participation in the selection of participants, or even in setting the agenda. These top-down initiatives do little more than provide the factions in conflict with a platform for posturing to external audiences. As peacemaking efforts these meetings consistently fail, because they ignore the underlying issues and indigenous processes of conflict resolution.

What makes the southern Sudan peacemaking program a special case is the process of grassroots dialogue. The process has stimulated feelings of interdependence among the parties in conflict. It emphasizes common identities and helps participants to understand the opposing positions. Grassroots peacemaking in the southern Sudan focuses on mutual human respect. The most effective dialogue often occurs when each side articulates its position and then listens to its opponent. In three grassroots Sudanese cases, women played that role very effectively, mobilizing to transform issues of conflict into opportunities for restoration through frank and honest encounter. One woman stated, "We have been told to believe in the truth, tell the truth. We learned this from our mothers, grandmothers, and it goes back to our ancestors."

The principal process of indigenous peacemaking is designing and carrying out intercommunity peace and reconciliation dialogues. The process is not limited to one event, but rather is continual, expanding to involve community after community. These peace conferences constitute a bottom-up approach, enabling communities to assume greater control of their own affairs. Below are three selected cases from the period ranging from 1994 to the year 2000.

Case 1: Upper Nile—Akobo Peace and Reconciliation Conference: Jikany-Lou Nuer Reconciliation

In 1993 the two Nuer groups, Jikany and Lou, fought over grazing land. This conflict resulted in a great number of lives lost on both sides. In August 1994 the local churches had to intervene to help resolve the conflict. The 1994 Akobo Conference was the beginning of the grassroots movement now known as the People-to-People Peace Process. The Nuer have a strong covenant tradition but no central authority and are without the formal political apparatus that is commonly associated with a federal system of governance. The Akobo Conference was not the first attempt to stop the intercommunity fighting among the Jikany and Lou Nuer. One liberation army faction, the Southern Sudan Independence Movement (SSIM) had tried and failed. It wasn't until the church got involved, calling on people to share Christian and traditional African values, that the chiefs, the commanders, and the grassroots people found common ground for reconciliation.

The first step was a dialogue between the Jikany and Lou Nuer chiefs. This opened the way to a larger community forum. The conference ultimately involved over five thousand participants, and was chaired by an elderly chief, Malual Wun, with over forty-four years of leadership experience. The conference sought agreement over the use of the water, fishing, and grazing lands, which had been the cause of violence. Ten Lou and twelve Jikany chiefs signed the agreement. The sacrifice of two white bulls sealed the covenant. Women played a particularly effective witnessing role at the conference, acting as an informal "truth commission." Each a *maan naath* (mother of the nation), the Nuer women would shout down any man whose accounts contained falsehoods. The shame of the women's hoots drove a number of men to revise their testimony, to avoid the embarrassment of being tainted as liars.

Immediately after the conference, the South Sudan Independence Movement/Army (SSIM/A), the liberation movement authority in the area, held a convention endorsing the resolutions of the Akobo Conference. Across the Nilotic community, people called for more dialogue, consultation, and commitment to locally based peacemaking. They called for more "bottom-up" grassroots approaches that allow communities to participate in the decision-making processes that affect their lives. Akobo thus became a pattern for future conferences, particularly the Dinka/Nuer Peace and Reconciliation Conference at Wunlit in early 1999.

Case 2: Equatoria—Ikotos Conference:
Eastern and Western Torit District

The Ikotos Conference resolved a conflict between the local Didinga ethnic community and the SPLA over land use. Following the SPLA's split in 1991, intercommunal conflict had increased in the Lotuko regions over the control of areas containing gold. There was also an increase of banditry and large-scale cattle rustling. In response, the Catholic and African Inland churches joined together to write a pastoral letter, read during Christmas ceremonies in 1994. The letter emphasized the local Lotuko concept of *emwara* (reconciliation).

Leaders of the Catholic Diocese of Torit began visiting villages to discuss the concept of intercommunity dialogue. In Equatoria, although local communities do not participate freely in peace activities (partly because of the secretive nature of the society), an undercurrent of popular resentment toward the controlling presence of the Dinka-dominated SPLA army had raised interest among the communities in dialogue with one another.

In January 1995, the diocese hosted a peace conference in Ikotos involving two thousand participants, including chiefs, community groups, and the SPLA leaders and members. The conference resolved many issues. For instance, escalating dowry prices were one reason for increased cattle rustling, so the conferees agreed to reduce the dowry from thirty to ten cows. Those caught raiding would be fined double their take. Compensation for wrongful death was set at twenty-two cows. Traveling outside one's home village with a gun was disallowed, with confiscation of the weapon as the penalty. SPLA soldiers would not be allowed to visit villages without specific orders from their commander. This conference produced the Dinka-Misseriya peace agreements. In the transitional zone between North and South, these agreements have more or less held (for reasons of commerce and deterrence) for seven years. Currently, however, they are under threat of collapse due to political instability in the area.

Case 3: Bahr el Ghazal—Wunlit Conference:
Dinka-Nuer Reconciliation

This was a regional Dinka-Nuer Peace and Reconciliation Conference encompassing the West Nile, North Bahr el Ghazal, and Bentiu areas. The NSCC organized this 1999 conference, which was also attended by observers, international journalists, and representatives of all the liberation army factions. To lay the groundwork of trust and to begin the healing process, an "exchange" of Nuer and Dinka chiefs and community leaders was organized. Chiefs were sent to the opposing territory to show their acceptance of dialogue. Those participating in the process were, in a very real sense, pledging their commitment to the process with their lives.

Wal Duany has described (1999) the exchange of the community leaders: "Our plan was to fly from Lokichoggio to pick up the Nuer chiefs, and then proceed to the exchange site in Dinka territory. [When the chiefs arrived] the reception in the Dinka village of Thiet was tremendous. Many SPLM/A soldiers and personnel, civil administrators, women's organizations, youth groups, and the general public were there. A white bull was sacrificed in accordance with the tradition for the reunion of brothers." The delegation then flew to Wunlit, where "the local chiefs and the crowds of people welcomed this combined delegation of Nuer and Dinka chiefs with songs and shouts of happiness. Local support for peace was demonstrated by the fact that an actual village had been constructed for the conference, including 150 *tukul* (huts), a conference hall, and latrines."

The first three days of the conference were set aside for storytelling between Dinka and Nuer. In this first round of dialogue, key issues were identified. Following that, working groups met to propose resolutions. Then the entire conference met for dialogue about the proposals and to reach a consensus on the final resolutions. Primary among the issues to resolve was conflict over shared grazing and fishing lands.

One pastor summed up the results of the conference:

Since Wunlit, the Dinka and the Nuer communities are now sharing grazing land and water pools. They are also rebuilding their villages, which were abandoned for ten years. Life is coming back and is good. Life is what matters to us. Anything that makes life meaningful is taken seriously. Peace is life. If you have life, you have something precious.

SIMILARITIES IN THE THREE CASES

Similarities in peacemaking activities generally are attributable to cultural similarities. More peace activities are ongoing in the Upper Nile and Bahr el Ghazal than in Equatoria, primarily because of a Nilotic openness and sense of individual freedom to speak out on issues of concern. In Equatoria, individuals do not express themselves freely. The reason is more cultural than political. Individuals share concerns privately, but avoid direct confrontation. Rather than engage in open dialogue, persons are more likely to remove themselves from a community and go apart with one another. In addition to cultural inhibitions, most communities are intimidated by SPLA control. Communities in Equatoria are not free to dialogue with one another unless the leadership of the SPLA first approves the activity.

Greater participation in peace activities tends to translate into higher production in the daily activities of the communities. In the years since the 1994 conference, the population of Akobo and the surrounding area has grown from
twenty thousand to over fifty thousand. More people have been able to produce
food for themselves because of stability in the region.

In spite of growing concern among the local communities about how to
resolve issues in their areas, church and community elders have difficulty facilitating peacemaking activities without some sort of outside support. The peacemaking in all three regions mentioned above reflects the influence of the
People-to-People Peace Process, as local churches have given the NSCC a trust
mandate to facilitate peace conferences in southern Sudan. During the year 2000,
peace activities increased in Equatoria, because local people were taking initiative to dialogue among themselves without permission from the SPLA. Still,
Equatoria stands in stark contrast to the Upper Nile, where community leaders
and the South Sudan Liberation Movement (SSLM) are working together to
restore law and order, and to provide a democratic forum where community
issues are discussed openly and without fear. Two results have been the establishment of local, traditional courts, where disputes are settled; and local regula-
tions regarding the use of arms.

DEVELOPING A CULTURE OF PEACE

In South Sudan indigenous conflict management mechanisms are still operational. Traditional social structures are the oldest institutions of civil society for
conflict resolution. In a study for the United States Institute of Peace, Wal Duany
found that the institutions of elders and community leaders have managed to
retain their status as important sociopolitical factors, influencing and guiding
everyday social and economic interactions within and between groups at the
grassroots level. "They appear to be the principal instruments for reconciling ethnic groups who contest such issues as grazing land, waterholes, and instances of
livestock raiding" (W. Duany 1997, 1-3).

The People-to-People Peace Process has strengthened traditional structures. It
is the most significant grassroots response to violence in the southern Sudan. It
demonstrates what can be accomplished when there is strong underlying motivation to resolve conflict in communities. The ground for peacemaking appears to
be especially fertile if the motivation for it is rooted in the teachings of the Christian Scriptures. The Sudanese churches have been a unifying center through
which people from all ethnic groups have found hope for reconciliation and forgiveness. Even those who did not identify themselves as Christians could participate in what was, in fact, a common struggle to restore broken relationships. The
Peace Process channeled that motivation, encouraging individuals and communities to rethink the terms and conditions of governance, and to establish self-
governing, democratic institutions that can sustain a culture of peacebuilding.

SUCCESS FACTORS

Peacemaking is finding a way to stop the violence. Peacebuilding is building upon the new relationships that have been established. This is a continuous process, demanding enormous resources, both material and human. The democratic system of civil institutions in the area must be restored in order to maintain the peace agreements. At the same time, resources for self-reliant living, such as seeds and health care, must be provided in order to minimize motivations for returning to conflict. This was particularly evident at the Akobo and Wunlit conferences, where conflicts over shared water, fishing, and grazing lands were seen as major problems. Sustaining a culture of peace really means sustaining a total way of life.

The following factors in particular have contributed to the success of the People-to-People Peace and Reconciliation Processes:

Initial Approach

Discussion began between partners and the local churches. Partners included ministers from international church bodies and members of the South's expatriate community. Those discussions launched a delegation of trusted, neutral "go-betweens," who approached the individual groups in conflict about initiating the reconciliation process. Initial contacts with the elders of each group led to requests for formal dialogue.

Needs Assessment

A preliminary mission by local churches conducted needs assessment, leading to a conference design. The design included formation of peace committees, including members from both groups, elected by their communities. As the process developed, representatives of the parties in conflict met. These representatives included women, youth, elders, traditional leaders, church leaders, traditional religious leaders, and intellectuals. An invitation to participate was extended to liberation army leaders, but later in the process the communities actually demanded their participation and support.

Conference Preparation

The preparation of a conference ideally involved close collaboration between the communities, the NSCC, and the liberation movement factions in the area. Responsibility for the daily activities and concerns of the conference rested with the host community, together with the NSCC. Activities and concerns included: selection of a conference site; identification of the issues to be discussed; preparation of a conference schedule; identification of approaches and materials to be used; the designing of the process; plans for administration and evaluation; and the drafting of a budget. Generally, the schema calls for churches and the NSCC to consult with resource persons on both sides, to prepare the conceptual tools that will guide the parties to sincere discussion. The resource persons are those who have been invited to play an advisory role, because they are regarded as experts or are knowledgeable about indigenous law and customs.

Logistics

Peace conference logistics required support from partners, NGOs, and the NSCC, since the success of a conference depended on the timely arrival of participants, arrangements for their transportation, security, water, food and lodging, and provision of other locally available services and amenities. If all of the logistics do not come together smoothly, there is a real danger that misunderstandings will break down the process. At Akobo and Wunlit, flexibility in the time line was crucial to the success of the conference.

The Conference Framework

The conference itself is a dialogue, under one roof, under the mediation of a chairperson or moderators chosen by consensus among the people. The People-to-People Peace Conferences were framed to incorporate both modern and traditional means of dialogue. The elders of the parties in conflict were key to keeping the conversation going until there was a definite conclusion. The elders then summarized it, and that statement became the group consensus. The consensus became the peace agreement. Two key elements signified commitment to the agreement. One was the traditional sacrifice of a white bull and sharing the meat together. The other was the modern signing of a written document by the leaders. In each case, the conference took many days (forty-five days at Akobo!). Conference organization also involved either open coproduction or open collaboration among the committees and the working groups in order to accomplish such tasks as writing up the actual peace agreement and follow-up activities (report writing and conference evaluation).

Implementation of the Peace Agreement

When a community initiates peacemaking, the process is one of forgiveness. When it moves toward peacebuilding, the process is justice. Implementation of a peace agreement is the process of restoring broken relationships on the basis of justice. It is a long-term process of community change. The peace agreement becomes a part of civil law, and the institutions of civil government enforce it. Implementation signifies a shift from chaos to order, from tyranny to self-rule.

CHALLENGES FOR THE CHURCHES

The Christian churches face two major challenges in responding to violent conflict. One is to realize that many things can go wrong with even the best approach. Indeed, any of the above steps can be misapplied. That is, the wrong target groups may be selected, or some of the right groups may be excluded; high-level support may be lacking; the needs assessment may be sloppy or superficial; guarantees of security may be weak; resources may be inadequate; there may be an inadequate commitment to implement the agreement; or there may be hidden agendas.

Parties or donors seeking to advance hidden agendas may support only the kind of peace program that enables them to achieve narrow, self-preserving objectives. The government of Sudan, for example, has used its participation in the IGAD forum to mislead the world that it is interested in peace, when it actually has not been. To the government of Sudan, the give-and-take nature of a peacemaking process has been seen as an obstacle, rather than as a solution to the North–South conflict.

A peacemaking program that puts tools for analysis, design, implementation, monitoring, and evaluation into the hands of people at the grassroots has, in effect, given them tools that could be used to disarm hidden agendas. No observer could fail to be struck by the nature of the concerns expressed by grassroots peace conference participants in South Sudan when they were given the opportunity to develop their own ideas on how to resolve problems. They uniformly proposed and sought very practical solutions involving community security, health enhancement, education, food production, and road building. The southern Sudanese cases make a strong argument for putting the necessary time and concentrated effort into developing grassroots, bottom-up approaches to peacemaking and peacebuilding.

The second challenge for the churches is to remember where their true strength lies. The church as an institution has been shut out of the IGAD peace process. The exclusion has forced the church to rediscover that its true strength is not in the power of the institution. Rather, it is in the transforming power of the gospel of forgiveness, reconciliation, and justice as it is worked out in the hearts and lives of individual grassroots people who live in the midst of conflict.

There has been a growing concern, too, that grassroots communities are losing their grip on the People-to-People Peace Process. One of the women leaders explained, "People who run the NSCC program have lost touch with reality in the villages. So we are looking at new ways of improving the peace initiative, to give it back to the people."

Several church leaders told us in the interviews that they have visited NSCC repeatedly and were not able to see the leaders with whom they wished to meet. "How many times have you gone to the NSCC office only to have an official tell you that nobody was there?" said one. "Peacemaking sells well and has become a big industry. It brings in thousands and thousands of dollars, which do not reach the people." People-to-People Peacemaking runs the risk of being derailed because it has lost some of the key people who started it and "who know what to do and what it takes to work with grassroots people."

CONCLUSION

Reconciliation and peacebuilding are complex challenges. But grassroots peacemaking is being accomplished in South Sudan. It is taking place through a flexible framework that integrates a coherent, comprehensive approach by the actors; a broad consensus on strategy and related interventions; a careful balance of microeconomic and political objectives; partnership between and the coordination of members of the communities; and the necessary financial resources.

It would be erroneous to think that the South Sudanese People-to-People Peace Process could have occurred without significant support from religious communities. In all three of the regions studied it was the religious leadership, both African-traditional and Christian, who represented the beliefs and sentiments of the people. They carried the power of the symbols and the responsibility vested in them by their respective constituents. It was the religious leadership who led their communities in reconciling people, both individually and collectively, with God, the spirits, and fellow human beings.

Religious networks that are indigenous to a given people in conflict clearly have a capacity to be significant actors in the process of peacemaking and reconciliation. They also have the capacity to call forth the best that is within people and to generate community pressure that can overcome cycles of violence. In this study it was evident that traditional belief systems and indigenous religion have capacities that offer potential for effective peacemaking and reconciliation, even in the midst of turbulent and chaotic times. In the Akobo and Wunlit cases the traditional leaders, who frequently were the custodians of the Dinka and Nuer religious customs, the local Christian churches, and the groups of women were key to the process of initiating and negotiating a settlement at the peace conferences.

The religious community exercises the power of the religious symbols and rituals that are commonly excluded from state institutions yet can be important elements in the reconciliation process. Similarly, it is more in the province of the religious community rather than the state to promote values education, stimulate awareness of the benefits of reconciliation, tolerance, and coexistence, and engage all sectors of the society in civic education, incorporating nonviolent methods of conflict resolution. The importance of education and awareness must not be underestimated, because those involved in the peacebuilding process must be well prepared and trained, understanding the culture and the way of life of the communities they seek to serve.

It would also be incorrect to think that the People-to-People Peace Process could have occurred without the involvement of as many people and sectors of society as possible. In seeking solutions to community problems, including violent conflict, the various sectors of society should be viewed as resources. Regardless of the magnitude of the problems, grassroots communities should not be ignored in resolution processes, because they are the ultimate stakeholders affected.

It is clear that reaching consensus or a peace agreement is not an end in itself. An ounce of prevention is better than a pound of cure. There is, therefore, a great need to create networks and platforms that promote coalition, coordination, and constituency building on the grassroots level. Grassroots peacebuilding creates new coalitions and strengthens those already existing between communities and organizations. Grassroots networks are created when groups are encouraged to seek common ground or to share scarce resources. Institution building should be stimulated at all levels of society to sustain reconciliation and peacebuilding. Particularly, the institutions of civil society must be in place to respond to community needs. Involving the grassroots or the base inhibits the elite from dominating the process and manipulating the issues.

There also is a need to establish preventive, early-response mechanisms. Ideally, local organizations will dedicate more attention and resources to preventing violent conflict than to reacting to it. In Akobo, the Presbyterian Church of the Sudan (PCOS) has formed a peace committee to monitor activities in the region, so that peaceful intervention may be initiated in the very early stages of conflict, before it escalates into armed violence.

The People-to-People Peace Process in South Sudan is a strategy that turns on understanding how a society actually functions and then working with it to achieve peaceful ways of life. The southern Sudanese experience gives a new dimension to the role of the church, challenging it to live up to its teachings, to seek synergies with traditional values, and to continue working at the grassroots level for peace among the people.

STATISTICAL TABLE
ASSOCIATED WITH CHAPTER 7 DATA

See pages 213-214 for an interpretation of this table. See chapter 1 for an explanation of variables.

TABLE 1. GENDER AND AGE AS FACTORS IN MOTIVATION FOR PEACEMAKING IN SOUTH SUDAN

	Practical Motivations	Relational Motivations	Ideological Motivations	Religious Motivations
Gender*	-.31**	-.22	-.13	.04
Age	-.37***	-.47***	.07	.23

    * Positive correlations indicate that women reported this type of motivation or activity more frequently than did men.

    ** $p = .07$.

    *** $p < .05$.

8

United States

Places of Sense/Senses of Place: Gang Violence, Positive Cultures Leadership, and Peacemaking

JOHN BROWN CHILDS

The role of community-based organizations that are working with youth in the streets is critical going into this next generation. This is because many of the folks who are working in these organizations are young people who used to be in the streets themselves, so they have a legitimate connection with the next generation. They can talk the language. They can understand some of the intimate details related to the problems they are dealing with that other people can't even see, let alone understand. So, support for these organizations is important because they have legitimate information, because they have legitimate ties to the street. I think it's almost criminal the way many of these organizations are being treated by people who have the resources to make things happen.

We know that the community-based approach works because "Community Based" means that folks live and work in that community. For me who has children, family, mom, dad and who lives in South Central Los Angeles to want to clean up the community, there is more of a real concern, a need, to make that a reality, as opposed to it just being a job. Because if the doors close at 5:00 and I go home, I still have to walk through that neighborhood and see what's going on. My kids have to go to school in that area. They have to get around the drive-by shootings. They have to get around the dope dealers and the prostitutes, and the other folks. So the

*community-based approach needs to be supported more if we are going to
really make a society without violence—a better society for everyone.*
> —Khalid Shah, former Los Angeles gang member, now
> director and founder of the Stop the Violence/Insti-
> tute the Peace Foundation, Los Angeles, California
> (interview in 2000 by Childs)

> *I have come to realize that there is a lot of healing that must take place
> in this world. In order to begin healing that pain we must first begin to look
> at our participation in causing such pain. For all of us, we have to be
> strong enough to examine ourselves individually and examine fault. But we
> also must look at ourselves collectively and learn about the disenfran-
> chisement of our world and how we participate in that. Working with youth,
> I realize that I have power. I must use that power for good and to empower
> the young with whom I work. The power is not mine to give. The power is
> already there. Our young people just have to be given the opportunity to
> use their power in the free expressions that they choose. When I fail at this,
> and I do, I must be willing to recognize these things and own them. I must
> repent for the sake of the relationships. Then I must work on reconciliation.
> Repentance is difficult. It means not only telling myself about my issues,
> but it also means confessing them to those around me. Through our rela-
> tionships we can work towards a better world, a world where we are all the
> body of Christ.* (Valenzuela n.d., 3)
> > —José Valenzuela, director of Family and Youth
> > Services, Trinity Lutheran Church, Brooklyn,
> > New York

Today, much of the United States is at war within itself. Youth gang violence
and conflict are killing and maiming many, from large cities to rural areas. Inter-
and intracommunal conflict, expressed in significant degree through gang organization, is a pivotal corrosive fact of societal life in key areas in and beyond
major urban centers of the United States. Killings by juveniles with firearms
quadrupled between 1984 and 1994, while the number of youth arrested for murder tripled during that same period. Although many overall crime rates have
declined in the past five years, there is the expectation that "the coming surge in
teen population could boost the juvenile murder total 25 percent by 2005.[1] Similarly, the Harvard Urban Seminar reports that "in recent years this problem has
become particularly acute for youths 15 to 20 years old whose rates of offending
and victimization have more than doubled" (Greenwood et al. 2000, 2). In a 1998
report, the U.S. Department of Justice noted that despite some decline in membership, gangs remain a serious problem. The California Wellness Foundation

---

[1] Statistics on juvenile crime rates are taken from Gest and Pope (1997, 164-66).

warns, "The cost of violence to individual and community well-being in California and elsewhere goes far beyond dollars. Violence has triggered an overwhelming sense of fear in major cities and a widespread feeling of insecurity in
the suburban areas that surround them" (California Wellness Foundation 2000,
4). A survey of prison wardens by a commission headed by U.S. Senator Paul
Simon in 1993 found that 85 percent considered prisons to be ineffective tools
for long-term violence reduction among youth and others (Childs, 1996, 40).

Out on the streets, youth and community activists with whom I spoke
expressed similar concerns about violence. One young man in Oakland, California, made this stark prediction: "The violence is not going to stop. [Youth] are
left to make their own decisions, and there's no one to guide them. It's the environment they hang around. If everything is negative . . . it changes their outlook.
If they see people dying, they'll think this is the way life is" (Anonymous, interview in 2000 by Byrd). Across the country in Brooklyn, New York, a young man
responded to the question, "Is there anything in your community that you feel
proud of?" by saying simply, "Nothing!" (Anonymous, interview in 2001 by
Alfonso).

Gang conflict and violence are compounded in the United States by the wide
and easy availability of firearms. It is usually estimated that there are enough
guns in the United States for every person to have three. Current gun purchasing
registration requirements do not prevent illegal use of guns. As two specialists on
gun use in the United States note, "Weapons frequently cross over from the realm
of the legal to the illegal" (Cukier and Shropshire 2000, 106-7). They also cite a
1996-1998 U.S. Bureau of Alcohol, Tobacco and Firearms study showing that 87
percent of the nearly thirty-five thousand weapons recovered from crime scenes
were not in the hands of the original purchaser at the time they were used in
crime. This indicates that resale and theft are major issues for gun trafficking
within the United States. Moreover, the diversion of originally legal weapons "to
illicit markets . . . blurs the lines between the legal and illicit trade," as Michael
Crowley and Elizabeth Clegg (2001, 51) point out in their analysis of the small
arms trade around the world. Youth, especially those involved in gangs, can and
do keep illicit guns at home, or at friends' homes for ready use. When "needed,"
the guns are available. As one teenage gang member in Santa Cruz County said
to me, "I can walk from school in five minutes and get a gun" (Anonymous,
interview in 2001 by Childs). With the relative ease of getting guns, well-armed,
often ethnically defined gangs, no matter how small a percentage of the total population, have a severe, corrosive impact on the communities within which they
operate.

But in the midst of this volatile situation, a positive current is swelling up and
gaining momentum in many of the hardest hit areas. I call this countercurrent
"positive cultures leadership," or PCL. This locally based leadership is creating
a myriad of safe places within which constructive interaction, nonviolent communication, and positive personal transformation are taking place. Positive cultures leadership organizations are creating "places that make sense" and are
simultaneously providing the opportunity for a constructive "sense of place" in

the midst of violence. I have identified 3,112 community organizations around the country that are working for urban peace and an end to (or at least a significant reduction of) youth violence (Childs 1996a, 41). Almost all of these organizations emphasize the creation of safe places within which young people can learn and be encouraged to practice nonviolence and cooperation. Simultaneously, these organizations usually have well-developed critical analyses of the larger society's economic, political, and cultural impacts on their communities. Generally, positive cultures leadership organizations merge the local with the national, and the immediate with the long-term as they work to address fundamentally pressing daily problems of violence and disruption in their communities.

José R. Valenzuela is a Brooklyn Lutheran lay leader of a youth outreach. During my visit to his Trinity Lutheran Church youth program in Brooklyn, New York, Valenzuela—known as *El Pastor* to the young people with whom he works—described an example of this positive cultures leadership: "Here kids can come to me and tell me what's in their hearts. They can play basketball. They can pray. They can tell the truth about their lives, their problems. They know the church is a home" (Valenzuela, interview in 2001 by Childs).

Similarly, Khalid Shah, director of the Stop the Violence/Increase the Peace Foundation in the Los Angeles area, emphasized the importance of a "community-based organization that can actually reach youth and others because we have legitimacy in the community" (Shah, interview in 2000 by Childs). Argelia Flores of the Santa Cruz Community Foundation described "a rich network of grassroots groups throughout the state that go largely unrecognized" (Flores, interview in 2001 by Childs). Hundreds of such community-based "places of sense," rooted in neighborhoods and other urban settings, some small, some larger, are in existence or are being created. Taken together, these diverse efforts constitute a major grassroots movement to (re)construct a positive cultural matrix for people who run the risk of being uprooted by harsh circumstances. In California, more than 90 percent of respondents to a 1999 survey supported "local community programs for youth and families," as a constructive response to violence and an alternative to incarceration (Fairbank, Maslin, Maullin and Associates 1999, 7).

TERMINOLOGY AND CONTEXT

My focus here is both on gang violence and on constructive, community-based, positive cultural leadership efforts to redress that problem.

By "gang" I mean a territorial (based in a neighborhood, city, or region) organization consisting primarily of youth predominantly between the ages of fifteen and twenty-four. The U.S. Department of Justice 1998 *National Gang Youth Survey* estimates that there are 28,700 youth gangs with an estimated 789,200 members. In 1998, 92 percent of gang members were male. Ethnically, 46 percent were Hispanic, 34 percent were African-American, 12 percent were Caucasian, 6 percent were Asian, and 2 percent were "other." An estimated 36 percent of youth gangs were of mixed ethnicity (U.S. Dept. of Justice 1998, iv-v).

In particular, highly organized "prison gangs" are almost always ethnically homogeneous in their membership. Consequently, when gang conflict occurs in prisons, it often tends to be ethnic in nature, unless it is intracommunal with competing groups from one ethnic population vying for influence. Such prison organizations often have links to and impact on communities, so their conflicts can and do sometimes translate into ethnic violence in the streets. It is also important to note that, given the high degree of ethnic residential compartmentalization/ segregation in U.S. cities, much gang violence takes place *within* ethnic communities. In these intra-communal settings, gangs, with their clothing of distinctive colors, territories, names, and histories take on a form that is itself very much like that of an ethnic group. So gang violence contributes to ethnic conflict and itself mimics ethnic conflict. As Ruben Chavez, a veteran community peace worker in Albuquerque, New Mexico, told me, "Blacks and Latinos out here on the streets hate each other. The ethnic conflict potential is like gasoline on a fire with regard to the youth in gangs, in the prisons, and out on the street" (Chavez, interview in 1999 by Childs).

The labels "gang" and "gangsters" must be used with caution. Community activists rightly complain that these labels are often officially used broadly and inaccurately to stigmatize youth simply for their age, ethnicity, color, and/or cultural styles. At the same time, communities are genuinely worried about "gangs" and use the term to describe real problems. Some young people refer to themselves as "gangsters" regardless of whether they belong to such groups or not. In some cultural settings "gangsta" and "my gangstas" can simply indicate comradeship and mutual respect among a benign group of young people. Caution and cultural alertness should therefore be exercised in the use of these terms.

Adding to the complexity are the fluidity and changing composition of gangs and related conflict. Conflict can be intensely dangerous at some moments, as Ruben Chavez describes above. But unexpected breakthroughs for peace, sometimes brought about primarily by people involved in the violence itself can alter these situations, at least temporarily. For example, in the same New Mexican environment described so accurately by Chavez, there had previously been peace efforts among African-American and Latino gangs. Shayn Obsataz, writing for the *Santa Fe New Mexican,* described the way in which members of the African-American Crips organization (originally formed in Los Angeles) and members of key Latino gangs such as the West Side Locos and East Side Homies agreed to a truce and expressed hope "for a peaceful future" (Obsataz 1994, 1). Such moments may last for years or for shorter periods. In Los Angeles, many truces arranged among rival African-American and Latino gangs following the Los Angeles riots of 1992 are still in effect. There is some evidence that they are now being eroded by younger generations that do not know the history of those peace efforts. And just as in other conflict areas of the world, apparently successful peace efforts can be rapidly undermined by wild-card incidents that break existing agreements. Nonetheless, that such truces and peace actions occur at all indicates that openings for peace over violence can crop up unexpectedly. It is precisely such fluidity, contradictions, and transformations among diverse individuals that any study of peacemaking and gang violence must incorporate.

Experienced peace activists with well-grounded understandings of their communities report that developing relationships with veteran gang members, often known as "Original Gangsters" or "OG's" of earlier generations can have positive potential. As a violence prevention youth worker in Los Angeles told me, "Minimally, any peace effort must make some contact with the OG's if it is to enhance nonviolence work out on the streets" (Anonymous, interview in 2001 by Childs).

RESEARCH APPROACH

My approach to the fieldwork for this study reflects these complex dynamic realities. My methods of inquiry were primarily ethnographic. Supporting survey data from various sources are also included. Moreover, for the past ten years I have worked for and continue to be affiliated with numerous urban peace organizations. The bulk of my research for this chapter was carried out through interviews and direct observation grounded in over a decade of direct community participation that has included writing about these organizations (see, e.g., Childs 1996a). My continuing long-term involvement in urban peace work, along with the interviews and observant participation conducted specifically for this study provide both information and a usefully nuanced understanding that goes beyond the usual academic "participant observation." I am a participant who observes and writes about what I see in ways that I hope will be of some value to the communities involved.

I employed the interview form that John Madge (1953, 71) called "nondirected," although some researchers call this format "open-ended interviewing." Nondirected interviewing delineates key themes to be covered but leaves open the questions to be asked in relationship to those themes. This interview format provides for a flexibility of response that encourages the respondents to introduce their own ideas, analyses, and outlooks. Such flexibility is important because even those directly involved do not know all that is happening "out on the street." As peace activist Daniel "Nane" Alejandrez once said to me, "Those who think they know, don't." All the more reason then for flexibility that encourages responses. The nondirected approach is also essential given the deliberately covert dimensions of gang activity and the constraints that these dimensions put on community peace activists. Those working to stop violence must always be on guard not to seem like interrogation police, or to be otherwise endangering those with whom they work, even as they elicit information and gain the confidence of gang members. Similarly, even when talking with peace activists, it was essential that I gave them room to broaden the parameters of what they wanted to disclose, rather than adopting an interrogatory style that would be viewed with suspicion and wariness. It was for all of these reasons that I employed the nondirected interview format.

A total of forty-one people were interviewed, some more than once; and thirty-two of these are community peace activists. Nine of the activists were under the age of twenty-one. Not all of these interviews are cited in this chapter. However, I have drawn upon examples from all those interviewed. I conducted thirty-five of the interviews myself. Two youths were employed as interviewers in order to effectively reach some gang members who were not accessible to me. One was in California, the other in New York. The interviews were conducted in Los Angeles (Inglewood), El Cajon, Santa Cruz, Watsonville, and Oakland, California; Brooklyn, New York; Hartford, Connecticut; and Albuquerque, New Mexico. The organizations at which interviews were conducted include the National Teen Action Research Center in Hartford, Connecticut, the Milagros Education Project in Watsonville, California, the National Coalition of Barrios Unidos in Santa Cruz, California, Stop the Violence/Increase the Peace in Inglewood, California, the Trinity Lutheran Church Youth Program in Brooklyn, New York, and Victory Outreach Church in El Cajon, California.

In addition to the more formal interviewing, I also spent considerable time "being there," listening and observing. I attended meetings, cultural events, and public speeches. I surveyed newspaper accounts and examined documents produced by organizations. Here also, respect for the often-sensitive issues of community organizations working with those who are viewed with suspicion by the authorities requires alertness to certain contextual requirements. Much of what I have written about here could only have been written because of my informal conversations and observations; and much of what I have seen in key moments would be invisible to the standard research interviewer who comes in to ask a set of questions after the fact.

An example of the importance of being present (as contrasted with formal interviewing) is in order here. A few years ago there was a gang-related murder in one of the cities in which I have community contacts. The community peace activist with whom I was working at that time became concerned about possible retaliation and a cycle of vengeance. He went to talk with members of the gang in which the murdered youth had been a member. I was invited to go with him. He spent the whole night talking, cajoling, and finally convincing them not to retaliate. The result was success in the sense that nothing happened. There was no retaliatory violence and so there were no news stories about the subject. Nor were any crime data produced. Rather it was the very absence of news and data that mark this moment as successful. Had I not been there I certainly would not fully have understood how successful his intervention was. Even if I had come across some information through a later interview, that could not replace the understanding that I gained from being at that place at that time. I have had many such opportunities.

In sum, the information, understandings, and analysis that I describe in this essay are developed through a combination of long-term community involvement, nondirected interviews, and more informal contacts, all enhanced by my already well established reputation for trustworthiness in the many communities.

I am told that I am viewed as a unique professor who cares enough to be directly involved in urban peace activism in a variety of organizations. "You're the only one from the university who we see down here," Lorenzo Abeyta of the Milagros Project once told me. The nickname "Doc," which has been assigned to me in different community settings, reflects this trust, for which I am deeply grateful.

STORIES OF POSITIVE CULTURES
LEADERSHIP ORGANIZATIONS

Advocates of positive cultures leadership are creating a wide range of community organizations around the country. Of the over three thousand organizations that exemplify PCL, 90 percent are primarily locally based. The rest are local community groups that are linked into larger organizational structures. Of the organizations that I examine in detail below, two are part of networks. One is Barrios Unidos in Santa Cruz, California, which is part of the multichapter National Coalition of Barrios Unidos. The other is Victory Outreach Church in El Cajon, California, which is part of a worldwide church of the same name. A somewhat mixed example of local and national is the Trinity Lutheran Church Youth Program in Brooklyn, New York, which on the one hand is obviously part of the larger Evangelical Lutheran Church, but which, as a specific program, is primarily limited to its own section of Brooklyn.

Whatever their form, be it local or networked, the peace organizations that I discuss here are part of a general positive cultures leadership movement that is creating a myriad of safe places within which constructive interaction, nonviolent practice, and positive personal transformation from violence to cooperation are taking place. Positive cultures leadership, of which the organizations discussed here are part, is giving people in violent settings locations to which they can go for sustenance, safety, and sanity. These locations are "places of sense," that also give people a "sense of place" in which they are encouraged and supported.

I now turn to specific organizational examples of positive cultures leadership engaged in the process of making "places of sense."

ONE: VICTORY OUTREACH CHURCH,
EL CAJON (SAN DIEGO AREA), CALIFORNIA

Victory Outreach Church is in El Cajon, in the San Diego, California, metropolitan area. The membership of El Cajon Victory Outreach reflects the predominantly Mexican-American population in this part of California. However, the church also has African-American and white members. The El Cajon church is part of the worldwide Victory Outreach Churches, which cut across racial, ethnic, cultural, and national boundaries. The El Cajon church was founded and is pastored by the Reverend Marco Evangelista.

Victory Outreach operates with paid staff and consistent volunteering by its membership. Victory Outreach makes clear its mission of reaching out, with "God's love," to

> individuals as well as families whose lives were once disrupted, almost destroyed by alcohol and drug abuse and involvement in the gang lifestyle that is found in the inner cities. (Victory Outreach n.d., 2)

For Victory Outreach, "the enemy" is not another person or group. Rather, it is violent behavior, be it violence of gang against gang, community against community, parent against child, spouse against spouse, or a person against him/herself. That behavior is viewed as nothing less than the work of Satan. It is Satan behind the gun, the knife, the fist, the drugs, the alcohol. If the enemy is violence prompted by Satan, then this also means that all people have positive potential if they choose (usually with guidance) to walk a spiritual path—the path of love through Jesus Christ. This characterization of "the enemy" as violent behavior rather than intrinsic human nature is characteristic of the PCL organizations, albeit with its own particular evangelical Christian emphasis on Satan. As we shall see, this emphasis on overcoming violent behavior is crucial to the ability of these organizations in reaching out with respect and caring to those who are deemed incorrigible by society at large.

The international Victory Outreach Church was founded by Sonny and Julie Arguinzoni in 1967. The Reverend Sonny Arguinzoni came to adulthood as a heroin addict on the mean streets of New York and "came to Jesus" through the work of David Wilkerson, whose book *The Cross and the Switchblade* (1963) described an early form of urban peacemaking. In their autobiography, Sonny describes his difficult escape from drugs, gangs, and violence and his coming to Jesus, in which he, like others with whom he works, "have been saved and delivered by the power of God" (Arguinzoni and Arguinzoni 1991, 102). Sonny Arguinzoni and his wife Julie created the first Victory Outreach Church in the predominantly Mexican-American inner city of East Los Angeles with their "East L.A. for Jesus" crusade. They also developed an approach that reached out to gang members who became known as "Gangsters for Christ." In typical positive cultures leadership fashion, this name, which at first glance may seem contradictory, helped Victory Outreach to move away from the stigmatization of youth, while also pulling them away from violence.

As an example of this search for the inner spiritual core of people, the Arguinzonis described one young man whom they referred to simply as "Cal." He started out as a violent gang member but then was transformed through spiritual power into a guide to other troubled youth:

> Cal had so much drive I soon noticed that his vision went beyond East L.A. He started praying for San Bernardino and sharing with me how the Lord was dealing with him about going there. San Bernardino is about an hour's drive from Los Angeles. I was just trying to reach our Jerusalem, East L.A.,

but now the Lord was taking us beyond and raising up a young man who was going to expand that vision. (Arguinzoni and Arguinzoni 1991, 182)

As with many positive cultures leadership organizers, Reverend Evangelista's own life is an inspiring and instructional example of escape from intractable violence into redemption and spiritual transformation. With this direct experiential knowledge, Evangelista reaches out to those on the margins of society, using several approaches to the complex problems of violence and despair. For Evangelista, the mission of the church is "to work with those whom the rest of society has cast off, just as Jesus went out to the marginal and the outlaws" (Evangelista, interview in 2001 by Childs).

The activities of Victory Outreach El Cajon include the following approaches. These are all taken from their organizational document *Treasures Out of Darkness* (n.d., 3-5).

Men's and Women's Homes
These are maintained "for the rehabilitation of substance abusers and alcoholics. . . . Our solution is not replacing one drug with another, but it is a whole solution, which is found in the spiritual experience with Jesus Christ."

Reentry Homes
Victory Outreach designed these homes to be "the final step toward re-integration into the outside society." In effect, they are actual, homelike "places of sense." From the Victory Outreach perspective, these sites provide safe settings where former gang members and ex-prisoners who are Christian believers "will establish a closer intimate relationship with Jesus Christ." The reentry home "integrates the individual into the local church." Those living in these sustaining settings learn to engage in and lead projects such as carpentry that help to make the homes economically self-sustaining. The residents must be in job training programs and/or seeking jobs as part of their involvement in the homes.

Prison Ministry
Victory Outreach works directly in county jails and many state and federal prisons. They provide prisoners with "visitation, counseling, and after release, placement to the Special Services homes." These "homes" are basically safe houses, where people can feel free to engage in positive actions without interference from those still in the gang life. Victory Outreach regards prison ministry as part of its call to "present the Good News of Jesus Christ to imprisoned persons, ex-offenders, and their families everywhere . . . and provide opportunities for inmates, ex-offenders, and their families to reach their potential in the Lord as they become productive members of society."

T.O.D. (Treasures Out of Darkness) Support Group
This is a support group whose goal is to "cause once hard-core gang members and long-term prisoners to become a force of transformed men influenced by the

vision of Victory Outreach International. These men empowered by the Holy Spirit will leave a lasting influence in the church."

T.O.D includes, "Bible Studies, Evangelism, Devotional Life Discipleship, Sports Activities, and Domestic Relations Seminars," in its work. All these activities involve a multifaceted emphasis on spiritual growth and positive social behavior that will aid those involved in reentering their communities without regressing back to gangs, drugs, and violence. The social settings in which cooperation and conflict solving are learned include sports fields, focus groups on domestic violence, and classes in Bible study. In all these settings, cooperative behaviors, not just the immediate objectives of the team, group, or class are emphasized.

Love Circles

In these gatherings, the approach is that of mutual respect and caring. The Love Circles are aimed at helping addicts by "challenging" those with chemical dependencies to "take control of their situation and change their lifestyles," through developing "a relationship with Jesus Christ." Addressing addiction is a vital part of Victory Outreach. Violence, both domestic and out on the street, as a part of gang life, is intimately intertwined with drug and alcohol use. Therefore, to help people escape from addiction is to help them escape from gang life and violence.

Public Rallies and Community Theater

In El Cajon and elsewhere, Victory Outreach is notable in its use of massive public rallies and theater productions for peace. The theater productions in particular offer powerful dramatizations of the dangers and pitfalls of a gangster life and life on the streets. Evangelista says that these events offer a way for youth to "go beyond their street life backgrounds" (Evangelista, interview in 2001 by Childs). With nonprofessional actors whose own experiences mirror the plays that are performed, these large public theater events erupt with intense realism about the seductions and consequences of violence, as well as the constructive alternatives available to those out on the streets and in the prisons. Usually held in large auditorium or stadium venues, the productions are free to the public. The language, sounds, and images of the street and of youth culture are used as familiar channels from which to reach out to the community. Concerning one of the first of such gatherings, Sonny Arguinzoni wrote:

> As the gang members walked into the auditorium, many of them were carrying weapons. Some were wearing them on or under their belts; others in their jacket pockets. . . . As we looked and experienced what God was doing we wept. Every kind of fallen humanity that you could ever imagine was streaming toward a better life—eternal life with Jesus. Murderers, prostitutes, dopers, bikers (motorcycle gang members), alcoholics, the forgotten, the lonely, forsaken souls were becoming God's new Treasures Out of Darkness . . . we don't turn away people because they are gang mem-

bers or prisoners. We treat them with respect and we reach out to them with the Message of Love of Jesus Christ." (Arguinzoni and Arguinzoni 1991, 89)

TWO: STOP THE VIOLENCE/INCREASE THE PEACE FOUNDATION, INGLEWOOD (LOS ANGELES METROPOLITAN AREA), CALIFORNIA

Khalid Shah created the Stop the Violence/Increase the Peace Foundation (STV/ITP) in 1989. Its headquarters is in Inglewood, a predominantly African-American district (along with Compton and South Central) in the Los Angeles metropolitan area. STV/ITP's roots are in the African-American community of the L.A. area, but the organization is open to all, regardless of ethnicity or race. STV/ITP has funding that allows for a paid staff as well as volunteers. Shah brought his well-developed organizational skills from his previous days as an organizer of gangs in Los Angeles in the early 1970s. Following his own pivotal transformation from violence to peacemaking, firmly believing in human potential for good, and knowing the harsh realities of life on the streets, Shah moved to build a positive community organization that directly addresses communities impacted by uprooted, disenfranchised youth. Shah regards such an organization as absolutely necessary. He describes the corrosive environment in the inner city areas where he works:

Now people have no regard for life, no regard for gender, no regard for anything and it's like the principles and everything are gone. The whole rules of the game have changed. Now it's about, I'm not even going to get my clothes dirty. I'm just going to shoot you. We have to redefine what our values are. (Quoted in Wright 1996, 36)

As Shah said to me, "Today we have drive-by shootings. We have teachers afraid of getting killed in class. Kids being afraid to go to school, being unable to learn anything because they are afraid of getting shot" (Shah, interview in 2000 by Childs). In turn, he says, the "school system reflects what's going on in the wider society. It reflects the chaos, the neglect, the moral decay, the lack of leadership . . . everything that is going wrong with our society" (Shah interview).

But Shah and his organization are also aware of the larger political picture. They emphasize that this state of affairs in the schools is directly related to the redirection of state policies away from support for education and toward support for the building of prisons. Rates of imprisonment are increasing, primarily among African-American and Latino peoples. Shah says: "You can look at statistics back in the fifties (in California) and see that schools were the number one spending priority for government in terms of building. . . . But here in the '90s the number one government building priority is prisons" (Shah interview).

Shah does not stop at this level of analysis. He faults corporate enterprises and government agencies that are not concerned with the inner cities with contributing to the negative situation there. To understand the big picture, he believes, one must consider the role of materialism and its origins in the economic system. Shah says that among the contributing circumstances to inner city problems is

> . . . greed on the part of people who think only in terms of profit. The people who say, "I didn't make that person buy the drugs, the alcohol" [or] "I didn't make that person turn on that violent program on television." I'm talking now about corporate leaders, business leaders who make money off of these productions. They are contributing in some way to the violence in our communities. This is greed on the part of people who take advantage of the situation. (Shah interview)

Looking at the larger socioeconomic picture is vital, says Shah, because such analysis involves necessary understanding of both the constraints and resources for building locally based peace organizations. For Shah, leaders and organizations that do not look at the big picture and so do not understand some of the complexities that they face are inadequate. Shah points to the need for what he calls "positive leadership." For him, positive leadership means those "who take into consideration the big picture, not just our families and community, but the whole society, what's going on in that." This "big picture" entails critical analysis of the economic system that puts profits before human needs. Shah says, "We need leadership not tied to corporate interest that's going to bring us things like Mad Cow Disease and lying to folks in the community. These elements contribute greatly to the demise of our community" (Shah interview).

But, as is common with positive cultures leadership organizations, Shah and STV/ITP never let the "big picture" divert them from the down-to-earth realities that their communities face. He also emphasizes the local loss of values reflected in family breakdown as part of the problem of violence. Shah says, for example, "Young people are the way they are because parents have stopped being parents." Consequently, there is a crucial need to emphasize individual responsibility: "People first need to start looking within themselves to make a commitment to break the cycle of violence within our own homes" (quoted in Wright 1996, 36).

It is clear that while Shah and STV/ITP emphasize individual, family, and home responsibility for ending of violence, they also focus on the need for grassroots activism to transform the broader social/cultural environment. For example, STV/ITP is deeply concerned about the negatively reinforcing impact of violence in the media, from MTV music videos to movies. It has organized boycotts of local radio stations for playing music that the organization sees as degrading and undermining of the very values that are being lost. As Bill Burgess, a Baptist minister and community-based outreach worker for STV/ITP said to me, "You look at television and there's blood spurting out all over the place. . . . When you hear that you know society is working against us. It is teaching the kids to resolve their problems with violence. This is totally against us. It's against our communities" (Burgess, interview in 2001 by Childs). In response, STV/ITP has launched a community campaign to educate people about media influences. They are also planning to put pressure on advertisers who support programs that, from

STV/ITP's perspective, glamorize violence, gangs, and drugs. (See similar grass-roots responses by Barrios Unidos and members of the Community Research Institute described below.)

However, it is also important to note that STV/ITP, along with other PCL efforts, does not simply restrict itself to being a "protest organization." Rather, any necessary direct advocacy or protest activity are linked to individual/family/community/educational/economic/cultural/ecumenical elements, all of which are important in relationship to each other and any one of which may require major focus at any given moment.

THREE: BARRIOS UNIDOS, SANTA CRUZ, CALIFORNIA

Barrios Unidos of Santa Cruz (known locally as "BU") is the founding chapter and headquarters of the National Coalition of Barrios Unidos, which has thirty-nine chapters, primarily in California, but also in the Southwest, Washington State, Virginia, and the District of Columbia. Barrios Unidos is located in the small city of Santa Cruz, California, about two hours south of San Francisco, along the Monterey Bay. Barrio Unidos in Santa Cruz operates both as the headquarters of all the national chapters and as a local chapter itself. For several years, I served on the Board of Directors of Barrios Unidos in Santa Cruz. During this time I had the opportunity to visit chapters in Virginia and Washington, D.C.

Barrios Unidos started from very humble beginnings. Daniel Alejandrez, known more commonly as "Nane," created it out of the trunk of his car, which was filled with silk-screening materials. Nane drove around the tough streets of Santa Cruz barrios offering silk-screening lessons for aspiring young artists. As he did so, Nane also both preached and modeled the importance of peace and constructive action against violence and the destructiveness of gang life. When I first met the Barrios Unidos people, they had moved into a small, rented office. BU now owns its own complex of buildings that provide ample room for school classes, a media lab, a computer room, a silk-screening production company, and an art studio, as well as low-priced housing for some staff, and a large room for community gatherings and other events. Barrios Unidos has come a long way from Nane's car trunk.

Although Santa Cruz has a population of only about sixty thousand and is known superficially for its beaches, boardwalk, and university, it also has an estimated seven hundred gang members. In the first five months of 2002 there were three shootings and a stabbing. This is a considerably high number for a small community. In this sense, Santa Cruz (and Watsonville, described below) illustrates the fact that youth and gang violence is not restricted to the big cities. For example, in 2001 three young Salvadoran men were murdered in downtown Santa Cruz in a gang-related drive-by shooting that actually turned out to be a case of mistaken identity.

There are two densely concentrated ghettoized areas in Santa Cruz. One is Neary Lagoon. The other, Beach Flats, is right behind the very visible and famous Santa Cruz boardwalk. There are also several low-income housing areas and motels that provide some of the only shelter for poor people in this community that is infamous for having the most expensive rental and housing market in the country. Unfortunately, many houses are used by those selling drugs and are owned by middle-class consumers who drive in from the suburbs to buy them, but who then can escape to the suburbs. This largely white, middle-class co-generation of inner-city crime and violence is a national pattern (see Childs 1991).

Barrios Unidos nationally works with a range of Mexican-American and Black Caribbean-Latino youth. In its national structure it crosses racial and ethnic lines. In Santa Cruz, where the Latinos of Mexican descent are the largest non-European ethnic group, Barrios Unidos primarily serves portions of that population. Nonetheless, cooperative ventures with similar African-American organizations are common. In 1995, for example, a cooperative youth peace summit was held in Santa Cruz that involved the Los Angeles Black Awareness Community Development Organization or BACDO, which had originally been founded in prison. As Jitu Sidiki, a former prisoner and leader of BACDO, said at the time:

We are in solidarity with what Barrios Unidos is doing, because it relates to what is happening in African-American communities as well. Along with national issues, we must maintain the relationship between Latinos and African-Americans. So this model of Black/Brown cooperation is extremely important when put in the context of where this country is moving and should move with regard to inner city youth. (Childs, field notes, 1995)

I have personally assisted in developing positive interaction between Barrios Unidos in Santa Cruz and Stop the Violence/Increase the Peace in Inglewood, California (described below). Most significant is the cooperative work developed with Gaylord Thomas, the African-American director of the Community Outreach Program of the Evangelical Lutheran Church headquarters in Chicago, which continues to yield highly beneficial networking results. Thomas has been instrumental in establishing links between Santa Cruz Barrios Unidos and the African-American "Simba Circle" peace organization in Chicago. I discuss this work on interethnic networking in later sections of this chapter.

The expressed vision of the National Coalition of Barrios Unidos is, "To stop the violence that is killing our youth by providing them with meaningful alternatives that will inspire positive change" (Barrios Unidos 1996, 5). Both nationally and in Santa Cruz, Barrio Unidos approaches violence as a multidimensional dilemma with multidimensional solutions. BU provides media workshops, computer training, art classes, conflict resolution, a successful silk-screening business and a community school, the Cesar Chavez School of Social Change. The objective of this school, which works in conjunction with the Santa Cruz County Office of Education, is to "provide an alternative high school" that has as its aims to "educate, train, and develop youth leaders" (Barrios Unidos 2001,1). Barrios Unidos also effectively intertwines the economic and the educational in its silk-screening production company, BU Productions. By providing artistic, technical, and business training for youth considered to be "high risk," it gives them an instructional framework within which they can apply their artistic talents previously used in spraying graffiti on buildings to economic production that is legal and rewarded rather than illegal and punished. BU Productions also produces some direct income for the organization itself.

With its local, statewide, and national links, Barrios Unidos embodies the locally rooted practical strengths and a vision of broad multiethnic bridge building typically found in positive cultures leadership.

FOUR: THE MILAGROS (MIRACLES) EDUCATION PROJECT, WATSONVILLE, CALIFORNIA

Since 2000, I have worked with and served on the Board of Directors of the Milagros Education Project in the small city of Watsonville, California. Watsonville is a predominantly Mexican-American city on Monterey Bay in an area of intensive agribusiness. Founded by Mike Chavez, a noted peace activist and former gang member, along with educator Lorenzo Abeyta, Milagros aims to reach youth involved in gang warfare. Unlike Victory Outreach and Stop the Violence/Increase the Peace, Milagros does not have a paid staff and relies completely on volunteers.

Despite its volunteer base and relatively small size, Milagros has a rich track record of proactive programs and outreach. In his position as a youth counselor, Chavez works tirelessly on the streets of Watsonville to keep youth out of gangs, while Abeyta does parallel work in the school system as an instructor. In one of its informational fliers, Milagros describes its work with youth and gangs as being structured in the following way:

Educational Presentations
Our staff is available to conduct educational presentations to schools, agencies, and community groups, concerning gangs, alcohol and drug abuse.

Gang Intervention
We work with groups of individuals involved or associated with gangs, or who abuse drugs or alcohol, to assist them in "breaking the chain" and developing self-esteem to succeed with a better outlook on life.

Violence Prevention
We work with young adults directly to reduce the consequences of gangs and violence and the after-effects of this life style.

Youth Cooperative Activities
We provide camping trips, mural painting, graffiti cleaning, car washes, barbecues, sporting events, and activities, group and individual counseling.

Milagros is working to redevelop earlier but now inactive after-school educational instruction and tutoring. Given limited resources, the historic and present tendency of this organization is to focus on developing diverse educational support structures for youth who are otherwise on the margins of the school system. As Lorenzo Abeyta noted to me, "Here in California we have more prison than school construction" (Abeyta, interview in 2000 by Childs).

Providing troubled youth with an alternative pathway that leads to real education, rather than prison, is a primary focus of this organization. Milagros is especially impressive in its attention to individual and family emergency needs. Milagros works hard to respond to those without adequate food or housing and those needing funds to travel to job interviews, or to provide some remembrance on holidays like Thanksgiving. The amounts given in such support are not large, but even relatively small amounts can go a long way. These acts of service reinforce the positive reputation of Milagros, thus advancing its efforts to help keep youth out of gangs.

Similar to Khalid Shah at Stop the Violence/Increase the Peace, Chavez and Abeyta undertake a broad analysis of the current socioeconomic system in the United States. In one meeting, they spoke about the way in which racial or ethnic populations were being increasingly marginalized economically and educationally. Chavez said, "As long as kids are expected to be criminals, they will be denied educational opportunity. That denial will cut them off from economic advancement. And that will turn them into criminals. It's a self-fulfilling prophecy that society does not have to do" (Chavez, interview in 2000 by Childs). They also pointed to the increase in prison construction and the implementation of harsher criminal penalties for relatively minor offenses alongside police brutality as important contexts within and against which they must work.

So, for Milagros, as for the other positive cultures leadership organizations described in this chapter, there is a direct link between highly personalized face-to-face work with youth and gang members, on the one hand, and the successful making of peace in their communities on the other. These positive cultures leadership activists fully recognize that, however successful their day-to-day local work, larger societal concerns must be taken into consideration by leadership at all levels of society if lasting and substantial peace is to be achieved. As a small, nonprofit organization of volunteers, they are restricted in their formal political activities. But in their discussions with youth and with other community members, they make these local, political, and economic connections, thus encouraging expanded thinking about more strategic responses to peacemaking.

FIVE: THE NATIONAL TEEN ACTION RESEARCH CENTER/COMMUNITY RESEARCH INSTITUTE, HARTFORD, CONNECTICUT

In the early and mid-1990s, Hartford witnessed violent gang warfare between two major street organizations that have ties throughout the northeastern and central states. As in other urban communities, such warfare impacts a wide range of families and institutions, especially schools, thereby eroding community solidarity and well-being. Although the violence has abated somewhat, gang and related drug activity are still serious problems.

The National Teen Action Research Center (NTARC), part of the Community Research Institute in Hartford, is unique among PCL organizations in its strong emphasis on "action research"—in other words, research that is applied and community-based. Action research entails involvement of youth from the community and objectives that directly address pressing problems from violence to AIDS. There is a twofold benefit to this approach. First, types of research that might not be conceived or carried out at all in more traditional university settings are designed and conducted. For example, NTARC conducted a location-by-location survey of the drug trade in Hartford, which had never been done before. Second, youth from the community become involved in such research and are encouraged and intellectually enriched through skill development, education, and the leadership enhancement that are required to carry out these studies and activities.

Nor are the organization's purposes restricted to research. NTARC also creates community-focused art and theater projects, such as plays about violence, or the painting of murals with social messages, which have similar intent and consequences. Importantly, research and cultural activity are not considered to be separate compartments as they usually are in university settings. Rather, culture (visual arts, theater, poetry, stories, etc.) and research are seen as assisting each other.

In 2001, I witnessed an example of this melding of art and research during an NTARC youth production of a strikingly powerful video drama on life, killing, and redemption on the street. I was invited to play a cameo role in the video production, and as with so many other "being there experiences," this aided me in gaining a more direct experiential sense of NTARC's unique approach. The resulting video program makes a powerful case for peace at both the personal and community levels in a style that effectively reaches the diverse youth population of Hartford. Before even writing the script for the video play, a highly motivated NTARC youth research team conducted fieldwork that included a statistical survey about violence in Hartford neighborhoods. Based on that research and their own life stories, the youth then went on to write a script, set up the production, and make the video. NTARC provided professional knowledge about field/survey research, theater, and video production to assist the youth. But this video project in all its stages, from research to production, was youth-led. The result is an outcome that has both educational and artistic merits. The video is being widely distributed in public schools and the community and so has an educational impact beyond that of a typical academic publication that might cover the same empirical ground.

NATRC is directed by Dr. Jean Schensul. In the essential positive cultures leadership fashion, Schensul is a guiding force behind the wide variety of NTARC's efforts, from the educational to the artistic, which in turn reflect the multidimensional problems faced by youth in Hartford. As Schensul said to me,

"We cannot just work with one area of concern. We have to deal with everything from violence to the media" (Schensul, interview in 2001 by Childs). Schensul believes that NTARC must work in close collaboration with schools, other community-based organizations, colleges, and universities.

Under the leadership of curator Lynne Williamson, NTARC houses a sizable community museum in its building. Exhibits, such as one that I visited on Taino indigenous culture in the Caribbean, are designed to be meaningful and significant to the diverse communities of the Hartford area, many of them with Caribbean roots. Culture and research go together at NTARC, as in other programs at the Community Research Institute, providing "a creative, new, and demonstrably successful approach to motivating young people of diverse ethnic backgrounds from high risk environments whose capacities have not yet been tapped in classrooms or community programs" (NTARC n.d., 1-3).

Hartford is an ethnically diverse city with a significant Spanish-speaking population primarily from the Caribbean, but with increasing numbers of people of Mexican descent. It also has a large, long-established African-American population. Reflecting the diversity of the Hartford population, NTARC's highly trained, professional staff is multilingual and multiethnic. Staff members engage in diverse, community-related research projects.

As is so common, a portion of the drug and prostitution trade related to gangs is fueled by middle-class, primarily white suburbanites, who are the consumers, but who use the inner city as a market in which they themselves do not have to live (see Childs 1991). In 2001, inner-city residents conducted anti-drug demonstrations in the suburbs after a young inner-city girl was killed in a gang shootout over the drug trade. Youth members of NTARC took part in these demonstrations.

NTARC also offers hands-on experiential learning to youth, both as a way of enhancing their school participation and of moving them away from life on the street. This experiential learning draws from actual life experiences and so values the youth as experts, while also providing them with analytical skills. In this experiential learning, and the research that emerges from it, youth seek real solutions to real problems in their schools and communities by gathering information from their peers and using it as a tool for change. The genius of NTARC is that its single projects, such as the video already mentioned, produce multiple positive results. Such work acts synergistically in many different areas of society, for example, this video drama, which can be shown widely in schools and other community settings. At the same time, the community also benefits from the development of professional skills and leadership among youth as well as through the spreading of a message of peace over violence. In its multifaceted typically positive cultures leadership approach, NTARC provides a wide range of possible venues for youth to work with professionals in ways that enhance their creativity, leadership capabilities, and intellectual breadth. As NTARC says, "By supporting teens in their effort to ask questions of social significance, collect and analyze information, and advocate for positive action through community forums, neighborhood projects, and educational materials, action research helps teens remain in school, consider higher education, develop long-term intimate relationships with positive role models, and avoid substance abuse, violence, antisocial behavior, and gang attachment" (NTARC n.d., 1).

In sum, NTARC is distinctive in its emphasis on combining applied research and cultural learning that engages and informs young people. While NTARC does not emphasize the more overt, broad political analysis that we see in Barrios Unidos, Milagros, and Stop the Violence/Increase the Peace, it does offer a strong foundation for youth to develop analytical skills and the capacity for social critique.

Six: Trinity Lutheran Church Family and Youth Office, Brooklyn, New York

Trinity Lutheran Church in the Sunset Park section of Brooklyn is the site of a newly developing youth program, organized and led by José Valenzuela. At the time of my visit in 2001, Valenzuela and his wife, Norma, had recently moved to Brooklyn from Texas. While his community-oriented youth outreach work is obviously part of the well-established church in Brooklyn, this setting is different from all those above insofar as it is, at the time of this writing, a one-man operation. Valenzuela, a layperson, was hired as director of youth programs because of his strong background in working in the community with young people in tough situations.

As I walked around the neighborhood and met with many people, it became increasingly clear to me that Valenzuela is affectionately regarded among the youth and adults in the Sunset Park area, who call him by the honorific title of "Pastor"—a term that really captures the essence of his dedication to the community. Valenzuela enthusiastically supports and organizes young people, using the church as the both a physical and a social site. Trinity Lutheran is a large building with room for many events, from meetings of Alcoholics Anonymous to youth gatherings. The church has a basketball court outside that is in almost constant use. Trinity Lutheran was originally built by and for a large Norwegian community in 1890 and also served Norwegian sailors who passed through the ports of the New York City area. Today there are still worship services in Norwegian for the older members of the church, as well as services in English for their descendants, and services in Spanish for the rapidly growing Mexican American population in Brooklyn.

The Sunset Park area of Brooklyn is a historic immigrant community. It is home to people in a wide range of situations, including hard-working immigrants with steady jobs, well-established families, numerous kids from disintegrated homes with one or no parents present, and newly arrived immigrants, some undocumented, who are subject to labor exploitation. Gangs, violence, and drugs are common problems. On the positive side, Caribbean- and Mexican-based voluntary associations and businesses with roots in rural communities of origin provide a societal foundation in the neighborhood. Much gang activity is linked to large organizations in other parts of New York City, some of which are part of regional networks connected to the same groups mentioned in the section on Hartford, above. Such extensive gang networking is important, because it makes the work of people like Valenzuela even more difficult. Conflict and flash points for violence can come from far-flung gang networks as well as from more immediate situations. Given this local/regional mix, Valenzuela must demonstrate understanding of and respect for youth in order to reach them successfully.

Valenzuela comes from a Mexican-American Lutheran family in New Mexico. Both of his parents are Lutheran ministers. His mother was the first Latina woman to be ordained by the Lutheran Church. Valenzuela works with approximately seventy youths in a number of different ministries. The youths are primarily Mexican-American, though a small number of white youngsters take part in the church's programs as well. Much of the youth culture described by Valenzuela and by John Alfonso, one of the student researchers who conducted interviews for this project, is heavily influenced by African-American urban cultural styles, with their distinctive language and clothing and tastes. For example, it is a mark of respect for Pastor Valenzuela (and his basketball ability) that the youth say to him in the language of the street, "Pastor, you a gangsta!" when he makes some particularly slick move on the court (Valenzuela, interview in 2001 by Childs). This term, as indicated in the introductory pages of this chapter, implies a strong, resolute, and trustworthy person who is part of the fabric of the neighborhood. To be called a "gangsta" in the sense conveyed by contemporary inner-city, hip-hop popular culture, is a sign of how much respect Valenzuela has earned among many youth in his community. Valenzuela says he came to Trinity Lutheran "to hit the streets, to walk around the neighborhood, and to build as many relationships as he can in the community" (Valenzuela interview). This he is doing very effectively. Every Wednesday is "high school night" on the basketball court. "I get about 50 kids," Valenzuela reports. "They all line up to hug me before they start" (Valenzuela interview).

As we walked together through the Sunset Park area, it became clear that Valenzuela is very well connected to people in that community. I heard various comments from young people and adults alike that showed how Valenzuela is considered to be a man with "heart" who won't back down and upon whom young people and the wider community can depend. Valenzuela explains that he comes from a community-organizing background that has taught him the value of engaging in "a lot of one-on-one direct personal interaction." Valenzuela spends a great deal of time on the streets, especially during the afternoon hours when school gets out, to talk with young people. This may sound simple. But the time period immediately after school is an important social moment in which youth are essentially on their own. One of the most impressive aspects of Valenzuela's outreach is that he is so knowledgeable about minute neighborhood details. He fulfills a function once carried out by neighbors in neighborhoods of yesteryear—that is, he watches out for the children. For example, when one young man whom he had asked to meet with him failed to show up one day, Valenzuela let it be known with tongue in cheek, and in the language of the streets, that he was "pissed." This message got back to the young man, who eventually showed up to say how sorry he was. In the midst of a potentially alienating, anomie-producing megalopolis, such interpersonal familiarity and mutual respect are nothing short of astonishing. The young people with whom Valenzuela works possess a strong sense of security rooted in their church. This security allows them to come to him with their troubles and difficulties, contributes to their self-esteem, and motivates them to grow in their Christian faith.

Along with his understanding of youth and gang life, Valenzuela is fully aware of the larger national political/economic/historical picture, invoking five hundred years of European colonization of the Americas and subsequent indigenous interpretations of it. Much of what he calls "the oppression of Mexican American youth" is, as he sees it, yet another chapter in the European invasion that disrupted already existing cultures. Valenzuela realizes that passing on such an understanding to youth will not solve immediate problems of violence. But when youths are made aware of this history, they are better oriented and motivated to play constructive roles in solutions that enrich them culturally. Valenzuela is therefore planning a play on the subject of identity and history of populations of Mexican descent to be held at his church, in which youth will play a prominent role, much like their counterparts at NTARC in Hartford and Victory Outreach in El Cajon.

As a positive cultures leader, Valenzuela emphasizes his commitment to listen to and provide a safe place for the stories of young people. He sees a supportive response from the church to the needs of youth as an absolute necessity. "The way I see it," he says, "if the church isn't there for these kids, then who is? If the church isn't doing it, then what else should the church be doing?" (Valenzuela interview). Clearly, for Valenzuela, the building blocks of positive constructive and spiritual development are intensely personal and interpersonal. All his work in the community is, as he says, "one on one" and all else flows from that. Like other dedicated positive cultures leaders whose work is chronicled in this chapter, Valenzuela bridges the personal and the societal; he can move from the realities of home and street to the profound depths of the human spirit. Because of his ministry, Trinity Lutheran is a place that "makes sense," where young people find a "sense of place."

BEYOND SOCIAL MOVEMENTS:
TOWARD A TRANSCOMMUNAL NETWORKING
OF POSITIVE CULTURES LEADERSHIP

A pivotal insight running through all the organizations described in this chapter is that the "enemy" is not young people or gangs per se. Rather, the enemy is violent behavior. For Victory Outreach Church, that enemy is personified as Satan. For Barrios Unidos, Milagros, and Stop the Violence/Increase the Peace, it is known as "the madness" or *la vida loca*. For NTARC, it is societal evils that must be studied and addressed. For José Valenzuela, it is the daily realities of "the street," not some intrinsic propensity of youth. This emphasis on behavior as opposed to labeling people as intrinsically bad allows all these positive cultures leadership groups and individuals to condemn violence while treating the human beings who are involved in violence with respect and a profound belief in their potential for positive transformation.

Overall, positive cultures leadership organizations, including the ones discussed here, are in effect reversing the tactical direction of the earlier civil rights movement and other social justice struggles in the United States. Those movements tended to aim for broad societal change (such as eradicating legal segregation based on race) to alter the overall society in the direction of equality and justice. Obviously, much of that hoped-for progress has occurred. But we also know that persistent inequality, systems of prejudicial exclusion, and a pattern of corrosive violence within and among communities remain essential problems. Broad social movements of earlier years did not resolve these problems; they still confront people every day, not just in the southern United States but throughout the nation.

By contrast, as described in the preceding pages, positive cultures leadership starts with on-the-ground realities of individual struggles to respond creatively within a disruptive and alienating context of deadening materialism and violence. This point of departure is based on direct and one-on-one personal work that addresses issues from gang violence to drug addiction. Through focusing on the personal potential of individuals and their transformation, PCL activists seek to strengthen communities with empowered and spiritually enriched young people. Out of such communities will arise a society transformed by justice and equality. Positive cultures leadership, as exemplified by the organizations examined in this study, combines visionary and pragmatic ways of being and thinking. Equally important, most of the leaders are people who have fundamentally transformed themselves from members of violent gangs or incarcerated offenders to constructive advocates of peace-oriented and justice-oriented community revitalization.

PERSONAL TRANSFORMATION

The transformation from violence to nonviolence, in the face of a society that generally says such change is not possible, is a key aspect of much PCL organizing. Some PCL leaders with whom I have worked for several years consistently testify both publicly and privately that while they were in the prisons, in the gangs, or in the thrall of drugs, they were known as dangerous people with little or no regard for life. They tell of vital, transformative moments, all of them personally intense, which led them to change. They speak about these transformations publicly, for the experience of vital change is itself an important aspect of their ability to reach others now living in harsh circumstances. As writer, peace activist, and former gang member Luis Rodriguez says about the possibilities of positive transformation, "I've talked with enough gang members and low-level dope dealers to know that they would quit today . . . if there was a viable alternative. If we all had a choice, I'm convinced nobody would choose *la vida loca* [the crazy life]" (Rodriguez 1993, 251).

Victory Outreach Church of El Cajon illustrates the power of transformation away from *la vida loca*, with a poster under the title of "Miracles of Progress" showing a man progressing from being a gangster with a gun to a churchgoer with Bible in hand. To further emphasize the positive potential for constructive transformation inherent in us all, Victory Outreach cites Isaiah 45:3, "I will give you the treasures out of darkness and hidden riches in secret places." The church's founder and pastor, Marco Evangelista, said to me, "I was a violent and dangerous man, now I am pastor of a Church that's helping others to escape from the evil of violence and drugs and alcohol" (Evangelista interview).

Khalid Shah, director of the Los Angeles-area organization Stop the Violence/Increase the Peace, had once been a key organizer of powerful gangs in Los Angeles. According to Shah, the paths that led to his personal transformation included his older brother's decision to quit the gang life; his mother's fundamental ethical values, which she instilled in him at an early age and to which he returned; and a paying job at a now-defunct War on Poverty organization called the "Economic and Youth Opportunities Agency." Equally significant for Shah was a defining moment in prison. He told me,

One time when I was in prison I had the job, the task of killing someone. But I suddenly thought of what my brother had told me. He said, "You can do almost anything else and make up for it, but if you take a life, it's gone forever." That really hit me and I didn't do it. That was a major step for me. (Shah interview)

Daniel "Nane" Alejandrez, founder of the National Coalition of Barrios, came from a drug gang background that was "hard, almost impossible to leave, and I was addicted too, but I got out and made a different person of myself with the help of others. So, I know it can be done and I am trying to do it with others at Barrios Unidos" (personal communication to author, 1995).

Such dramatic, life-affirming transformations are not common to all PCL leaders, nor are they essential to their leadership. However, all such leaders must recognize the capacity for change of gang members, and of those in prison. The fact that so many who now assert peace and nonviolence were once themselves in the same situation as those in gangs, in prison, and/or addicted to drugs, carries a tremendous amount of weight. Those who have "been there" win the respect of those who are still there. Moreover, these transformed peace activists have not lost the knowledge that they gained in their former lives. They can speak with great experiential authority about violence directly, and not abstractly or "academically" from a distance. As Marco Evangelista of Victory Outreach said to me, "The gang members, the hustlers, they have to have energy, initiative, and intelligence to survive. We don't ask them to give that up. We help them to change so that they can use all that strength for positive rather than negative purposes" (Evangelista interview).

Like Jonah emerging from the belly of a "great fish," these transformed peace activists have been "in the belly of the beast," but have come forth to carry out their prophetic callings of personal and community reconstruction.

VISIONARY LEADERSHIP

In turn, the great significance of such personal transformation directly connects to the visionary leadership of PCL organizations. The leaders who have gone through such change, and who are now directing organizations working directly in troubled communities, usually bring with them an associated magnetism emanating from their victory over despair and hopelessness as well as from their organizational successes. The founding and pivotal leaders of many organizations such as those described above possess leadership stemming from the exceptional transformative crossings in their lives.

This does not mean that such leaders must have been directly involved in the prison/gang/street scene to be effective. José Valenzuela, the son of Lutheran ministers, did not go through that kind of experience, yet his ability to reach youth by interacting with them in ways that fit into and respect their urban culture is no less impressive. When he plays basketball with the young men of the community they compliment his knowledgeable and tough approach by saying in the local parlance, "You a 'gangsta' pastor!" This means, in effect, "you are one of us" since "gangsta" does not necessarily mean gang member. Rather, it signifies a grounded, experienced, and knowledgeable person who can be respected, trusted, and looked up to.

Neither does Jean Schensul of NTARC in Hartford come from a "street" background. But she has long and distinguished record of work for social justice both in the United States and internationally. Vision and practical organizing capabilities combine in Schensul to maker her a charismatic community leader.

Also in Hartford, Yedalis Ruiz, NTARC's "prevention research" educator, effectively reaches high school students and other young people through her tremendous facility with urban youth culture. In one meeting with her, for example, I was struck by her ability to explain how she cracked the coded glamorization of the dangerous drug "Ecstasy" in a popular song, well known on television. I knew the song, but its message, which was opaque to me, was clear to young people. Ruiz said to me, "I can go out to the schools and talk straight to them about what this song is about and what drugs are about and show them the contradictions without coming down on them like adults and the police do" (Ruiz, interview in 2001 by Childs). She was also involved in creating a for-school-use project through NTARC, using portable murals about media glamorization of violence against women, which is a part of drug culture, and which in turn is connected to gang violence through the drug trade as business.

In common with her counterparts in Inglewood, Santa Cruz, Watsonville, and Brooklyn, Ruiz demonstrates her understanding of wider political/legal elements when she adds, "This music is about making drugs seem glamorous but we can't censor it. . . . What we have to do is to educate the kids about the dangers, and about who really makes money off of this poison. We are using art and research to do this in the schools and churches and elsewhere" (Ruiz interview).

PRACTICAL LEADERSHIP

While the leaders described in this chapter are strongly visionary, leading in part by the force of their ideas, such urban peace activists are also highly pragmatic in their organizational activity. They combine the visionary with the practical, and the immediate with the long-term.

In turn, this pragmatic capability of visionary peace activists means that they are able to attract multiskilled individuals to join them in their work. These workers can handle the multifaceted tasks of organizations that must address the personal, the interpersonal, the spiritual, the cultural, the economic, and the educational in immediate, intermediate and mediate ways if they are to be successful. All of the organizations described in this study have achieved this type of capability, although there are limitations based on resources available to them for supporting paid staff or attracting and maintaining volunteers.

No one response can work in the midst of complex problem matrices; several direct practical approaches are necessary. Stopping a fight among rival groups will not solve economic problems. But being able to stop such a fight is still absolutely necessary. Such success lays the groundwork for other forms of cooperative interaction.

IMPLICATIONS FOR FUTURE TRANSCOMMUNAL SOCIAL ACTIVISM

The visionary and practical PCL organizations that I have described in this chapter have deep roots in their communities. Their ability to address everyday issues along with long-range and broad outlooks gives them a solid grounding for expanding social justice networking in this new century. For positive cultures leadership organizations, the building process is central and ongoing. Thousands of such organizations are now in place; what is needed now is the creation of cooperative networks—that is, more effective, nonhierarchical methods of cooperation based on mutual respect and interpersonal relations among these many organizations. Nationwide social justice action must be rooted in myriad local autonomous organizations rather than imposed from above by a handful of people, no matter how well meaning. Because of the growth of positive cultures leadership, we are now poised on the edge of an important sociopolitical development: a twenty-first century mode of organizing for justice and dignity that I call "transcommunality" is emerging.

By "transcommunality" I mean the constructive and developmental interaction occurring among distinct communities and organizations. This interaction develops through interpersonal relations of people engaged in common tasks. Transcommunalists do not employ a "melting pot approach" in which particular community and organizational allegiances are obliterated in order for cooperation to occur. On the contrary, transcommunal action and interaction become possible precisely because people emerge from and work within distinctive communal and organizational settings. They have roots. So, rather than being an abstract, top-down call for unity of the kind so common in the nineteenth and twentieth centuries, transcommunality flows from practical action around common problems, which in turn leads to increasing communication, mutual respect, and understanding (see Childs 2002).

Positive cultures leadership organizations see part of this broad transcommunal development occurring in many parts of the world (Childs 2002). Positive cultures leadership organizations are laying the groundwork for transcommunal cooperation across ethnic lines in the United States. The next step is for a more concerted, egalitarian, and constant effort to amplify contacts among the already well established organizations that in multifaceted ways are all working toward urban peace and justice.

Such transcommunal networking is not only a dream for a better future. It exists in the here and now, while needing expansion. Let me suggest two such concrete transcommunal examples, which demonstrate both its practical reality and its future possibilities. One is the 1993 National Urban Peace and Justice "Gang Truce" Summit held in Kansas City, Missouri, which I attended as an advisor to Barrios Unidos. The other is the more current, ongoing collaboration between Santa Cruz Barrios Unidos and the Chicago-based Simba Circle with the assistance of Gaylord Thomas of the Evangelical Lutheran Church's Community Outreach Program.

The National Urban Peace and Justice Summit was organized in part by Daniel "Nane" Alejandrez and Barrios Unidos, along with Carl Upchurch of the National Urban Peace and Justice Coalition. They worked alongside a diverse variety of Latino/African-American/white community organizations, religious leaders, and community peace groups. Dedicated to the memory of farm labor organizer Cesar Chavez, the summit brought together gang members and peace activists from around the country to meet at the predominantly African-American St. Stephen Baptist Church. All those associated with the Summit charted new ground as they crossed over gang, ethnic, and racial lines around the common goal of creating peace on the street. The summit brought together representatives of some of the largest urban nations or gangs, including the Black Disciples, Black Souls, Bloods, Crips, Cobras, Gangster Disciples, Latin Kings, El Rukhyns, Stones, Conservative Vice Lords, Sureños and Norteños, who worked in concert with one another and with community peace activists. Without their involvement, the Summit, dedicated to promoting peace and justice would have been meaningless. As Sharif Willis, minister of justice for the Conservative Vice Lords, said, "Anytime you can bring together those whom society has defined as incorrigible you have accomplished something" (Childs 1993, 50).

The core message of the summit, agreed to by its diverse participants, was for an activist peace that stops violence while improving overall economic/societal conditions. "Racism has pulled us apart," said one gang member about the importance of crossing racial boundaries. Steering committee member Fred Williams, who had been involved in earlier truces among Crips and Bloods in Los Angeles, observed, "This country has never had young African-Americans and Hispanics come together on the premise that we are not here to shoot each other. Our destinies are tied together." Similarly, Marion Stamps, an indomitable peace worker from the violence-torn Cabrini Green housing projects in Chicago, stated that the Summit "signified the reunification of black poor and oppressed communities" (Childs 1993, 50).

The summit was wide-ranging in its participants and fully cognizant of broad socioeconomic impacts on the cities. But the summit was made possible only because of already well established, community-rooted, positive cultures leadership organizations that work on the daily, visionary, and practical basis described earlier in this chapter; these created the "places of sense" and "senses of place" from which the summit organizing could succeed. At the end of the summit, Daniel "Nane" Alejandrez spoke of the need to take its message of nationwide cooperation back to the ghettos and barrios. As positive cultures leadership increases and strengthens, such cooperation becomes ever more possible.

For example, an ongoing relationship between the predominantly Mexican-American Barrios Unidos and the predominantly African-American Simba Circle is continuing and growing in what is called "the Warriors' Circle." This is a gathering of at-risk youth from California, Chicago, Brooklyn, and other places, who come to a retreat at the Mount Cross Lutheran Bible Camp every summer. The Warriors' Circle is actively supported by Gaylord Thomas, who works as an advisor to the Simba Circle and whom I described earlier as a key inspirational figure in the Evangelical Lutheran Church's Community Outreach Program. The Warriors' Circle offers a "place of sense/sense of place" retreat that aims to "show boys raised in gang-infested neighborhoods that they don't have to commit violence to be a man" (Harlick 2002, 1). The gathering is centered on the message of nonviolence and "the philosophy of shared values that transcend all races, ethnicity, and nationalities. As one young man said about his experience in the Warriors' Circle, "This has showed me how to be strong. I don't have to do drugs. I know I can do it" (Harlick 2002, 1).

As with the Kansas City summit, which in turn helped to lead to multi-organizational, transcommunal cooperative efforts such as the Warriors' Circle, this gathering is possible only because Barrios Unidos and the Simba Circle have deep community roots. The roots are deep because these organizations engage in the everyday practical issues such as direct prevention of violence and personal transformation from gang member to peace leader among youth. The minute, everyday aspects of positive cultures leadership that combine the visionary and the practical are the twenty-first century foundation for nationwide cooperation for peace. This cooperation will go beyond the organizing forms characteristic of twentieth-century social movements, with their national leaders and broad agendas. Rather, it will involve transcommunal networks that respect and draw from the distinctive locations, needs, and resources of highly diverse kinds of positive cultures leadership action.

CONCLUSION: PROSPECTS AND OPPORTUNITIES
FOR CHURCHES AND OTHER CHRISTIAN COMMUNITIES

The cooperative work that I have already described taking place between Barrios Unidos and Simba Circle is an excellent example of respectful, sensitive, and helpful support among allies concerned with pressing urban problems of violence. Instructively, Gaylord Thomas, as a peace outreach worker, does not tell community organizations what to do. But he and the Evangelical Lutheran Church do offer various kinds of appropriate support, such as assistance in developing transcommunal youth peace gatherings. Significantly, Thomas is highly ecumenical in his outreach; he does not work only with Lutheran-based organizations. Thomas flexibly respects a range of beliefs from different Christian groups to indigenous spirituality as well as more strictly secular analysis. Given the range of approaches that we see in the PCL organizations, such a truly ecumenical outreach approach is necessary for any real alliance and supportive role to be played by Christian communities.

Another important area of concern for any would-be supportive role for Christian communities involves being in the process for the long haul. The problems facing these positive cultures leadership organizations can range from those of immediate crises, to longer-range needs for educational opportunity, to big picture analyses of national/global politics and economic impacts. All such issues occur in the context of continuous, traumatic gang violence, which disrupts families and erodes communities. Also, given the difficulties faced by individuals trying to escape from gangs, violence, addiction, and poverty, it is not surprising to see "backsliding" by some—all of which requires constant patience, faith, and stamina by positive cultures leadership activists and organizations. The fact that a gang member says one positive thing and then does something negative cannot be grounds for dismissal. Rather, the peace activists must start all over again. It is such patience that is one of the features distinguishing positive cultures leadership from the more immediately retributive "criminal justice system." As Bill Burgess of Stop the Violence/Increase the Peace said to me in response to a question of how he keeps his spirit up, "Well, I am a spiritual man. I believe that God has a design for everything and that we will be able to stop the violence. But I won't see it in my lifetime. That's okay, it's not about me. It is about peace for our grandchildren. We have to think about them" (Burgess, interview in 2001 by Childs).

With all of this in mind, Christian communities in the United States will have to think about how to provide such respectful, long-term support for positive community efforts. Unfortunately, the general picture is that many Christian communities operate more on an immediate, "response to crisis" mentality. Obviously there are major crises in the world, and helpful responses to them are needed. But a recent nationwide survey by Mark Chaves found that "[most] religious congregations typically engage in short-term emergency help rather than long-term social service provision. They are more likely to provide emergency food, shelter, and clothing, for example, than to run programs that focus on long-term face-to-face education or counseling" (Chaves 2001, 11).

According to Chaves, the National Congregations Study data indicate that "congregations are not very involved at all in holistic levels of social services" (Chaves 2001, 12). A key question is this: Can Christian communities work respectfully and effectively as allies with positive cultures leadership organizations in the long-term, multifaceted struggle for peace and justice? Such long-term commitment is absolutely necessary, given the deeply ingrained problems of violence that are complexly linked to a range of factors from education to the economy to guns to discrimination.

So, there is much room for growth of expanded respectful and tangible collaboration of currently noninvolved Christian communities with positive cultures leadership. Given the already developing networks of local groups in some cases, it would be especially useful to facilitate more transcommunal, face-to-face gatherings such as the Kansas City summit and the Warriors Circle. Christian community support, much like that provided by Gaylord Thomas and the Evangelical Lutherans, can have an important positive impact on such transcommunal developments and on the daily, pressing realities facing urban peace organizations. Such support would also help to bridge the racial and class divides between inner cities and suburbs.

In his classic work *Where Do We Go from Here: Chaos or Community?*, Martin Luther King, Jr., spoke of the need for sustained support of community network building as essential for social justice. King wrote that we must "have people tied together in a long-term relationship instead of evanescent enthusiasts" (King 1967, 187). More than ever, today's positive cultures leadership organizations deserve such long-term support from Christian communities.

9

The Mystery of Transformative
Times and Spaces

Exploring a Theology of Grassroots Peacebuilding

JOHN PAUL LEDERACH

Inside the Maze

"My fear of peace?" he asks.
We sit hunched under bunks.
Men with tattoos bring us tea,
Roll cigarettes,
And watch even our breathing.
"That at the end of the day,"
he says to me twice,
"That at the end of the day,
I'll be back in this prison visitn'
me children's children."

I wrote this poem following a conversation with a prisoner in the Maze on April 24, 1995. It is filled with ambiguity, much like the moment was experienced. Why would someone fear peace? How is it that so many settings of deep-rooted violent conflict have these generational cycles, where the worst-case as opposed to the best-case scenario defines reality? At the time of this conversation, the cease-fires in Northern Ireland were recent and clearly those who had been involved in the violence were leery about the possibility of their success. Now six years later I am writing the early lines of this article at the Maryknoll Center in New York. John Brewer, our research colleague from Northern Ireland prayed this morning for the talks on the Island where the peace seems precarious, the political leaders are meeting in emergency session, sectarian murders have recently erupted, and the parading season is in full swing. This could just as easily be July from any decade over the past four. My commander friend from the Maze is now out of prison, but his cautionary words are hauntingly prescient. While I have given most of my professional and academic life to pursuing peace, it remains an elusive, sometimes fearful mystery.

My contribution to this research project on grassroots responses of Christians to violence has been to reflect on the process, findings, and discussions from a theological point of view. When I first received the phone call from Tom Bamat about participating in the Maryknoll initiative I thought he had made a mistake.

"You know I am a sociologist and a practice-oriented conciliator?" I inquired at the other end of his first phone call. "I am not a theologian. In fact, even though I find it annoying, you should know that many of my theological colleagues critique my work by saying it has no theology."

"We know you are not a theologian," he responded. "What we want is simple. Just talk about what you see theologically from the standpoint of your experience and insights."

So it was that a Mennonite sociologist-mediator type agreed to provide theological reflections for a Catholic-initiated research endeavor. And herein lie the introductory caveats. This chapter represents my best efforts to put on the "logos-lens" of the divine while looking, listening, and interacting with the messiness of how everyday people in grassroots communities respond to the overwhelming challenges of war and deadly conflict. While I have enjoyed every minute of interacting with this widely diverse set of researchers and the case studies and the research challenges they represented, I must confess that I often felt overwhelmed by my task. To develop a comprehensive and rigorous theology of grassroots response to violence and peace is not only beyond the scope of a single chapter; it is well beyond my personal capacities and preparation. So I soon put aside any notion of being something I am not, or doing something that I am not prepared to do, and decided to concentrate on what I can offer. I almost feel you should be forewarned: Reader beware! You are about to enter the zone of a conciliator-sociologist who was given permission to muse and ramble about the theology of grassroots peacebuilding.

In the end, as Tom suggested, my approach was simple. I am writing directly from what I know best, what I see, and what I feel—and not worrying whether it is theologically correct or formally rigorous. I have worked with many grassroots community leaders all over the world who are courageously attempting to forge peace in the midst of violence. I come from a practical approach of working at conflict transformation and peacebuilding, particularly in efforts aimed at conciliation, sustained dialogue, and nonviolent social change. And I come from and am active in a peace-oriented faith tradition that has informed my personal motivation, sustained my work, and provided me with a lens to go beyond the professions of sociology and mediation.

When I interacted with the seven case studies of this project I was drawn immediately to three arenas of reflection that form the structure of this chapter: theologies of space, time, and mystery. Early on it was suggested I look at spaces and times in the plural, since in each case I was clearly looking at multiple ways that these were formed and reformed in my own experiences and in the cases produced by the research colleagues. While I had explored some of these themes in earlier work, I found in this project a new and invigorating opportunity to go further with my reflection and to let the research emerging from on-the-ground ethnographies and surveys change, reorient, and reinforce my conceptual frameworks and biases. This chapter is an effort to attest to and recognize the invisible: the miraculous way that God is present and moves people and history toward a redeemed and transformed humanity and creation.

A THEOLOGY OF SPACES

To talk about a theology of spaces may sound conceptually odd to the casual reader, like some kind of esoteric or obscure philosophical exercise. I would suggest the opposite. Building and sustaining peaceful transformation of deadly conflict is perhaps first and foremost the process of creating and keeping alive transformed spaces of interdependence and interaction between real people in real communities with histories of struggle and division. In fact, in nearly all the study's cases the specificity of conflict was a history of struggle over access to land and recognition of the rights of people to exist in shared space. And most importantly, these were struggles for power over who would decide the fate of space and its proper occupants. From Northern Ireland to Sri Lanka, Guatemala to South Sudan, the conflict could be understood as a conflict over whether coexistence in the same space could be achieved. However, when it came to peacebuilding I was nervous about suggesting a theology of spaces to the research group until I saw the title of John Brown Child's chapter on responses to urban gang violence in the United States: "Places of Sense, Senses of Place." Then I knew the time had come to give more serious attention to this theology.

I do not want to use the pages given to this chapter to explore the deadly, negative, and violent struggles for access to and control of space that underpin so many conflicts at the grassroots. Clearly, one of the most important aspects of these situations is the use and abuse of power, particularly hegemonic and dominant power aimed at excluding and marginalizing people from their own places. But my intention is rather to explore how space is articulated, defined, and redefined by people engaging in grassroots peacebuilding as a response to those situations. I propose not so much to explore the verbal externalization of what grassroots peacebuilders say they do and are, but rather to explore the meaning of their lives and action across dimensions that more often than not remain in the domain of the invisible, the unspoken, and the symbolic. When I started to look at this more carefully, two important dimensions of spaces with theological meaning stood out: the geography of peace and prophetic bridge building.

THE GEOGRAPHY OF PEACE

One of the remarkable aspects of listening to the researchers and reading through the case studies was the multiple references to grassroots communities initiating a process to reappropriate a claim on their own space. In every instance this was local, a movement to take action, to speak to others about the right to a safe place, a place that can be called "ours," a community—whether its realization was the zones of peace in Mindanao, fields of cooperative agriculture in Sri Lanka, or an old house in a Los Angeles neighborhood where gang-traumatized citizens meet to formulate alternatives. These were what John Brown Childs called "locally rooted places as sites on which to build constructive multidimensional reinforcements for positive life."

This emphasis on creating a geography that is life-giving seems at the base of "grassroots" peacebuilding in a literal sense. Home is where the roots and the heart lie. There is a sociological component that accompanies this orientation, namely, that people seek a voice in that which most directly affects their lives at home. But it simultaneously represents a series of profound theological affirmations.

First, grassroots peacebuilding suggests that creating and sustaining life begin close to where life, survival, and nourishment actually take place. Peace is not exclusively nor primarily the responsibility or mandate of those far off and higher up. It is the duty and domain of those who are close to home. The marked localization of peace efforts in the case studies—in other words, the consistent pursuit of transforming violent conflict starting in our backyards and communities—suggests a theological understanding of God present in the everyday and immediate.

Second, localization and creating grounded spaces of peace indicate an incarnate understanding of faith and belief. Life giving in the face of life-destroying contexts moves people to reflect the presence of the divine in everyday, proximate relationships. It is as if, to quote the first verses of the Gospel of John, the "Word pitched a tent and dwelt among us" (John 1:14). This is not a distant, esoteric, or even rhetorical peace. Peace is embodied in the redefinition of violent spaces into safe and livable places—owned, created, guarded, and sustained by the people who actually live and make life in them.

In contrast, the more dominant views of peace from the standpoint of national negotiations processes and structures, on the one hand, and—paradoxically—much of the peace research focused on systemic policy and macrostructural changes, on the other, seem to suggest that peace requires a massive institutional change. Sustained movement toward justpeace* will undoubtedly require such institutional change. However, the grassroots theological view rising from the research is not one that is daunted or paralyzed by the massive level of change

---

*Lederach introduced this term in "Justpeace: The Challenge of the 21st Century," in *People Building Peace: 35 Inspiring Stories from Around the World* (Utrecht: European Centre for Conflict Prevention, 1999), 27-36.—*Eds.*

required. Rather, it infuses the immediate situation with a local and microchange understanding that seems to operate on a principle of accessibility: "We will work to create and redefine a local space that is within our reach and that demonstrates the kind of changes we seek more broadly." In this sense, as suggested by Karl Gaspar in the course of our research meetings, a geography of peace is microutopian, requiring an eschatology of "on earth as it is in heaven." This theology suggests that God transforms the world through the weak, the small, the foolish, and the local. And it says that God is invoked and made visible in the actual relationships that define everyday living in "homeland" spaces. In this sense, defining geographies of peace that are concrete and accessible and that touch the immediacy of everyday lives is a profound act of empowerment and hope.

PROPHETIC BRIDGE BUILDING

Throughout the descriptions of actions taken up by grassroots community peacebuilders was that of moving between conflicting groups. In Northern Ireland, Mindanao, and South Sudan, to mention a few cases, the forms of intermediary action were varied. Sometimes it was oriented toward a preventive action—how to head off the rapid rise of tensions before they translated into full-blown violence. At other times it was clearly about a process of seeking remedies and solutions, and deescalating existing cycles of violent conflict between individuals or groups within the community. Sometimes the interviewees referred to this with the formal terminology of mediation; more often it seemed to be captured in a metaphorical language of "bridge building" or "dialogue." This type of action, by my reading of the breadth of the case studies in this book, was among the very few examples of grassroots activity that were present in all of the cases. The ubiquitous nature of bridge building begs reflection as to the theological underpinnings of it as metaphor and action.

Let us start with a few observations on the metaphor of bridge building as situated in the context of the grassroots examples given in the preceding chapters. First, one of the characteristics that leaps out from the descriptions is the fact that those building the bridge are not the sociological ideal-type mediators described in much of the academic and prescriptive literature about third-party roles (see, e.g., Moore 1996). They are not outside of the relationships, nor are they neutral or impartial. Grassroots peacebuilders are located in the web of relationships wherein the conflicts are spun. They are individuals seen as coming from a particular side or identity within that context. They are, in the terms I have used in a previous work, "inside-partials" (Lederach 1998).

I am reminded of what a colleague from the Philippines once commented: "You don't build a bridge starting from the middle." This I believe points to a theology of intermediary action that is reflected in the case studies. Invariably in both the qualitative and quantitative aspects of the research, men and women involved in grassroots peacebuilding identified "relationship building" as core, at the center of what they were engaged in. This was particularly true of the intermediary examples, where the purpose of the activity was to restore relationships, heal divisions, or find solutions to bring people back together. Here the existing identities, close and connected to the actual people involved in the fighting and division, were seen as a resource rather than an obstacle.

The folk forms of intermediary work were not concerned with neutrality in a professional sense but with the building and rebuilding of trust. One interpretation is that this type of action in a context of deeply divided relationships represents the development of intermediary activity as the process of creating authentic community. In this sense, grassroots intermediary activity is profoundly prophetic. We typically understand the prophetic tradition as framed in the form of denouncement. On closer examination, and pushed by what we find in these case studies, the prophetic tradition is equally oriented toward calling people to authenticity in their relationships. This is the prophetic action of creating the space of genuine relationship, engagement, and healing.

The question then becomes how such a space is created from the eyes of grassroots reconcilers. The examples we find here are those of creating space for healing between enemies who live in the same communities, action aimed at breaking down the dividing walls of hostility. In the case studies, people carried out the intermediary action by creating relationships on both or on multiple sides of the division. A relationship-based approach creates legitimacy of action not on the basis of professional role development and presentation, sustained by certificates of formal training and skill, but essentially on the quality of trust and respect in and through the persons serving as the bridge. To return to our metaphor, the bridge must have strong footing in the shores, often requiring grassroots people to think creatively in terms of teams and networking. Here the very form that the intermediary work takes is the building of connections and cooperative action of a "cross-community" team in Northern Ireland, or an interfaith initiative in Mindanao. The process is not lodged in the individual as mediator, but in the space created in the set of relationships of those providing a bridge.

The cases suggest another analogy emerging from the idea of serving as a bridge. The primary purpose of a bridge is to allow people to cross over it. By its very definition then, a bridge points to a set of attributes and disciplines of those who serve as the linkages that transcend social boundaries. The key attributes emerging from the cases seem to be humility, patience, and sacrifice, all of which are deeply imbued with a spiritual and theological content, whether they come from one religious tradition or another.

Humility was referred to time and again as people spoke of "simple actions" required by the necessity of day-to-day response to survival. These were not grandiose or arrogant efforts aimed at receiving a peace prize, but rather the humble action of people finding a way forward in the midst of violent chaos, expecting absolutely no recognition for their work. Patience comes in the examples of South Sudan, Guatemala, and Sri Lanka, where the community bridge builders labored not for days and weeks, but literally for years and even decades in their efforts to build and sustain relationships at community levels. Sacrifice can be found in all the cases where these community peacebuilders pursued their efforts to create a new relational space at great personal risk, not only from the need to move toward an enemy group to engage them, but from the pressures of their own people, who questioned what they were doing. In all these instances, what we find is not an elaborated theology that then leads to action. It is rather an incarnated life and action—characterized by the highest disciplines of spirituality by any standard—that in retrospect can be interpreted theologically from the actions taken.

Perhaps in the bridge building more than in any other source, we find the degree to which grassroots peacebuilding represents an embodied theology emergent from action more than a doctrinal or canonical theology that deductively suggests values and life action. This is due in large part to the *locus* of the peacebuilding itself. Grassroots, by definition, means that the location of the actor and action is among the poor, the affected communities who have little or no alternative recourse vis-à-vis their situation. People located higher up in the affected population, at the middle and highest levels of leadership, have the luxury of picking and choosing when they might encounter an enemy and carefully planning the peacebuilding process. People at the grassroots live in the caldron of predefined necessities and boundaries that render them immediately interdependent with their enemies, conducting their lives in the physical and direct proximity of their enemies. Theirs is a theology and encounter of necessity.

A THEOLOGY OF TIME

We turn our attention to the challenge of time and peacebuilding. From a theological point of view there are significant connections. In the broadest of strokes, key and central themes of theological concern about peace are found in time dimensions described by the psalmist in Psalm 85:9-12. For example, truth as it relates to relationships broken by violence and conflict often focuses on the *past* seeking to establish clarity about what happened, responsibility for the brokenness, and what and how it will be remembered. Justice addresses a concern in the *present* for how the brokenness and wrongdoing will be addressed and redressed with some form of accountability. Mercy and hope raise the horizon of the *future* and the restoration of the relationship. Peacebuilding is always dealing with some conjugation of time energies in the past, present, and future.

It was particularly intriguing to engage this conjugation from the standpoint of the case studies and the ways in which they found local communities dealing with the ongoing legacy of violent conflict. Each of the major themes of the psalm verses referred to above—truth, justice, mercy, and hope—found an inherent tension that played itself out within the communities, a tension that at times could appear to yield contradictory voices appealing to God and promoting theological interpretations for very different sorts of action. The emphasis on truth, for example, within a Rwandan or Northern Irish context, could appeal to the memory of losses and violations against a community as a necessary part of restoration and healing, wherein the chosen memory of certain histories was not shared by opponents on the other side of the conflict who chose to remember different aspects of history. A key across all the cases, however, would seem to be that the core of truth is the capacity to make a public recognition of wrongdoing. Justice could at times appeal for revenge or, on the other hand, for a rebalancing of what had been wrong. Mercy could be used to pacify, to forget in order to move forward, or could be mobilized in the direction of a mutual recognition of humanity. Likewise, peace itself could be called upon to hold an apparent harmony on the surface, where there was not more shooting, but where not everything had been healed or made right in terms of historic transgressions or oppression. Alternatively, peace could point toward the radical transformation of immediate relationships. Being at a grassroots level did not, according to the cases studied here, assure unanimity of voice and perspective on the meaning of these deep theological themes.

Where we did find more consistency across the cases—in terms of how grassroots communities experienced and developed an implicit theology of time—was in reference to two key perspectives. First, when communities and community leaders stepped into peacebuilding roles at considerable risk to themselves, they very often justified it by saying "we do this on behalf of our children." Interestingly, this view articulates an eschatology which suggests that action is taken in the present, risky as it may be, in order to align oneself with a view of how the future should look. In other words, hope for the future indicates how to live today. Second, these community actions seemed to be advocating a social and community right that goes well beyond the common notion of human rights: We have the right to leave our children a better future than we have experienced.

At another level these communities also articulate a view of time related to the nature of their struggle. Time and again in the case studies there was a view that this was a long-term process. Theirs was like wandering in the desert for forty years (Num. 32:13). This is not a metaphor. This is literal. Many of the people in these cases studies lived and understood their context of violent conflict as a generational phenomenon that swept them, their families, and their communities into processes that had lasted and might well last twenty, thirty, even forty years. In their views, therefore, we find a parallel to many of the great Bible stories of transformation of people and peoplehood across decades and generations, rather than quick transitions gauged in days or months. Sudan has had a conflict of over forty years. "The troubles" in Northern Ireland are over thirty years in duration and not yet over. The Sri Lankan conflict dates back across decades. This, I think, is of theological importance in reference to the sense of lifelong processes of transformation. It requires one to think of stories like the people of God wandering in the desert learning about themselves, their God, and the nature of human community. It calls our attention to the story of Jacob and Esau, two brothers torn apart by jealousy and division, who spent a lifetime finding a way back together, passing through decades-long processes of moving apart, inner struggle, and then moving back toward encounter with each other.

The case studies in this volume are about these kinds of contexts. They teach of communities who understand survival and change in terms of decades and generations, in terms of lifelong processes of transformation. This is a welcome and I think realistic antidote to contemporary global situations where politics, economics, and social planning envision change and prescriptions for problems as processes requiring quick, logical fixes, but little suffering and struggle. If these case studies teach us anything about time and peacebuilding, it is simply the need to expand our horizons in order to develop a long view of history—with an equally long view of our children's children's future.

THEOLOGY OF MYSTERY

As part of their contribution to this study, research partners in Northern Ireland, Sri Lanka, and the Philippines inquired about the images of the divine held by respondents from their various communities. The images varied. There were some who found a deep feeling of despair, a sense that God had left them. For other respondents, God was close at hand, in spite of the duress of violence, like a protective father or nurturing mother. Still other images suggested a God who would judge and bring justice to wrongdoers. However, what I found most fascinating was not the specific content of words used to describe the divine, but rather the sense of the corresponding responses to violence required if those responses were to represent the building of peace and the solidification of reconciliation in war-torn communities. The predominant sense was of an entry into the spaces of the Divine, for the very journey of response was an entry into a land unknown. It was a journey into mystery. This was entry into a sacred land because it was a place not known.

Mystery calls us toward the spiritual and the sacred. God is and remains Mystery, even to the most fervent believer. In many regards, mystery and faith relate significantly. Take, for example, the explanation of faith by the author of Hebrews:

> Now faith is the assurance of things hoped for, the conviction of things not seen. Indeed by faith our ancestors received approval. By faith we understand that the worlds were prepared by the word of God, so that what is seen was made from things that are not visible. (Heb. 11:1-3)

The examples that follow are of heroes of faith, which we could easily call heroes of mystery. Abraham left on a journey for a promised land that he would receive in inheritance: "He set out not knowing where he was going" (Heb. 11:8). Sara believed she would conceive a child though she was past the age when that was possible, and yet she lived as if it were true (see Heb. 11:11). Noah built an ark in preparation for the flood before there was any sign that it was even raining (see Heb. 11:7). "What is seen was made from things that are not visible." This is faith. This is mystery. This is the space of the sacred. This is the journey of building reconciliation in settings destroyed by violence in people's daily lives by people who chose to walk toward a place they believed possible without knowing where they were going.

Herein we find the explanations of peace and reconciliation as grassroots community people attempt to give words to their action and journey. The cases indicate a deductive approach, where the theory of words gave pathway to their action. Time and again the interview and questions of the researcher gave pause to the respondent, who then tried to give words that explained their actions. Thus the words and explanations seem simple. "It is the right thing to do. We believe in stopping violence. Peace is God's way." But most importantly, as researchers described the case studies, it did not seem that a well-articulated theology of action was in place, precisely because, I would suggest, work for reconciliation embodies mystery.

As I read through the case studies, the following stands out: Reconciliation is the mystery of entry into an arena, a space, not well defined by doctrine or the logic of cognitive, rational explanation. Mystery is intuitively a journey toward the divine, toward a sacred place, like the burning bush, where the presence of God is encountered. But such a journey requires faith because the destination is not known, nor is the pathway familiar.

In one of our conversations, John Brewer of Northern Ireland made a remarkable reply to my suggestion that a fundamental response of grassroots communities emerged from a theology of mystery. I paraphrase here from the notes I jotted as he reflected on the cross-community work in Northern Ireland and how peoples' responses give flesh to such a theology.

> In our context of thirty plus years of troubles, violence, fear, and division are known. Peace is the mystery! People are frightened of peace. It is simultaneously exciting and fearful. This is mystery. Peace asks a lot of you. Peace asks you to share memory. It asks you to share space, territory, specific concrete places. It asks you to share a future. And all this you are asked to do with and in the presence of your enemy. Peace is mystery. It is walking into the unknown.

Returning for a moment to our earlier discussion about time, I recall that a colleague once explained to me the linguistic concept of how time may be seen differently from the eyes of at least one group in Africa, as opposed to the eyes of the West. In the West, by and large, we have a concept that time flows forward, that we are moving from the past and through the present toward a future. And of course within that view, the West has a strong sense that we can forge the future according to our designs. In a workshop in Kenya, one participant explained that in her native tongue of Kalinga, it would be said: "The past lies before us and the future lies behind us." She went on to explain that the ancestors are what we keep our eyes on, they are that which is known. Our face, our eyes and vision, can see their example. Therefore they lie before us. It is toward joining the ancestors that our journey takes us. But the future is not known. It is ambiguous at best, hazy, and unclear. The future lies behind us, where our eyes cannot see, for we back into the future not knowing our path predictably.

On the other hand, in the course of our discussions Bernard Rutikanga shared the story of a respondent who, when asked how he saw reconciliation, had a sense of despair combined with hope. Bernard reported this response from a man who was in prison following the Rwandan genocide:

> Let us do something for our children. For us, we are dead. But for you who are outside, try to prepare a better Rwanda for our children. Nothing can be done to heal the present generation. If something can be done, focus on the future, for the present cannot be healed; it is dead.

Herein we find the paradoxical mystery of building peace and reconciliation from the actions of grassroots communities. On the one hand, as described so clearly in many of the cases, the communities are backing into the future of new relationships, entering a space hardly known on a journey that is unpredictable, but also faith-based. On the other, they hold out hope for a transformed relationship in the future, a hope for their children and grandchildren. As John Brown Childs put it, the action of former gang members who now work as street mediators and peacebuilders combines ancestors and grandchildren into an "embodied future." It is not hard to see mystery linked with St. John's Gospel, which starts with these powerful statements:

> In the beginning was the Word, and the Word was with God and the Word was God. (1:1)

> All things came into being through him. . . . What has come into being in him was life. (1:3)

> And the Word became flesh and lived among us. (1:14)

Clarence Jordan, author of the "cotton patch" versions of the Gospels and a founder of Koinonia Farm[1] once translated the idea of word becoming flesh in the phrase "the Word pitched its tent and lived with us" (Jordan 1970). This is the mystery we find in grassroots peacebuilding, the embodiment of peoples' hopes with their eyes fixed on what is known while backing into the sacred unknown.

CONCLUSION

I started this chapter with a poem I wrote nearly seven years ago about a jailed commander involved in paramilitary violence. He spoke of his fear of peace

---

[1] Begun in 1942 in Americus, Georgia, Koinonia Farm was a bold Christian experiment in interracial community. Today it is known as Koinonia Partners. See K'Meyer 1997.

because his own experiences had taught him that cycles of violence are hard if not impossible to break. Throughout the case studies this harsh voice of reality made its voice known. People at the grassroots know the realities of violence on a daily basis and harbor no doubts about the challenges of survival and the pitfalls of hatred. While they do not always articulate it as such, they intuitively know they are swept up in a system that is beyond themselves and their making. At the same time, they are part of a cloud of witnesses, heads high above the fray, moving forward with a deep sense that these hard realities can and must change (Heb. 12:1). Theirs are stories of hope, but not a cheap hope easily belittled as Pollyannaish idealism. Their hope is hard won from hands and feet that walk the mysterious journey of forging new life and relationships in the midst of the violence. In the words of Irish poet and playwright Seamus Heaney, these are people whose lives bespeak the "hope for a great sea-change on the far side of revenge." May the Mystery of their journey shed a light for us all.

10

A Theology of Power and Spirituality of Empowerment

SR. MARY JOHN MANANZAN, O.S.B.

Seven countries that are home to different races, cultures, and historical traditions nevertheless share one thing in common: an experience of war, conflict, and violence. In Northern Ireland, the conflict involves Catholics and Protestants; in Rwanda, Hutu and Tutsi; in Sri Lanka, Tamils and Sinhalese; in Mindanao in the Philippines, Muslims and Christians; in the southern Sudan, a variety of ethnic communities; in Guatemala, the state and its citizens; and in urban centers in the United States, street gangs. For three years researchers from these countries went into volatile areas to study grassroots peacemaking attempts, particularly those that involved Christian communities. It was their belief that such research could benefit churches throughout the world, both in their particular mediating efforts and in their larger endeavor to be a peace-inspiring presence in all spheres of life. Another goal of the research was to advance the current understanding of cross-cultural Christian mission. A third and most important goal was to help local ministers, laity, and overseas missioners seeking to defuse conflicts in the volatile areas where they live and serve.

As I grew to understand the conflicts and peacemaking efforts in the countries listed above, it occurred to me that the use of power is a critical ethical variable in understanding both the use of violence and the means of counteracting it. In her book *Truth or Dare: Encounters with Power, Authority, and Mystery* (1987), Starhawk, an indigenous American ecofeminist, offers a reflection on power based on her experience in a detention camp. She and six hundred other women were held in the camp after peacefully blockading the Livermore Weapons Lab, where nuclear weapons are designed and developed.

THE NATURE OF POWER ACCORDING TO STARHAWK

Starhawk sees three categories of power: "power over," "power from within," and "power with." "Power over," according to Starhawk, is essentially linked to domination and control, "power from within," to the mysteries that awaken a person's deepest abilities and potential, and "power with," to the social power and influence people wield among their equals. Each type of power is rooted in a mode of consciousness and a worldview. Each has its own language and mythology and depends on distinct motivations.

POWER OVER

The consciousness that underlies "power over" is a world seen as an object, made up of separated parts that have no intrinsic life, awareness, or value. Consciousness is fragmented and disconnected; the language of "power over" is "the language of law, of rules, of abstract generalized formulations enforced on the concrete realities of particular circumstances" (Starhawk 1987, 14). In the worldview of "power over," human beings have no inherent worth; their value must be earned or granted.

"Power over" motivates through fear. It instills fear and then offers the hope of relief in return for compliance and obedience. Disobedience is met with force and violence. "Power over" works through threatening the sustenance, comforts, and esteem of the dominated. It has a clear material base and is grounded on the ability to punish by imposing physical or economic sanctions. Thus "power over" is inherently related to war and violence:

> Power-over comes from the consciousness I have termed estrangement: the view of the world as made up of atomized, nonliving parts, mechanically interacting, valued not for what they inherently are but only in relation to some outside standard. It is the consciousness modeled on the God who stands outside the world, outside nature, who must be appeased, placated, feared, and above all, obeyed. . . . Power-over is ultimately born of war and the structures, social and intrapsychic, necessary to sustain mass, organized warfare. Having reshaped culture in a martial image, the institutions and ideologies of power-over perpetuate war so that it becomes a chronic human condition. (Starhawk 1987, 9)

POWER FROM WITHIN

"Power from within"—in other words, *empowerment*—traces its meaning from the root of the word "power," which is "to be able." This kind of power is what is manifested when children develop new abilities: standing erect, speaking, reasoning, and so on. It arises from one's sense of connection with other human beings and with the environment. It stems from a consciousness that sees the world as a living being, made up of dynamic aspects, where all have inherent value and are interconnected.

The language of "power from within" is:

> poetry, metaphor, symbol, ritual, myth . . . of "thinking in things", where the concrete becomes resonant with mysteries that go beyond its seeming solid form. Its language is action, which speaks in the body and to all the senses in ways that can never be completely conveyed in words. (Starhawk 1987, 15)

"Power from within" is the unsuspected deep source of strength and energy that allows a person to survive the most excruciating pain and overcome almost insurmountable difficulties. It is the capability of transcending victimhood to become a survivor and an advocate. Ultimately it is not only an individual gift, but has a communicable and transformative quality that can enable others to bloom and develop to their full potential.

POWER WITH

"Power with" can be confused with "power over" because it involves influencing others. "Power with," however, comes not from commanding but from the power to suggest and be heard, to begin something and see it develop. Its source of effectiveness is not in fear but in the willingness of others to listen to other people's ideas. The relationship of "power with" is among equals. "Power with" affirms, shapes, and guides collective decision, but it does not enforce its will on the group or push it to actions contrary to the communal will.

"Power with" bridges the value systems of "power from within" and "power over." It sees the world as a pattern of relationships, but its interest is in how that pattern can be shaped, molded, and shifted. Like "power from within," it recognizes the inherent worth of things but it can also make comparisons, valuing some things above others. The language of "power with," according to Starhawk, is "gossip." She explains:

> Gossip has a bad reputation as being either malicious or trivial. But in any real community, people become interested in each other's relationships within the group, love affairs, quarrels, problems. The talking we do about each other provides us with invaluable information; it makes us aware of whom we can trust and whom we distrust, of whom to treat carefully and whom to confront, of what we can realistically expect a group to do together. Gossip maintains the social order in a close-knit society more effectively than law. (Starhawk 1987, 15-16)

"Power with" or the ability to gain influence, to persuade, and to use this ability to empower others comes naturally or intuitively to so-called charismatic leaders, but ordinary individuals can observe and learn these characteristics to improve their own leadership effectiveness.

In the pages that follow, I will attempt to analyze the various conflict situations represented in this volume from the perspective of the "power over" category; I will use the "power from within" and "power with" categories to interpret the dynamics of the various peacemaking efforts. Finally, I will endeavor to develop a spirituality of empowerment for and from those already embarked upon the lengthy, risky, and uncharted paths of grassroots peacemaking.

A THEOLOGY OF POWER

KYRIARCHY, VIOLENCE, AND WAR

The Kyriarchal World

The interpretation and exercise of power as "power over" is manifest in our kyriarchal world. *Kyriarchy* is a neologism coined by Elisabeth Schüssler Fiorenza to denote the rule of the emperor/master/lord/father/husband/ over those in his power. This includes but goes beyond patriarchy, which was used to mean the absolute rule of the father in early societies and denotes the oppression of women by men. Some believe that such feminist analyses reduce everything to gender-based conflict, but this is not so; Schüssler Fiorenza clarifies: "As its basic analytic categories it [feminist analysis] does not simply employ androcentrism and patriarchy, which are generally understood in dualistic terms as the oppression of all women by all men. Rather, a critical feminist analysis radically shifts its focus from gender analysis to a complex system analysis of the multiplicative structures of oppression" (Schüssler Fiorenza 1995, 13). In order to express this more precisely, she opts not to use *patriarchy* to describe these varied forms of domination that are mainly associated with gender oppression but coins the word *kyriarchy*—or the rule of the *kyrios* or master. Kyriarchal power operates not only along the axis of gender but also along those of race, class, culture, and religion. Kyriarchy denotes a complex social pyramid of graduated dominations and subordinations. Schüssler Fiorenza further explains:

> With this term, I mean to indicate that not all men dominate and exploit all women without difference and that elite Western educated propertied Euro-American men have articulated and benefited from women's and other "nonpersons'" exploitation. As a consequence the hermeneutical center of a critical feminist theology of liberation cannot simply be women. Rather, it must be constituted and determined by the interests of women who live at the bottom of the kyriarchal pyramid and who struggle against multiplicative forms of oppression. The term "kyriocentric," in turn, refers to ideological articulations that validate and are sustained by kyriarchal relations of domination. Since kyriocentrism replaces the category of androcentrism, it is best understood as an intellectual framework and cultural

ideology that legitimates and is legitimated by kyriarchal social structures and systems of domination. (1995, 14)

Christian Legitimation of Kyriarchy

Although the legitimation of Western kyriarchy had Greek origins, specifically in classical Aristotelian philosophy, it is also found in Christian Scriptures. Western kyriarchal structures of domination were not invented by Judaism or Christianity but found their way into them. One scriptural legitimation of kyriarchal structure is Genesis 1:26-28. These verses express God's having given man (as in *male*) the power "to have dominion over the fish of the sea and over the birds of the air and over every living thing that moves upon the earth." *Dominium terrae* has been interpreted as a God-appointed role of dominance given to man (as in *male*) over the natural world, which justifies his conquest of nations, his ruling of the waves, and his exploitation of the earth. The male's relationship of superiority to both women and nature is subsumed under his relationship with God. This interpretation of the Genesis text offers a totalitarian view of the human being's relationship to God and thereby legitimates holding power over those lower than oneself on whatever scale of being. Ecofeminist theologian Anne Primavesi (1991, 220) warns of its consequences:

> The ramifications of this concept of power are of theological concern today in that it sanctions violence against the natural world. Its violent overtones build up strategies of destruction against that world. It trains us to see spirit as severed from the material world and from the world of political, economic and environmental action.

A kyriarchal interpretation of Genesis was prevalent among the church fathers including Jerome, Ambrose, and Augustine. Augustine wrote and preached extensively in this vein on the Genesis narrative. And when Constantine adopted the cross as a symbol of victory in the battles of the Roman Empire, violence, in the name of the perfect flesh of Christ against the flesh of the unbaptized and the pagan, was justified. Military metaphors up to our present day abound in hymns sung in Christian worship—"Onward Christian Soldiers" is one obvious example. In 405 C.E., Augustine gave his approval to the use of force by the Roman state for the purpose of "reuniting" with the Catholic Church the Donatist congregations, who were considered heretical. According to Primavesi (1991, 214), Augustine thus exemplified the view that "the hierarchical structures of authority that gave cohesion to society might be called upon to support the Catholic Church." On the same page, Primavesi comments:

> This link between Christianity and physical violence forged in the name of church expansion or spiritual good is one of the ugliest manifestations of its hierarchical character and its perception of power. It sanctioned military, domestic and economic violence of the cruellest kind. Rape and pil-

lage are the inseparable companions of war, and religious wars have been no exception.

Augustine's ethic lives on. Some Christians in Northern Ireland today believe that the conflict there is the Lord's battle and that in participating actively in violent acts, they are being true to God's will. At a meeting of the researchers in preparation for this volume, John Brewer recounted the story of a Protestant pastor who was imprisoned for ten years after being involved in gun-running and pipe-bomb attacks on the homes of Catholics. According to Brewer, the pastor regarded attacks on individual Catholics as part of the Lord's battle to defeat evil and to resist unification with a popish Ireland.

Similarly, in Rwanda, bishops, priests, and nuns actively participated in massacres. These publicly religious people felt no sense of contradiction between their Christian beliefs and their partaking in violent acts, carried out primarily in the name of Hutu supremacy. For example, sisters in charge of sanctuary houses allowed soldiers to enter, resulting in the massacre of their charges. The international press reported the case of a Benedictine, Sr. Gertrude, who was brought to Belgium, tried, and convicted for just such acts. Priests and bishops did not prevent killings that they could have prevented, and some are accused of actually having themselves engaged in the killing. An even more terrible truth is that most of the genocide was carried out by ordinary Catholics against fellow Catholics. Even women and children went on a spate of killing. When Bernard Rutikanga interviewed them in prison (see chapter 5), they did not understand how they could have done what they did. He cited as a probable explanation the daily radio propaganda, which had one message: Kill or be killed. Widely accessible hate propaganda on the radio had a stronger claim on the hearts of people in this Catholic nation than the Fifth Commandment: "You shall *not* kill" (Exod. 20:13, emphasis added).

Kyriarchy and Military Consciousness

Although kyriarchal values are embedded in all structures—economic, political, sociocultural, and religious—they are most consciously promoted in military institutions. Military training is, inescapably, training for *machismo*. Further, it is a training to kill in order that one not be killed—a training to "shoot" and ask afterwards. Military personnel have to go through a process of brutalization in order to become organized killers. The initiation of recruits begins with hazing, which is intended to "toughen" them. In the Philippines, there have been widely publicized cases of actual torture resulting in death during this initiation process in military academies.[1]

---

[1] Documentation available on the web site of the *Philippine Daily Inquirer*, www.inq7.net: "Hazing law won't apply to PMA, says prosecutor," April 18, 2001; "Lessons of Sept. 21, 1972," September 20, 2001; "PMA cadets, officers sign covenant to fight abuses," October 8, 2001. Accessed June 5, 2002.

There is also the question of military consciousness and the possibility of peace. When one has been trained to be a professional soldier with no other occupation, what is one's stake in peace? When there is war, professional soldiers feel that they are serving, doing what they have been trained to do, and their status derives from this. In peace, where is their prestige? What sense of significance do they have? Conflicts and wars are perpetuated by people profiting from them monetarily (such as those who trade in weapons) and psychologically (such as professional soldiers). In chapter 6, ShirleyWijesinghe corroborates this in the case of Sri Lanka:

[The] war economy provides employment to Sinhalese and Tamil youth, personal profits to arms dealers, and power, prestige, and wealth to both government forces and militants. Those who benefit from the war economy shudder at peace initiatives. Their influence is so widespread and entrenched that there is no massive grassroots movement for peace in the country. Any such movement in the making would come under attack from both extremist Sinhalese and Tamil sectors.

Consequences of a Kyriarchal Interpretation and Exercise of Power

Luise Schottroff, an ecofeminist theologian, points out the consequences of exercising "power over":

Animals and foreign nations are hunted game when the capitalist master comes. All natural resources, the earth, animals and humans are objects of his so-called economic enterprise and rapacious attacks. . . . Entire populations are killed for a slight power advantage. (Schottroff 1997, 30)

Besides having dominance as its main value, kyriarchy is characterized by hierarchical structure, exploitation or oppression of lower beings, fear of the "other," exclusion, segregation, discrimination, and finally, the use of violence.

Kyriarchy sees reality as hierarchy, which refers to the "system of elitist privileges and graded subjugation that permeates every aspect of human society, including religion and the church" (Aquino 2000, 163). There is a pecking order that has God on top in theistic societies followed each in turn by the male, female, animals, plants, and inanimate elements of nature. There is a legitimation of the subordination of lower beings to those higher than they. Any monopoly of power necessitates exploitation and oppression. So women are subordinated to men; colonial powers exploit and conquer underdeveloped countries; the white person discriminates against the person of color. Those who hold power are forever insecure about losing their power. They therefore see "the other" and "otherness" as threats. In order to subdue peoples and to hold on to power, the use of violence is inevitable.

From this perspective, one can see that the violent conflict situations in the seven countries examined in this volume are caused or perpetuated in defense of power. Each of these conflicts can in some way be traced to the interests of colonial or neocolonial powers. Until well into the twentieth century, the British Empire reigned in Ireland, Sri Lanka, and the Sudan. The Belgians ruled Rwanda until 1962. The Spanish and Americans colonized the Philippines, whereas in Guatemala, Spanish rule gave way to military domination and economic exploitation by the United States. In the United States itself, indigenous and mestizo peoples of the Southwest were subjugated and became targets of racial discrimination.

Early colonial conquests were usually for gold, glory, and gospel, which stand for economic exploitation, political domination, and religious conversion (or cultural subjugation). Colonial masters imposed their political power on the countries and henceforth exercised economic and cultural domination over the peoples. In the case of Rwanda, the Belgians artificially developed the Tutsi as a local elite, thus fanning the flames of ethnic conflict with the Hutu. In the Philippines, the colonial government's policy of relocating Bisaya citizens to Mindanao sowed the seeds of conflict there, just as in Sri Lanka the government-sponsored settlement of Sinhalese farmers in Tamil areas exacerbated tensions there.

After the colonies gained their independence, the colonial masters continued to exercise power by tying new countries to their economic apron strings—through what is known as neocolonialism. In many of these former colonies, governments run by local elites soon developed strong military or dictatorial forms of rule as in Guatemala, Sudan, Rwanda, and in the Philippines. This, in turn, gave rise to revolutionary liberation movements that were suppressed violently and plunged the countries into a state of civil war.

At least three of the conflicts—those in Mindanao, Philippines, Northern Ireland, and Sri Lanka—have religious aspects. The actual root of these conflicts, however, is either economic or political. In Mindanao, land grabbing by Christian settlers from the North, the negligence of the government in developing the area, and the interests of multinational corporations in exploiting the natural resources of the region are certainly among the major causes of the conflict. John Brewer writes in chapter 3 of the conflict in Northern Ireland:

> It is supposedly a religious war fought over doctrinal principles between people for whom religion is their primary identity, yet religion disguises the conflict's inherently political character. The conflict is over the legitimacy of the state and access to its political, economic, and cultural resources, but religious affiliation defines the boundaries of the groups that are in competition.

In Sri Lanka, the Sinhalese Buddhist majority has feared that its language and culture could be swept away by Hindu Tamils, potentially backed by multitudes of Hindus in India—just a few miles of island and ocean to the north. In the end, then, even when religion has a high profile within a conflict, the root of the problem is not religious differences, but imbalance or misuse of power.

A particularly valuable aspect of this volume is the fact that most of the studies herein address an often-overlooked topic: the impact of armed conflict on women. Often, in a war or a battle, when a city or a country falls to the victor, the women of the vanquished are raped. But even in the ordinary course of the war, while no victory is as yet ascertained, the women of both contending parties are vulnerable to rape by the enemy. Many stories of rape have been recorded among the political prisoners and *desaparecidas* of Guatemala. In chapter 6, ShirleyWijesinghe quotes Daya Somasundaram (1998, 244) on the incidence of rape as a component of the Sri Lankan conflict:

> [Rape] was carried out with considerable brutality and impersonality, where the victims were publicly defeminized and destroyed. . . . Chastity is traditionally considered one of the supreme virtues of women, to be safe-guarded with the same diligence as their life. The screams and pleading of a young, attractive girl, whom three soldiers were trying to rape at gun point, still echoes [*sic*] in my ears. She fell at their feet and begged, "Please brother, shoot me, but don't do this." Fortunately for her, her pleading got through to an officer who took pity and let her go, after slapping her.

Furthermore, according to Wijesinghe, "A young girl who is raped may never be able to marry; if a married woman is raped, she runs the risk of abandonment by her husband. No female is immune to this danger; even women well past menopause have been brutally raped."

Many women are left widows. For thousands of these, the psychological burden of losing a spouse, as well as the financial support that the spouse may have provided, has been aggravated by witnessing the killing of their own children or the burning of their home and possessions. Already having to earn their living through hard labor, they must now work even longer hours to make ends meet; in addition, they become sexually vulnerable. Some of them are driven to prostitution. Wijesinghe writes, "The prostitution practiced in the sacred city of Anuradhapura is a product of the war economy; soldiers make up most of its clientele, while destitute young women from the villages on the borders of the war zone have become its victims." Wijesinghe also describes the suffering of women living in refugee camps, crowded into cramped spaces with unhygienic conditions. Many succumb to melancholy and suicide.

A GOD OF WAR?—THEOLOGICAL AND ETHICAL QUESTIONS

In many of the conflict situations studied, people invoke God to justify their positions—the Protestant Evangelicals of Northern Ireland, the Muslims and the Christians in Mindanao, the Buddhists and Hindus likewise in Sri Lanka. Bishops, priests, and religious were involved in the Rwandan genocide. General Efraín Ríos Montt, under whose regime horrendous massacres were carried out in Guatemala, was a member of the California-based Church of the Word—which was, according to Susanne Jonas (1991, 153), "initially an instrument of counterinsurgency used to combat a Catholicism influenced by Liberation Theology."

A God of War?

Is God a God who can be invoked to grant one side victory in war? Battles fill the pages of the Old Testament. Constantine fought the Battle of Milvian Bridge with the standard of the cross. Fighters for the Crusades were recruited from the pulpit of medieval churches. The *jihad* was and is fought in the name of Allah. The colonial wars fought in the name of the Gospel invoked such a warlike God. And down through the ages to our own, people have continued invoking this God. José María Vigil (2001, 99) characterizes such a God as follows:

> The God of war is a God of power, of pyramidal, hierarchical, oligarchical and monarchical, vertical order, which justifies "someone having to be at the bottom." There is a whole class of person, of philosophy, of psychology (and of religiosity) that echoes this model of God. . . . The God of war is a God who remains passive in the face of the suffering of the poor, accepting that "things have always been the same" . . . [The God of war] demands human sacrifices: someone has to accept the harsh side of reality; someone has to be at the bottom; someone has to die so that we can live, prosper, develop. It is "natural" and is inevitable that there should be losers, people left on the margins, excluded.

Yet Christians hail Christ as the "Prince of Peace" foretold by Isaiah (9:6). Christ proclaimed peacemakers "blessed" (Matt. 5:9), forgave his killers (see Luke 23:34), and rebuked Peter for attempting to take up a sword against the slave of the high priest (see John 18:10-11). Psalm 34 urges Jews and Christians alike to "Seek peace and pursue it" (v. 15), and all wisdom's paths are peace (see Prov. 3:17).

Islamic scholar Mohammed Abu-Nimer notes, "When one searches the Library of Congress subject categories for resources on *Islam and nonviolence*, fewer than five items appear on the screen. However, thousands of items are listed when *violence and Islam* are on the screen" (2000-2001, 218). But in fact, argues Abu-Nimer, the Prophet Muhammad preached "a clear message to avoid the use of violence and prevent aggression by Muslims against Muslims and non-Muslims" (254); many Muslims throughout the world are actively engaged in peacemaking. Hinduism, Buddhism, and most indigenous/traditional religions have strong peace traditions as well.

Yet God is invoked in war. That "God" is a patri-kyriarchal god, a god made in the image and likeness of man (as in *male*), a god, to borrow Starhawk's category, who exercises "power over." A challenge to the peacemaker is to confront the reality that people keep making "God" in their own image and likeness to rationalize and justify what they want to do and to defend their interests. This is also a challenge to churches who so easily condemn revolutions but bless the army's weapons of death. Such challenges lead us to the question of whether it is ever morally justifiable to take sides in a conflict.

Taking Sides—An Ethical Question

In conflict situations, Albert Nolan points out that people often say: "We must be fair, we must listen to both sides of the story, there is always right and wrong on both sides. If we could only get the contending parties to talk to one another to sort out their misunderstandings and misconceptions, the conflict could be resolved" (1984). This sounds very Christian. But what is wrong with it? It is based, according to Nolan, on three mistaken assumptions:

1. That all conflicts are based on misunderstanding and there is always blame on both sides. In fact, in some conflicts one side is right and the other wrong, one side is oppressive and unjust, while the other is the victim of its injustice and oppression.

2. That a person can be neutral in all cases of conflict. Not only is neutrality not possible in all conflicts; there are conflicts where one should not be neutral.

3. That Christians should always seek harmony and a "middle way" in every dispute and that tension and conflict are worse evils than injustice and oppression.

Nolan explains why these assumptions are often inadequate:

If we do not take sides with the oppressed, then we are, albeit unintentionally, taking sides with the oppressor. Bringing the two sides together in such cases is actually extremely beneficial to the oppressor, because it enables the status quo to be maintained; it hides the true nature of the conflict, keeps the oppressed quiet and passive and it brings about a kind of pseudo-reconciliation without justice. The injustice continues and everybody is made to feel that the injustice doesn't matter because the tension and conflict have been reduced. (1984)

In the Scriptures, God commands people again and again to oppose tyranny. In fact it was considered a sin of the Jewish people that they attempted to be reconciled with their oppressors so that when they shouted "Peace, peace," Jeremiah responds by saying there is no peace without change or conversion (Jer. 6:14). Christ himself sided with sinners, prostitutes, and tax collectors in their conflict with the self-righteous Pharisees. He was not neutral. He condemned, in no uncertain terms, the Pharisees and pronounced blessings on the so-called sinners. He made a distinction between the peace that the world wants (see John 14:27) and the peace that God wants. The peace that the world wants is a superficial peace that compromises truth and covers up injustices. The peace that God wants is a peace that is based on justice, truth, and love. It is not a false but a true and lasting peace.

To make a responsible option in a conflict situation, therefore, one needs to keep in mind certain principles. First, it is necessary to make a rigorous and honest analysis of a conflict. And if one sees that one side is right and the other is wrong, one should side with what is right, doing so, ideally, with nonviolent means. If in some cases both sides are basically right, reconciliation is to be pursued. And if both sides are wrong and are both part of the oppression, then both must be confronted. Second, it is important to think in structural terms. In some cases there is a structural conflict between the oppressor and the oppressed. It is not just a personal squabble. The very way society is structured may itself be wrong. However personally honest and sincere a person may be, he or she may still occupy a structurally oppressive position. In this case, when we side with the oppressed we are working for the good of all—even of the oppressor.

SUMMARY

We live in a world of violence and conflict. Some of us, in fact, live in a culture of violence. There is personal and structural violence. There is economic violence, political violence, cultural violence, racial violence, gender violence, and ecological violence. There are long-standing conflicts and wars between nations, between governments and their own people, between members of different ethnic groups and different religions, and there are wars between street gangs. As a framework for understanding such conflicts, I chose the perspective of patri-kyriarchy within feminist liberation theology. From this perspective, I have interpreted violence within an overarching framework of domination that looks upon and exercises power primarily as "power over," that sees the world as a hierarchy with the economically and politically dominant (usually men) at the top tracing their legitimation from God "Himself." Those at the top look upon anyone who is "other" as a threat to their power and interest and justify the exclusion, subordination, exploitation, and oppression of people with force, if necessary. They believe that they have the mandate to likewise dominate and exploit nature to their interests. They worship a God of war and a God of profit. In some conflicts, it may appear that people are fighting among themselves, but a deeper analysis will often reveal either in the history of the conflict or behind the actual combatants, higher stakes and transnational interests. Peacemakers have to question this understanding of power and the religious legitimation it claims. In the exercise of "power with," peacemakers have to take sides with the oppressed. This gives rise to the following questions: Can they take sides and still work for peace? Can they take sides yet be critical when necessary of the side they have opted for? What does it take to bring about not just peace, but a *justpeace?*[2] These are some questions for peacemakers to ponder.

A SPIRITUALITY OF EMPOWERMENT IN PEACEMAKING

In the midst of worldwide conflicts and war, there are peace initiatives going on, not just on the official level of negotiations but among grassroots people—people who themselves are directly affected by the conflict, people who have to survive and live their lives amid the dangers and uncertainty of war situations. What motivates these people in their actions? What keeps them going? What do they really want to bring about?

---

[2] See preceding chapter.

WHY DO PEOPLE WORK FOR PEACE?

What motivates the people at the grassroots to work for peace? Those who are in war zones seem to do so for sheer survival. They have to go on with their lives, and this involves earning a living, seeing to their children's schooling, and carrying out a range of family and community responsibilities. For them, peacemaking is a necessary and urgent task that is not optional. For people not living in war zones, engaging in peace activities may come about through care and concern for relatives and friends in combat areas, commitment to humanitarian values, or religious beliefs.

Although religion is an exacerbating factor in some of the conflict situations, it is also a factor in peacemaking. Some peacemakers, mostly men, cite religious beliefs as a motivation—surprising, given that women are more likely than men to become members of religions and join religious organizations, engage in more public and private devotional activities, and generally take responsibility for the religious education and formation of their children. Men may cite religious motivations more frequently for their peacemaking involvement out of a need to attribute higher motives to what they do, while women just do what has to be done in their particular situations. Men may also typically have greater access to religious education at higher levels than do women. Both women and men report that they have been encouraged and strengthened by their faith.

Some peacemakers regard the enemy as a child of God like themselves, who should be forgiven. In chapter 3, on Northern Ireland, former Loyalist prisoner Jim McKinley affirms, "Jesus preached a message of nonviolence and those who follow Him are called to be peacemakers in this world." Whether they are aware of it or not, peacemakers like Jim McKinley are living out a spirituality of empowerment.

Such a spirituality requires a serious commitment to justpeace as a continuous process—not an off-and-on launching of projects, but rather a way of life. By "spirituality" I am referring not to any specific religious affiliation but to a commitment to a goal or vision that transcends oneself and entails the harnessing of all the resources of one's spirit and of one's community. Here is where power becomes "power from within" and "power with."

SELF-EMPOWERMENT (POWER FROM WITHIN)

There is, first of all, the necessity of self-empowerment, because we cannot give what we do not have, nor can we empower if we ourselves have not somehow been empowered. Self-empowerment distinguishes seriously committed peacemakers. Paula Green, an international peace activist, explains:

We remind ourselves that to create peace we must "be peace." There exists, in other words, a seamless web: between being and doing, between the inner state of mind and its outward interpersonal or worldly expression. Just as one cannot achieve peace by preparing for war on the sociopolitical level, one cannot be peaceful in interpersonal relationship without a certain amount of equanimity, awareness and control of violent tendencies internally. Thus we acknowledge that peace begins at home, the internal home that each of us must guide and monitor with great vigilance. (Green 1997, 2)

The process of self-empowerment begins with reconciliation with one's self, with one's personal history, and with the process of becoming oneself. It might entail some healing of memories, without which one risks projecting onto others one's aggression toward significant childhood figures. Effort must be made to reconcile with one's family, with one's neighbor, with the earth, and with God. The "bully" inside—the violent tendencies that may be coming from unconscious needs—has to be confronted and transformed with love.

Indeed, as in any spiritual journey, becoming a peacemaker usually begins with some sort of personal conversion. This conversion may vary in intensity— it may be serious or dramatic, but somehow there is a deep enough experience to inspire a person to invest him- or herself seriously in peacemaking. At the beginning of chapter 3, Jim McKinley gives a testimony of his "conversion." He was born into a poor Unionist Loyalist family in Northern Ireland and got involved in a paramilitary organization. He was arrested by the security forces and sentenced to life imprisonment. He writes:

As I settled into the routine of imprisonment, very slowly I started to question my beliefs and values. For the first time in my life I actually read the Bible. As I read about the life of Jesus, I came to a conclusion that grows stronger with each passing day—that Jesus preached a message of nonviolence and that those who follow Him are called to be peacemakers in this world. It is easy to preach the message of peacemaking, harder to practice it, yet God wants us to live it in our everyday lives. I learnt this in prison and have tried to follow it since.

In chapter 8, John Brown Childs cites similar examples of personal transformation in his research on peacemaking among the urban gangs in the United States. The life of Marco Evangelista, now pastor of Victory Outreach Church in El Cajon, California, moved from "intractable violence into redemption and spiritual transformation." Daniel "Nane" Alejandrez left behind gangs and drugs to found the National Coalition of Barrios Unidos out of the trunk of his car. Childs underscores the importance of these examples of personal transformation in the work for peace:

[Positive Cultures Leaders] with whom I have worked for several years consistently testify both publicly and privately that while they were in prisons, in the gangs, or in the thrall of drugs, they were known as dangerous people with little or no regard for life. They tell of vital, transformative moments, all of them personally intense, which led them to change. . . . [T]he experience of vital change is itself an important aspect of their ability to reach others now living in harsh circumstances.

Yet becoming a peacemaker is hardly the exclusive preserve of the formerly violent. People with no prior military or paramilitary involvement, no prison records, no drug backgrounds, also experience a conversion—from apathy to activism, perhaps, or (to borrow John Brewer's terminology in chapter 3) from the relative safety of passive peacemaking to the gritty, risky realities of active peacemaking.

Peacemaking has its own asceticism. Since a justpeace cannot be achieved without *truth*, *justice*, and *interdependent well-being* on a personal and a social level, peacemakers have always to strive after truth, justice, and interdependent well-being also in their personal lives before they can promote it among the conflicting groups they work with.

What do I mean by truth, justice, and interdependent well-being? *Truth* is not just refraining from telling a lie. It is an abiding characteristic. It is expressed better in the word *authenticity*. Authenticity requires that one strive toward self-knowledge and self-acceptance; that one has a realistic and healthy perception of reality and is honest in dealing with others; that one can accept and correct one's mistakes and is therefore trustworthy. *Justice* is giving others what is due them. On a personal level, this means fairness and respect for the dignity of all human beings; it precludes prejudice. *Interdependent well-being* is a term used by the United Nations Educational, Scientific, and Cultural Organization (UNESCO) in various documents on building a culture of peace. It means having for oneself and others the means to maintain good mental and physical health; beyond the fulfillment of basic necessities, it refers to the availability of leisure and the opportunity to enjoy and appreciate beauty. Interdependent well-being is much in the spirit of the labor anthem penned by James Oppenheim and sung by striking textile workers marching through the frigid streets of Lawrence, Massachusetts, in 1912: "Hearts starve as well as bodies; give us bread, but give us roses!" (Fowke and Glazer 1973, 71).

Indispensable to an effective peacemaker is a habit of personal reflection. For people of faith, this means the practice of contemplative prayer or meditation. Human beings are vulnerable to self-delusion, and it takes long periods of silence to expose one's egoistic motives masquerading as altruism. Times of silent reflection are likewise indispensable to the calming of the spirit—to the development of serenity that should characterize a person of peace. Everyone has within him- or herself an inexhaustible source of strength and power. Christians believe this is so, because the Holy Spirit dwells in each person. Hindus hold the firm conviction that "Shiva is in you *as you*," and Buddhists believe that this source of strength and power is the real *you* that is buried under the impacted sediment of small egoisms. But one has to be in touch with this inner source in order to harness its inexhaustible wellspring of strength and power. The most direct access to this wellspring is through meditation. The effectiveness of meditation as a method of spiritual self-empowerment has been borne out in thousands of years of practice.

It must be noted that this study has yielded some interesting findings about the ways in which peacemakers do *not* differ from nonpeacemakers. When researchers in Sri Lanka, Northern Ireland, and the Philippines asked respondents about their images of members of the opposing group, they found that the images held by peacemakers are not more positive than those held by nonpeacemakers. One does not stop having likes and dislikes when one becomes a peacemaker, nor, as suggested earlier, does one refrain emotionally from taking sides. The decision to pursue peace despite holding persistent negative perceptions of one's opponents is all the more remarkable. It indicates that the decision to work for peace is not contingent on whether one likes the enemy. Rather, negative images of the opponent are superseded by the values described above.

COMMUNAL EMPOWERMENT (POWER WITH)

In peacemaking, one is never completely alone, even when working on one's own. Integral to peacemaking is mutual empowerment and acting together for peace. The pages of this volume abound with effective examples of communal empowerment, both in the midst of violent conflict and during the post-violent period of healing. This example from Sri Lanka (chapter 6) shows the audacious creativity of Sinhalese and Tamil farmers who joined together in an effort to cultivate rice paddies in a disputed territory:

> [A]bout a thousand women, men, and children from Sinhalese and Tamil farm families met at Palaiyadyvattai in the disputed territory to prepare the fields for cultivation. But upon seeing each other, emotions overflowed; they embraced one another in tears and celebrated the reconciliation with a festive meal right in the heart of the disputed territory. From this day onward, the Sinhalese and Tamil farmers have worked together in their fields under banners reading *Keth bimata samaya,* "Peace to the Rice Fields." Henceforth, both the government forces and the militants would learn that the presence of banners meant that there were unarmed farmers in the fields. Furthermore, the farmers pleaded with the warring parties not to roam the rice fields, the unofficial peace zone of the farmers.

In chapter 8, John Brown Childs provides an example of a communal effort to prevent a retaliatory killing:

> A few years ago there was a gang-related murder in one of the cities in which I have community contacts. The community peace activist with whom I was working at that time became concerned about possible retaliation and a cycle of vengeance. He went to talk with members of the gang in which the murdered youth had been a member. I was invited to go with him. He spent the whole night talking, cajoling, and finally convincing them not to retaliate. The result was success in the sense that nothing happened. There was no retaliatory violence and so there were no news stories about the subject. Nor were any crime data produced. Rather it was the very absence of news and data that mark this moment as successful.

Even after the cessation of the violent phase of conflict, one cannot conclude that peace has been achieved. As women in the South Sudan told Julia Aker Duany (see chapter 7), "Peace is a total way of life." People must be empowered, therefore, not only to work against violence committed by others, but to accept responsibility for their own violent deeds. Restorative justice must be effected. Repentance must be awakened. Forgiveness must be evoked. Only then is reconciliation possible. These processes immediately following the cessation of violent conflict do not come easily and demand tremendous effort from people who have hurt each other and/or killed each other's loved ones. In some instances, the guilty parties cannot or will not accept responsibility for their criminal deeds. That is why in Guatemala, there remains a pervasive sense that the conflict is not yet resolved; many people cannot forgive, because nobody is asking for forgiveness. At a research meeting, Kuldip Kaur shared with us a quote from her interview with Juan Manuel Gerónimo:

> They say peace will exist when we put the past behind us. It's easy for those who haven't lost family members or suffered in other ways to ask for peace. But when you witness from a distance the massacre of 264 people then are ordered by the same killer to bury the dead in less than eight hours, you don't forget. My children were there that day; they were receiving classes on baptism. But we can't forget, because no one has asked for forgiveness, we can't forgive. Only when they recognize what they did and can be accountable can we start to talk about peace.

Forgiveness and love of enemy, which are essential to genuine reconciliation, are virtues that one cannot simply draw from one's pocket at the negotiating table. They presuppose a lifelong practice of outstanding generosity and humility that can hardly be expected from most people. Christian peacemakers believe in a God who is Love and who, out of that love, took on the human flesh, shared in human suffering, forgave his accusers and tormentors, and empowered his followers to forgive as well. There are some transgressions that make forgiveness seem impossible; only grace makes it possible to forgive the unforgivable.

HOPE'S PLACE IN A SPIRITUALITY OF EMPOWERMENT

In chapter 3, John Brewer describes the sophisticated, well-funded, long-standing, and perhaps most systematic "peacemaking industry" in the world, which exists in Northern Ireland. Yet, he observes, peace is long in coming, perhaps because:

> First, there is personal and family safety. Peacemakers at the grassroots often have to put themselves and their families in hard places; if not putting off some people, this can at least predispose them quite naturally to "safer" forms of peacemaking. . . . More dangerous peacemaking, like mediation and conflict resolution, cries out for greater involvement, but this is just the

sort of grassroots work that leads people to be accused of "selling out" their community, and it makes them vulnerable to harassment and attack from paramilitary organizations on their "own side." . . . Peace asks too much of [people]. It asks them to address the image of themselves, in which they might find bigotry and culpability; it asks them to be more open to the other by embracing the other in trust; it asks them to redefine their identity and group interests away from zero-sum notions and "all or nothing demands"; and peace requires them to share—space, territory, privilege, and power. This is too much for too many people, so they are afraid of peace, at least at the moment.

In some other places like Guatemala, the Sudan, and Mindanao, the root causes of the conflicts have not yet been successfully addressed. As long as truth, justice, and interdependent well-being have not been accomplished to a sufficient degree, the situation remains like a dormant volcano ready to erupt at any moment. In chapter 6, ShirleyWijesinghe points to another discouraging factor: the business of arms and those who profit from it.

An economy dependent on war is a severe obstacle to peace in Sri Lanka. Those involved in the war industry are reported to be earning fabulous sums of money. In a sense, both the Sri Lankan military and Tamil militia have gained through the war. Some enjoy economic benefits and power which would be unthinkable in peaceful circumstances. This is true even at the grassroots level, where the home guards resist peace efforts for fear of losing their employment.

Not only local enterprises, but also foreign interests supply arms to combatants in countries such as Rwanda, Sudan, Guatemala, Sri Lanka, and the Philippines.

With so many factors against them, the lack of tangible, long-lasting success in many peacemaking efforts is enough to discourage the fainthearted. And yet in spite of constraints, frustration, and disappointments, attempts at peacemaking continue. Hope is one of the most important attributes of the peacemaker—not hope that is floating in the clouds, but hope based on small victories: a violent retaliation prevented; a piece of land peacefully cultivated to nourish people from both sides; a glimmer of understanding of an opponent's beliefs; the miracle of forgiveness from someone whose whole family was massacred. The peace-maker's hope is anchored in one's memory of God's fidelity, of unexpected, unplanned intervention of the Holy Spirit in seemingly hopeless situations. It is a hope that surges from the inexhaustible source of power within, which, emboldened by love, empowers others to shape their common future for the good of all. It is a hope that keeps alive the eternal dream of God and of humanity for the dawning of a day when:

> They shall beat their swords into plowshares,
>   and spears into pruning hooks;

nation shall not lift up sword against nation,
   neither shall they learn war anymore. (Isa. 2:4)

And likewise,

   The wolf shall live with the lamb,
     the leopard shall lie down with the kid
   the calf and the lion and the fatling together
     and a little child shall lead them.
   The cow and the bear shall graze
     their young shall lie down together;
     and the lion shall eat straw like the ox.
   The nursing child shall play over the hole of the asp,
     and the weaned child shall put its hand on the adder's den.
                            (Isa.11:6-8)

Finally,

   God will wipe every tear from their eyes,
     And death will be no more. (Rev. 21: 4)

11

Grassroots Artisans of Peace

A Theological Afterword

ROBERT J. SCHREITER, C.PP.S.

What is the Christian contribution to peacemaking—not just at a conceptual level, but on the grassroots level, where it makes such a difference? To be sure, the grassroots picture that emerges from this study, in both the qualitative and quantitative results, provides some hope. One sees acts of great courage, astounding acts of forgiveness, and many stories of profound human endurance. At the same time the results of this study of communities in conflict, and of persons and groups within them who become artisans of peace, are complex. Despite rather clear implications and challenges with regard to peace education, some results do not lead to clear-cut conclusions. Others may be a little disheartening. For one thing, as Thomas Bamat and Mary Ann Cejka point out in the introduction and first chapter of this volume, while Christians committed to peacemaking in these conflicts frequently cite explicit Christian motivations for their peacemaking work, they cite other types of motivations even more. A lot of what they do is prompted by what might be called basic human decency. One can be left with the lingering question as to whether all the Christian rhetoric about peacemaking, forgiveness, and reconciliation may be no more than just that—wonderful words which may make little difference in how conflict and violence are prevented, endured, and resolved.

The question of an explicitly Christian contribution to peacemaking is especially important now, at the beginning of the twenty-first century, when the relation of religion and violence is being scrutinized in a special way. The linking of religion to violence in many conflict settings around the world today, and a rereading of such linkages made in the past, have prompted some to say that religion's enduring connection to violence is as a source of legitimation of violence rather than as a resolution of it. In fact, some have averred that religion's purported contribution to peacemaking and social reconstruction pales in comparison to how it can motivate groups to violent action. Bamat and Cejka take up this question too in the introduction, citing works by David Martin and R. Scott Appleby. In the larger contemporary discussion of this issue, the matter is far from resolved. The complexity of the roots of violence and the emotions and ideas that sustain it do not admit of easy attribution of causes.

Yet the question must be asked. Are the contributions religion makes to violence in any way comparable to the resources religion offers to peacemaking, the pursuit of justice, and the prospects of reconciliation? No discussion of religion and violence today can escape offering an opinion on this matter, if not some more definitive answer.

Within Christianity, there has been an ever-growing literature since the 1960s on the contribution of the Christian message of peace and peacemaking. That literature in turn rests upon a much longer tradition about war and peace reaching back, in the Christian West, to Augustine. In this Afterword, I cannot pretend to rehearse all the arguments or re-present the positions here. Rather, a somewhat different approach seems in order. The more we look at concrete experiences of living in conflict and pursuing peace, the more we might be able to learn about how we might best articulate a theology of peace and peacemaking that can go beyond the articulation of general principles to respond to the concrete situations in which people find themselves today. This will help us mark the contours of a theory and praxis of peace that might prove more helpful to people trying to respond to violence at the grassroots level.

A TWO-PART THEOLOGY OF PEACE

I would like to contribute to this discussion by suggesting that the Christian tradition (building upon its Jewish roots) offers a two-part theology of peace which responds to the situations articulated in this book. On the basis of that reflection, some of the thorny questions raised by this study, and by other situations of violence in our world today, might come into sharper focus. In this manner, the responses of grassroots Christians that we see in this book might be better situated in a view and praxis of peace that can be of benefit not only to Christian peacemakers, but to others as well.

A study of the Jewish and Christian Scriptures suggests a two-part theology of peace, with one theology building upon the other. The first theology of peace finds its roots in the soil out of which Israel came forth and remains the enduring fundament for a theology of peace for both Jews and Christians. The second theology of peace grows out of Christians' experience of the passion, death, and resurrection of Jesus and the implications those events hold for our understanding of God's work in the world toward peace. I would call the first theology a theology of peace *revealed*; the second, a theology of peace *redeemed*.

PEACE REVEALED

The first theology finds its origins in the covenant that God made with Noah and his family (Gen. 9:1-17). In this covenant God reveals the nature of the world order—how human beings are to live with one another, with the animals, and with the earth. Of special importance here is an injunction against taking the life of another human being (Gen. 9:5), something for which the descendants of Noah—that is to say, all human beings—will be held accountable.

Jewish theology has reflected extensively on what it calls the Noachide laws, that is, the law of the order of nature that God revealed in this first covenant with humankind. It is the basis for reaching a common understanding between peoples about the nature of their relationships, both within groups and even more importantly, between them. What we have here is what is called in the Catholic tradition of Christianity the basis for natural law and a natural theology.

One can read from this a pattern of relationships revealed by God, yet embedded deeply in the evidence of creation itself. We are intended, as creatures of God, to live in right relationship with one another. The result of living in right relationship is that we fulfill our destiny as human beings. Inasmuch as we are created in God's image (something that the Noachide covenant reaffirms, echoing Gen. 1:27), that pattern of right relationships mirrors the very life of God. The Jewish concept of *shalom*, the peace and well-being which is the fruit of living in right relationship with God, one another, and God's creation, flows from this idea. In the Scriptures, *shalom* is expressed in harmonious relationships, prosperity, long life, and children. It is the goal of life together; it is the end we try to achieve in all that we do.

Even though *shalom* is the outcome of these relations, there is a keen sense, too, that this peace is a gift from God. The Scriptures are also keenly aware of human sinfulness and all that blocks the achievement of these relationships. That God gives the gift of peace to those who strive to live in right relationship underscores the fact that God is with creation at all times and is not a distant god who creates the world and then leaves it to its own deserts.

By rooting this idea in the Noachide covenant, Jewish theology sees this not as a special revelation to Israel, but as a revelation made to all of humankind. Similar ideas and patterns recur in societies around the world. Especially in small-scale societies, where the society's survival depends on the cooperation of all for the sake of a common well-being, the pursuit of right relationships is the definition of justice and of harmony. What God reveals about God's very nature and about what human beings are intended to be can be seen as a revelation, but these are also so imprinted upon the world that they appear self-evident.

The Catholic tradition of a theology of peace builds upon this theology of peace revealed. The rootedness of our nature in God's creation gives us a kinship with all creation (as John XXIII proposed in his encyclical *Mater et Magistra* §157). The dignity of the human person, as created in the image and likeness of God, is at the center of the theological vision of the human which has animated the theology of Pope John Paul II, from his first encyclical, *Redemptor Hominis*, through his social encyclicals such as *Sollicitudo Rei Socialis* and *Centesimus Annus*, to his articulation of a "culture of life" in *Evangelium Vitae*. The doctrine of the dignity of the human person and the relation of humanity to God is the bedrock upon which a theology of peace is built.

I think this theology of peace, rooted in creation itself, is much in evidence in the self-expressed motivations and actions of the grassroots peace agents in this book. To seek the common ground between actors in violent situations is a recurring motif in a number of the studies presented here. We are reminded that the one God is the source of all life (Sudan), and that a common humanity binds us all, despite our differences (Rwanda, United States). Dialogue, therefore, is not just a strategy for ending conflict, but something that grows out of our very humanness (Philippines). The appeals to God, to common humanity, to a dialogue that expresses life, while they may seem general and even generic, bespeak nonetheless a profound theology of peace rooted in the Noachide covenant—a covenant to which all human beings have access. There is, therefore, a theology at work here that may initially be considered human common sense (which it is), but its roots can be seen as profoundly theological. Living in peace and harmony is intended to be our natural state, an imaging forth of the harmony of God in our relationships.

This theology of a peace revealed is important especially when the actors in violence do not share a common religious faith (or even belief at all). In so many of the conflicts today (evident here in those reported from the Sudan, Sri Lanka, and the Philippines),[1] there is not only religious difference, but the difference of religion may be appealed to as itself a justification for conflict. The capacity to reach beyond religious difference to a common view of humanity can be an important moment in the peacemaking process. It can also serve the mobilization of religion for peacemaking by introducing interreligious dialogue, wherein the respective traditions seek their own vision of humanity as a basis for speaking to each other and working together.

PEACE REDEEMED

One can trace a second theology of peace in the Jewish and Christian Scriptures as well. If the first is rooted in the covenant that revealed the order of creation and God's intention for the world, the second focuses on the cessation of violence and the reconstruction of society. Its origins can be seen especially in the classical prophets of the Jewish Scriptures, who look to the reconstruction of Israel after the exile. A remembrance of what had been in the past and what God intended; a memory of the disruption, dislocation, and return of exile; and the dreams of a new society, which is at a once a restoration and something new,

---

[1] Since Catholicism and Protestantism are both expressions of one religion (Christianity), the divide in Northern Ireland is between Christian denominations rather than between religions.

create a complex experience of peace that embraces past, present, and future. This embrace of the totality of time—in its brokenness, in its dislocation in the present, in its hope for the future—recognizes at once the complexity of the consequences of violence and the complications of creating a different kind of future.

In the Christian Scriptures, this experience of peace finds its clearest expression in the story of Jesus. He preached the forgiveness of sins and the advent of God's rule over the earth. He brings about that turning point from the past into a new future in his own body—in his suffering and death, and God's raising him up to new and transfigured life. Christ is indeed our peace (Eph. 2:14), a peace from God greater than the *Pax Romana,* which ruled the world in which Jesus and his disciples lived. If *shalom* was ultimately a gift from God because it represented the life of God, the peace of Christ showed the divine origin of that condition even more clearly. As Christians were to develop this idea, the peace of Christ revealed the relationships within God, that is, the relation of the Persons of the Holy Trinity.

Out of that complex of the experience of violence and alienation, one recalls the entire story of disruption and the reestablishing of relations on the part of God for our sakes. If the first peace, based on creation, is peace revealed to all humankind, then this peace is a peace redeemed, one that results from an acknowledgment of the incapacity of human beings to extricate themselves entirely from the mess they have made of God's creation, and God's intervention to make of us a new creation (see 2 Cor. 5:17). It is thus a story of redemption that we could not achieve by ourselves.

Christian understandings of justice and reconciliation grow out of this experience of God's work in Jesus Christ. Justice is real and an ineluctable part of God's plan. The advent of real justice in earthly life is always partial, even fragmentary due to the extent of havoc wreaked upon creation by human wrongdoing. It also represents the human capacity to create greater damage than it can possibly repair. For that reason, justice always has an eschatological dimension. Justice is promised and assured. Its full enactment, however, remains elusive in terms of human effort and human achievement. It can be met only in the reconciling of all things which God is working in Christ. For this reason, the Christian belief in and commitment to reconciliation reaches beyond the empirical situation in which we find ourselves, even as it is committed to that situation. Like the peace of which it is a harbinger, reconciliation is profoundly an act of God and a gift from God, in which we, at best, participate. The capacity to undo the wrong we have wreaked upon one another can be met only by the grace of a God who is the author of all dignity and all relationships.

The language of this theology of peace embraces the complexity of this story of alienation and redemption. One finds it in the stories of peacemaking recounted in this book. The notion of sin as a definition of this wrongdoing appears (Philippines, Northern Ireland), as well as the need for conversion (Philippines, United States). Likewise, the need to pursue justice to right the effects of wrongdoing (Guatemala), and to seek forgiveness (Rwanda) are concepts that bring the acknowledgment of wrongdoing and the search for a way to repair it. Visions drawn from Catholic teaching emerge as well, from the work of Popes Paul VI and John Paul II (Philippines), as well as biblical images, such as that of the shepherd (Rwanda). To pursue a civilization of love (Paul VI) and a culture of life (John Paul II) are visions growing out of church teaching which can give coherence and direction to actions for peacemaking.

A theology of peace redeemed is, of course, an explicitly Christian one. As it is described here, it is also explicitly Catholic. Within Christianity itself, there will be common voices (as indicated by some of the explicitly Catholic examples of peacemaking recounted in this volume, as well as the responses to gang violence in the United States described by John Brown Childs), using the language of sin, conversion, and reconciliation. But there will also be sharp differences, as the accounts from Guatemala reveal between Catholics and evangelical Protestants, and even among Catholics themselves; in Northern Ireland, the conflict is given a harsh confessional (Catholic versus Protestant) profile. But the divide of greatest significance here is between what would be a Christian theology of peace redeemed, and the visions of peace that might be offered out of the heart of other traditions such as those represented in some of the countries in this study—primarily, Muslim, Hindu, and Buddhist. To be sure, these traditions are not any more uniform internally than is Christianity. But the vision of redemption and reconciliation of Christians is one that is not shared in these other traditions. Justice is certainly central to Islam. Past deeds and ignorance play roles, in Hindu and Buddhist traditions respectively, that get little hearing within Christianity. What needs to be underscored here is that each of the great religious traditions of the world has a vision of peace. The second strand of a Christian theology of peace—peace redeemed—represents its specific contribution.

To finish this brief sketch of a two-part Christian theology of peace: both parts are in evidence in the stories recounted here. Christians often tend to emphasize the second part, peace redeemed, at the expense of the first, peace revealed, perhaps because the second is so specifically Christian. Yet both are part of Christian tradition. The first may be more important in situations of interreligious encounter. The second is most useful for dealing with violence among Christians themselves (as in Rwanda and Northern Ireland, where this language is especially in evidence). It is perhaps for this reason, at least partially, that what would count as "motivation" among Christian peacemakers seems to draw less on explicit Christian teaching (read: a theology of peace redeemed) in these stories. I would argue that Christian motivation is present in all of these stories through the clear commitment to a theology of peace revealed.

ISSUES IN CHRISTIAN PEACEMAKING

The Pastoral Constitution on the Church in the Modern World from the Second Vatican Council (*Gaudium et Spes*) calls us to be "artisans of peace" (§ 77). The studies collected here raise a number of other questions about peacemaking and the role of Christian traditions of peacemaking in the lives of grassroots artisans of peace. A few of them can be noted here.

IMAGES OF GOD

One explicit object of investigation in this study was the ways in which images of God were operative in the lives and actions of grassroots peacemakers. The coordinators of this project distinguish between three kinds of images: power-over images, agentic images, and immanent images. They note that all three sets are in evidence in peacemakers, although agentic images are somewhat more common than power-over and immanent ones.

The data gathered on images of the divine are what social scientists call correlational. As Cejka explains in chapter 1, causal relationships cannot be inferred between them and other aspects of peacemaking examined in this volume. All one can say is that the various images of God are more common or less common in relationship to these other variables. But the next step is to speculate a bit on the relative salience of how each of these sets of images may be at work.

Power-over images of God are indeed present. I would think of the "God first" language found in the study of gangs in the United States, the emphasis on providence in the Philippines study, and the importance of conversion in several of the studies as reflecting power-over images. Power-over images are especially important, it seems to me, when one feels overwhelmed by the evil being encountered, or when one comes from a small-scale society that reflects clear hierarchical arrangement (such as Mindanao). Evangelical Protestant language, as (at least initially) a language of the dispossessed, would reflect this same characteristic. A strongly theocentric approach to peace would find its image of God most likely in what is called here power-over language. Moreover, power-over images are not out of line with the affirmation that justice, peace, and reconciliation are ultimately the work of God in our world, transcending our efforts to right the wrong we have inflicted on others or to repair the damage we have experienced at others' hands.

Agentic language, with its images of God as healer, liberator, or redeemer, may be more likely employed when one feels some power to alter or direct the situations of violence and conflict. When one feels that resistance or other strategies to change the situation of violence could be beneficial, one may be more likely to invoke a God who is perceived as active in history and the efficacy of oneself as an agent as well. Strong models of service as part of a peacemaking activity might also have saliency here. Those who had been influenced through their catechists by a theology of liberation in Guatemala might be found in this group. The sharp difference reported between these Catholics, on the one hand, and charismatic Catholics and evangelical Pentecostals, on the other, might be accounted for in some measure by different images of God.

It is more difficult to speculate about immanent images of the divine and their connection, if any, with a particular context or aspect of peacemaking. One might suspect that immanent images would prompt peacemaking in the form of relationship building, but the data do not bear this out.

Again, it is important to remember that people's images of God do not sort out that neatly. But this study's findings on images of the divine caution us not to assume that agentic language, for example, is always preferable over the others, or that power language is always inadequate or even wrong. Circumstances shape our experiences, and our relative experience of agency, power, and capacity to relate will doubtless affect how we read situations. Experience itself may reveal God to us in different ways. At the same time, it is important to remember that our circumstances in themselves do not determine our beliefs or responses.

IMAGES OF THE ENEMY

One of the results emerging from the study was the lack of significantly more positive images of enemies among peacemakers than among non-peacemakers. At one level, this might seem surprising, since one would think that agentic or immanent images of God might influence or be influenced by images of the enemy. But put against a wider range of experiences of conflict, violence, and reconciliation, this discrepancy is not as surprising as it may seem.

One reading of a Christian theology of peace would suggest that seeking peace with or loving and forgiving one's enemies, as urged by Jesus in the Gospels, should be accompanied by more generous characterizations of the enemy. The inference would be that those who come to forgive and even love their enemies must start from a different point in their relationship to their enemies than those who cannot come to love or to forgive them. Some of the moving stories of forgiveness from Rwanda in this volume, when juxtaposed with those stories of unfulfilled justice from Guatemala, for example, could prompt such an inference.

If one works from a theology of peace revealed, as outlined above, that inference of difference of starting point might well be justified. Different perceptions lead to different relationships. But a theology of peace redeemed opens up another point of view. Enemies are enemies. They threaten our well-being and see us as obstacles to their goals. The transformation of our view of enemies has less to do with our capacity to see them differently—at least initially—than with our experience of how God heals us in the act of reconciliation and, in turn, brings us to a different place. Because of the different vantage point at which we have arrived, thanks to the grace of God, it becomes possible to imagine a different future for our enemies. It is because we can begin to imagine the relationship of *God* to our enemies—not *our* relation to them—that the possibility of forgiveness opens up. Psychologically speaking, forgiveness becomes possible only when we are able to see the action and motivation of the wrongdoer from a different point of view. This does not change the overt or conscious motivation of the wrongdoer, but allows us to see that motivation in a wider perspective. In the theological sense of forgiveness, we may be able to arrive at a different view of our enemy because we believe God has a point of view different from ours (even if we cannot enter that different point of view). Such a view of forgiveness of enemies could emanate, therefore, from a power image of God: that is to say, we trust God's view of the enemy, even when it is not our own. In so doing, we may be able to enter in a different way so as to come to alter our image of the enemy.

Such an act of faith can be augmented by our own human experience of the complex motivations for wrongdoing. For example, when people in Guatemala tried to keep their sons or pupils out of the army, yet were unable to do so, they may have come to a better appreciation, as parents and as teachers, of the many pressures and influences that prompted government soldiers to act as they did.

A commitment to right relationships, even with those who were enemies, may be a belief that can override one's experience of the enemy and what an enemy has done. No causal relationship between images of God and images of forgiveness can be inferred on the basis of this study, but those committed to peace must be able to imagine how people might come to quite different conclusions than we do. This is necessary in order to understand the astounding acts of forgiveness that do take place after situations of violence and conflict.

Connected to this is understanding, from the perspective of the relation of justice to forgiveness, that in the second theology of peace—peace redeemed—forgiveness does not mean forgoing justice. One can forgive an enemy and still insist that, in justice, the enemy needs to be punished. This is for the sake of the reconstruction of the social order. Punishment may not bring back the dead, but it says that such behavior will not be tolerated in the reconstructed society. And as was pointed out in the study of Guatemala, punishment meted out in the name of justice can redeem innocence: justice done says that the wrongdoing was against innocent people, not guilty ones, as had been claimed.

Yet forgiveness can happen even when justice has not been done, as has been documented in truth and reconciliation hearings around the world. The reason for this is that, if forgiveness always depended on punitive or restorative justice being done, then it could rarely happen, because most often justice is not achieved. Forgiveness, at least at the personal level, has to do with the victim's relationship to the event that happened in the past. Forgiveness means that the victim is no longer controlled by or held hostage to the event and the wrongdoer. It is about being able to remember the past—both the wrongdoer and the deed—in a different way. This is possible for the victim because the victim believes that God sees the wrongdoer and the deed as well. God sees them in all their wrongfulness and does not forget what has happened. God's justice will be enacted. (Or for some of the Achi of Guatemala, the ancestral spirits will enact justice in the next life.)

Here an idea from the first theology of peace might be seen to be at work: that we are all created in God's image and are accorded thereby a certain dignity. Even though wrongdoing represents a terrible diminution of our capacity to image forth God, we do not lose the intrinsic capacity to do so. It is because of this that redemption and forgiveness are possible, even though they may not always occur. It is because of this that a Christian can hope for a future that is different from the past—that is, the past need not determine the future.

BELIEF IN A "JUST WORLD"

The phenomenon of belief in a "just world" posits a world in which relationships are *already* right, and which operates as a closed system. If people get what they deserve and deserve what they get, then only a finite amount of justice can circulate within the system. Justice can be meted out, but there is no room for anything beyond it. The second theology of peace, of peace as redemption, believes that God infuses more value, as it were, into the system. God's mercy reaches beyond what our justice might be able to offer, not by negating our justice but by embracing it and taking things even further. This is because justice, and peace, come from God and are not something we produce ourselves. The concept of a universe infused with limitless grace is already embodied in the first theology of peace, where *shalom*, too, is recognized as a gift from God. The peace of Christ, at the center of the second theology of peace, is a "peace which the world cannot give," as John's Gospel puts it. It brings more into the world than was there in the first place. It is what makes the idea of a "new creation" possible.

That belief in a "just world" does not correlate strongly with peacemaking, then, is not a surprise. Peacemaking—either as a commitment to right relationships we cannot yet imagine, or a forgiveness which at this moment reaches beyond the horizons we have set for ourselves—always has a surplus value that cannot be reduced to the value we human beings create and distribute within our finite systems. This seems to be the sense of "peace" as it is spoken of in the Gospel of John and in Paul's letters—a peace that reaches beyond our closed systems.

RELIGION AND VIOLENCE

No discussion today of peacemaking can avoid examining, at least in some measure, what religion contributes to the promotion of violence. Christian peacemakers are more wont to dwell on what religion can contribute to the pursuit of peace. They share with those committed religionists of other traditions the conviction that their own tradition—Christianity—is a tradition of peace. The use of religion to instigate or to sustain violence is a misuse and a perversion of religion's deepest intentions.

One of the values of studies of violence and peacemaking such as the one in this book is to show that the roots of violence are complex. The hostility of Muslims to Christians in Mindanao, or among religionists in Sri Lanka, or among Christians in Northern Ireland and Rwanda cannot be wholly accounted for on religious grounds. Religion is often used to legitimate other motivations for violence, such as a lust for power, greed for natural resources or land, or the pursuit of a sense of honor. These other motivations for conflict must be recognized for what they are and not be allowed to hide behind an inferred religious legitimation.

Moreover, religious difference can be a handy index for defining difference in general. An index of difference is a necessary category for making neighbors into "the other" or "the enemy." When the religious index coincides with ethnic difference or territorial difference, it becomes especially potent, since it implies that what makes our enemy different is not something as superficial as territorial location or language difference or outer appearance: it is rather something deeply and disturbingly transcendental.

It is because of this religious identification with the roots of violence that religious legitimation, more than ethnic or racial legitimation, can be especially lethal. And it is for that same reason that the role of religion in promoting violence must be specified as clearly as possible. Is the motivation really traceable to religious belief and practice, or is it simply a mask for some other element of power or greed? Religious identification of the roots of a conflict is very suspect in a given situation, for example, when people of different religious faiths have been able to live together in the past, or manage to live together peacefully elsewhere in the present. Such examples of interreligious harmony undercut the sure identification of religion with the need to promote violence. Examples of peaceable existence, and, as in this volume, of joint peacemaking, are of particular value.

At this point, one further, urgent question arises from the studies collected here: If religion is not seen as providing strong motivation for peacemaking, might such an attitude not arise from a belief that religion has not contributed much to the origins of the violence, and so has little to say about the resolution of violence, no matter how it might otherwise appear to outsiders examining the situation? I raise this here only as a query. Put simply, if religion is not seen as part of the problem, is it then not seen either as part of the solution? In other words, religious belief, no matter how important it might otherwise be for people, may not be seen as contributing to peace because the real issues are not about religious difference or religious faith. Religion might prompt some individuals to undertake peacemaking efforts, but it does not present itself as a structural element for changes in conditions and relationships that are essential to reconstructing a society. One may want to question the place religion might have in this worldview. But as a description of attitudes of those inside the situation, it may well explain the apparent absence of religion from peacemaking.

Even having said all this about the peripheral place religion may hold in the legitimation of violence, there is still ample evidence of how religion has been harnessed, legitimately or illegitimately, to promote real and deadly violence. Here, what religious traditions say about concepts of justice, possibilities of forgiveness, images of the other and of the enemy, the intervention of God in our world, and boundaries of belonging and not belonging must be examined. How religion is used to constitute memory of the past, how it is used to create the future, and how it serves to redeem what can be saved of the present (John Paul

Lederach's thoughts on these matters in chapter 9 above are useful here) have to figure into the planning and the action of Christian peacemakers.

GRASSROOTS ARTISANS OF PEACE

So just what can Christian peacemakers contribute to grassroots peacemaking? One can agree, perhaps, on general tenets of a Christian theology of peace, but how do those tenets translate into grassroots action? Let me touch on several ways that acts of peacemaking such as those described in this volume carry deep theological significance.

The first is the fact that they *create new social spaces*. As was noted in some of the studies presented here, social peacemaking has a greater capacity to contribute to societies where the structures of civil society are in place, such as in Northern Ireland and the Philippines. The presence of civil society implies that there are practices and institutions that sustain a minimal amount of trust upon which relationships can be built, ideas can be tested, and new arrangements for society can be suggested.

Both theologies of peacemaking articulated here can contribute to the creating and enhancement of such social spaces. The theology of peace revealed holds to the intrinsic value and worth of each human being, because we have all been created in the image and likeness of God. Consequently, each human being is to be valued. As we have seen, this is at the basis of Catholic social teaching and of Pope John Paul II's vision of a culture of life. What this means concretely is that a social space must be created within our communities that is at once both *safe* and *hospitable* for human relationships and human community. Spaces are safe in that they promote relationships of trust. Trust is the basic building block of human society. Without trust, there can be no sense of safety and security. It is upon trust that more complex relationships can be built.

Conflict and war are about the breakdown of trust—both in the sense of the trustworthiness of our neighbor and in the sense of security against extinction. When people have been through the trauma of violence, the basic bonds of trust are sundered. Rebuilding those bonds is essential for the reconstruction of society.

Here a theology of peace redeemed contributes the idea that trust betrayed or trust broken can be restored. The graciousness of God who heals those bonds in Christ, who is making peace through the blood of his cross (Col.1:20), makes a new creation possible. If we are left to rearrange the relationships we have within our societies without the hope of anything new being added, the situation can indeed look hopeless. What a theology of peace redeemed adds to the first theology of peace revealed is precisely this sense of graciousness, of gratuity that reaches beyond what we deserve or what can be meted out within the canons of justice. It is this graciousness (called by Christians "grace") that marks the hospitality of the social space created. It is given to us not on the basis of what we deserve, but in view of our larger destiny as children of God, as bearers of the image of God.

In all of this, a Christian theology of peacemaking can contribute to a new beginning for a society, not by predetermining the future but by offering a place of safety and graciousness which makes thinking in a different way a possibility.

Second, Christian peacemaking can *redeem memory.* The potential power of the REMHI project of the Archdiocesan Office of Human Rights in Guatemala underscores this potential contribution. Memory plays a central role in how the future will be lived. The REMHI project insisted on remembering the past, rather than trying to erase it. Remembering the voices of those who have been silenced, remembering the real pain suffered, and not treating suffering as something to be suppressed and forgotten underscore a key element of a theology of peace revealed: we are all creatures of dignity before God, and what happens to us is not something of no consequence. To remember is to reassert dignity.

Acknowledgment of the past is the first step in the redemption of memory. The second is how we choose to remember that past. Will those memories keep us bound to that past in a way that mortgages the future, or can the past serve in some other way of creating a future where the past will not be repeated? The remembering of the past as past is the first step; seeing the past as instructive of a different kind of future is the second. If in the present we try to create a future that does not repeat the past, which changes the social conditions under which the past happened, we are creating a new possibility. That, it seems to me, is an essential part of the reconstruction of a new, peaceful society. It is a redemption of the past; that is, it does not repeat the past but sees the past as a way of creating a different kind of future.

The memory of the suffering and death of Christ could have been a story that repeats an age-old truism: the powerful of this world always win out and destroy dreams of something different. The suffering and death of Jesus were not something he deserved or earned; it was rather the efforts of earthly power to reassert its control over the vision he had preached. God's raising up of Jesus from death put the lie to those power relationships. Because of the resurrection of Jesus, Christians can never believe that the past determines the future. In the paradox of the peace created by the blood of Christ's cross, the blood of those who suffer today is not silenced. It continues to cry out. And it points to a social arrangement different from that held out for us by the powers-that-be.

Third, the twin belief in the intrinsic dignity of each human being (in a theology of peace revealed), and in God's working something new (in a theology of peace redeemed) creates *a source of hope,* which is essential for peace to be more than the cessation of conflict. If peace is to lead to the reconstruction of society in such a way that the past is not repeated, it needs a continuing source of hope. Hope for the Christian is not the same as optimism. Optimism is something that comes from our estimation of our own vision and our own efforts. Optimism gives us reason to believe that we can make things better. In the aftermath of Rwanda, in the social devastation of Mayan cultures in Guatemala, in the decades of war—yet to be resolved—in the Sudan, optimism can seem rather feeble. Hope is a gift from God, something that draws us into a future that is not completely of our own imagining. Hope is not without an anchor in the reality we experience in the present or remember from the past. But it represents something that keeps us moving even when everything seems blocked. It is a reminder that peace and reconciliation are not things we create, but are gifts from God we learn to recognize and make our own.

CONCLUSION

Christian peacemaking at the grassroots level can be seen in the different aspects of peacemaking that have emerged from this study. Its commitment to right relationships can press it into action in pre-conflict situations of engaging in actions that work against conflict and violence. In the midst of conflict, its memory of human dignity and hope for a peaceful tomorrow prompt it into acts of rescue, of resistance, and of mercy which cannot be reduced to the relationships of the past. In its efforts toward the reconstruction of post-conflict society, it has shown its potential to retrieve memory, to pursue justice, and to establish those social spaces in which a new society can come about. The actions of Christian peacemakers resemble those of others committed to peace in many ways, because they share some common convictions about the nature and destiny of humankind. Ultimately, however, a vision of a world redeemed in Christ can sustain them; in that world, every tear will be wiped away, and the things longed for become, indeed, the way of life.

Contributors

THOMAS BAMAT is Director of the Center for Mission Research and Study at Maryknoll, New York. A sociologist and a lay missioner, he has worked for many years in Latin America as well as in the United States. Among his publications are works on human rights, politics, religious movements, and popular Christianity.

JOHN D. BREWER is Professor of Sociology at The Queen's University Belfast and is actively involved in peacebuilding in Northern Ireland. The author of thirteen books, Brewer has written on ethnic and religious conflict, crime, policing, and qualitative research methods. In 1998 he was elected a Fellow of the Royal Society of Arts.

MARY ANN CEJKA is a social psychologist serving as Associate Researcher at the Center for Mission Research and Study at Maryknoll. A longtime activist for peace and justice issues and church reform, she has published a wide variety of articles in both pastoral and scholarly journals.

JOHN BROWN CHILDS is Professor of Sociology at the University of California, Santa Cruz. Among his numerous works is a recent volume on "transcommunality" from Temple University Press. Childs works with urban community peace organizations dedicated to ending youth violence constructively.

JULIA AKER DUANY is a researcher with the Workshop in Political Theory and Policy Analysis at Indiana University. Her doctorate is in education. Forced to flee her country in the 1980s, Duany has returned regularly in recent years. She writes on the war in the Sudan and has been actively engaged in efforts to bring peace to its people.

KARL M. GASPAR, C.SS.R., is Coordinator of the Redemptorist Itinerant Mission Team. He has a doctorate in Philippine Studies. Gaspar has worked with the Asian Social Institute and the National Secretariat for Social Action, Justice, and Peace. He is a member of the Ecumenical Association of Third World Theologians and of the Mindanawon Initiatives for Cultural Dialogue.

KULDIP KAUR is an anthropologist currently doing doctoral studies at the University of London. She has worked as a researcher in Guatemala with the Myrna Mack Foundation, the Latinamerican Faculty of Social Sciences (FLACSO), and the Association for the Advancement of Social Sciences (AVANCSO).

JOHN PAUL LEDERACH was founding director of the Conflict Transformation Program at Eastern Mennonite University. He is now a professor at the Kroc Institute for International Peace Studies at the University of Notre Dame. Lederach has extensive global experience as a peacebuilding practitioner, trainer, and consultant and has published numerous works on reconciliation and conflict transformation.

MARY JOHN MANANZAN, O.S.B., is a Missionary Benedictine Sister who directs the Institute of Women's Studies at St. Scholastica's College, Manila. She has served as president of St. Scholastica's and as executive secretary of the Ecumenical Association of Third World Theologians. She is currently doing research on women and Asian spirituality.

BERNARD NOEL RUTIKANGA is Lecturer in History at the National University of Rwanda, and vice-president of the national chapter of the Organization for Social Science Research in Eastern and Southern Africa. A former refugee himself, Rutikanga has served as a counselor and has written both poetry and scholarly work on African refugees.

ROBERT J. SCHREITER, C.PP.S., is Bernardin Center Professor of Vatican II Theology at Catholic Theological Union, Chicago. A member of the Congregation of the Precious Blood, he is a popular lecturer worldwide. His many books include *Constructing Local Theologies, The New Catholicity*, and *Reconciliation.*

SHIRLEY LAL WIJESINGHE is a Senior Lecturer at the University of Kelaniya in Sri Lanka. He holds a doctorate in Biblical Exegesis from the Catholic University of Louvain, Belgium, and has lectured on exegesis and hermeneutics in the Philippines and Italy. He is currently engaged in research on the theology of peace at the Centre for Society and Religion, Colombo.

Bibliography

Abu-Nimer, Mohammed. 2000-2001. "A Framework for Nonviolence and Peacebuilding in Islam." *The Journal of Law and Religion* 15:217-65.

Adams, Richard. 1993. "Etnias y Sociedades (1930-1979)." In *Historia General de Centroamérica,* edited by Hector Pérez Brignoli, 165-243. Guatemala City: FLACSO.

Adams, Tani. 1978. "San Martín Jilotepeque: Aspects of the Political and Socio-economic Structure of a Guatemalan Peasant Community." Master's thesis, University of Texas, Austin.

African Rights. 1995. *Rwanda: Death, Despair and Defiance*. London: African Rights.

———. 1999. *Resisting Genocide: Bisesero April-June 1994*. London: African Rights.

Akenson, Donald H. 1992. *God's Peoples: Covenant and Land in South Africa, Israel and Ulster*. London: Cornell University Press.

Albino, Oliva. 1970. *Sudan: The Southern View*. London: Oxford University Press.

Alecio, Rolando. 1995. "Uncovering the Truth: Political Violence and Indigenous Organizations." In *The New Politics of Survival: Grassroots Movements in Central America,* edited by Sinclair Minor. Washington, D.C.: EPICA.

Alejo, Albert E. 2000. *Generating Energies in Mt. Apo*. Quezon City: Ateneo de Manila University.

Alfaro, Rosita. 2000. "Rabinal: Las Cofradías." Master's thesis, University of San Carlos, Guatemala.

Amodio, Richard R. 1992. "The Relationship of Projection, Nationalism, and Empathy to the Phenomenon of 'Enemy Images.'" Ph.D. diss., University of Cincinnati.

Anderlini, Sanam N. 2000. *Women at the Peace Table: Making a Difference*. New York: United Nations Development Fund for Women (UNIFEM).

Anderson, Shelley. 1998. "When Will We Get the Chance? IFOR Women on the Move." *Fellowship* 64:14-15.

Appleby, R. Scott. 2000. *The Ambivalence of the Sacred: Religion, Violence and Reconciliation*. Lanham, Md.: Rowman and Littlefield.

Aquino, María Pilar. 2000. "Patriarchy." In the *Encyclopedia of Third World Theology,* edited by Virginia Fabella and R.S. Sugirtharajah, 163-65. Maryknoll, N.Y.: Orbis.

Arguinzoni, Sonny, and Julie Arguinzoni. 1991. *Treasures Out of Darkness*. La Puente, Calif.: New Leaf Press.

Balasuriya, Tissa. 1986. "Theology and Ethnicism." *Logos* 25:1-84.

Ball, Patrick, Herbert Spirer, and Louise Spirer. 2000. *Making the Case: Investigating Large Scale Human Rights Violations*. New York: American Association for the Advancement of Science (AAAS).

Bardon, Jonathan. 1992. *A History of Ulster*. Belfast: Blackstaff.

Barrios Unidos. 1996. *BU Productions*. Santa Cruz, Calif.: Barrios Unidos.

———. 2001. *Program Statement: Cesar Chavez School of Social Change*. Santa Cruz, Calif.: Barrios Unidos.

Bastos, Santiago, and Manuela Camus. 1996. *Quebrando el Silencio: Organizaciones del Pueblo Maya y sus Demandas*. Guatemala: FLACSO.

Baum, Gregory, and Harold Wells, eds. 1997. *The Reconciliation of Peoples: Challenge to the Churches.* Maryknoll, N.Y.: Orbis; Geneva: WCC Publications.

Bazivamo, Christopher. 2001. "Elections: Engine for Good Governance in Rwanda." Kigali.

Beshir, Mohamed Omer. 1968. *The Southern Sudan: Background to Conflict.* London: C. Burst and Co.

Blaney, Roger. 1996. *Presbyterians and the Irish Language.* Belfast: Ulster Historical Foundation.

Block, Gay, and Malka Drucker. 1992. *Rescuers: Portraits of Moral Courage in the Holocaust.* New York: TV Books.

Boulding, Elise. 2000. *Cultures of Peace: The Hidden Side of History.* New York: Syracuse University Press.

Brewer, John D. 1991. "Northern Ireland's Experiences of the Parallels between Sectarianism and Racism in Terms of the Models of Work, Classroom Issues and Preparation for Practice." Report for the National Steering Group on the Teaching of Race and Anti-Racism in the Personal Social Services, Central Council for Education and Training in Social Work.

———. 1992. "Sectarianism and Racism, and Their Parallels and Differences." *Ethnic and Racial Studies* 15:352-64.

———. 1998. *Anti-Catholicism in Northern Ireland 1600-1998: The Mote and the Beam.* London: Macmillan.

Brintnall, Douglas. 1979. *Revolt Against the Dead: The Modernization of a Mayan Community in the Highlands of Guatemala.* New York: Gordon and Breach.

Bunch, Roland. 1982. *Two Ears of Corn: A Guide to People-Centered Agricultural Improvement.* Oklahoma City: World Neighbors.

Byran, Dominic. 2000. *Orange Parades.* London: Pluto.

California Wellness Foundation. 2000. *Violence Prevention Initiative.* San Francisco: California Wellness Foundation.

CBCP and CIRD. 1991. "Dialogue and Proclamation: Reflections and Orientations on Interreligious Dialogue and the Proclamation of the Gospel of Jesus Christ." Manila: Catholic Bishops' Conference of the Philippines and the Commission for Inter-religious Dialogue. Unpublished manuscript.

CEH (Commission for Historical Clarification). 1999. *Guatemala: Memoria del Silencio, Vol. I-XIII.* Guatemala: UNOPS. http://hrdata.aaas.org/ceh/.

Cejka, Mary Ann. Forthcoming. "Which God Is on Whose Side and How? Religious Orientation, Social Attitudes, and the Common Good." In *Lived Theology in America: The Practice and Promise of Reconciling Communities*, edited by Tracy E. K'Meyer and Charles Marsh.

Centro Ak'Kutan. 1994. *Evangélio y Culturas en Verapaz.* Coban, Guatemala: Centro Ak'Kutan.

Chaves, Mark. 2001. "Question and Answer with Mark Chaves on the National Congregations Study." *Nonprofit Research News* 8:10-13.

Cheksy, Laurel. 2002. "GUNS: Facts and Protocol." *The New Haven Advocate* (March 14): 17.

Chelsea House Educational Communications, Inc. 1977. *Paper Bullets: Great Propaganda Posters of the Axis and Allied Countries, WWII.* New York: Chelsea House Publishers.

Che Man W. K. 1990. *Muslim Separatism: The Moros of Southern Philippines and the Malays of Southern Thailand.* Quezon City: Ateneo de Manila University.

Childs, John Brown. 1991. "Partners in Crime: Middle Class Co-Generation of the Ghetto Drug Trade." *Z Magazine* 4 (June): 92-96.

————. 1993. Field Notes. Santa Cruz, Calif. Unpublished typescript notebook.

————. 1994. "The Value of Transcommunal Identity Politics: The Peace and Justice Gang Truce in Kansas City." *Z Magazine* 7 (July/August): 48-51.

————. 1995. Field Notes. Santa Cruz, Calif.: Unpublished typescript notebook.

————. 1996a. "Peace in the Street: The New Youth Peace Movement." *Z Magazine* 9 (November): 40-43.

————. 1996b. "Transcommunality: A 21st Century Social Compact for Urban Revitalization in the United States." In *Villes et Politiques Urbaines au Canada et aux Etats Unis,* edited by Jean Michel Lacroix, 180-214. Paris: Sorbonne University.

————. 2002. *Transcommunality: From the Politics of Conversion to the Ethics of Respect.* Philadelphia: Temple University Press.

Chrétien, Jean P. 1995. *Rwanda: Les Médias du Génocide.* Paris: Editions Karthala.

CIIDH (International Center for Human Rights Investigations). 1996. *Draining the Sea: An Analysis of Terror in Three Rural Communities in Guatemala (1980-1984).* Guatemala: GAM.

Collins, Robert O. 1999. "Africans, Arabs, and Islamists: From the Conference Tables to the Battlefields in Sudan." *African Studies Review* 42:105-23.

Commission for Historical Clarification. *See* CEH

Constantino, Renato. 1975. *The Philippines: A Past Revisited.* Quezon City: n.p.

Crowley, Michael, and Elizabeth Clegg. 2001. "Enhancing Controls on Legal Transfers." *Seton Hall Journal of Diplomacy and International Relations* 2:51-62.

Cukier, Wendy, and Steve Shropshire. 2000. "Domestic Gun Markets: The Licit-Illicit Links." In *Running Guns: The Global Black Market in Small Arms,* edited by Lore Lumpee, 105-28. London: Zed Books.

Delli Sante, Angela. 1996. *Nightmare or Reality: Guatemala in the 1980s.* Amsterdam: Thela Publishers.

Des Forges, Alison. 1999. *Leave None to Tell the Story: Genocide in Rwanda.* New York: Human Rights Watch.

De Silva, K. M. 1981. *A History of Sri Lanka.* London: Hurst.

Detmold Confession. 1996. *Signe d'espoir pour le Rwanda,* a conference report prepared in Detmold, Germany.

De Waal, Alex, ed. 1997. *Food and Power in Sudan: A Critique of Humanitarianism.* London: African Rights.

Dobbs, Michael. 2000. *Madeleine Albright: A Twentieth-Century Odyssey.* New York: Henry Holt and Company.

Dorsey, Learthen. 1994. *Historical Dictionary of Rwanda.* Lanham, Md.: Scarecrow.

Duany, Julia Aker. 1997. "Making Peace: A Report on Grassroots Peace Efforts by Women in South Sudan." *African Journal of Institutions and Development* 3:19-34.

Duany, Wal. 1997. "Religion and Reconciliation in the Sudan: Institutional Requirements for Religious Tolerance and Pluralism." Bloomington, Ind.: South Sudanese Lens, 1-3. http://www.southsudanfriends.org.

————. 1999. "The Diaspora Briefings: A Report on the Wunlit Dinka-Nuer Peace and Reconciliation Conference." Prepared for the executive secretary of the New Sudan Council of Churches (NSCC), Nairobi, Kenya (July-August).

Duany, Wal, and Julia Duany. 2000. "Genesis of the Crisis in the Sudan." In *White Nile, Black Blood: War, Leadership, and Ethnicity from Khartoum to Kampala,* edited by Jay Spaulding and Stephanie Beswick, 167-82. Lawrenceville, N.J.: Red Sea Press.

Dupuis, Jacques. 1997. *Toward a Christian Theology of Religious Pluralism.* Maryknoll, N.Y.: Orbis.

EAFG (Guatemalan Forensic Anthropology Team). 1995. *Las Masacres en Rabinal.* Guatemala: EAFG.

Economic, Social and Human Cost of the War in Sri Lanka, The. 2001. Colombo: National
  Peace Council of Sri Lanka.
Ecumenical Association of Third World Theologians (EATWOT). 1996. "Search for Jus-
  tice, Challenges to Theology." Unpublished conference statement.
Emmanuel, S. J. 1999. "Asian Churches for a New Evangelization: Chances and Chal-
  lenges." *East Asian Pastoral Review* 36:252-75.
European Centre for Conflict Prevention. 1999. *People Building Peace: 35 Inspiring Sto-
  ries from Around the World.* Utrecht: European Centre for Conflict Prevention.
Evans-Pritchard, E. E. 1968. *The Nuer: A Description of the Modes of Livelihood and
  Political Institutions of a Nilotic People.* London: Oxford University Press.
Fairbank, Maslin, Maullin and Associates. 1999. *Resources for Youth.* Santa Monica,
  Calif.: Fairbank, Maslin, Maullin and Associates.
Faith and Politics Group. 1991. *Remembering Our Past: 1690 and 1916.* Belfast: Inter-
  church Group on Faith and Politics.
————. 1996. *Forgive Us Our Trespasses . . . ?* Belfast: Interchurch Group on Faith and
  Politics.
————. 2001. *Transitions.* Belfast: Interchurch Group on Faith and Politics.
Falla, Ricardo. 2001. *Quiche Rebelde: Religious Conversion, Politics and Ethnic Identity
  in Guatemala.* Austin: University of Texas Press.
FARG (Fond National pour l'Assistance aux Réscapés du Génocide et des Massacres au
  Rwanda). 2000a. *Raporo y'Imirimo y'Umwaka w'1999.* Kigali: FARG.
————. 2000b. *Raporo y'Inkunga Yatewe Hatarimo Kubaka no Gusana 1998-2000.*
  Kigali: FARG.
————. 2000c. *Etats Financiers Exercice 1999.* Kigali: FARG.
————. 2000d. *Plan Triennal du FARG 2001-2003.* Kigali: FARG.
Fernandez, Francis. 1999. "Towards New Horizons in Interreligious Dialogue." *Mission
  Today* 1:88-100.
Fond National pour l'Assistance aux Réscapés du Génocide et des Massacres au Rwanda.
  See FARG
Foster, Robert F. 1988. *Modern Ireland 1600-1972.* London: Penguin.
Fowke, Edith, and Joe Glazer. 1973. *Songs of Work and Protest.* New York: Dover.
Furnham, Adrian, and Edward Procter. 1989. "Belief in a Just World: Review and Critique
  of the Individual Difference Literature." *British Journal of Social Psychology* 28:365-
  84.
Gailey, A. 1975. "The Scots Element in North Irish Popular Culture." *Ethnologia
  Europaea* 7:2-22.
Gálvez, Victor, et al. 1997. *¿Qué Sociedad Queremos?* Guatemala: FLACSO.
Gardner, Katy, and David Lewis. 1996. *Anthropology, Development and the Post-Modern
  Challenge.* London: Pluto Press.
Garrard-Burnett, Virginia. 1998. *Protestantism in Guatemala.* Austin: University of Texas
  Press.
Gasibirege, Simon, and Stella Babalola. 2001. *Perceptions About Gacaca Law in
  Rwanda: Evidence from a Multi-Method Study.* Baltimore: Johns Hopkins University
  School of Public Health, Center for Communication Programs.
Gaspar, Karl M. 1994. *Readings on Contemporary Mindanao Church Realities.* Quezon
  City: Claretian Publications.
————. 1997. "Abante, Atras, Abante: Patterns of the Mindanao Catholic Church's
  Involvement in Contemporary Social Issues." In *Civil Society Making Civil Society,
  Philippine Democracy Agenda,* Vol. 3. Quezon City: Third World Studies Center.
Gaspar, Karl M., Elipidio A. Lapad, and Ailynne J. Maravillas. 2002. *Mapagpakamalina-*

won: A Reader for the Mindanawon Peace Advocate. Davao City: Alternate Forum for Research in Mindanao.

Gest, Ted, and Victoria Pope. 1997. "Crime Time Bomb: Rising Juvenile Crime." In *Criminal Justice 97/98*, edited by John J. Sullivan and Joseph L. Victor, 164-66. Guilford, Conn.: Duskin/McGraw-Hill.

Gleijeses, Piero. 1992. "La Reforma Agraria de Arbenz." In *500 Años de Lucha Por La Tierra*, edited by Julio Castellanos Cambranes, 349-77. Guatemala: FLACSO.

Gourevitch, Philip. 1998. *We Wish to Inform You That Tomorrow We Will Be Killed with Our Families: Stories from Rwanda.* New York: Farrar Straus and Giroux.

Gouteux, Jean P. 1998. *Un génocide secret d'état: La France et le Rwanda 1990-1997.* Paris: Editions Sociales.

Goyvaerts, Didier, ed., 2000. *Conflict and Ethnicity in Central Africa.* Tokyo: Tokyo University of Foreign Studies, Institute for the Study of Languages and Cultures of Asia and Africa.

Green, Paula. 1997. "Teaching Non-Violence in a Violence Addicted World." *ReVision: A Journal of Consciousness and Transformation* 20. http://www.karunacenter.org/article-teaching.html.

Greenwood, Peter W., Jeffrey Wasserman, Lois Davis, Allan Abrahamse, Peter D. Jacobson, and James Chiesa. 2000. "The California Wellness Foundation's Violence Prevention Initiative: Findings from the Evaluation of the First Five Years." Paper presented at the Youth Violence in Urban Communities Harvard Urban Seminar: www.ksg.harvard.edu/urbanpoverty/Sitepages/UrbanSeminar/Violence/Papers/Greenwood-paper.pdf

Guatemalan Forensic Anthropology Team. *See* EAFG

Gurr, Ted Robert. 2000. *People Versus States: Minorities at Risk in the New Century.* Washington, D.C.: United States Institute of Peace.

Handy, Jim. 1994. *Revolution in the Countryside.* Chapel Hill: University of North Carolina Press.

Harlick, Jean. 2002. "A Healing Circle." *The Santa Cruz Sentinel* Online Edition (4 April): http://www.santa-cruz.com/archive/2002/April/04/local/stories/0/local.htm

Hempton, David, and Myrtle Hill. 1992. *Evangelical Protestantism in Ulster Society 1740-1890.* London: Routledge.

Holmes, F. 1985. *Our Irish Presbyterian Heritage.* Belfast: Presbyterian Church in Ireland.

Holt, P. M., and M. W. Daly. 1986. *A History of the Sudan: From the Coming of Islam to the Present Day.* New York: Longman Group.

Houtart, Francois. 1974. *Religion and Ideology in Sri Lanka.* Bangalore: Theological Publications of India.

Human Rights Task Force. 1992. *Annual Report 10 August 1991-10 August 1992.* Colombo: Human Rights Task Force.

———. 1993. *Annual Report 10 August 1992-10 August 1993.* Colombo: Human Rights Task Force.

———. 1994. *Annual Report 10 August 1993-10 August 1994.* Colombo: Human Rights Task Force.

Human Rights Watch/Africa. 1994. *Civilian Devastation: Abuses by All Parties in the War in Southern Sudan.* London: Human Rights Watch.

IBON. 2000. "The Recent Skirmishes in Brief." *IBON Fact and Figures* 23:13-14.

Inter-Church Council. 1993. *Sectarianism: A Discussion Document.* Belfast: Irish Inter-Church Meeting.

Inter-Church Group on Faith and Politics. 1989. *Living the Kingdom.* Belfast: Inter-Church Group on Faith and Politics.

International Center for Human Rights Investigations. *See* CIIDH

Jayawardena, Kumari. 1986. *Ethnic and Class Conflicts in Sri Lanka*. Colombo: Centre for Social Analysis.

Johnson, Douglas, and Cynthia Sampson, eds. 1994. *Religion: The Missing Dimension of Statecraft*. New York: Oxford University Press.

Jonas, Susanne. 1991. *The Battle for Guatemala: Rebels, Death Squads, and U.S. Power.* Boulder, Colo.: Westview.

————. 1997. "The Peace Accords: An End and a Beginning." *NACLA Report on the Americas* 30 (May-June): 6-10.

Jordan, Clarence. 1970. *The Cotton Patch Version of Matthew and John*. New York: Association Press.

Keen, Sam. 1986. *Faces of the Enemy: Reflections of the Hostile Imagination*. San Francisco: Harper & Row.

Kennaway, B. 1997. "What Is the Orange Order?" *Lion and Lamb* 13:8-9.

Kimonyo, Jean P. 2000. *Revue Critique des Interprétations du Conflict Rwandais*. Butare: Editions de l'Université Nationale du Rwanda.

King, Martin Luther, Jr. 1967. *Where Do We Go from Here: Chaos or Community?* New York: Bantam.

K'Meyer, Tracy E. 1997. *Interracialism and Christian Community in the Postwar South: The Story of Koinonia Farm*. Charlottesville, Va.: University Press of Virginia.

Lavie, Smadar. 1990. *The Poetics of Military Occupation: Mzeina Allegories of Bedouin Identity Under Israeli and Egyptian Rule*. Berkeley: University of California Press.

Le Bot, Yvon. 1993. "El Palimpsesto Maya: Violencia, Comunidad y Territorio en el Conflicto Guatemalteco." In *Representaciones del Espacio Político En las Tierras Altas de Guatemala*, edited by Alain Breton, 17-28. Mexico: Centro de Estudios Mexicanos y Centroamericanos.

Lederach, John Paul. 1998. *Building Peace: Sustainable Reconciliation in Divided Societies*. Washington, D.C.: United States Institute of Peace.

Lesch, Ann Mosely. 1998. *The Sudan: Contested National Identities*. Bloomington: Indiana University Press.

————. 1999. "Sudan: The Torn Country." *Current History* 98 (May): 218-22.

Les Dossiers de Golias. 1999. *Rwanda, L'honneur Perdu de l'Eglise*. Villuerbanne Cedex: Editions Golias.

Levenson-Estrada, Deborah. 1994. *Trade Unionists Against Terror: Guatemala City 1954-1985*. Chapel Hill: University of North Carolina Press.

Liechty, Joseph. 1993. *Roots of Sectarianism in Ireland*. Belfast: Irish Inter-Church Meeting.

Liechty, Joseph, and Cecilia Clegg. 2001. *Moving Beyond Sectarianism*. Dublin: Columba Press.

Linden, Ian. 1999. *Christianisme et Pouvoirs au Rwanda (1900-1990)*. Paris: Editions Karthala.

Loganathan, Ketheshwaran. 1996. *Sri Lanka. Lost Opportunities. Past Attempts at Resolving Ethnic Conflict*. Colombo: Centre for Policy Research and Analysis.

Logiest, Guy. 1988. *Mission au Rwanda: Un Blanc dans la Bagarre Tutsi-Hutu*. Bruxelles: Didier Hatier.

MacIver, M. A. 1987. "Ian Paisley and the Reformed Tradition." *Political Studies* 35:359-78.

Madge, John. 1953. *The Tools of Social Science*. London: Longmans, Green.

Majul, Cesar A. 1973. *Muslims in the Philippines*. Quezon City: University of the Philippines.

Malwal, Bona. 2000. *Sudan Democratic Gazette* XI (August): 1-4.

Marcus, George E. 1995. "Ethnography in/of the World System: The Emergence of Multi-Sited Ethnography." *Annual Review of Anthropology* 24:95-117.

Martin, David. 1997. *Does Christianity Cause War?* New York: Oxford University Press.

Mbiti, John S. 1970. *Concepts of God in Africa.* London: S.P.C.K.

McClintock, Michael. 1985. *The American Connection: State Terror and Popular Resistance in Guatemala.* London: Zed Books.

Mendoza, Fe Teresita. 2001. "Basic Ecclesial Communities—Authentic Formation and Interreligious Dialogue: A Lonerganian Perspective." Ph.D. diss., Pontifical Universitas Gregoriana, Rome.

Mercado, Eliseo R. 1990. "The Moro People's Struggle for Self-Determination." *Mindanao Focus Journal* 24:10-15.

———. 1999. *Southern Philippines Question.* Cotabato City: Notre Dame.

Miller, D. W. 1978. *Queen's Rebels: Ulster Loyalism in Historical Perspective.* Dublin: Gill and Macmillan.

Minow, Martha. 1998. *Between Vengeance and Forgiveness: Facing History After Genocide and Mass Violence.* Boston: Beacon.

Monaghan, P., and E. Boyle. 1998. *Adventures in Reconciliation: Twenty-Nine Catholic Testimonies.* Guildford: Eagle.

Montada, Leo, and Melvin J. Lerner. 1998. *Responses to Victimizations and Belief in a Just World.* New York: Plenum.

Moore, Christopher. 1996. *The Mediation Process.* San Franscisco: Jossey-Bass.

Muligande, Benjamin. 2000. "Gahini: Une Mission Anglicane au Buganza, Role Religieux, Politique, Economique et Socio-Culturel (1922-1980)." Ph.D. diss., National University of Rwanda.

Myers, David G. 1993. *Social Psychology.* New York: McGraw-Hill.

National Human Rights Commission of Rwanda. *See* NHRC

National Teen Action Research Council. *See* NTARC

National Unity and Reconciliation Commission. *See* NURC

Navarette, Sergio. 1999. "The Meanings of Marimba Music in Rural Guatemala." Ph.D. diss., University College of London.

NHRC (National Human Rights Commission of Rwanda). 2000. *First Annual Report of the National Human Rights Commission, June-December 1999.* Kigali: NHRC.

———. 2001. *Raporo ya Komisiyo Umwaka w'i 2000.* Kigali: NHRC.

Nolan, Albert. 1984. *Taking Sides.* Catholic Institute of International Relations and Catholic Truth Society.

NTARC (National Teen Action Research Council). n.d. *Developing Kids by Changing Communities.* Hartford, CT: NTARC.

NURC (National Unity and Reconciliation Commission). 2000a. *Nation-Wide Grassroots Consultations Report: Unity and Reconciliation Initiatives in Rwanda.* Kigali: NURC.

———. 2000b. *Annual Report of Activities by the National Unity and Reconciliation Commission February 1999-June 2000.* Kigali: NURC.

Obsataz, Shayn. 1994. "Gang Truces." *Santa Fe New Mexican* (October 2): 1.

Ochaita, Liliana. 1974. "Pervivencia de las Cofradías Indígenas en Rabinal, Guatemala." Unpublished Thesis, Universidad Rafael Landivar, Guatemala.

OLS (Operation Lifeline Sudan). 1995. "Weekly Update." Nairobi: UN World Food Program.

Ostrom, Vincent. 1997. *The Meaning of Democracy and the Vulnerability of Democracies.* Ann Arbor: University of Michigan Press.

Peterson, Scott. 2000. *Me Against My Brother: At War in Somalia, Sudan, and Rwanda.* New York: Routledge.

Pieris, Aloysius. 1988. *An Asian Theology of Liberation.* Maryknoll, N.Y.: Orbis.

Playboard Northern Ireland. 1990. *Play Without Frontiers.* Belfast: Playboard Northern Ireland.

PNUD (United Nations Development Program) 2000. *Guatemala: La Fuerza Incluyente del Desarrollo Humano.* Guatemala: United Nations.

Pollner, M. 1989. "Divine Relations, Social Relations, and Well-Being," *Health and Social Behavior* 30:92-104.

Primavesi, Anne. 1991. *From Apocalypse to Genesis: Ecology, Feminism and Christianity.* Minneapolis: Fortress.

Prunier, Gérard. 1995. *The Rwanda Crisis: History of a Genocide.* New York: Columbia University Press.

Psalidas-Perlmutter, Foulie. 2000. "Ethnic Conflicts: The Interplay of Myths and Realities." *Orbis* 44 (Spring): 237ff.

Rafferty, Oliver P. 1994. *Catholicism in Ulster 1603-1983: An Interpretative History.* Dublin: Gill and Macmillan.

Ramsey Marshall, Donna. 2000. *Women in War and Peace: Grassroots Peacebuilding.* Peaceworks No. 34. Washington, D.C.: United States Institute of Peace.

Rasmusen, Eric B. 2000. *Oil in the Sudan.* Bloomington, Ind.: South Sudanese Friends International. http://www.southsudanfriends.org.

Recovery of Historical Memory Project. *See* REMHI

REMHI (Recovery of Historical Memory Project). 1998. *Guatemala: Nunca Más,* Vols. 1-4. Guatemala: ODHAG.

———. 1999. *Guatemala Never Again.* Maryknoll, N.Y.: Orbis.

Rights Action. 2000. "Rio Negro's Fight for Reparations: The Massacre That Won't Go Away." http://www.rightsaction.org/urgent_com/c061000.htm.

Rodil, B. R. 1990. "The Resistance and Struggle of the Tribal Peoples of Mindanao 1903-1935." *Mindanao Focus Journal* 29:33-59.

———. 1994. *The Minoritization of the Indigenous Communities of Mindanao and the Sulu Archipelago.* Davao City: Alternate Forum for Research in Mindanao.

Rodriguez, Luis J. 1993. *Always Running, La Vida Loca: Gang Days in L.A.* New York: Simon and Schuster.

Rojas Bolaños, Manuel. 1993. "La Política." In *Historia General de Centroamérica,* edited by Hector Pérez Brignoli, 85-162. Guatemala: FLACSO.

Ruane, Joseph, and Jennifer Todd. 1996. *The Dynamics of Conflict in Northern Ireland.* Cambridge: Cambridge University Press.

Rummel, R. J. 1994. *Death by Government: Genocide and Mass Murder Since 1900.* New Brunswick, N.J.: Transaction.

Salgado, Pedro. 1990. "The Rape of Mindanao-Sulu." *Mindanao Focus Journal* 30:3-25.

Sama Jeevanaya "Youth for Peace": Final Report. 1999. Colombo: Centre for Society and Religion.

Sande, G. N., G. R. Goethals, L. Ferrari, and L. T. Worth. 1989. "Value-guided Attributions: Maintaining the Moral Self-image and the Diabolical Enemy Image." *Journal of Social Issues* 45:91-118.

Schefer-Hughes, Nancy. 1992. *Death Without Weeping.* Berkeley: University of California Press.

Schirmer, Jennifer. 1993. "The Seeking of Truth and the Gendering of Consciousness: The Comadres of El Salvador and the CONAVIGUA Widows of Guatemala." In *Viva!: Women and Popular Protest in Latin America,* edited by Sarah Radcliffe and Sallie Westwood, 30-64. London: Routledge.

———. 1998. *The Guatemalan Military Project: A Violence Called Democracy.* Philadelphia: University of Pennsylvania Press.

Schottroff, Luise. 1997. "The Creation Narrative—Genesis 1.1-2.4a." In *A Feminist Com-*

panion to Genesis, edited by Athalya Brenner, 25-35. Sheffield, England: Sheffield Academic Press.

Schüssler Fiorenza, Elisabeth. 1995. *Jesus, Miriam's Child and Sophia's Prophet: Critical Issues in Feminist Christology.* New York: Continuum.

Scott, James C. 1985. *Weapons of the Weak: Everyday Forms of Peasant Resistance.* New Haven: Yale University Press.

Scott, William Henry. 1993. *Internationalization of the Bangsamoro Struggle.* Quezon City: University of the Philippines.

————. 1994. *Barangay: Sixteenth Century Philippine Culture and Society.* Quezon City: Ateneo de Manila University.

————. 1997. *The Filipino Muslim Armed Struggle 1900-1972.* Manila: Filipinas Foundation.

Sharp, Gene. 1973. *The Politics of Nonviolent Action.* 3 volumes. Boston: Sargent.

Shawcross, William. 2000. *Deliver Us from Evil: Peacekeepers, Warlords, and a World of Endless Conflict.* New York: Simon and Schuster.

Shenk, Gerald. 2000. "Anonymous Are the Peacemakers." *Christianity Today* (December 4): 34-40, 81.

Siebers, Hans. 1990. "El Trabajo Pastoral y La Institucionalización de la Iglesia Católica en la Actualidad." In *Guatemala: Retos de la Iglesia Católica en una Sociedad en Crisis,* edited by Oscar Sierra, Hans Siebers, and Luis Samandú, 111-62. San Jose, Costa Rica: DEI.

Silverstein, Brett, and Robert R. Holt. 1989. "Research on Enemy Images: Present Status and Future Prospects." *Journal of Social Issues* 2:159-75.

Sitbon, Michel. 1998. *Un génocide sur la conscience.* Paris: L'esprit Frappeur.

Smith, Carol. 1990. "Origins of the National Question in Guatemala: A Hypothesis." In *Guatemalan Indians and the State,* edited by Carol Smith, 72-95. Austin: University of Texas Press.

Smock, David R. 1997. *Creative Approaches to Managing Conflict in Africa: Findings from USIP-funded Projects.* Washington, D.C.: United States Institute of Peace.

————, ed. 2002. *Interfaith Dialogue and Peacebuilding.* Washington, D.C.: United States Institute of Peace.

Somasundaram. Daya. 1998. *Scarred Minds: The Psychological Impact of War on Sri Lankan Tamils.* Colombo: Vijitha Yapa.

Starhawk. 1987. *Truth or Dare: Encounters with Power, Authority, and Mystery.* San Francisco: Harper and Row.

Statistical Abstract of the Democratic Socialist Republic of Sri Lanka. 1991. Colombo: Ministry of Policy Planning and Implementation.

Stoll, David. 1993. *Between Two Armies in the Ixil Towns of Guatemala.* New York: Columbia University Press.

Stop the Violence/Increase the Peace. n.d. *Vision Statement.* Inglewood, California.

Tambaiah, S. J. 1986. *Sri Lanka: Ethnic Fratricide and the Dismantling of Democracy.* Chicago: University of Chicago Press.

Tan, Samuel K. 1993. *Internationalization of the Bangsamoro Struggle.* Quezon City: University of the Philippines Press.

————. 1997. *The Filipino Muslim Armed Struggle 1900-1972.* Manila: Filipinas Foundation.

Tilley, Terence W. 1995. *Postmodern Theologies: The Challenge of Religious Diversity.* Maryknoll, N.Y.: Orbis.

Tracy, David. 1988. "The Question of Criteria for Inter-Religious Dialogue: A Tribute to Langdon Gilkey." In *The Whirlwind in Culture,* edited by Donald W. Musser and Joseph L. Price, 246-62. Bloomington, Ind.: Meyer Stone Books.

Tschuy, Théo. 1997. *Ethnic Conflict and Religion: Challenge to the Churches.* Geneva: WCC Publications.

Tudtud, Bienvenido S. 1988. *Dialogue of Life and Faith.* Quezon City: Claretian Publications.

UNIFEM (United Nations Development Fund for Women). 2000. *Women at the Peace Table: Making a Difference.* New York: UNIFEM.

United Nations Development Program. *See* PNUD

U.S. Department of Justice/Office of the Juvenile Justice and Delinquency Prevention. 1998. *National Youth Gang Survey.* Washington, D.C.: Department of Justice.

Valenzuela, José. n.d. "Reflections on Community Healing." Trinity Lutheran Church, Brooklyn, NY.

Victory Outreach. n.d. *Treasures Out of Darkness.* El Cajon, Calif.: Victory Outreach Church.

Vigil, José María. 2001. "The God of War and the God of Peace with Justice." *Concilium* 2:94-101.

Vitug, Maritess Danguilan, and Glenda Gloria. 2000. *The Crescent Moon: Rebellion in Mindanao.* Quezon City: Ateneo de Manila Center for Social Policy and Public Affairs and the Institute for Popular Democracy.

Wai, Dunstan M. 1981. *The African-Arab Conflict in the Sudan.* New York: Africana Publishing.

Wallensteen, Peter, and Margareta Sollenberg. 1996. "The End of International War? Armed Conflict 1989-95." *Journal of Peace Research* 33:353-70.

Wallis, Roy, and Steve Bruce. 1986. *Sociological Theory, Religion and Collective Action.* Belfast: Queen's University of Belfast.

Warren, James. 1985. *The Sulu Zone 1768-1798.* Quezon City: New Day Publishers.

Warren, Kay B. 1998. *Indigenous Movements and Their Critics: Pan-Maya Activism in Guatemala.* Princeton, N.J.: Princeton University Press.

Waylen, Georgina. 1996. *Gender in Third World Politics.* Boulder, Colo.: Lynne Rienner Publishers.

Wells, Ronald A. 1999. *People Behind the Peace: Community and Reconciliation in Northern Ireland.* Grand Rapids: Eerdmans.

WFP (Witness for Peace). 1995. *A People Damned: The Impact of the World Bank on the Chixoy Hydroelectric Project in Guatemala.* http://witnessforpeace.org/adp.html.

Wilkerson, David R. 1963. *The Cross and the Switchblade.* With John and Elizabeth Sherill. New York: B. Geis and Associates/Random House.

Williams, T., and A. Falconer. 1993. *Sectarianism.* Dublin: Dominican Publications.

Wilson, Richard. 1994. "Anchored Communities: Identity and History of the Maya' Q'eqchi." *Man* 28, no. 1:121-38.

Winter, Greg. 2002. "Los Angeles Street Wars Grow Deadlier." *The New York Times* (April 11): A24.

Witness for Peace. *See* WFP

Wright, Robin. 1996. "Stop the Violence, Increase the Peace." *Hope Magazine* 1 (March/April): 36.

Wulff, David M. 1991. *Psychology of Religion: Classic and Contemporary Views.* New York: John Wiley & Sons.

Ziselsberger, Georg. 1990. *The Vision of Dialogue of Bishop Bienvenido S. Tudtud.* Zamboanga City: Silsilah Publications.

Zur, Judith. 1998. *Violent Memories: Mayan War Widows in Guatemala.* Boulder, Colo.: Westview.